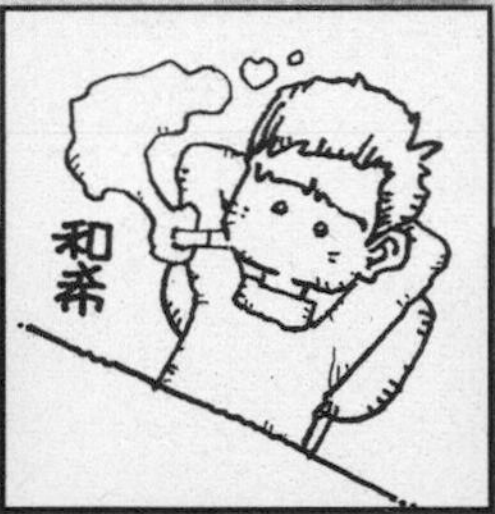
和希

KAZUKI TAKAHASHI

The new series *Yu-Gi-Oh! ARC-V* starts this spring, and Miyoshi-kun is on the planning team! Keep an eye out for it!

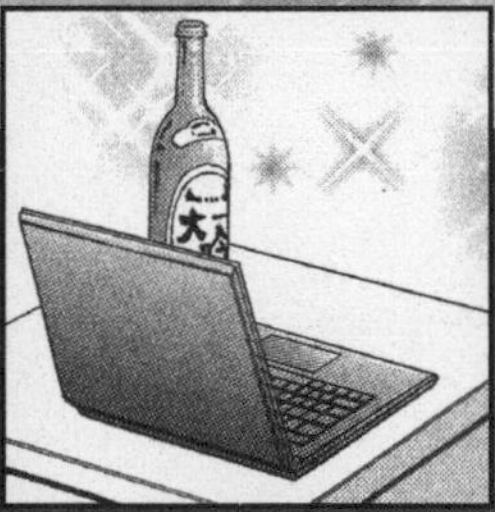

SHIN YOSHIDA

My work on the anime is over, so now I'm concentrating on the manga. Not like I wasn't concentrating on it before, though! (lol) I'll work hard to make sure the manga moves people in its own unique way!

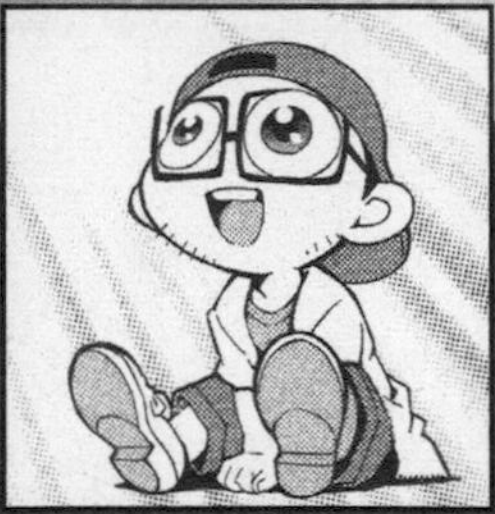

NAOHITO MIYOSHI

When volume 6 comes out, the *ZEXAL* manga will have been running for three full years. I never dreamed I'd be part of such a big project. I'll do my best to stay humble and keep working hard!

YU-GI-OH! ZEXAL

Volume 6
SHONEN JUMP Manga Edition

Original Concept by KAZUKI TAKAHASHI
Production Support: STUDIO DICE
Story by SHIN YOSHIDA
Art by NAOHITO MIYOSHI

Translation & English Adaptation TAYLOR ENGEL AND IAN REID, HC LANGUAGE SOLUTIONS
Touch-up Art & Lettering JOHN HUNT
Designer STACIE YAMAKI
Editor MIKE MONTESA

Printed in the U.S.A.

VIZ media
www.viz.com

RATED T FOR TEEN
PARENTAL ADVISORY
YU-GI-OH! ZEXAL is rated T for Teen and is recommended for ages 13 and up. This volume contains fantasy violence.
ratings.viz.com

SHONEN JUMP
www.shonenjump.com

YU-GI-OH! ZEXAL

VOLUME 6:
Sins Revealed!!

Original Concept by **KAZUKI TAKAHASHI**
Production Support: **STUDIO DICE**
Story by **SHIN YOSHIDA**
Art by **NAOHITO MIYOSHI**

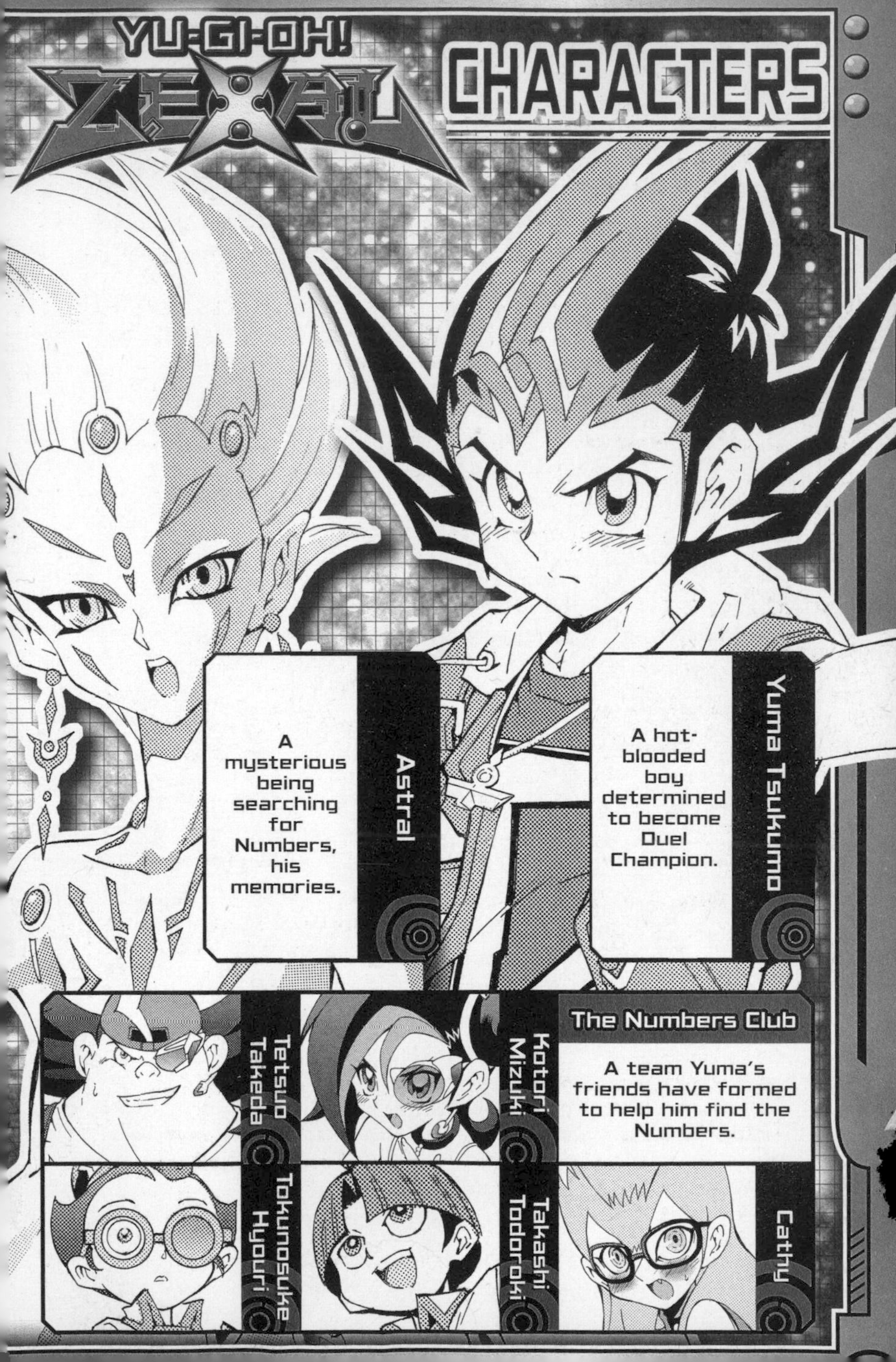

YU-GI-OH! ZEXAL
CHARACTERS
Yuma Tsukumo
A hot-blooded boy determined to become Duel Champion.
Astral
A mysterious being searching for Numbers, his memories.
The Numbers Club
A team Yuma's friends have formed to help him find the Numbers.
Kotori Mizuki
Tetsuo Takeda
Cathy
Takashi Todoroki
Tokunosuke Hyouri

Kyoji Yagumo

Kyoji hunts the Numbers cards for Dr. Faker.

Ryoga Kamishiro

Goes by the nickname "Shark." His fate is tied to Yagumo's.

Kaito

A Numbers Hunter who is searching for Numbers to save his little brother.

Mr. Heartland | Dr. Faker

These two villains are collecting Numbers to destroy the Astral world.

Luna

She is trying to destroy the numbers cards along with Ryoga.

Haruto

He possesses the power to destroy the Astral world.

Yuma Tsukumo is crazy about dueling. One day, during a duel, the charm his parents had left him—"the Emperor's Key"—triggered an encounter with a strange being who called himself Astral. Astral was a genius duelist, but his memories had turned into special cards called "Numbers" and were lost. Yuma began working with Astral to find them!

Standing in their way are Dr. Faker, who's trying to use the power of the Numbers cards to destroy the Astral World, and Kaito, who's hunting the Numbers to help his little brother! Ryoga and Luna are also working to wipe out the Numbers. Meanwhile, Yagumo joins forces with Dr. Faker and declares war on Yuma and friends! The Numbers War begins.

In the middle of all this, Ryoga and Kaito clash. However, during their duel, they fall into Shadow's trap…!!

Yu-Gi-Oh! ZEXAL

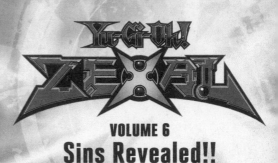

VOLUME 6

Sins Revealed!!

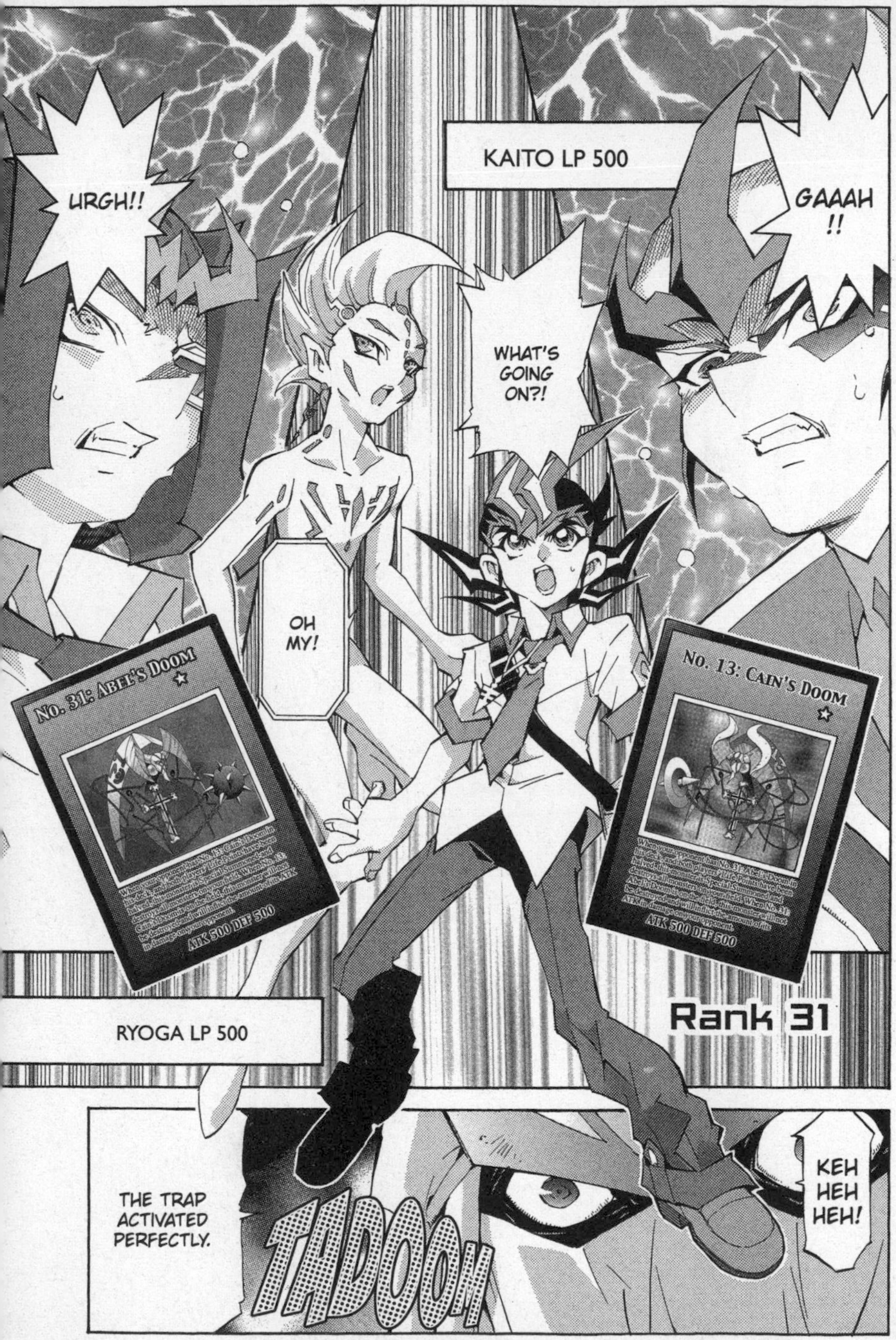
GAAAH!!
KAITO LP 500
URGH!!
WHAT'S GOING ON?!
OH MY!
No. 13: Cain's Doom
ATK 500 DEF 500
No. 31: Abel's Doom
ATK 500 DEF 500
Rank 31
RYOGA LP 500
KEH HEH HEH!
THADOOM
THE TRAP ACTIVATED PERFECTLY.

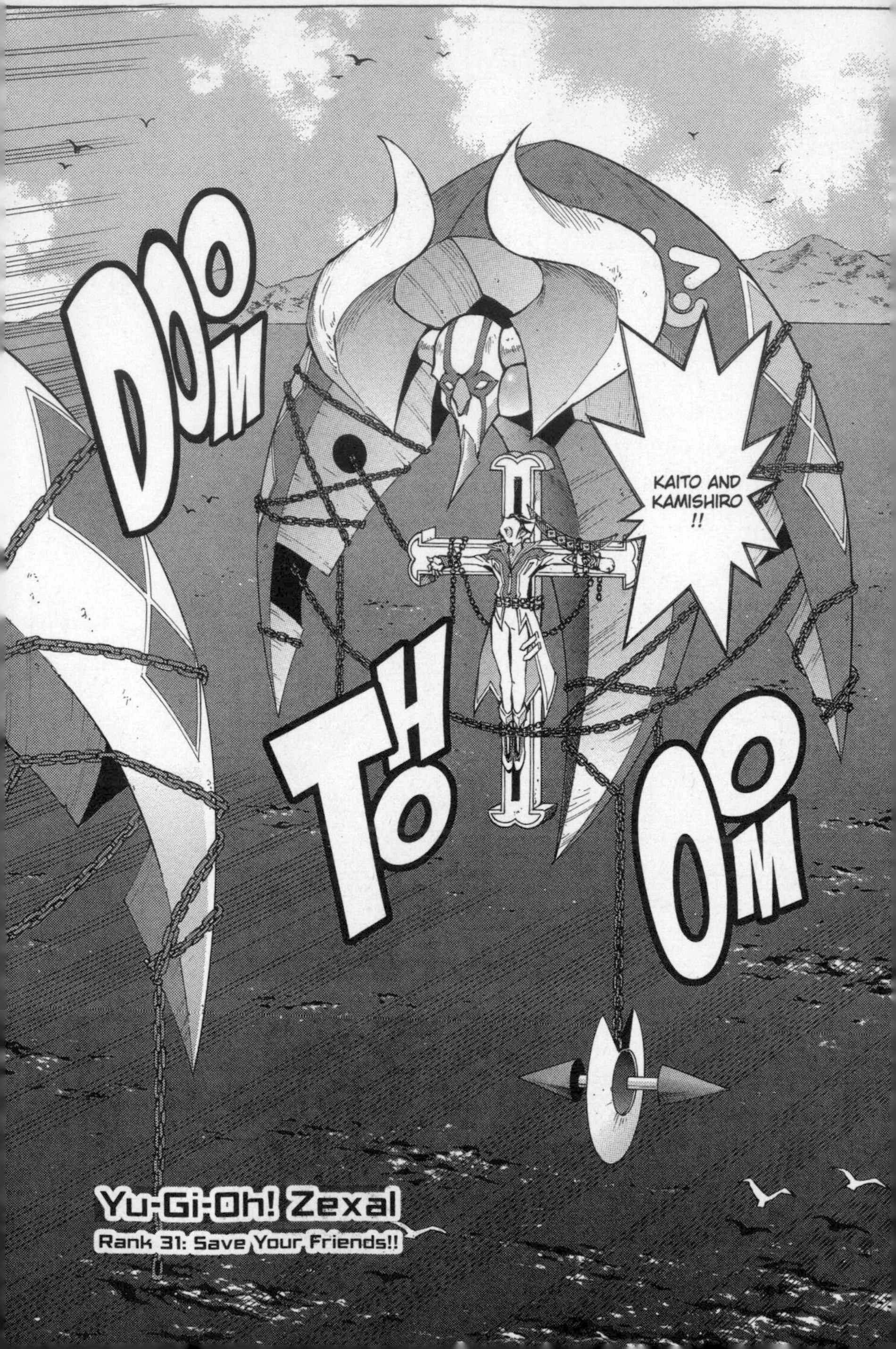
KAITO AND KAMISHIRO !!
DOOOM
THOOOOM
Yu-Gi-Oh! Zexal
Rank 31: Save Your Friends!!

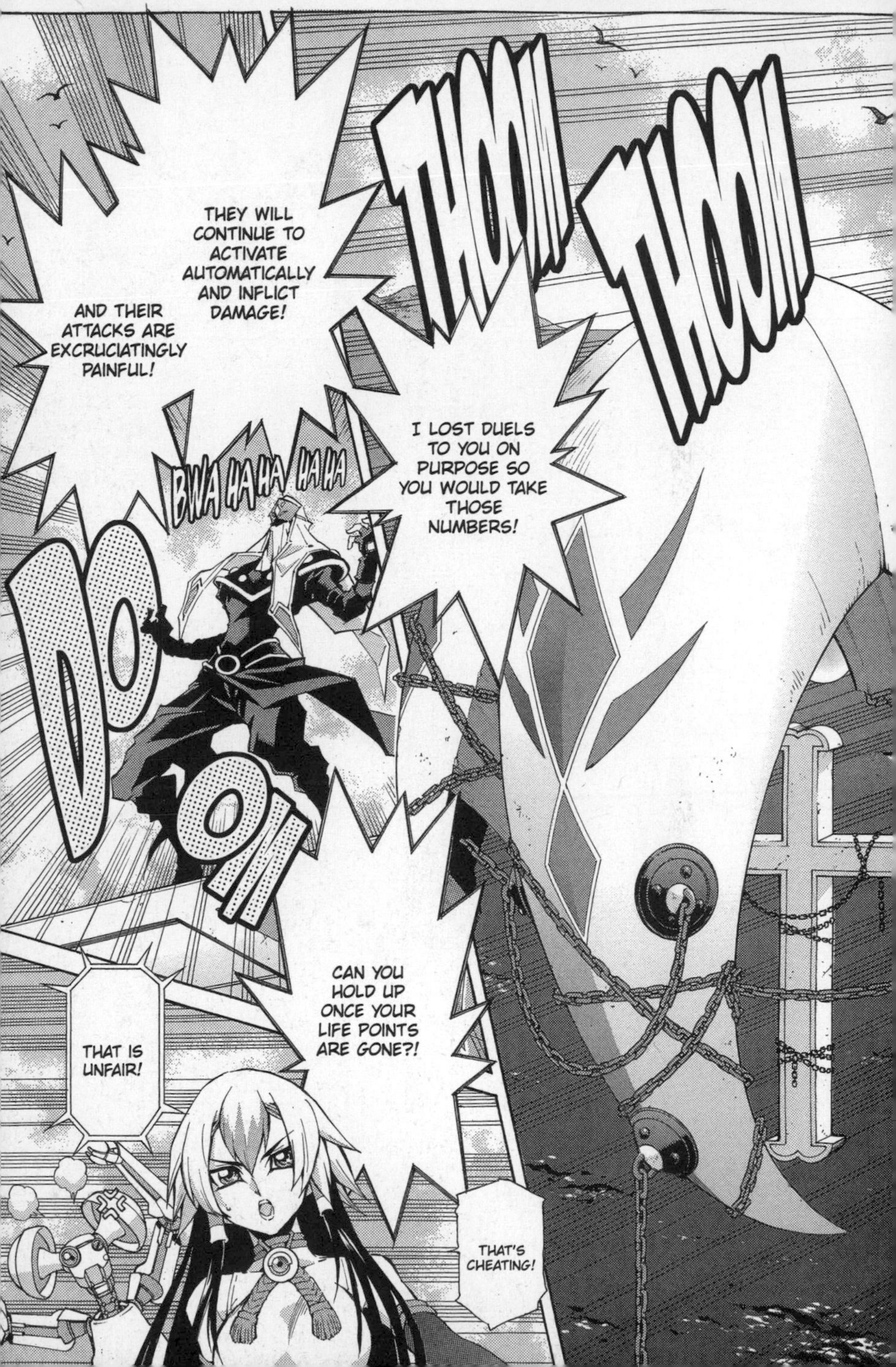
THOOM
THOOM
THEY WILL CONTINUE TO ACTIVATE AUTOMATICALLY AND INFLICT DAMAGE!
AND THEIR ATTACKS ARE EXCRUCIATINGLY PAINFUL!
I LOST DUELS TO YOU ON PURPOSE SO YOU WOULD TAKE THOSE NUMBERS!
BWA HA HA HA HA
DOOM
CAN YOU HOLD UP ONCE YOUR LIFE POINTS ARE GONE?!
THAT'S CHEATING!
THAT IS UNFAIR!

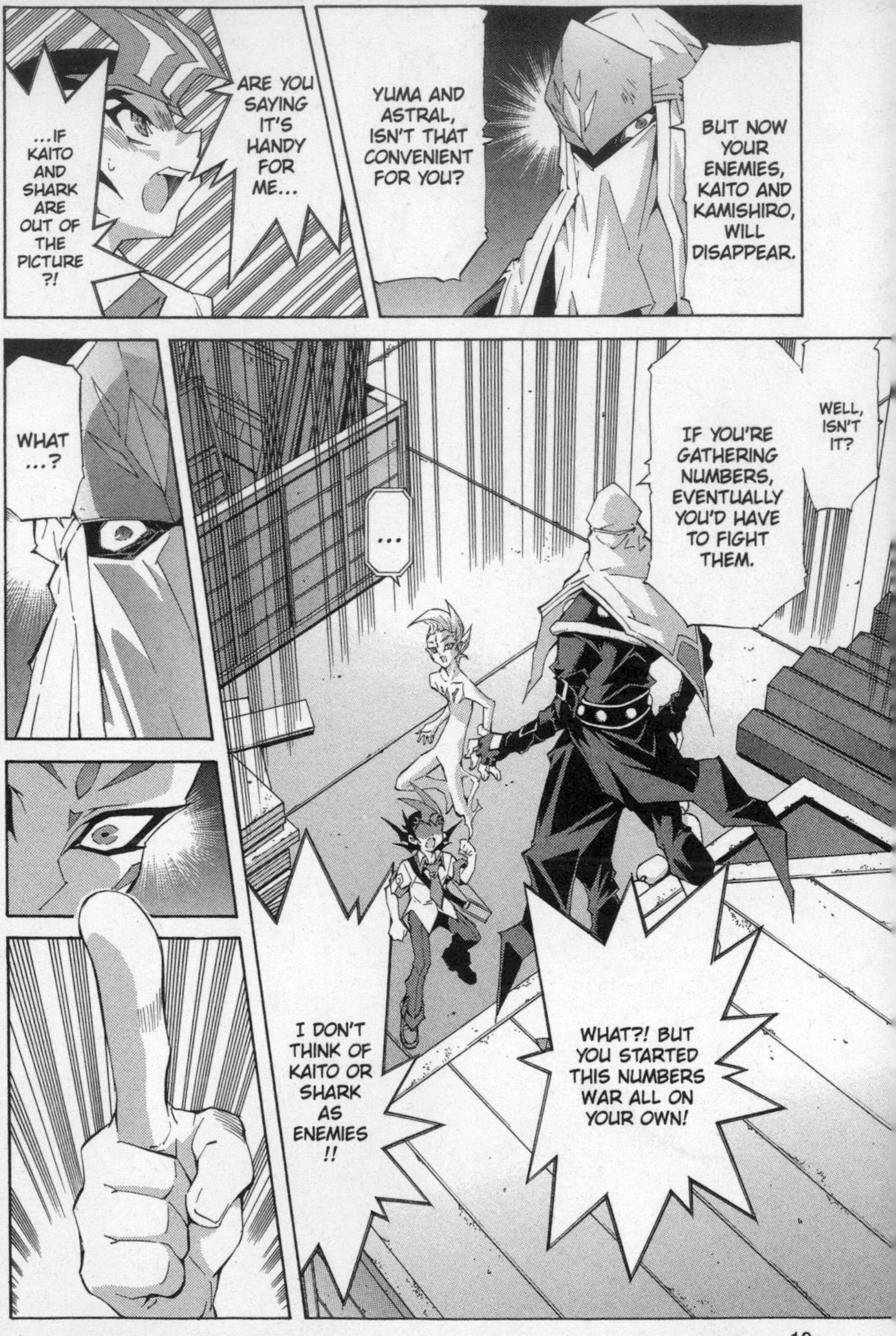
BUT NOW YOUR ENEMIES, KAITO AND KAMISHIRO, WILL DISAPPEAR.
YUMA AND ASTRAL, ISN'T THAT CONVENIENT FOR YOU?
ARE YOU SAYING IT'S HANDY FOR ME...
...IF KAITO AND SHARK ARE OUT OF THE PICTURE ?!
WELL, ISN'T IT?
IF YOU'RE GATHERING NUMBERS, EVENTUALLY YOU'D HAVE TO FIGHT THEM.
...
WHAT?! BUT YOU STARTED THIS NUMBERS WAR ALL ON YOUR OWN!
I DON'T THINK OF KAITO OR SHARK AS ENEMIES !!
WHAT ...?

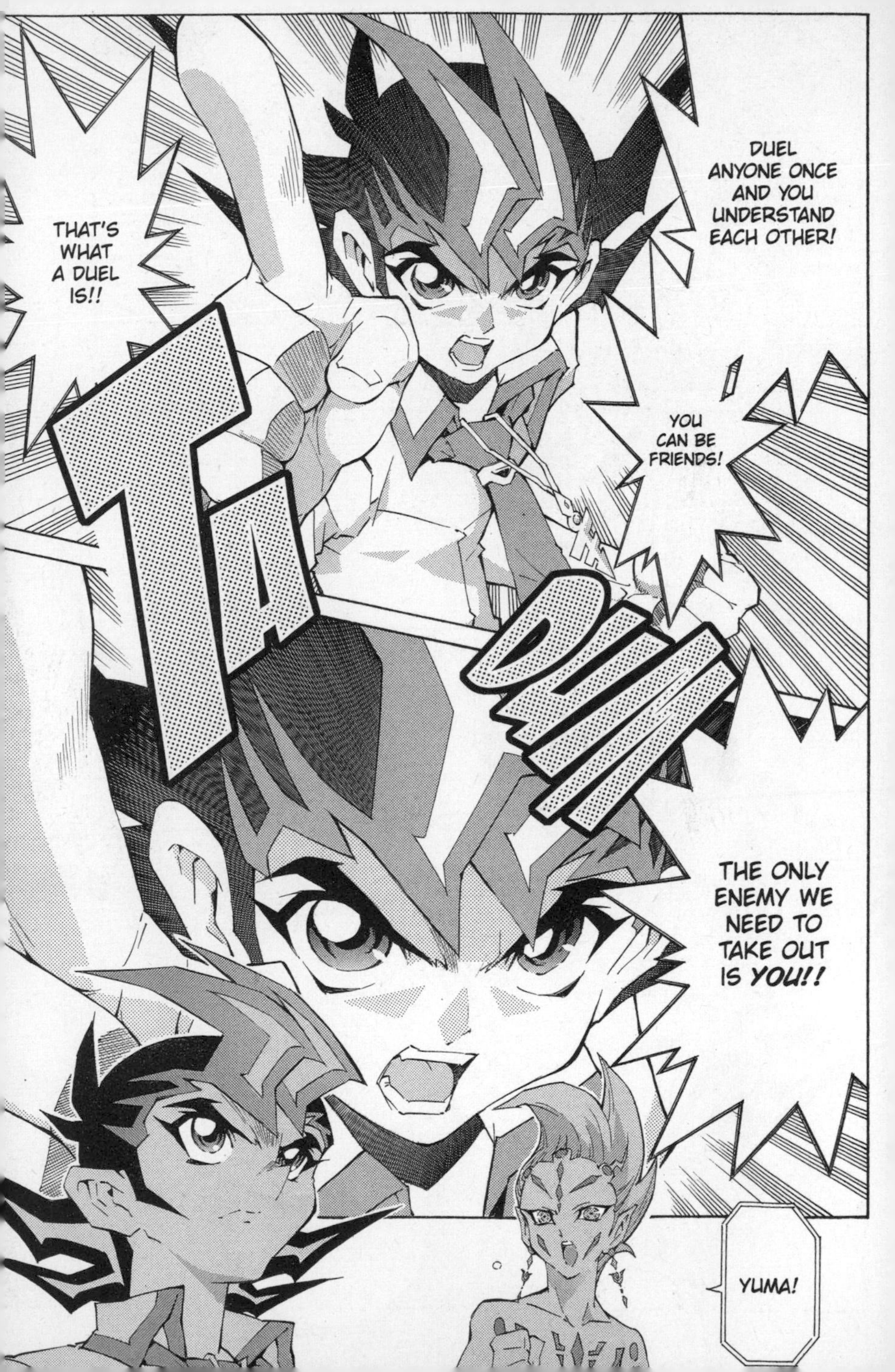
DUEL ANYONE ONCE AND YOU UNDERSTAND EACH OTHER!
YOU CAN BE FRIENDS!
THAT'S WHAT A DUEL IS!!
THE ONLY ENEMY WE NEED TO TAKE OUT IS *YOU!!*
YUMA!

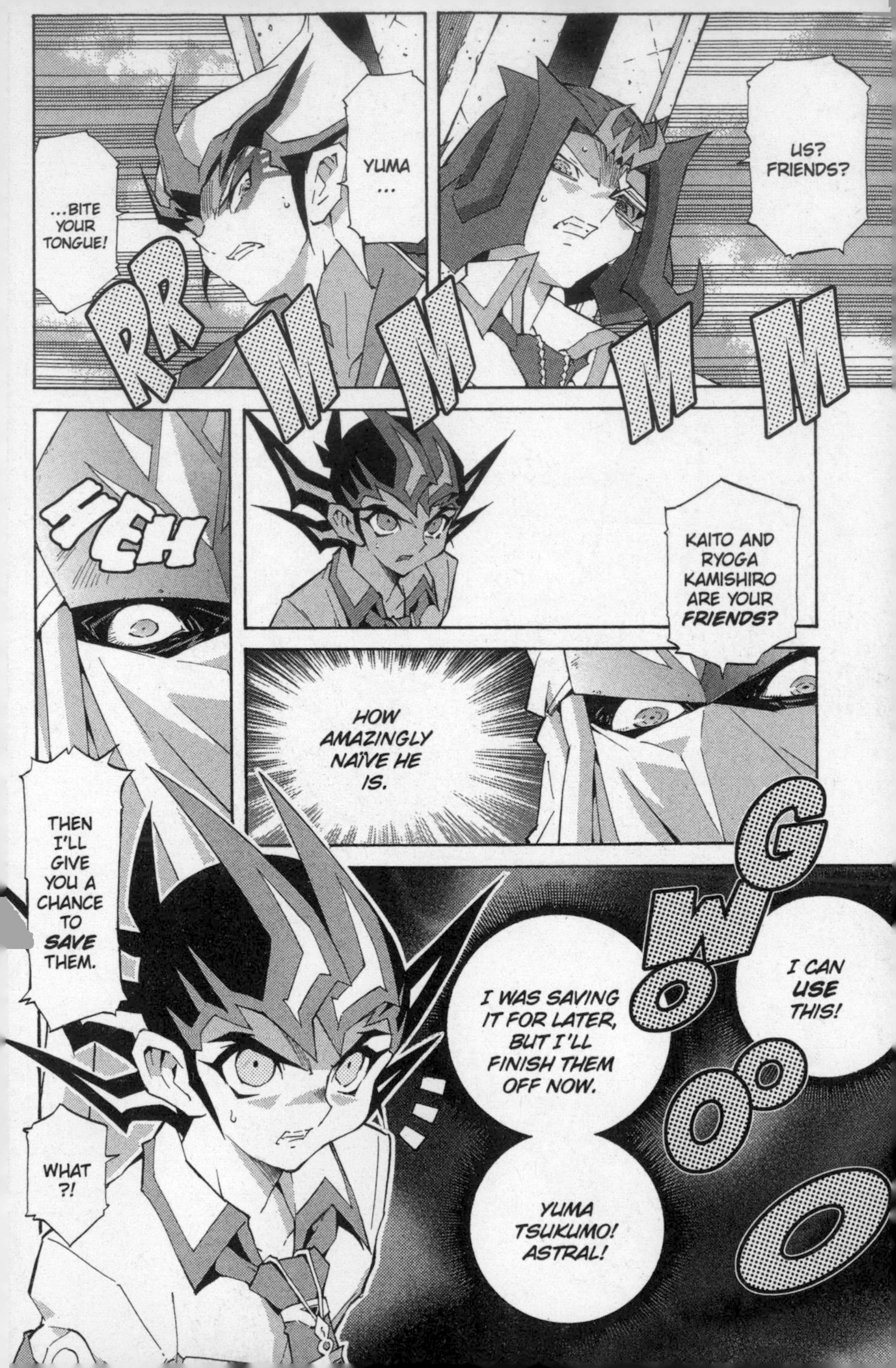
US?
FRIENDS?
YUMA
...
...BITE
YOUR
TONGUE!
RRMMMMM
KAITO AND
RYOGA
KAMISHIRO
ARE YOUR
FRIENDS?
HEH
*HOW
AMAZINGLY
NAÏVE HE
IS.*
THEN
I'LL
GIVE
YOU A
CHANCE
TO
SAVE
THEM.
*I CAN
USE
THIS!*
GWOOOOO
*I WAS SAVING
IT FOR LATER,
BUT I'LL
FINISH THEM
OFF NOW.*
*YUMA
TSUKUMO!
ASTRAL!*
WHAT
?!

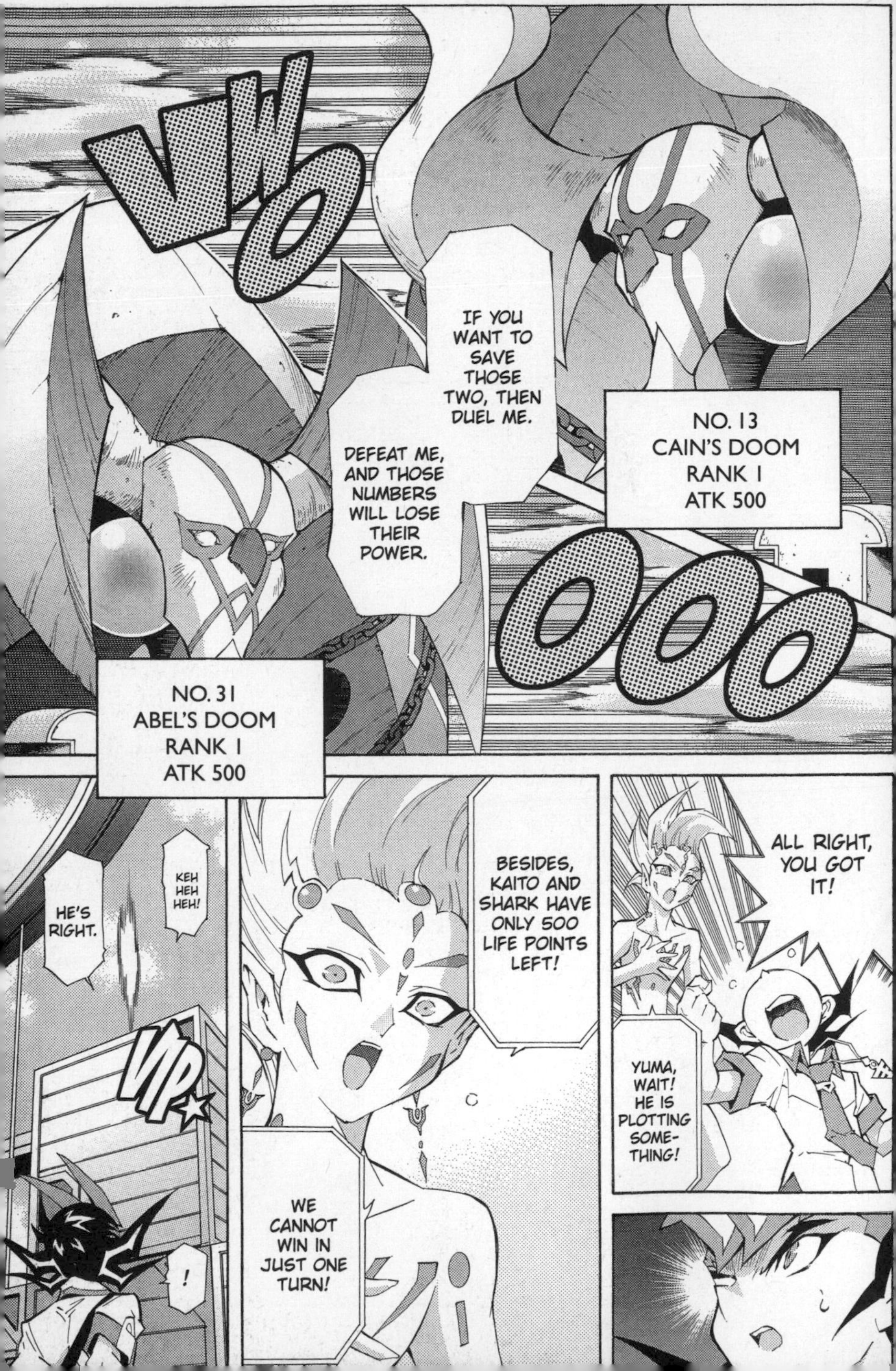
NO. 13
CAIN'S DOOM
RANK 1
ATK 500
IF YOU WANT TO SAVE THOSE TWO, THEN DUEL ME.
DEFEAT ME, AND THOSE NUMBERS WILL LOSE THEIR POWER.
VWOOOO
NO. 31
ABEL'S DOOM
RANK 1
ATK 500
ALL RIGHT, YOU GOT IT!
YUMA, WAIT! HE IS PLOTTING SOME-THING!
BESIDES, KAITO AND SHARK HAVE ONLY 500 LIFE POINTS LEFT!
WE CANNOT WIN IN JUST ONE TURN!
KEH HEH HEH!
HE'S RIGHT.
VIP☆
!

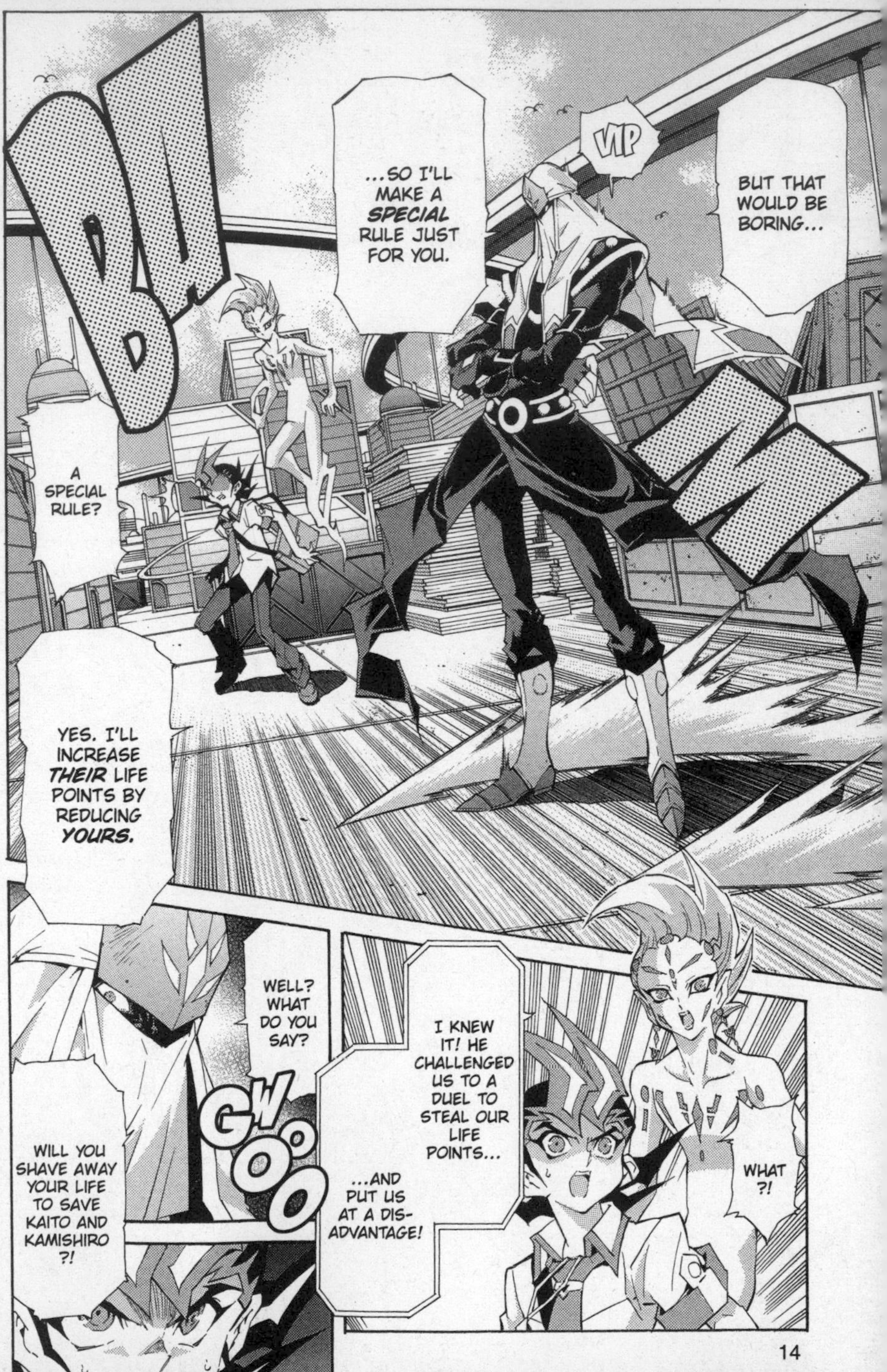

BUT THAT WOULD BE BORING...
VIP
...SO I'LL MAKE A *SPECIAL* RULE JUST FOR YOU.
BA!
A SPECIAL RULE?
YES. I'LL INCREASE *THEIR* LIFE POINTS BY REDUCING *YOURS.*
WHAT ?!
I KNEW IT! HE CHALLENGED US TO A DUEL TO STEAL OUR LIFE POINTS...
...AND PUT US AT A DIS-ADVANTAGE!
WELL? WHAT DO YOU SAY?
GWOOO
WILL YOU SHAVE AWAY YOUR LIFE TO SAVE KAITO AND KAMISHIRO ?!

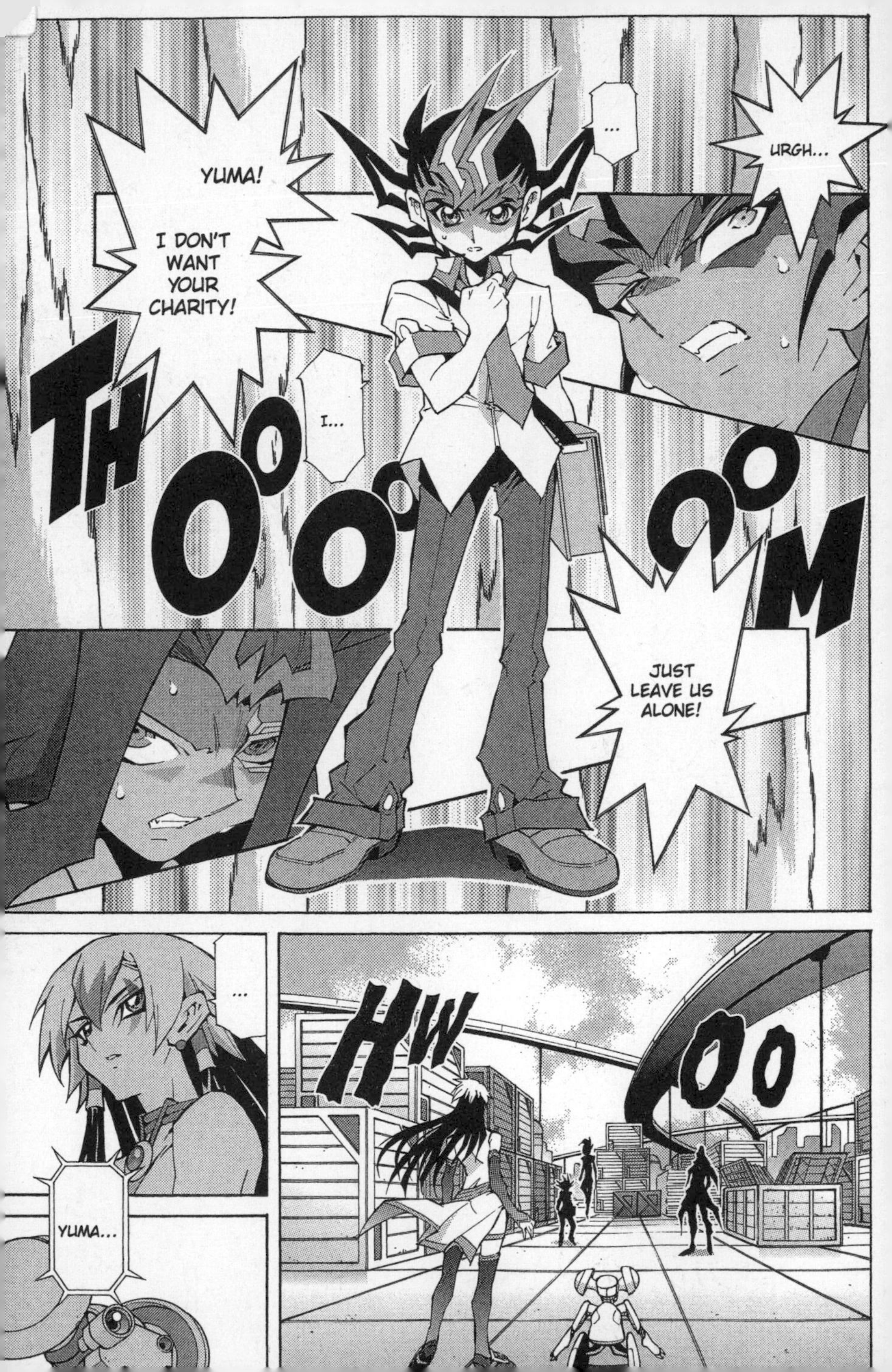
URGH...
...
YUMA!
I DON'T WANT YOUR CHARITY!
I...
THOOOOOOM
JUST LEAVE US ALONE!
HWOO
...
YUMA...

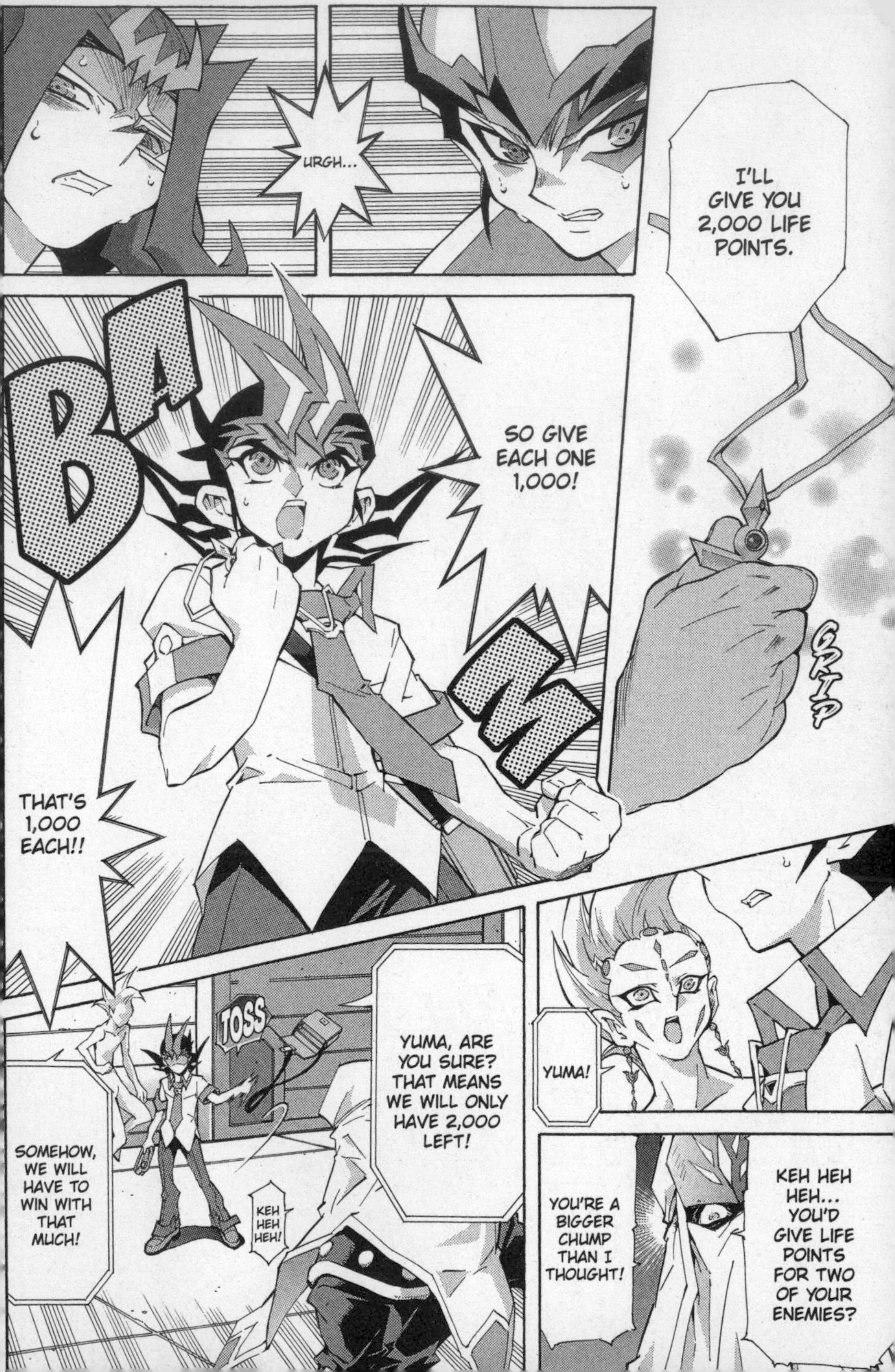
I'LL GIVE YOU 2,000 LIFE POINTS.
GRIP
URGH...
BAM
SO GIVE EACH ONE 1,000!
THAT'S 1,000 EACH!!
YUMA!
KEH HEH HEH... YOU'D GIVE LIFE POINTS FOR TWO OF YOUR ENEMIES?
YOU'RE A BIGGER CHUMP THAN I THOUGHT!
YUMA, ARE YOU SURE? THAT MEANS WE WILL ONLY HAVE 2,000 LEFT!
TOSS
KEH HEH HEH!
SOMEHOW, WE WILL HAVE TO WIN WITH THAT MUCH!

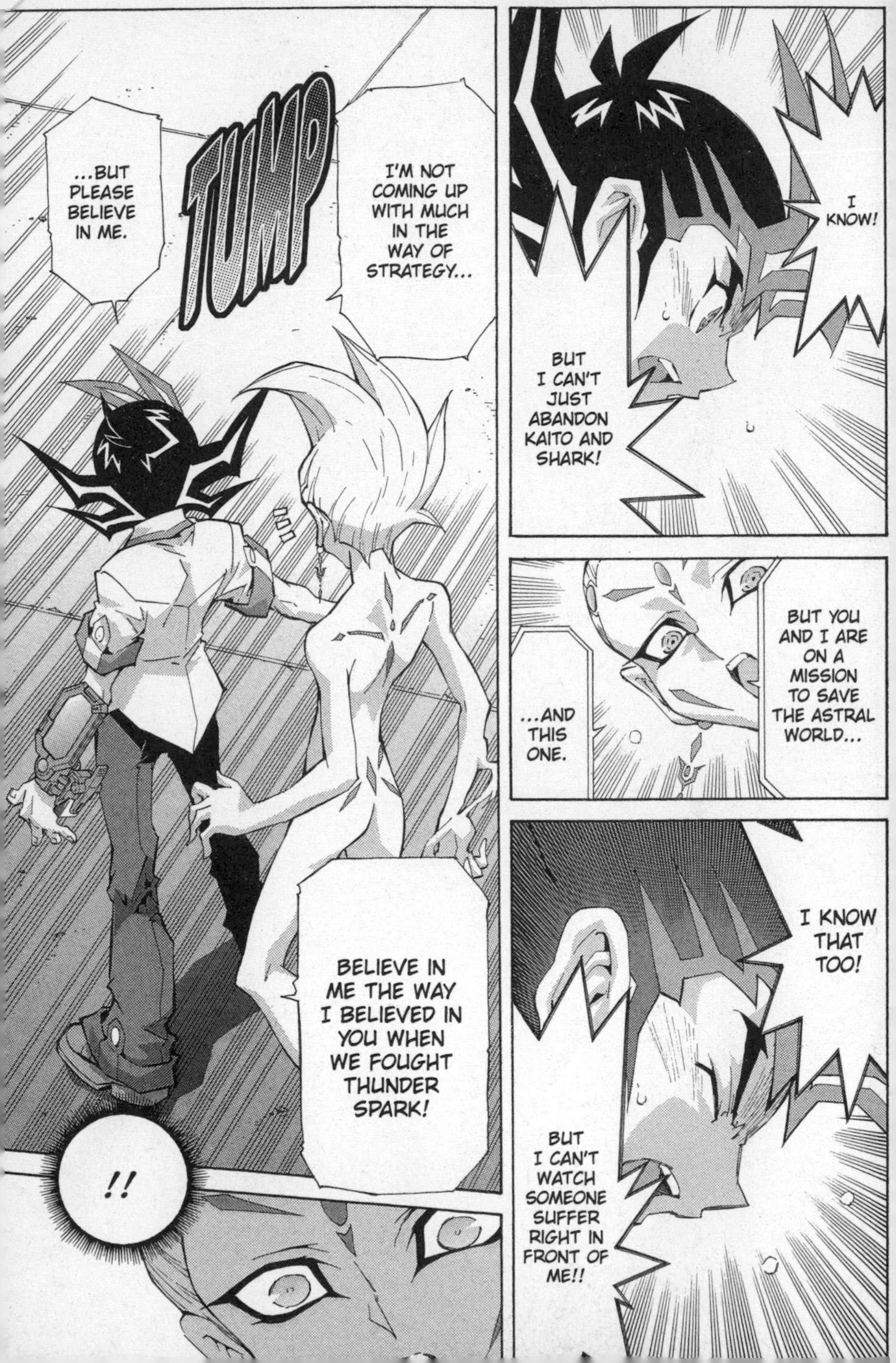
I KNOW!
BUT I CAN'T JUST ABANDON KAITO AND SHARK!
BUT YOU AND I ARE ON A MISSION TO SAVE THE ASTRAL WORLD...
...AND THIS ONE.
I KNOW THAT TOO!
BUT I CAN'T WATCH SOMEONE SUFFER RIGHT IN FRONT OF ME!!
I'M NOT COMING UP WITH MUCH IN THE WAY OF STRATEGY...
TUMP
...BUT PLEASE BELIEVE IN ME.
BELIEVE IN ME THE WAY I BELIEVED IN YOU WHEN WE FOUGHT THUNDER SPARK!
!!

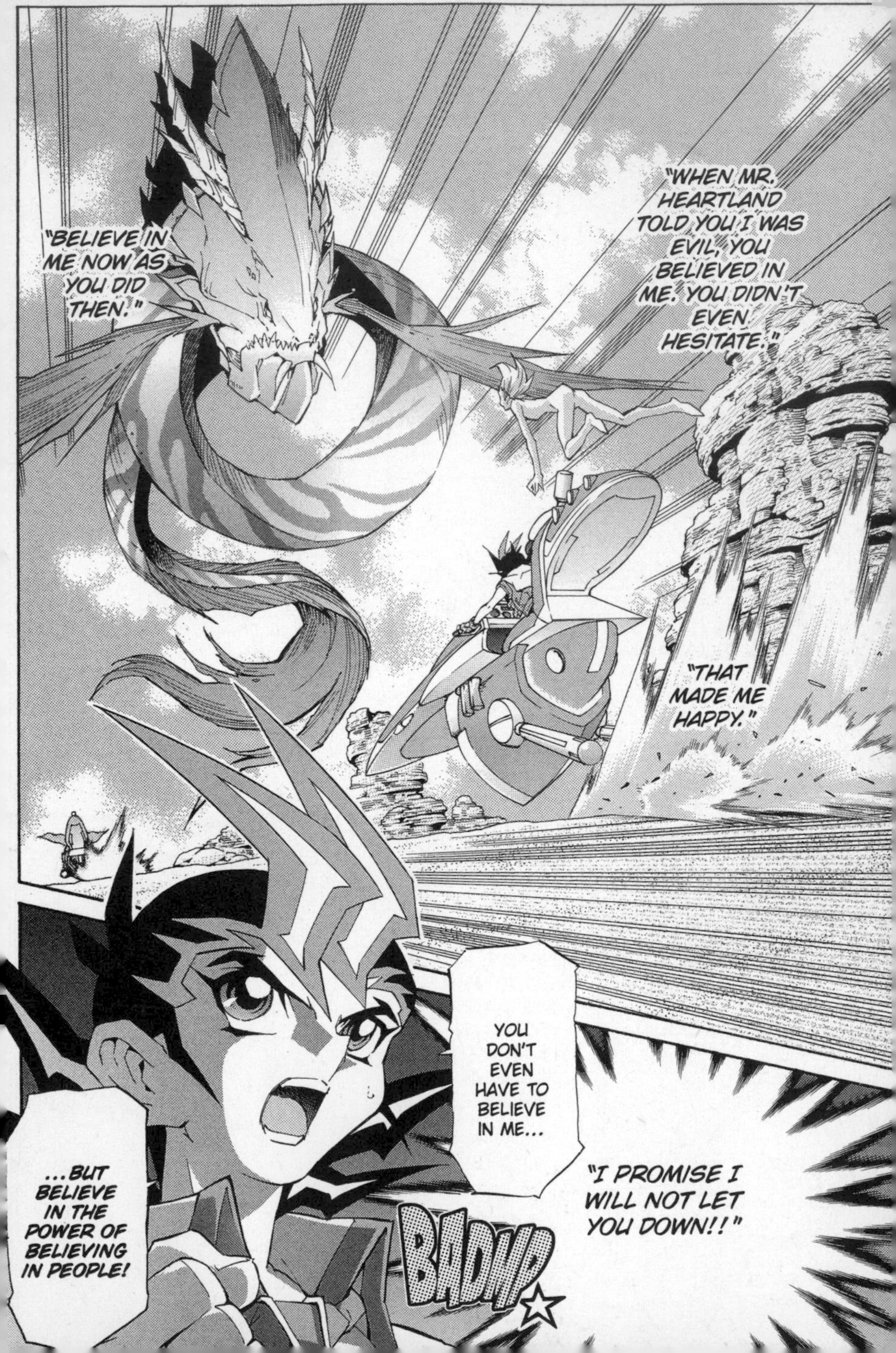
"WHEN MR. HEARTLAND TOLD YOU I WAS EVIL, YOU BELIEVED IN ME. YOU DIDN'T EVEN HESITATE."
"THAT MADE ME HAPPY."
"BELIEVE IN ME NOW AS YOU DID THEN."
"I PROMISE I WILL NOT LET YOU DOWN!!"
YOU DON'T EVEN HAVE TO BELIEVE IN ME...
...BUT BELIEVE IN THE POWER OF BELIEVING IN PEOPLE!
BADMP☆

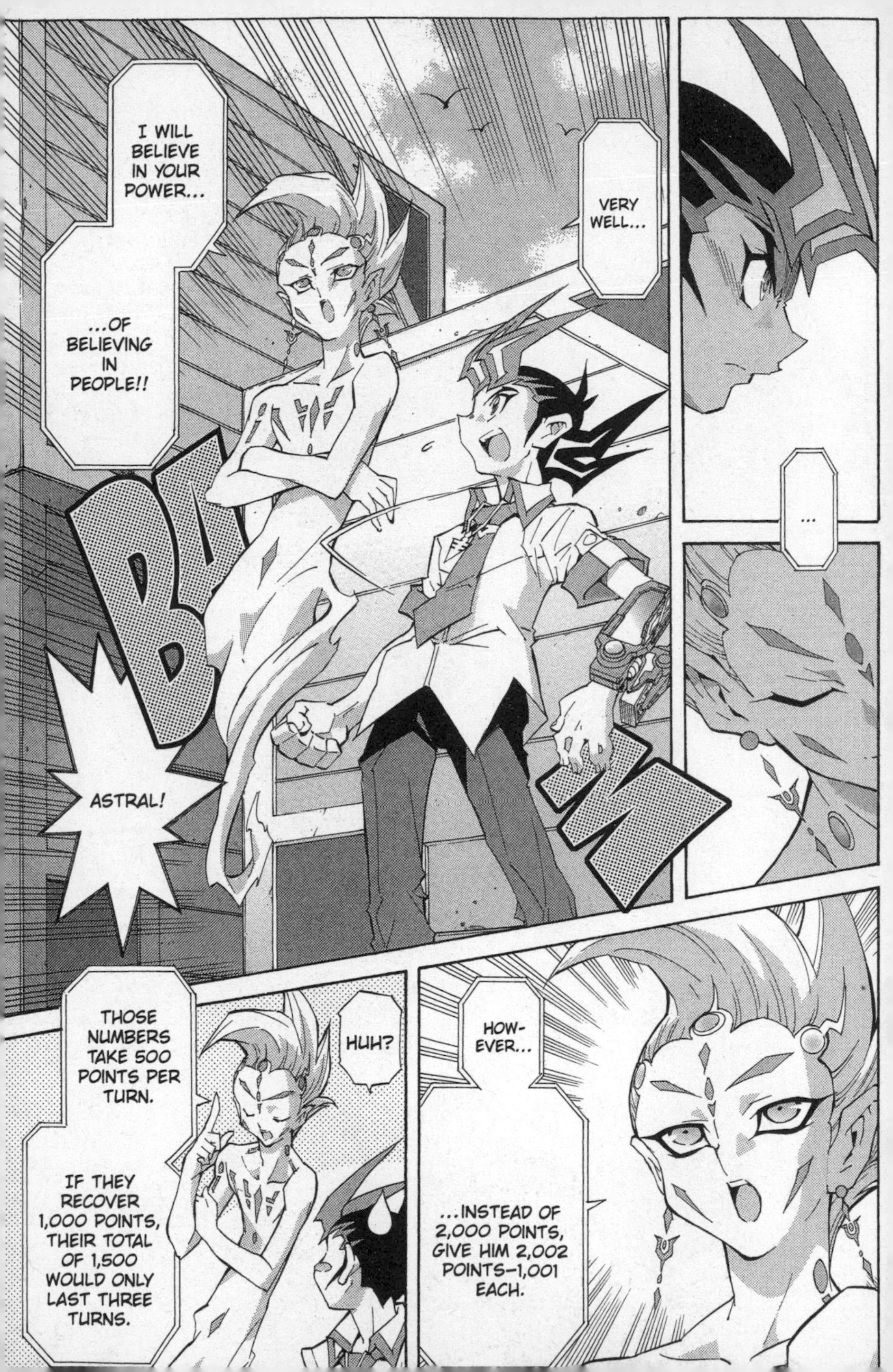
...
VERY WELL...
I WILL BELIEVE IN YOUR POWER...
...OF BELIEVING IN PEOPLE!!
BUM
ASTRAL!
HOW-EVER...
...INSTEAD OF 2,000 POINTS, GIVE HIM 2,002 POINTS—1,001 EACH.
HUH?
THOSE NUMBERS TAKE 500 POINTS PER TURN.
IF THEY RECOVER 1,000 POINTS, THEIR TOTAL OF 1,500 WOULD ONLY LAST THREE TURNS.

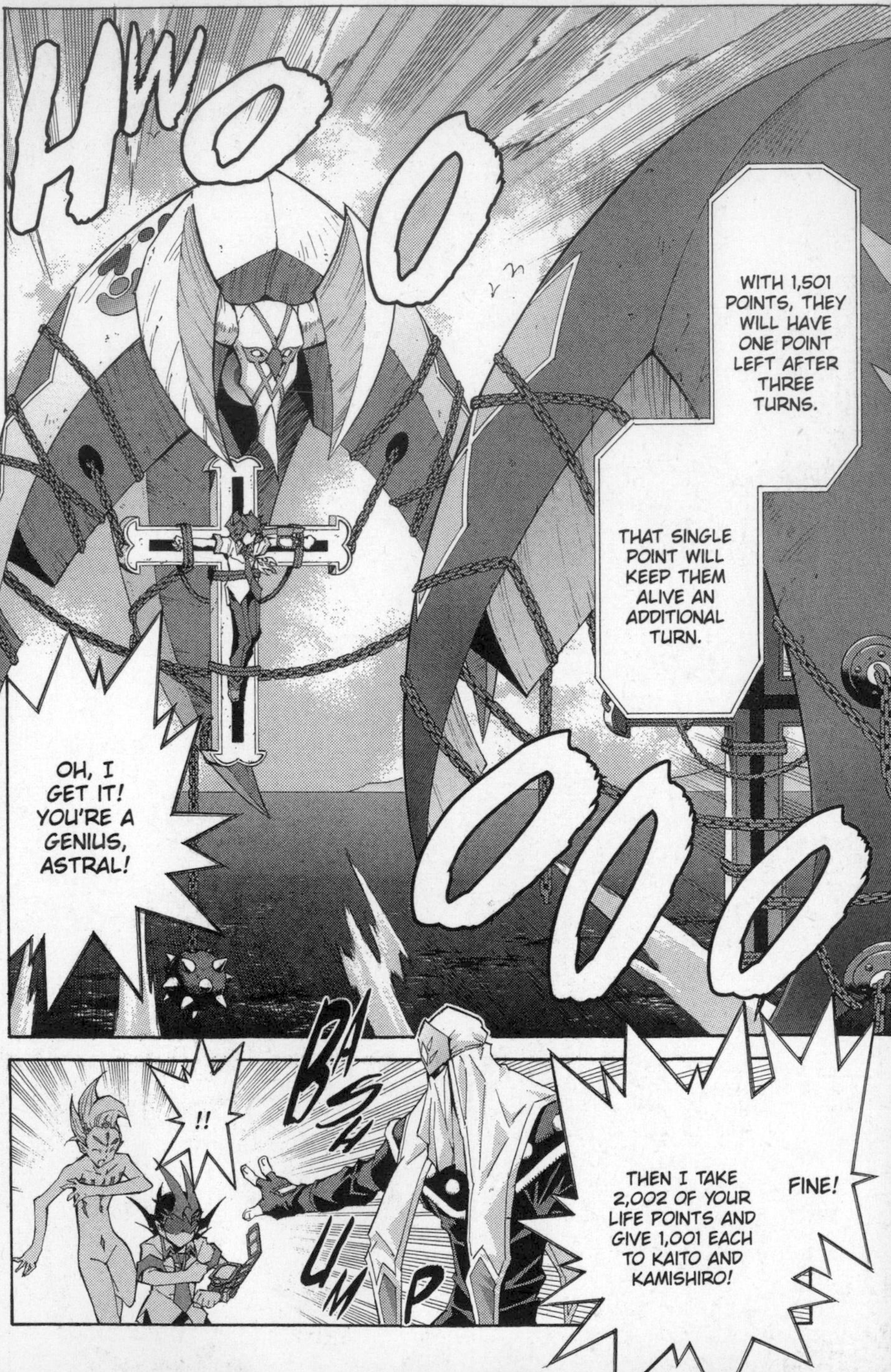
WITH 1,501 POINTS, THEY WILL HAVE ONE POINT LEFT AFTER THREE TURNS.
THAT SINGLE POINT WILL KEEP THEM ALIVE AN ADDITIONAL TURN.
HWOOOOO
OH, I GET IT! YOU'RE A GENIUS, ASTRAL!
FINE!
THEN I TAKE 2,002 OF YOUR LIFE POINTS AND GIVE 1,001 EACH TO KAITO AND KAMISHIRO!
BASH
UMP
!!

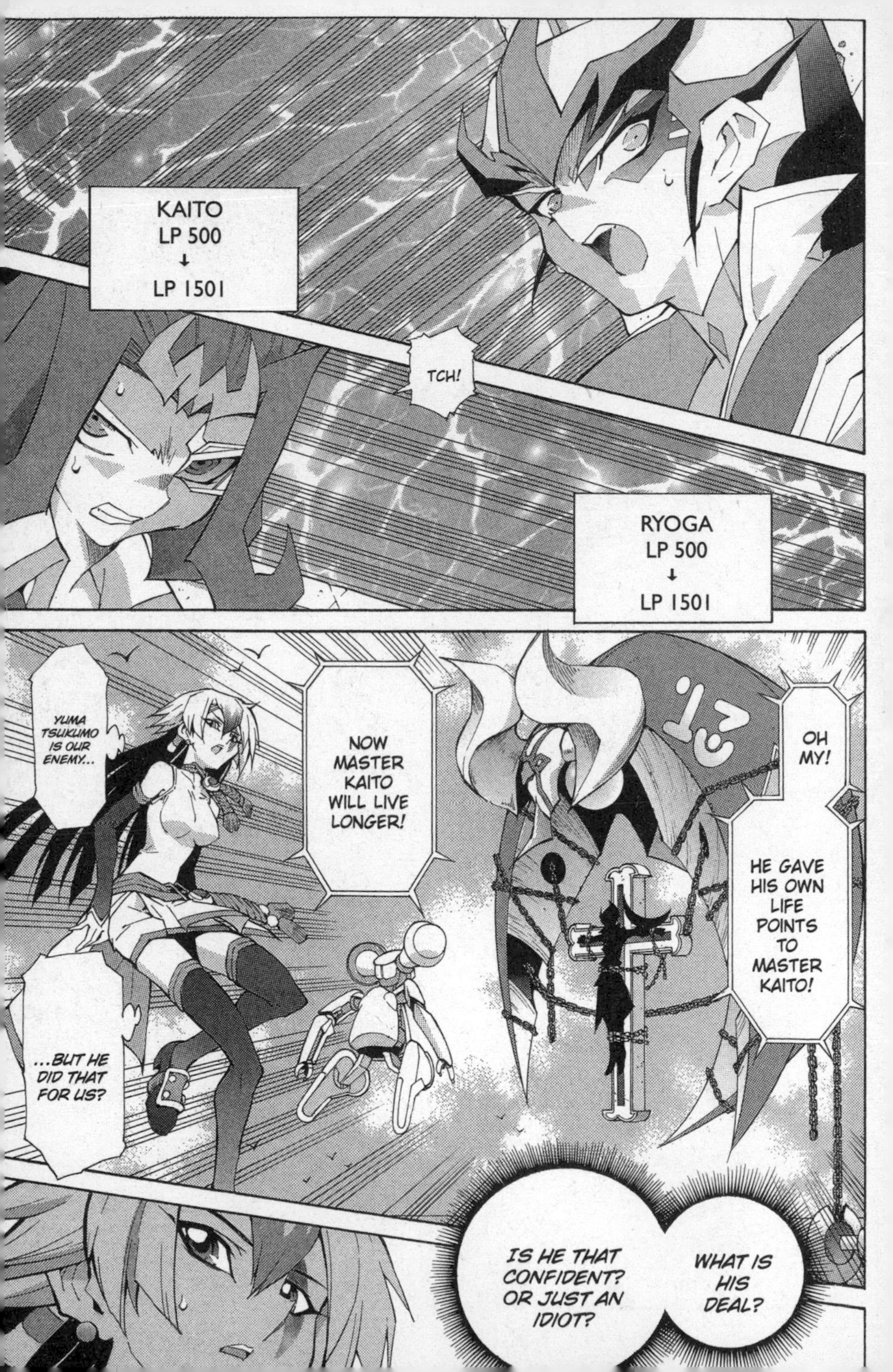

KAITO LP 500 ↓ LP 1501
TCH!
RYOGA LP 500 ↓ LP 1501
OH MY!
HE GAVE HIS OWN LIFE POINTS TO MASTER KAITO!
NOW MASTER KAITO WILL LIVE LONGER!
YUMA TSUKUMO IS OUR ENEMY...
...BUT HE DID THAT FOR US?
WHAT IS HIS DEAL?
IS HE THAT CONFIDENT? OR JUST AN IDIOT?

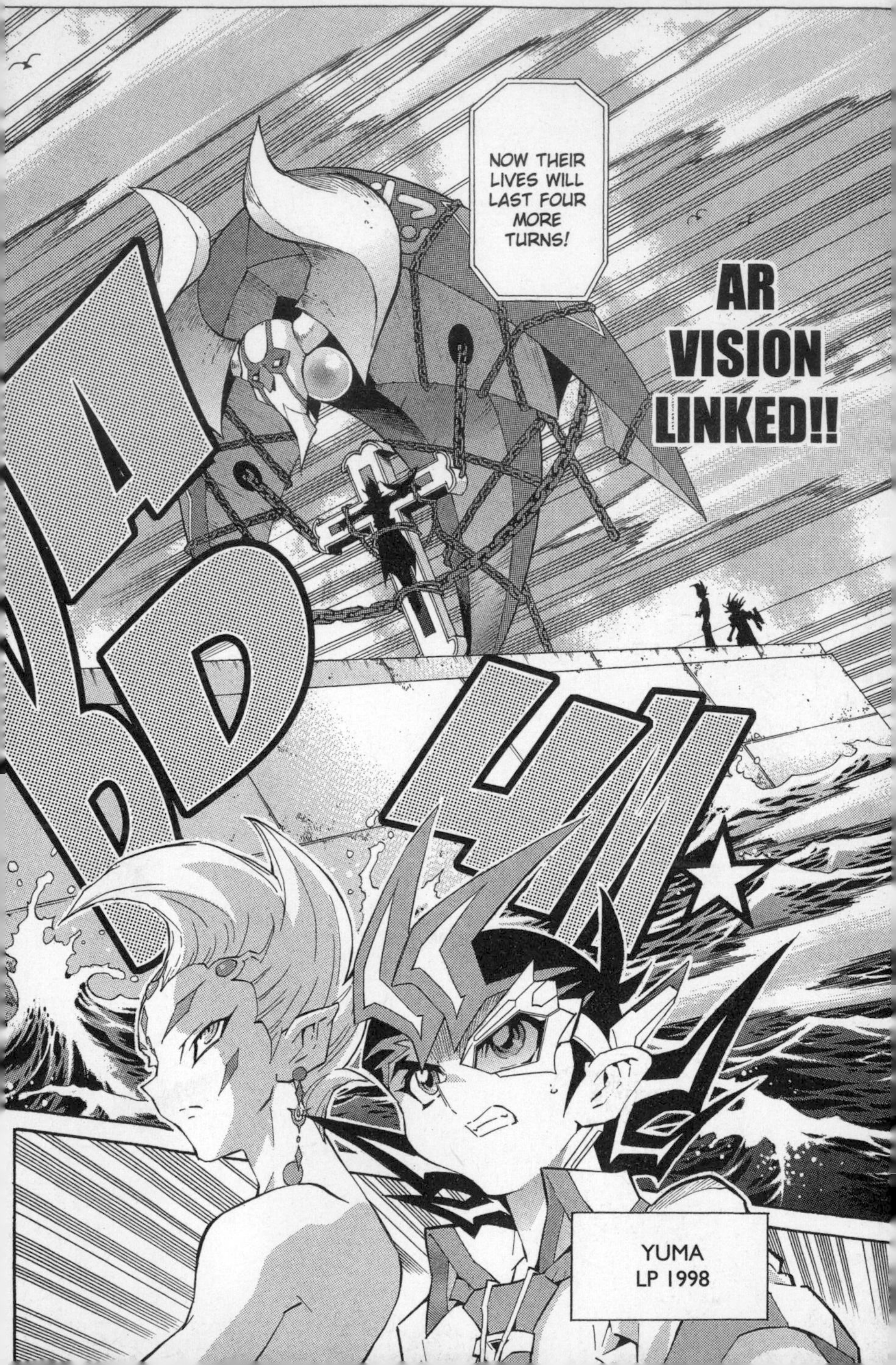

NOW THEIR LIVES WILL LAST FOUR MORE TURNS!
AR VISION LINKED!!
YUMA
LP 1998

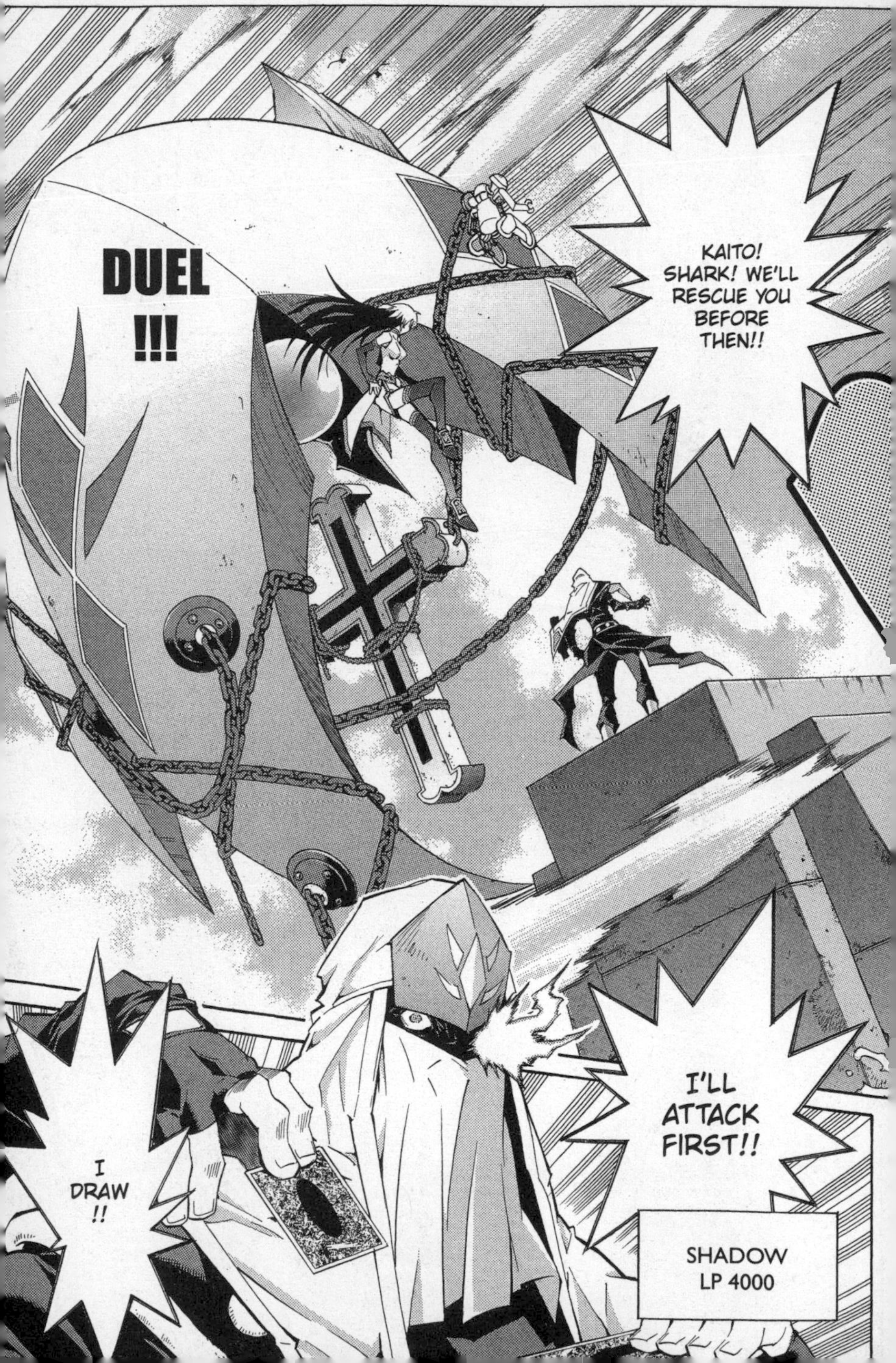
KAITO! SHARK! WE'LL RESCUE YOU BEFORE THEN!!
DUEL !!!
I'LL ATTACK FIRST!!
SHADOW LP 4000
I DRAW !!

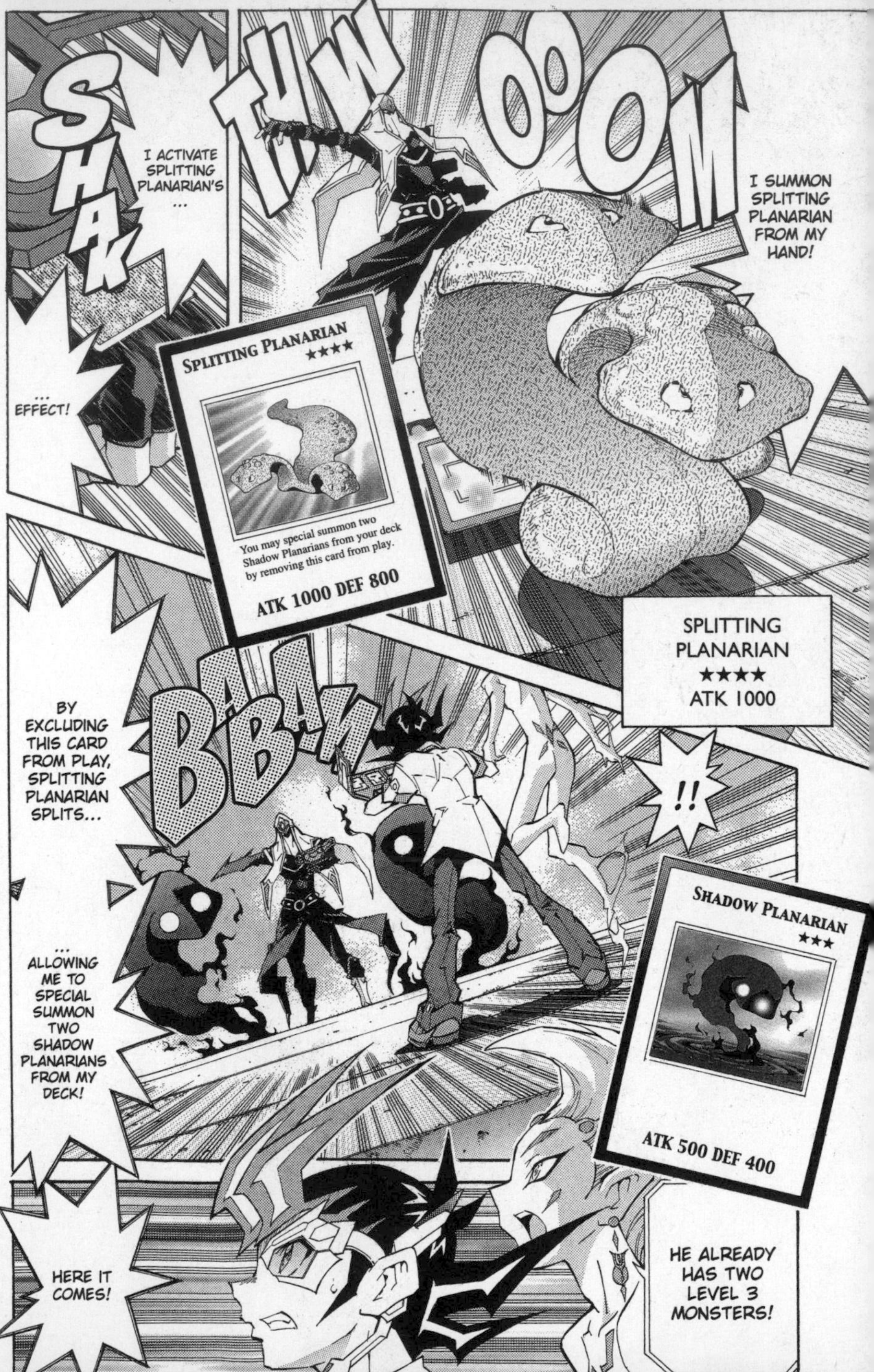

THWOOOOM
I SUMMON SPLITTING PLANARIAN FROM MY HAND!
SPLITTING PLANARIAN ★★★★
You may special summon two Shadow Planarians from your deck by removing this card from play.
ATK 1000 DEF 800
SPLITTING PLANARIAN ★★★★ ATK 1000
SHAK
I ACTIVATE SPLITTING PLANARIAN'S ...
... EFFECT!
BABAM
!!
BY EXCLUDING THIS CARD FROM PLAY, SPLITTING PLANARIAN SPLITS...
... ALLOWING ME TO SPECIAL SUMMON TWO SHADOW PLANARIANS FROM MY DECK!
SHADOW PLANARIAN ★★★
ATK 500 DEF 400
HE ALREADY HAS TWO LEVEL 3 MONSTERS!
HERE IT COMES!

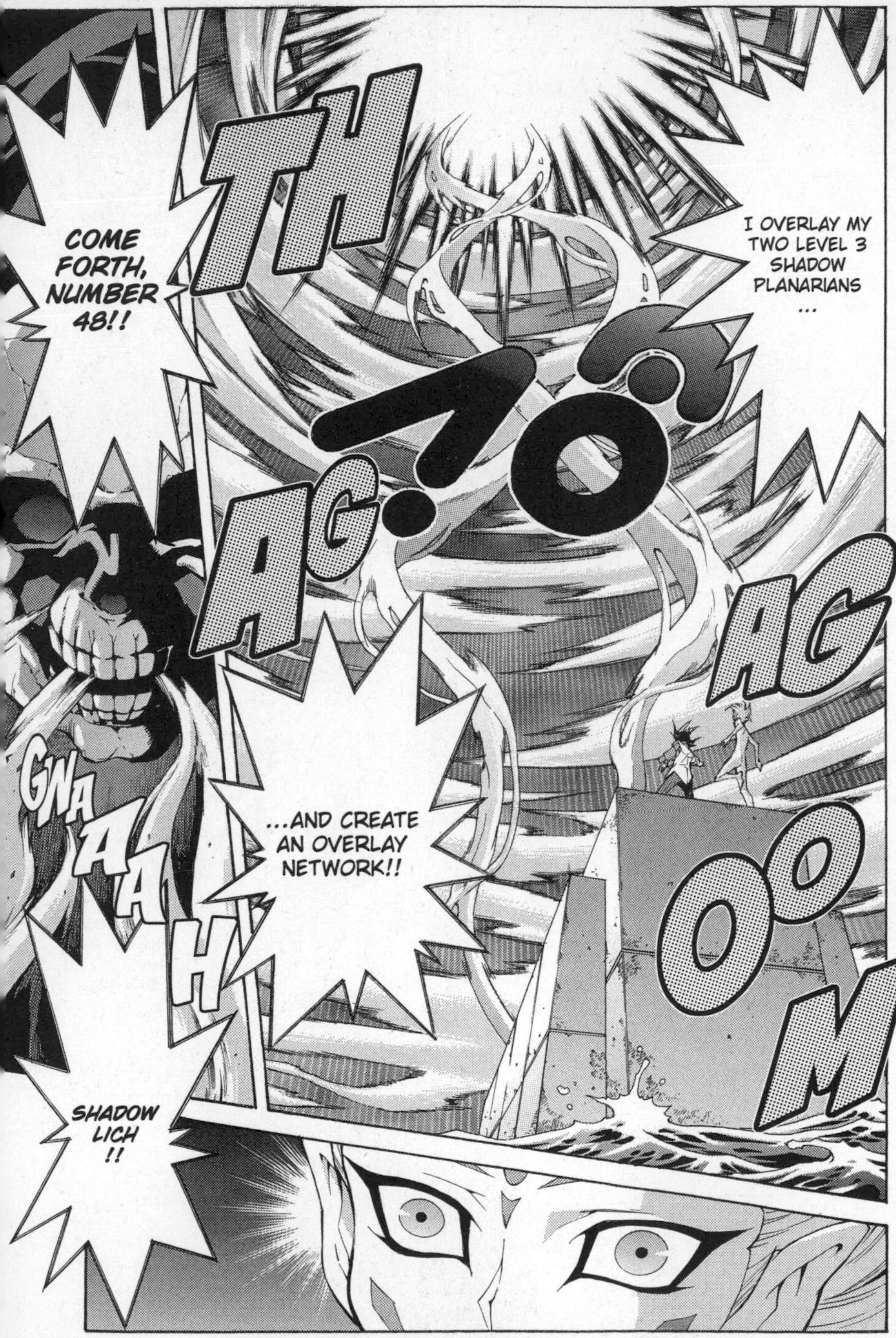
I OVERLAY MY TWO LEVEL 3 SHADOW PLANARIANS ...
...AND CREATE AN OVERLAY NETWORK!!
COME FORTH, NUMBER 48!!
GWAAAH
SHADOW LICH !!

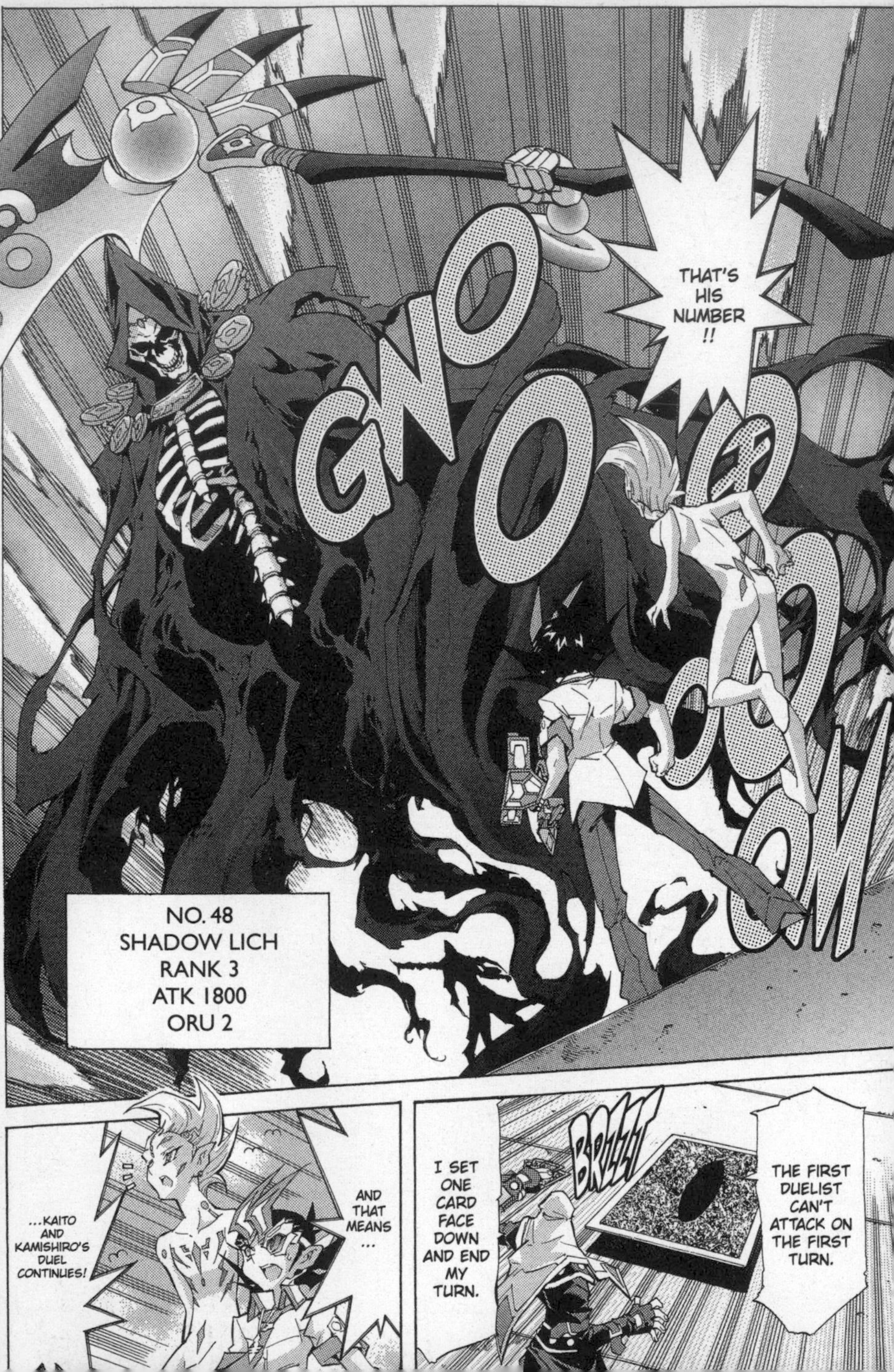
THAT'S HIS NUMBER !!
NO. 48
SHADOW LICH
RANK 3
ATK 1800
ORU 2
THE FIRST DUELIST CAN'T ATTACK ON THE FIRST TURN.
I SET ONE CARD FACE DOWN AND END MY TURN.
AND THAT MEANS ...
...KAITO AND KAMISHIRO'S DUEL CONTINUES!

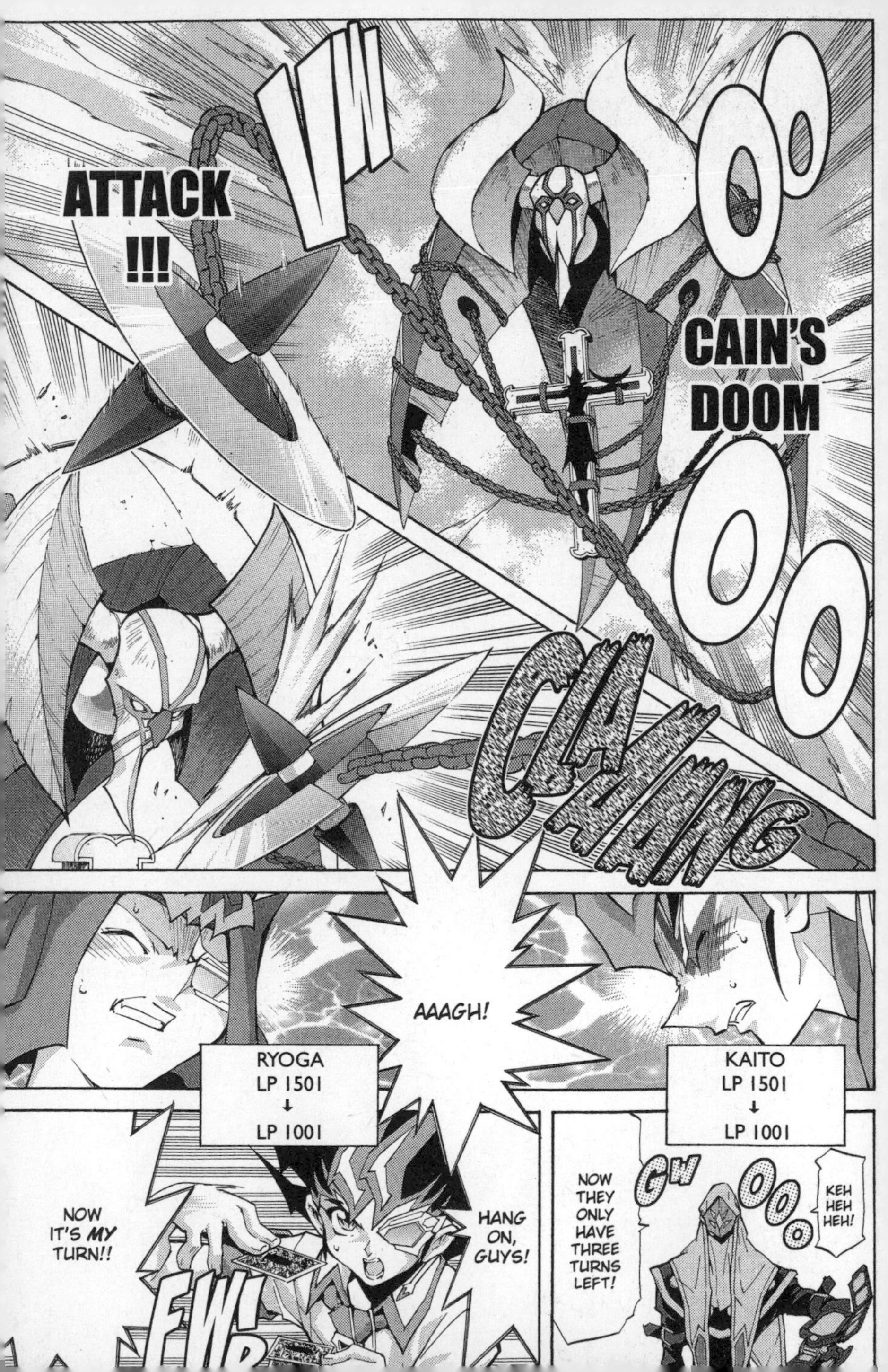

CAIN'S DOOM
VWN
ATTACK !!!
KAITO LP 1501 ↓ LP 1001
AAAGH!
RYOGA LP 1501 ↓ LP 1001
KEH HEH HEH!
NOW THEY ONLY HAVE THREE TURNS LEFT!
HANG ON, GUYS!
NOW IT'S *MY* TURN!!

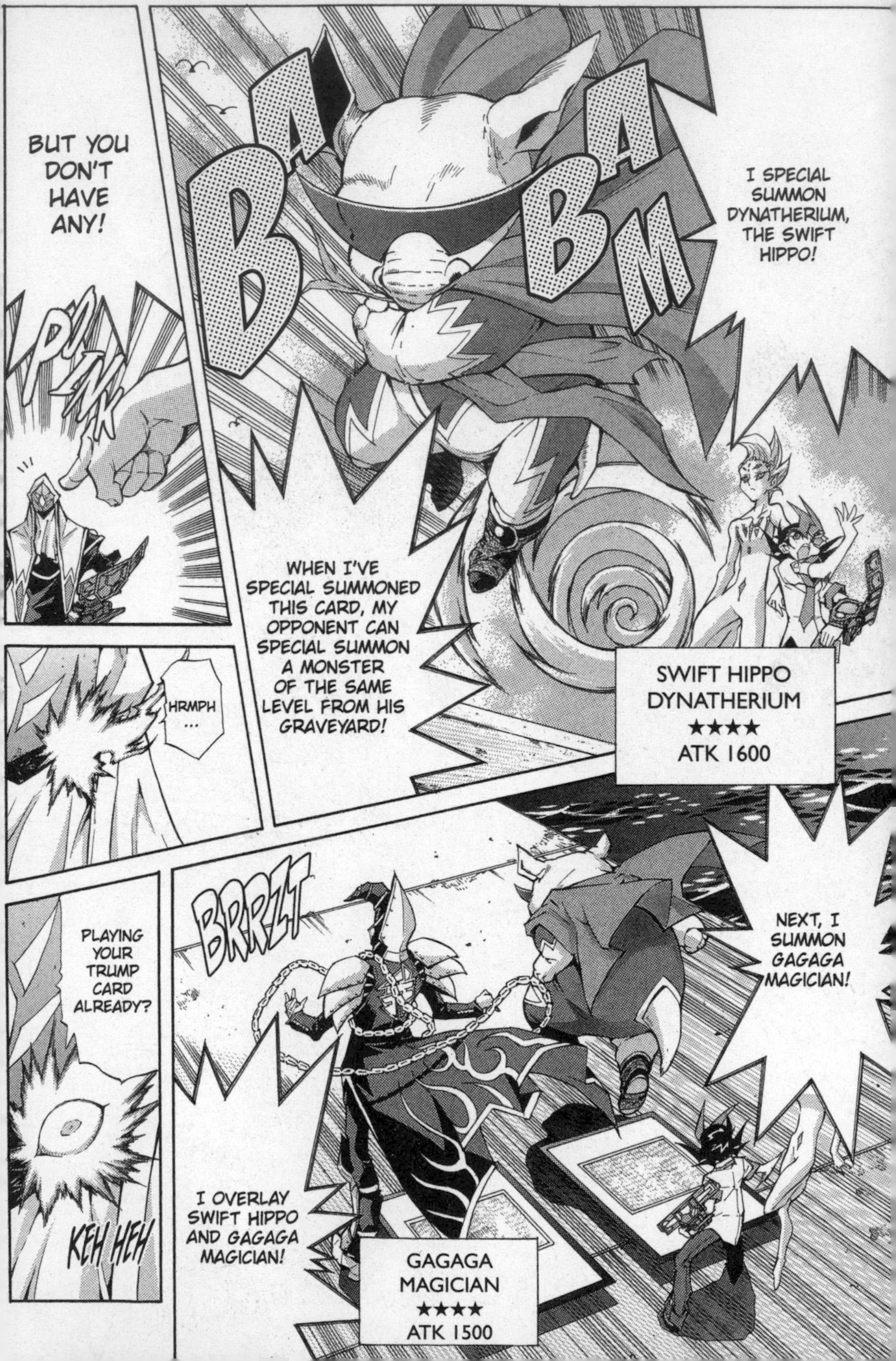
BABAM
I SPECIAL SUMMON DYNATHERIUM, THE SWIFT HIPPO!
WHEN I'VE SPECIAL SUMMONED THIS CARD, MY OPPONENT CAN SPECIAL SUMMON A MONSTER OF THE SAME LEVEL FROM HIS GRAVEYARD!
SWIFT HIPPO DYNATHERIUM ★★★★ ATK 1600
BUT YOU DON'T HAVE ANY!
PLINK
HRMPH ...
NEXT, I SUMMON GAGAGA MAGICIAN!
BRRZT
I OVERLAY SWIFT HIPPO AND GAGAGA MAGICIAN!
GAGAGA MAGICIAN ★★★★ ATK 1500
PLAYING YOUR TRUMP CARD ALREADY?
KEH HEH

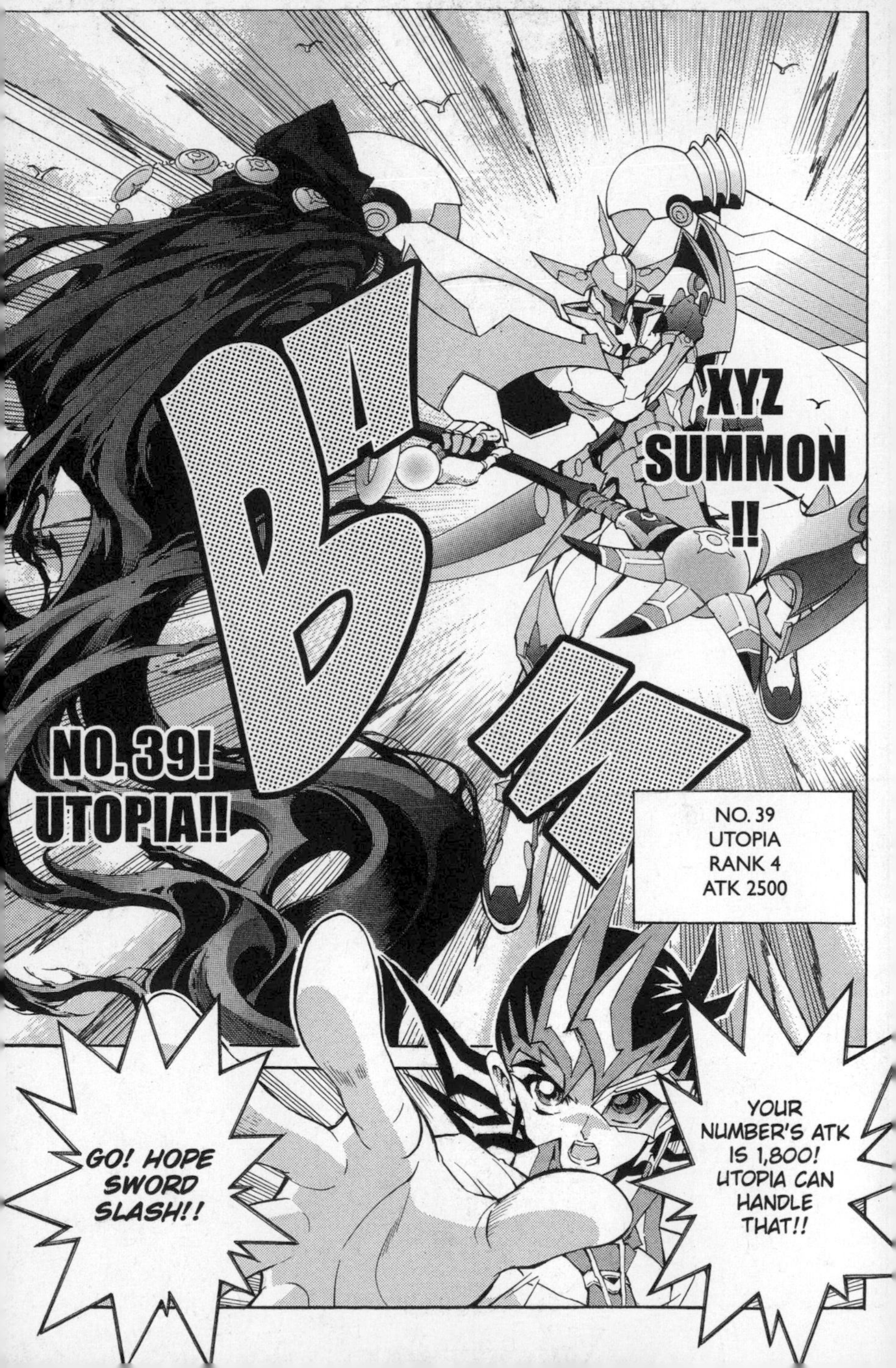
XYZ SUMMON!!
NO. 39! UTOPIA!!
NO. 39 UTOPIA RANK 4 ATK 2500
YOUR NUMBER'S ATK IS 1,800! UTOPIA CAN HANDLE THAT!!
GO! HOPE SWORD SLASH!!

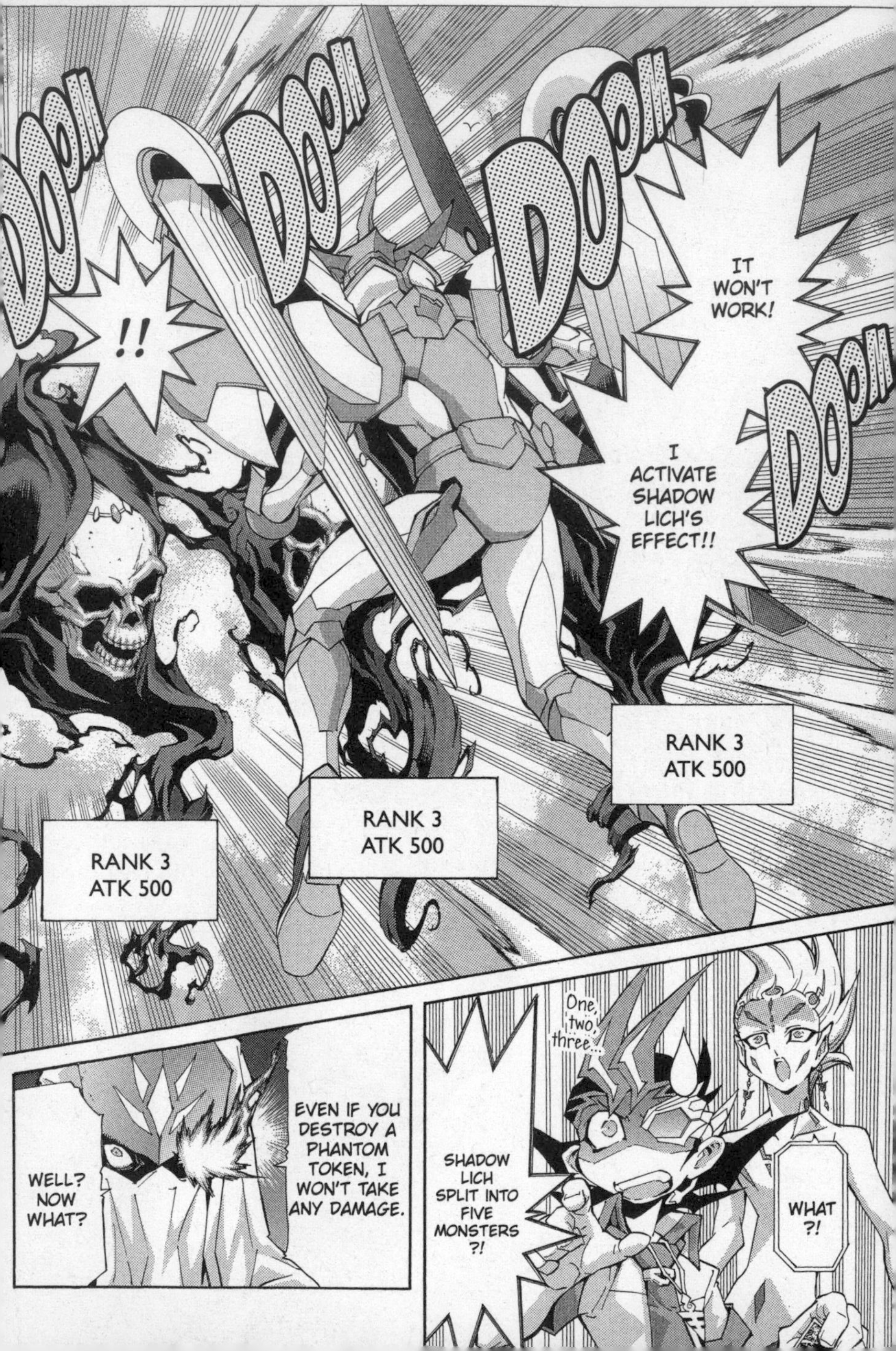
IT WON'T WORK!
I ACTIVATE SHADOW LICH'S EFFECT!!
!!
RANK 3 ATK 500
RANK 3 ATK 500
RANK 3 ATK 500
WHAT ?!
One, two, three...
SHADOW LICH SPLIT INTO FIVE MONSTERS ?!
EVEN IF YOU DESTROY A PHANTOM TOKEN, I WON'T TAKE ANY DAMAGE.
WELL? NOW WHAT?

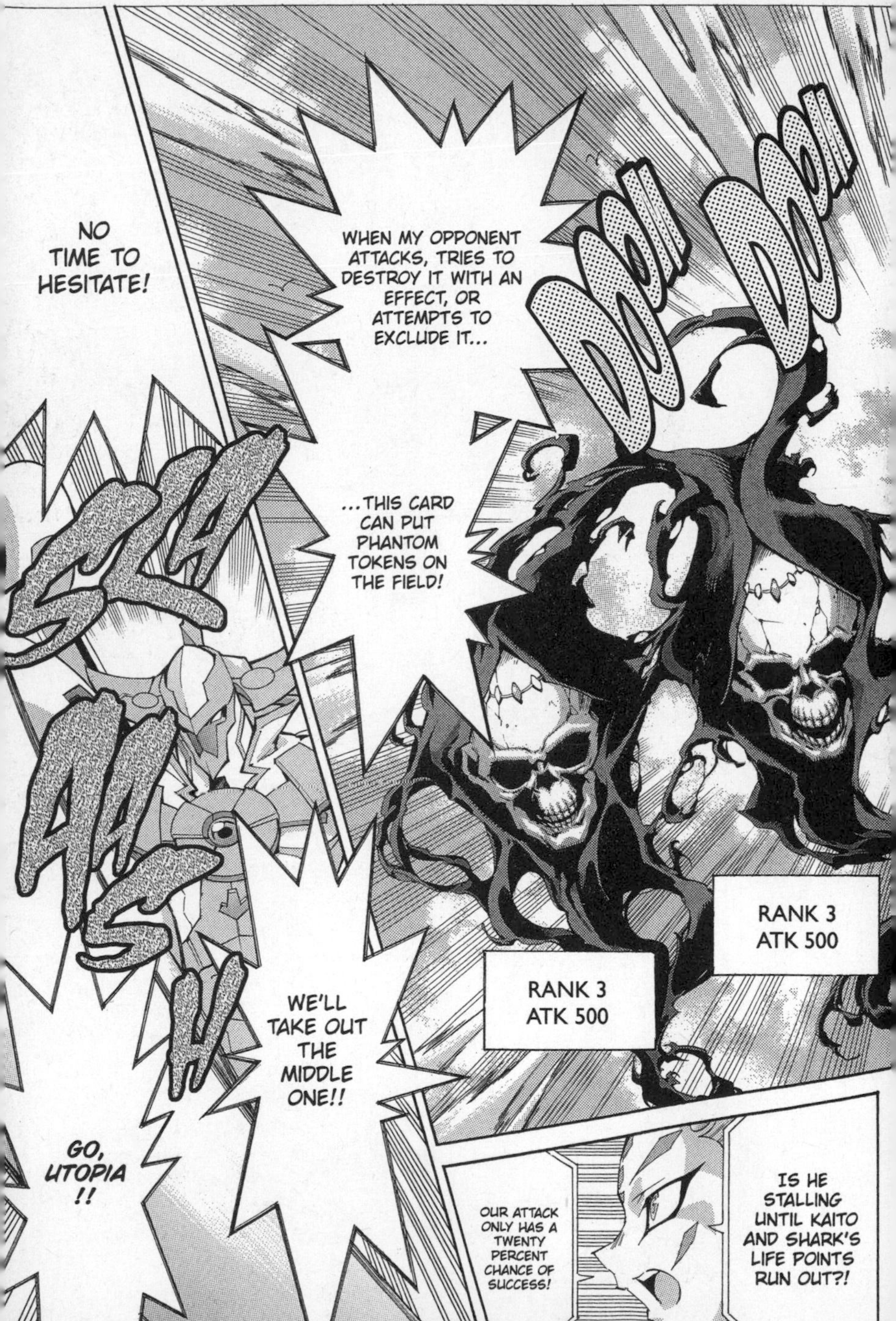
DOO!! DOO!!
WHEN MY OPPONENT ATTACKS, TRIES TO DESTROY IT WITH AN EFFECT, OR ATTEMPTS TO EXCLUDE IT...
...THIS CARD CAN PUT PHANTOM TOKENS ON THE FIELD!
RANK 3 ATK 500
RANK 3 ATK 500
IS HE STALLING UNTIL KAITO AND SHARK'S LIFE POINTS RUN OUT?!
OUR ATTACK ONLY HAS A TWENTY PERCENT CHANCE OF SUCCESS!
NO TIME TO HESITATE!
SLAAASH
WE'LL TAKE OUT THE MIDDLE ONE!!
GO, UTOPIA!!

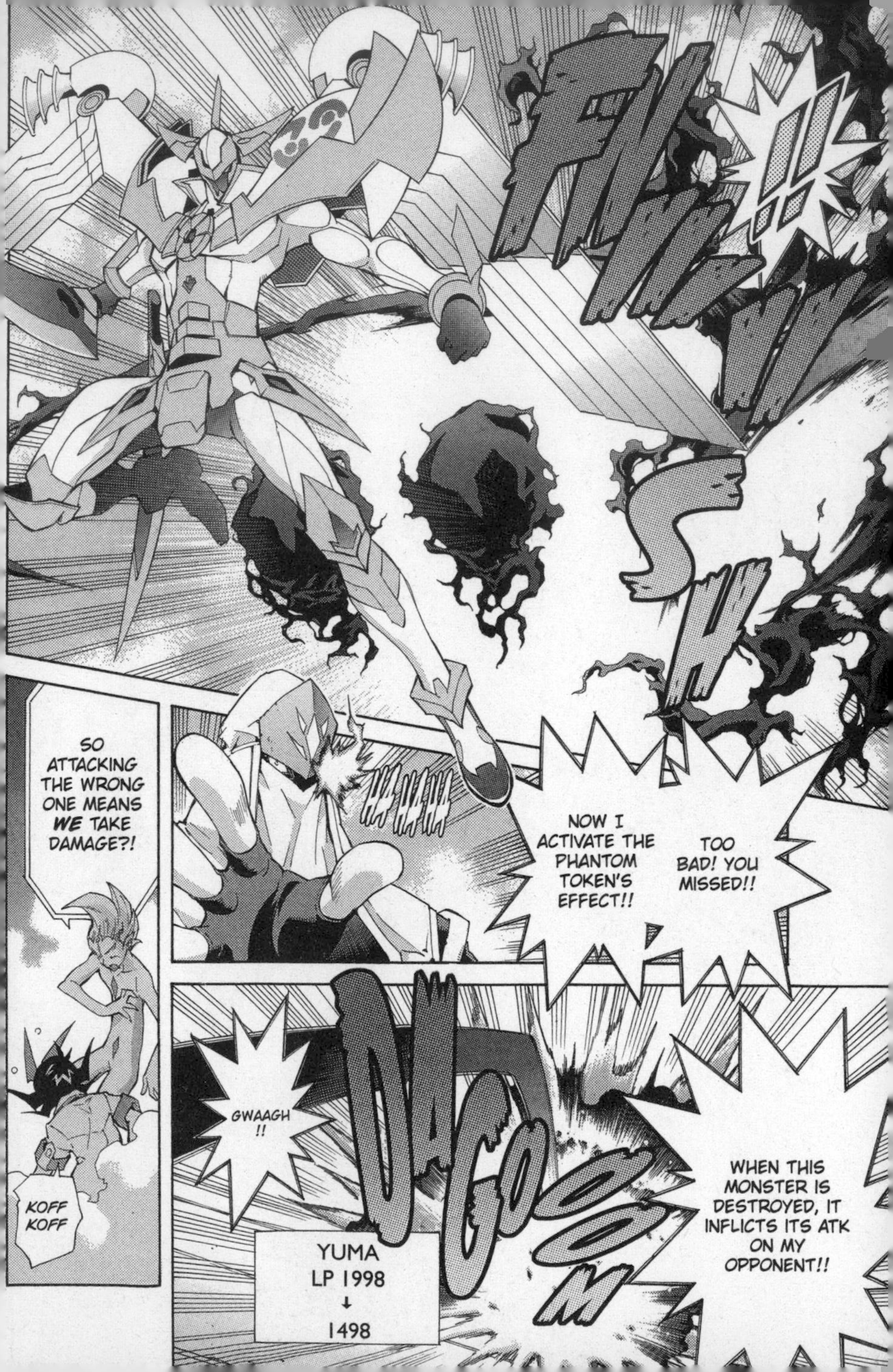
TOO BAD! YOU MISSED!!
NOW I ACTIVATE THE PHANTOM TOKEN'S EFFECT!!
WHEN THIS MONSTER IS DESTROYED, IT INFLICTS ITS ATK ON MY OPPONENT!!
GWAAGH !!
YUMA LP 1998 ↓ 1498
SO ATTACKING THE WRONG ONE MEANS *WE* TAKE DAMAGE?!
KOFF KOFF

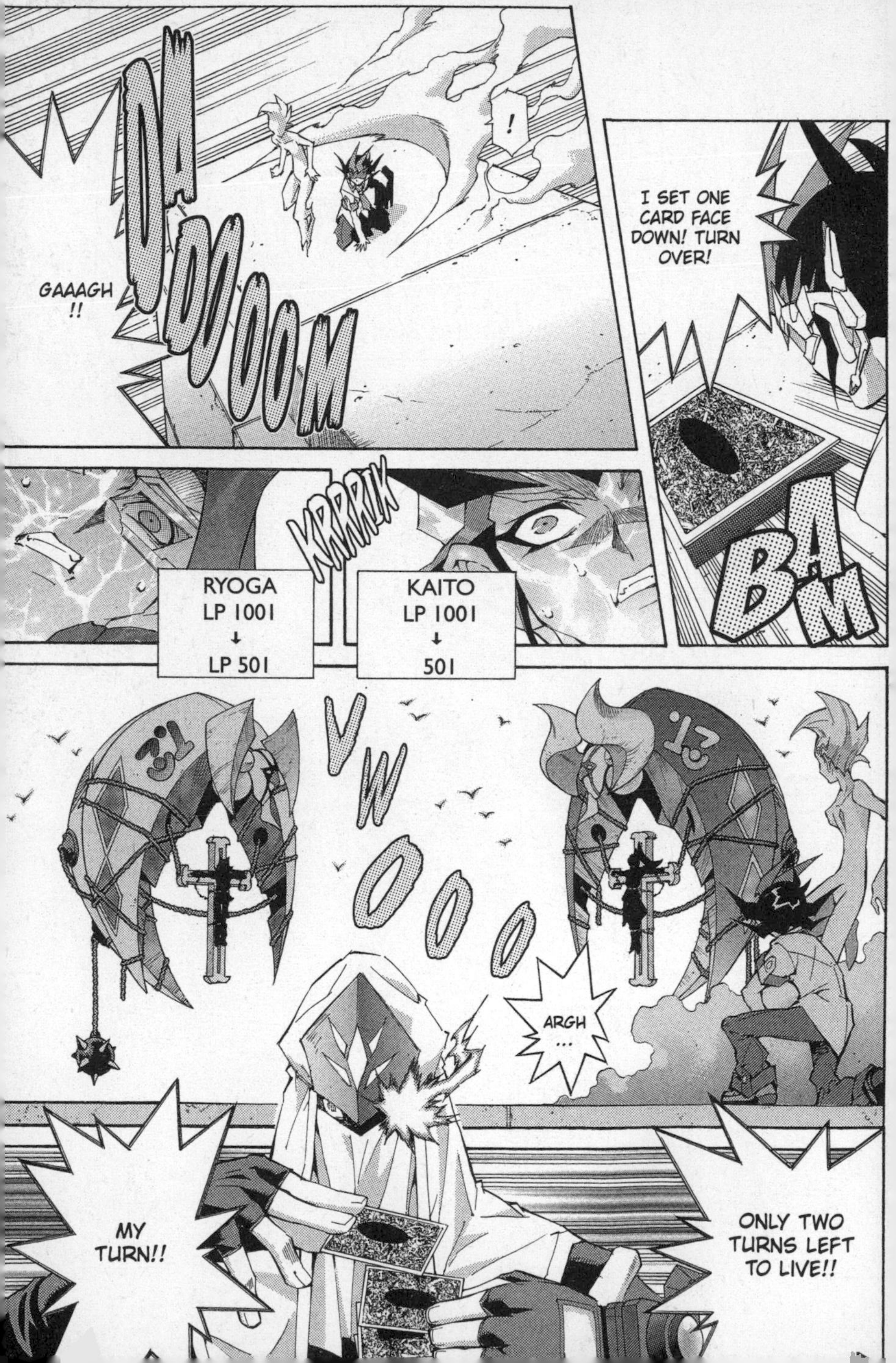
I SET ONE CARD FACE DOWN! TURN OVER!
BAM
!
DOOOOM
GAAAGH!!
KRRRIK
KAITO LP 1001 ↓ 501
RYOGA LP 1001 ↓ LP 501
VWOOOO
ARGH...
ONLY TWO TURNS LEFT TO LIVE!!
MY TURN!!

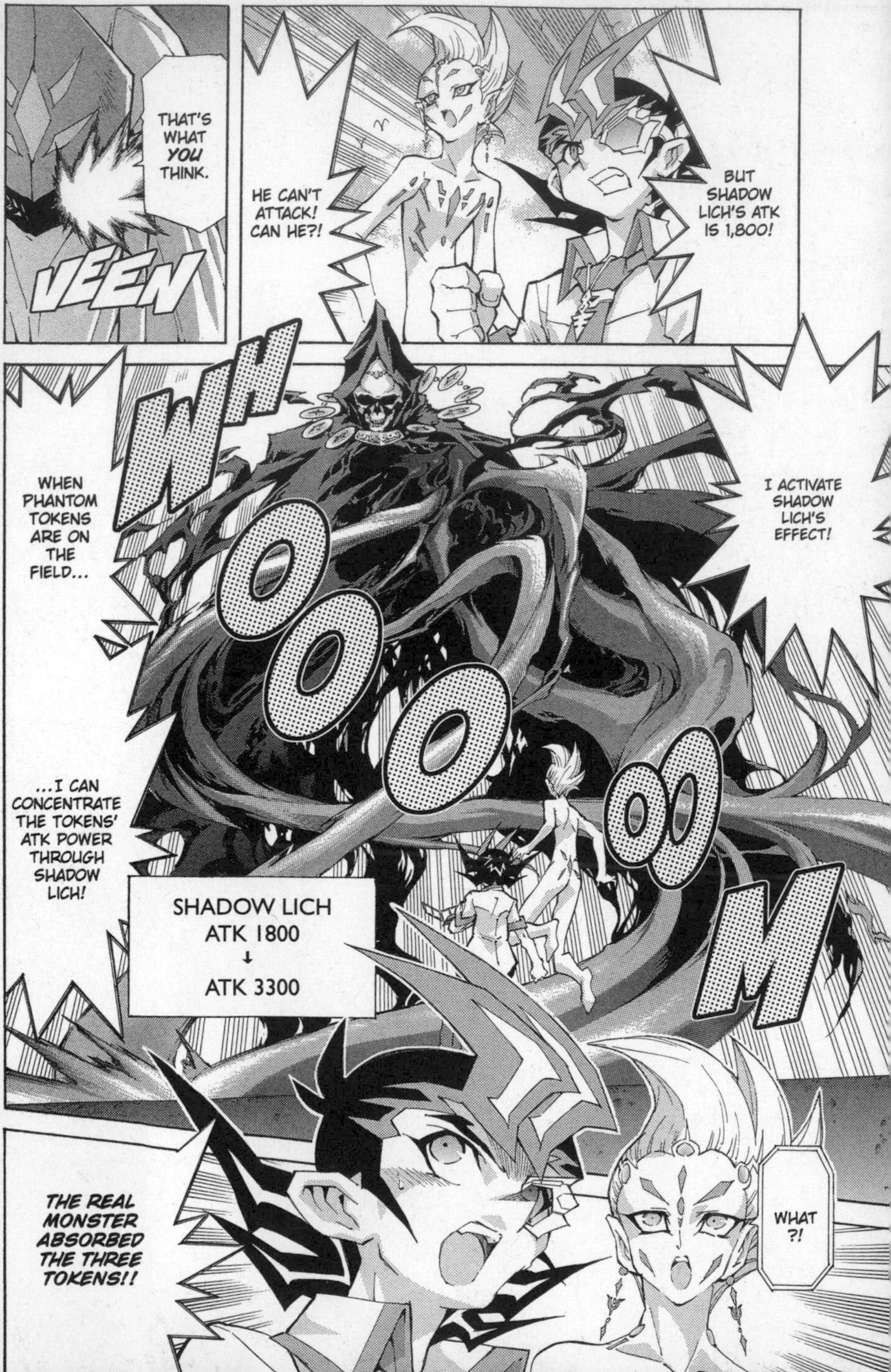
BUT SHADOW LICH'S ATK IS 1,800!
HE CAN'T ATTACK! CAN HE?!
THAT'S WHAT YOU THINK.
VEEN
I ACTIVATE SHADOW LICH'S EFFECT!
WHOOOOOOM
WHEN PHANTOM TOKENS ARE ON THE FIELD...
...I CAN CONCENTRATE THE TOKENS' ATK POWER THROUGH SHADOW LICH!
SHADOW LICH ATK 1800 ↓ ATK 3300
WHAT?!
THE REAL MONSTER ABSORBED THE THREE TOKENS!!

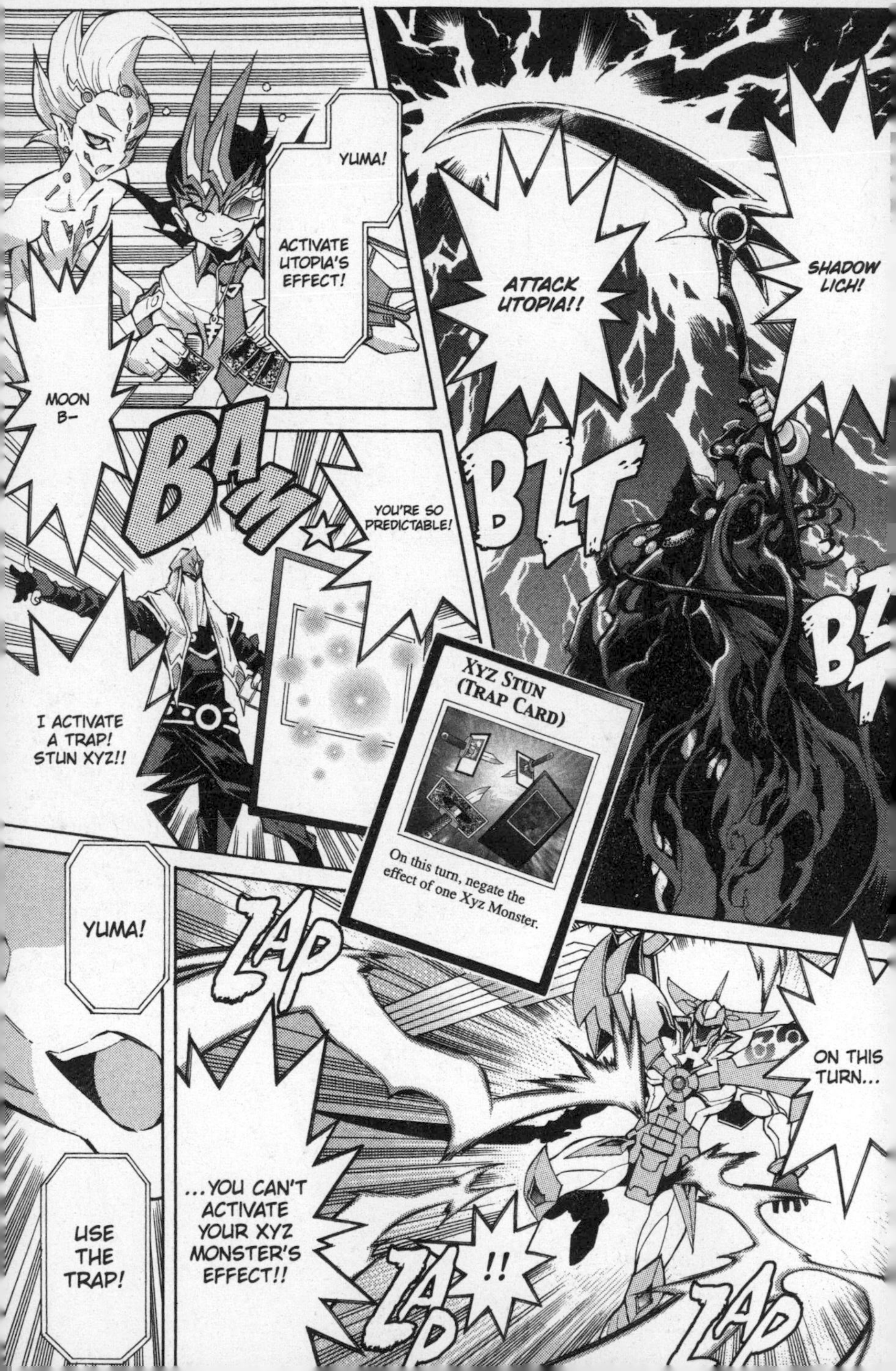
SHADOW LICH!
ATTACK UTOPIA!!
BZT
BZ
YUMA!
ACTIVATE UTOPIA'S EFFECT!
MOON B–
BAM
YOU'RE SO PREDICTABLE!
I ACTIVATE A TRAP! STUN XYZ!!
XYZ STUN (TRAP CARD)
On this turn, negate the effect of one Xyz Monster.
ON THIS TURN...
...YOU CAN'T ACTIVATE YOUR XYZ MONSTER'S EFFECT!!
ZAP
!!
ZAP
ZAP
YUMA!
USE THE TRAP!

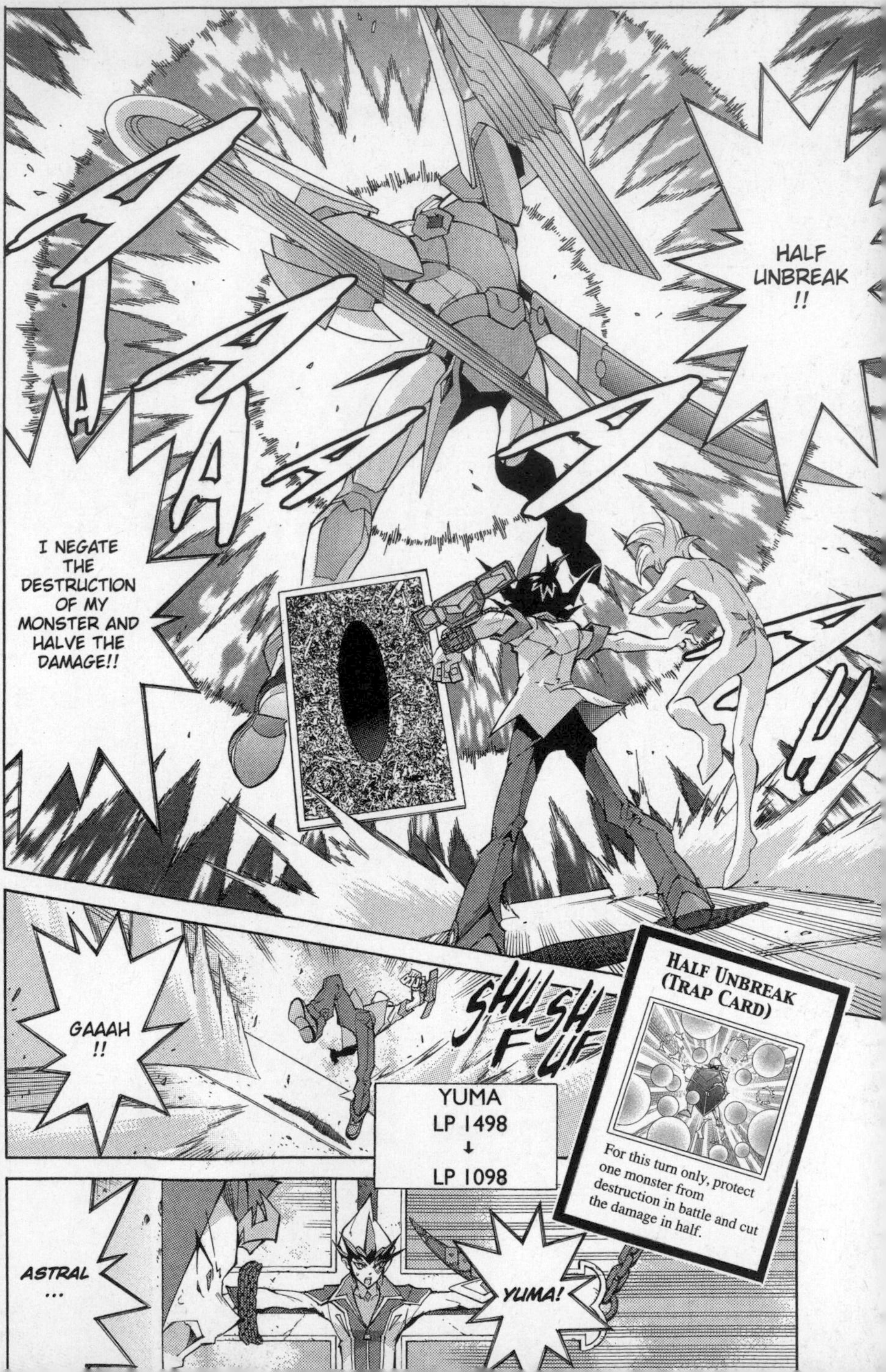
HALF UNBREAK!!
I NEGATE THE DESTRUCTION OF MY MONSTER AND HALVE THE DAMAGE!!
HALF UNBREAK (TRAP CARD)
For this turn only, protect one monster from destruction in battle and cut the damage in half.
SHUSH
FUF
YUMA LP 1498 ↓ LP 1098
GAAAH!!
YUMA!
ASTRAL...

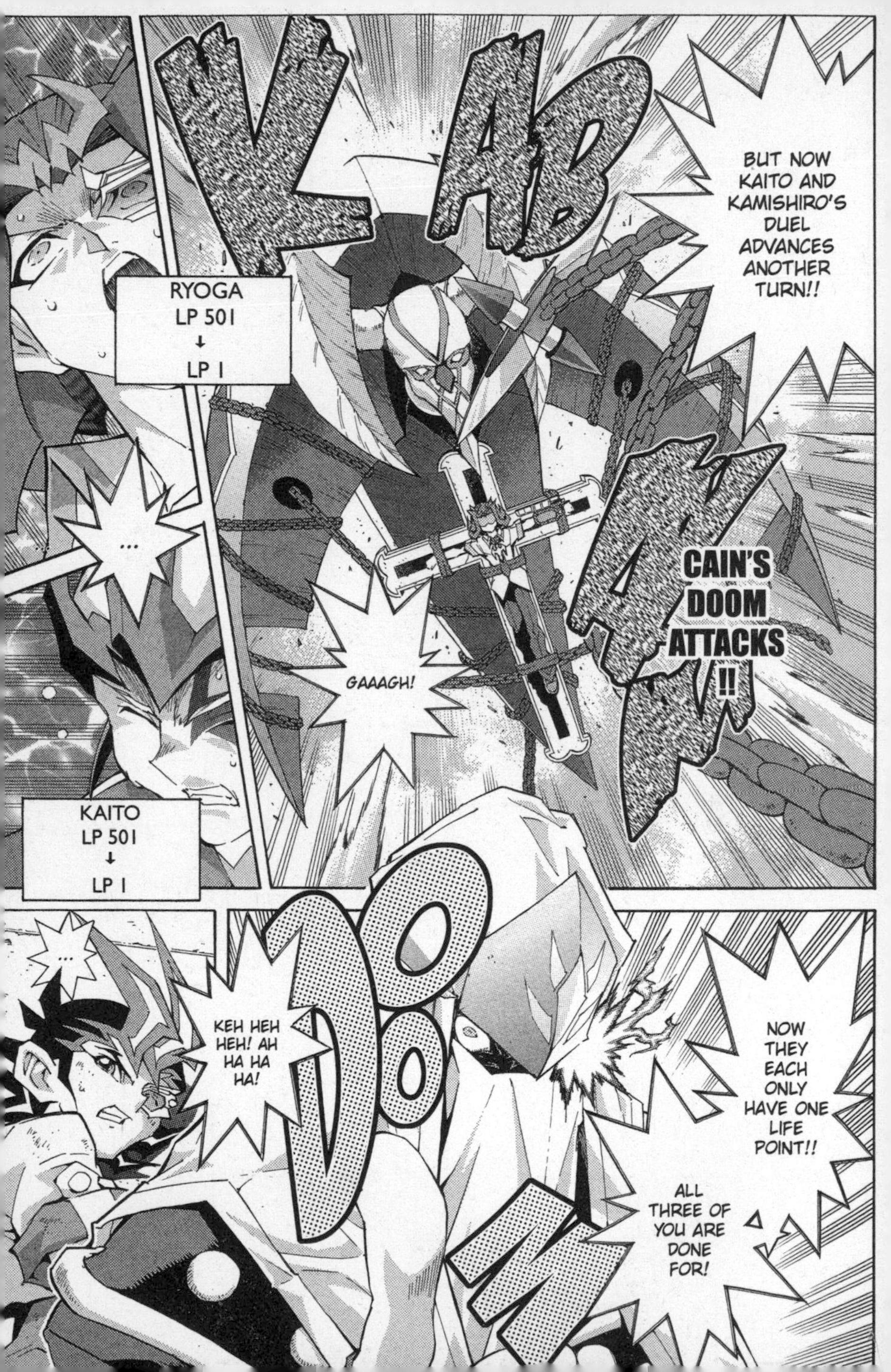
BUT NOW KAITO AND KAMISHIRO'S DUEL ADVANCES ANOTHER TURN!!
CAIN'S DOOM ATTACKS!!
GAAAGH!
RYOGA
LP 501
↓
LP 1
...
KAITO
LP 501
↓
LP 1
NOW THEY EACH ONLY HAVE ONE LIFE POINT!!
ALL THREE OF YOU ARE DONE FOR!
KEH HEH HEH! AH HA HA HA!
...

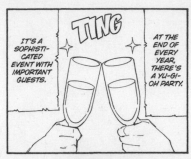

astral's Journal #8
TING
AT THE END OF EVERY YEAR, THERE'S A YU-GI-OH PARTY.
IT'S A SOPHISTICATED EVENT WITH IMPORTANT GUESTS.
MIYOSHI'S FIRST TIME WAS IN 2010 AT TAKAHASHI SENSEI'S HOUSE.
SINCE THEN, IT'S BEEN HELD AT AN ITALIAN RESTAURANT.
OPEN
MIYOSHI IS ALWAYS IN A HURRY AT THIS TIME OF YEAR.
This year, I'll finish the manuscript before the party for sure!!
MIYOSHI-SAN, YOU STILL HAVE WORK. YOU SHOULD GO.
AWWW!
IT'S THE SAME EVERY YEAR.
EDITOR
FEAST♡

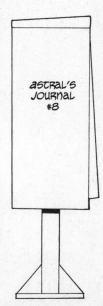

Rank 32

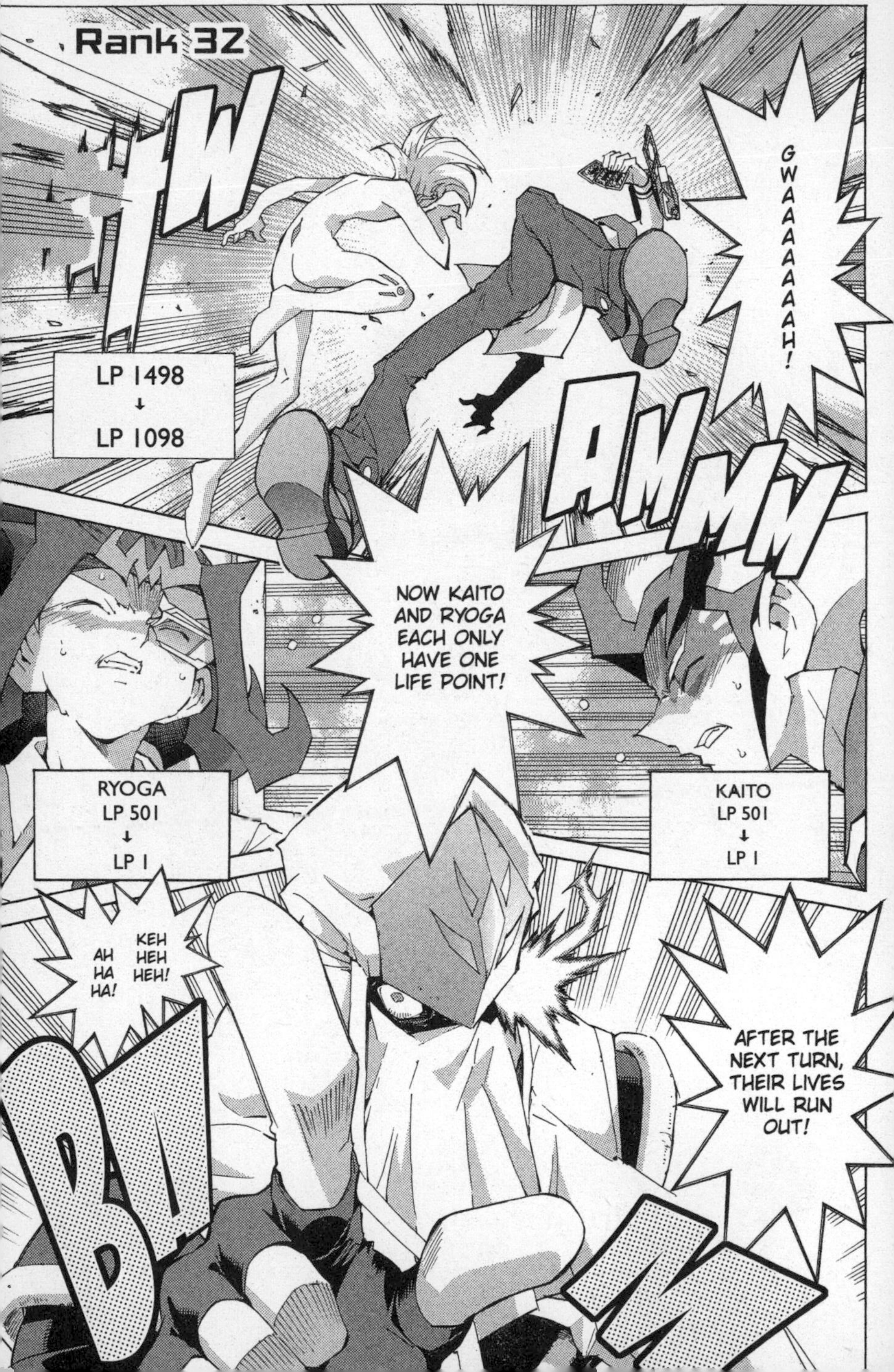
GWAAAAAAAAAH!
LP 1498 ↓ LP 1098
NOW KAITO AND RYOGA EACH ONLY HAVE ONE LIFE POINT!
KAITO LP 501 ↓ LP 1
RYOGA LP 501 ↓ LP 1
AFTER THE NEXT TURN, THEIR LIVES WILL RUN OUT!
KEH HEH HEH!
AH HA HA!

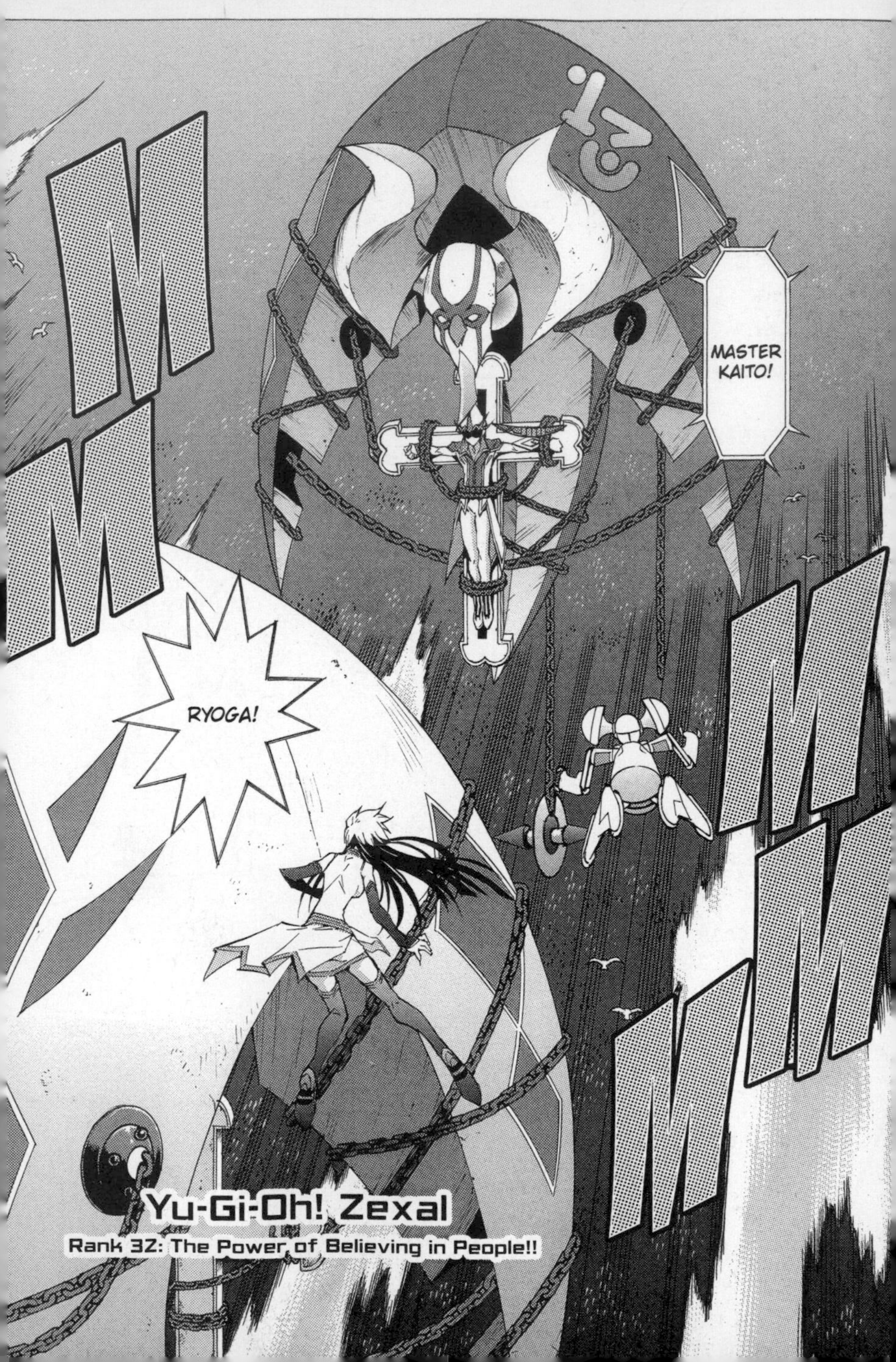
MASTER KAITO!
MMMM
RYOGA!
MMM

Yu-Gi-Oh! Zexal

Rank 32: The Power of Believing in People!!

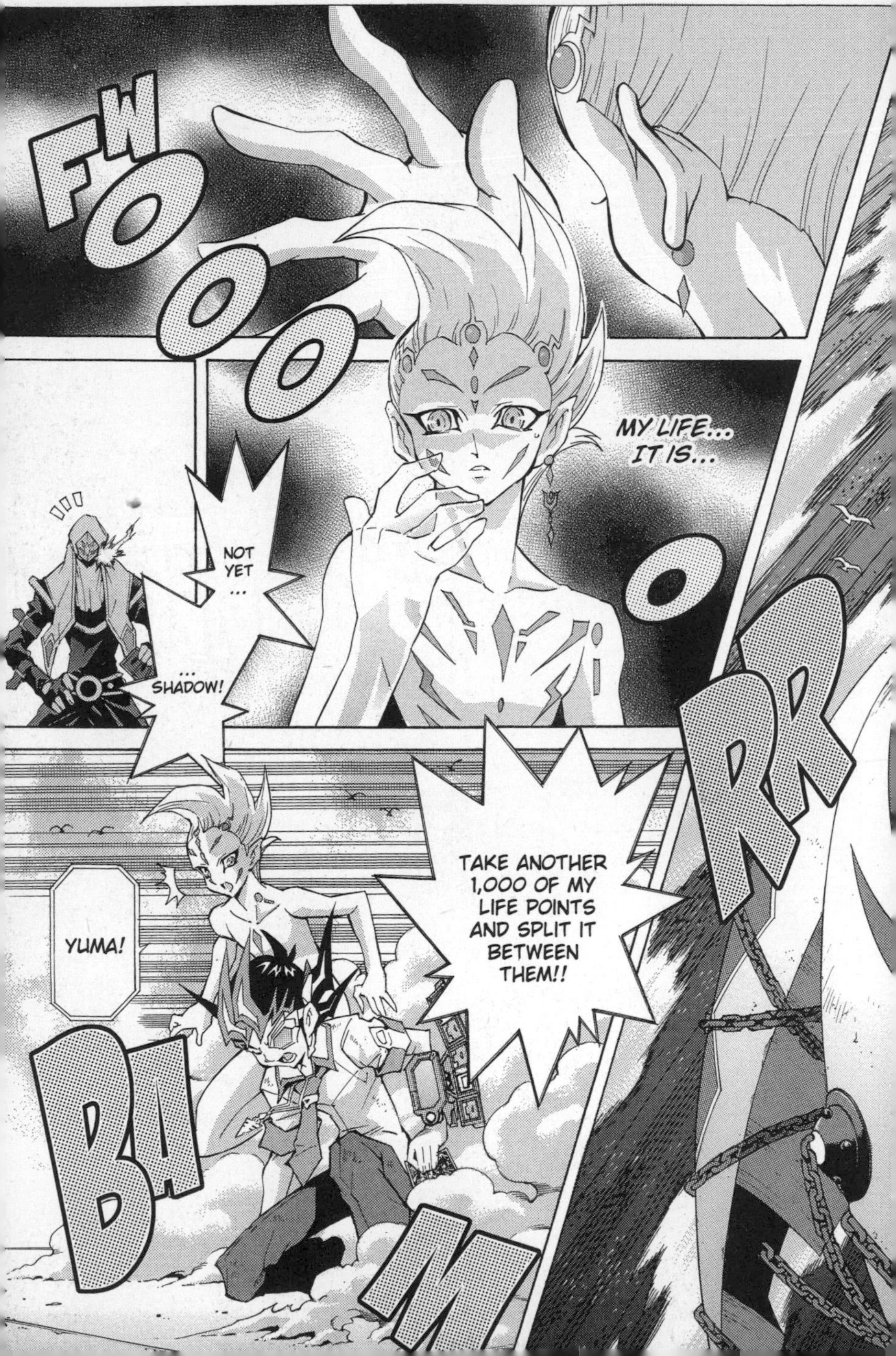
FWOOOORR
MY LIFE... IT IS...
NOT YET ...
... SHADOW!
TAKE ANOTHER 1,000 OF MY LIFE POINTS AND SPLIT IT BETWEEN THEM!!
YUMA!
BAM

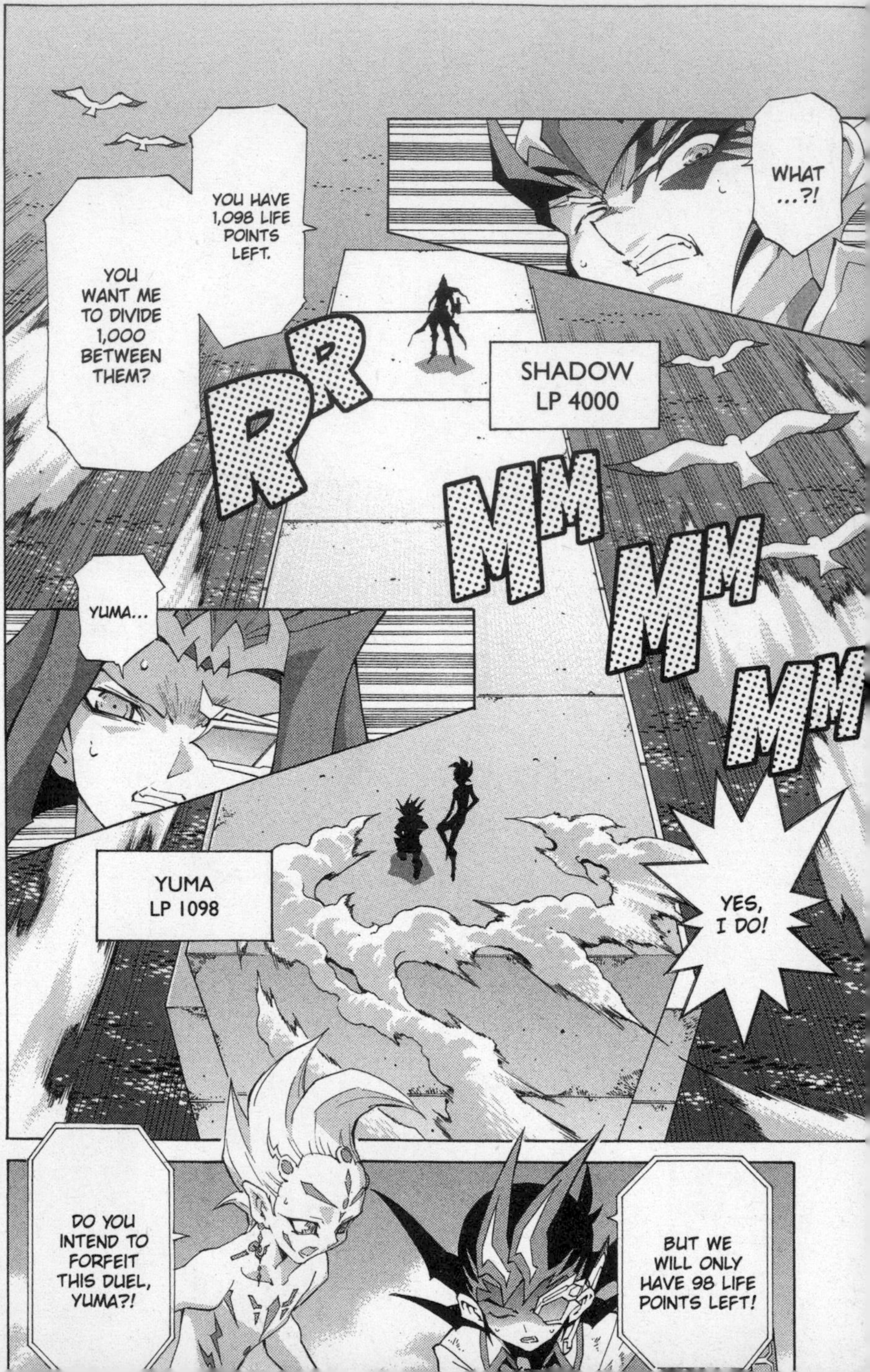
YOU HAVE 1,098 LIFE POINTS LEFT.
YOU WANT ME TO DIVIDE 1,000 BETWEEN THEM?
WHAT ...?!
RR
SHADOW LP 4000
MMM
MMM
MMM
YUMA...
YES, I DO!
YUMA LP 1098
BUT WE WILL ONLY HAVE 98 LIFE POINTS LEFT!
DO YOU INTEND TO FORFEIT THIS DUEL, YUMA?!

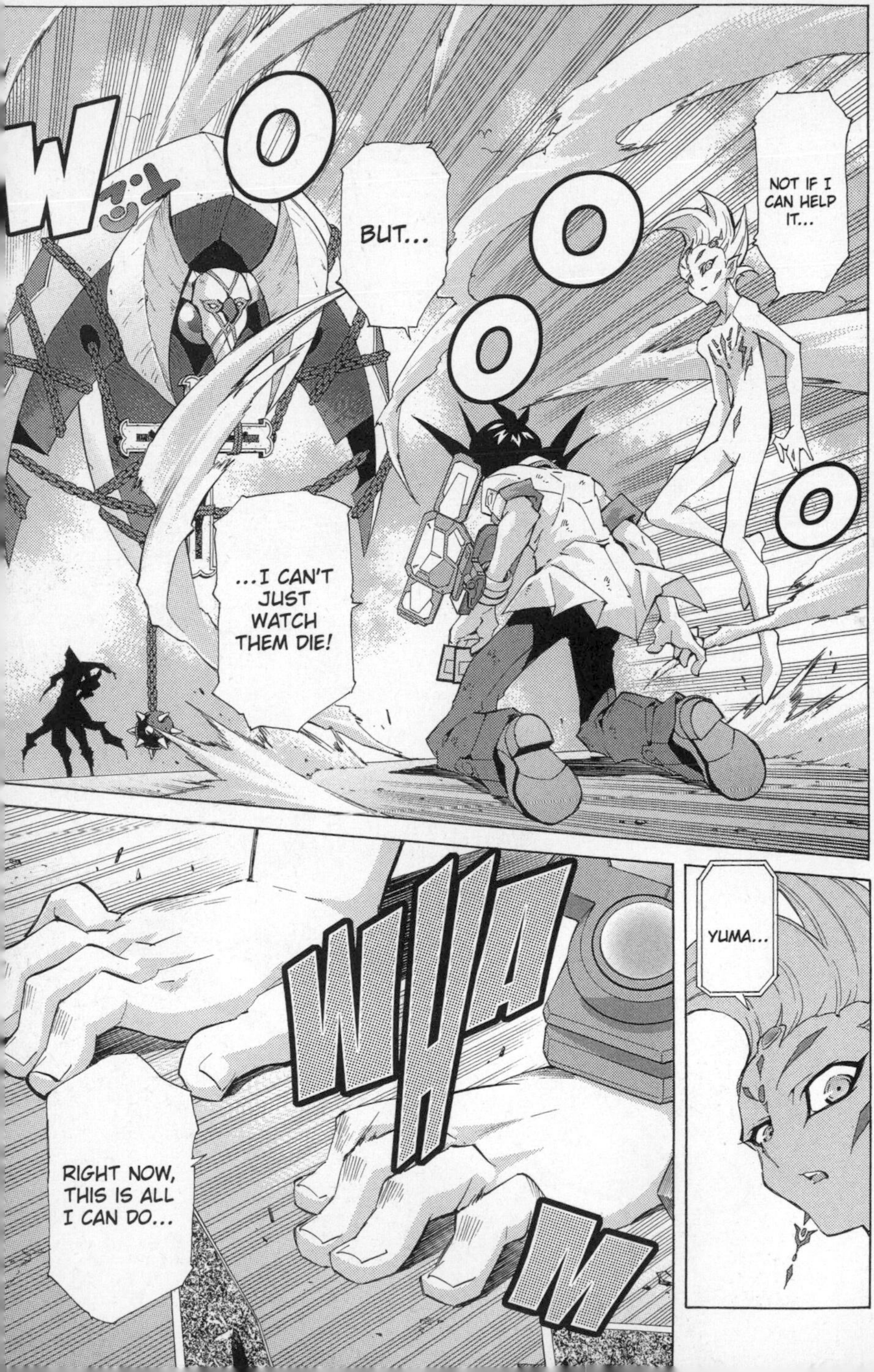
NOT IF I CAN HELP IT...
BUT...
WOOOO
...I CAN'T JUST WATCH THEM DIE!
YUMA...
WHAM
RIGHT NOW, THIS IS ALL I CAN DO...

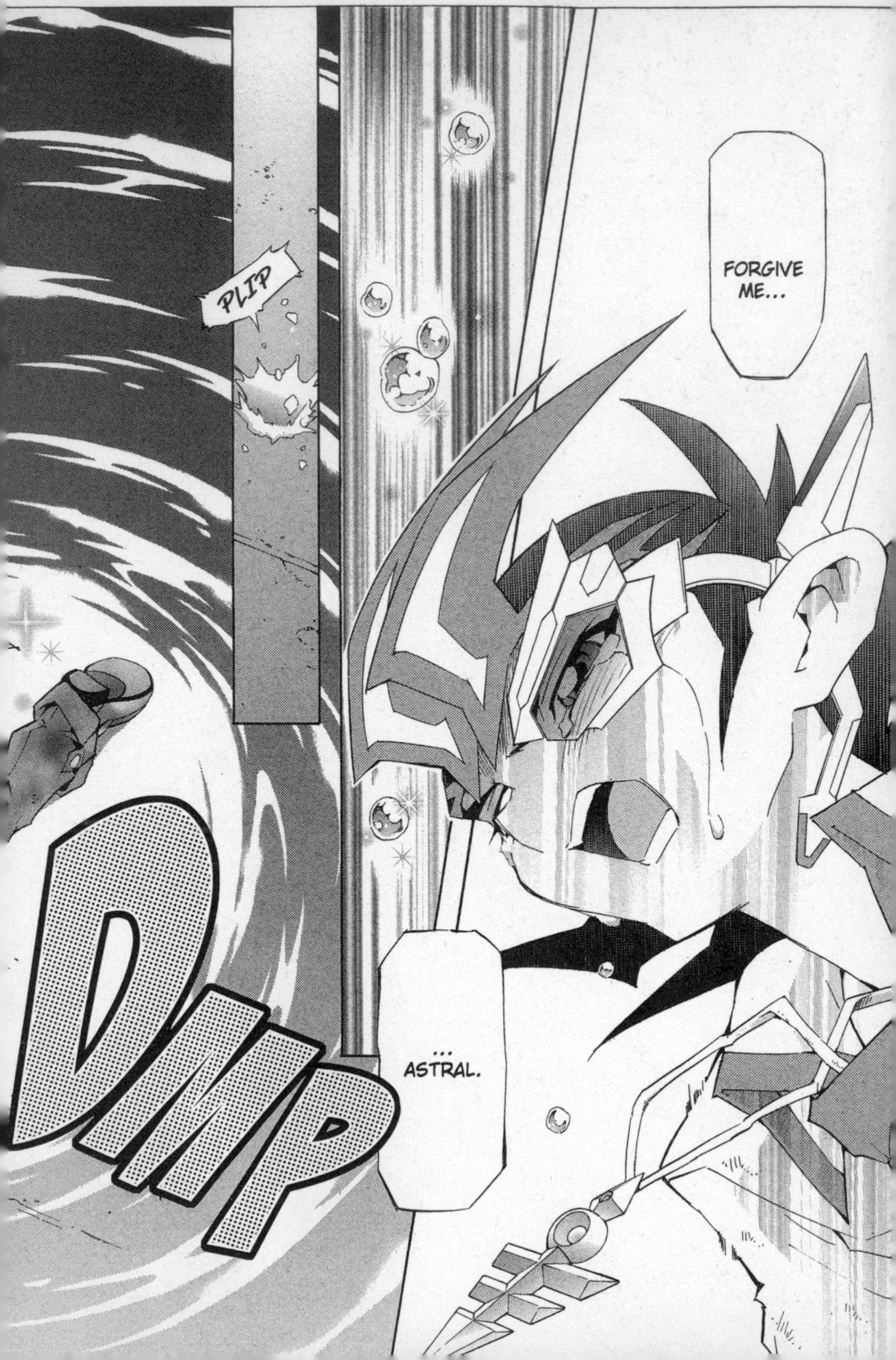
FORGIVE ME...
... ASTRAL.
PLIP
DMP

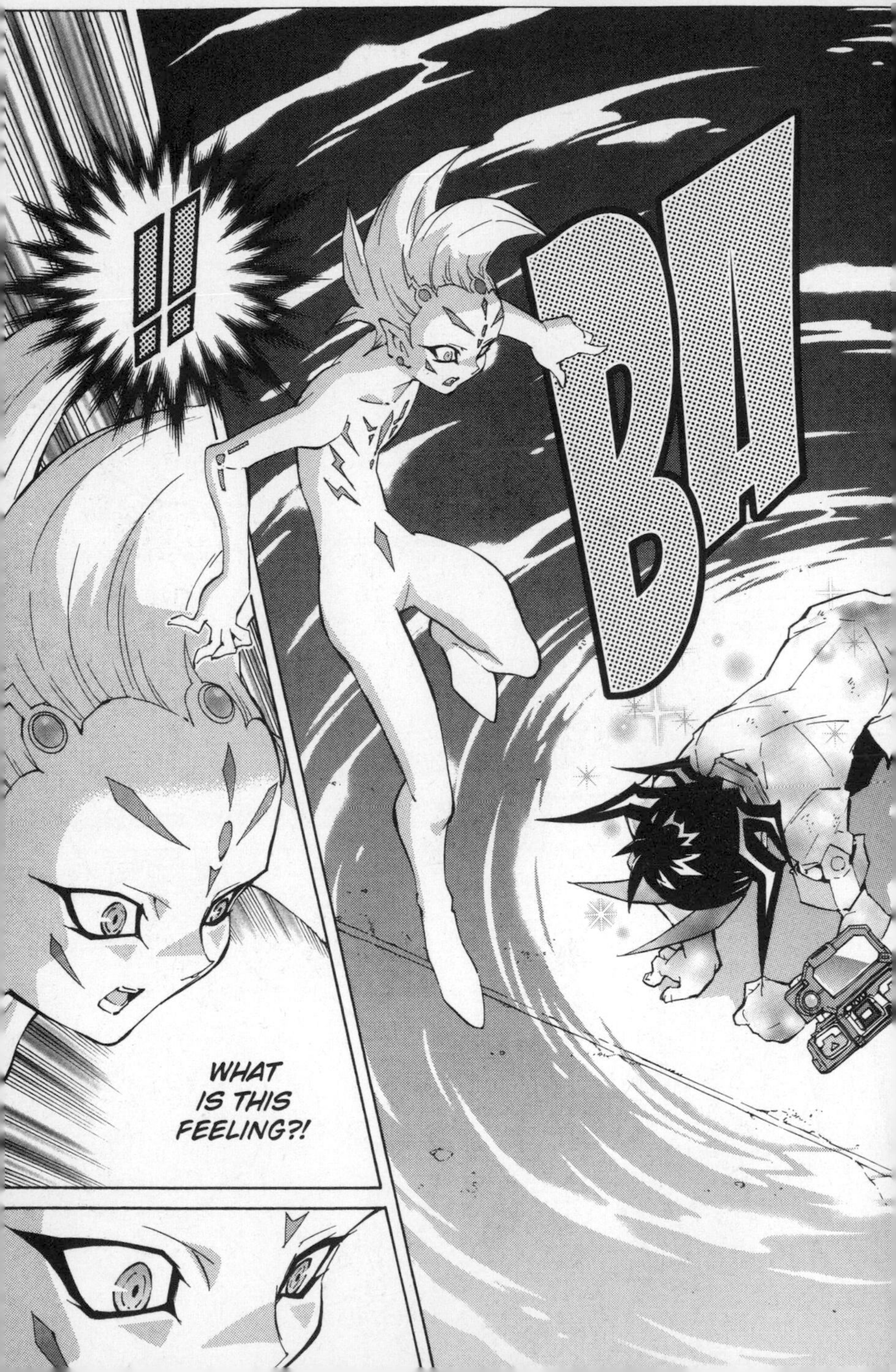
BA
!!
WHAT IS THIS FEELING?!

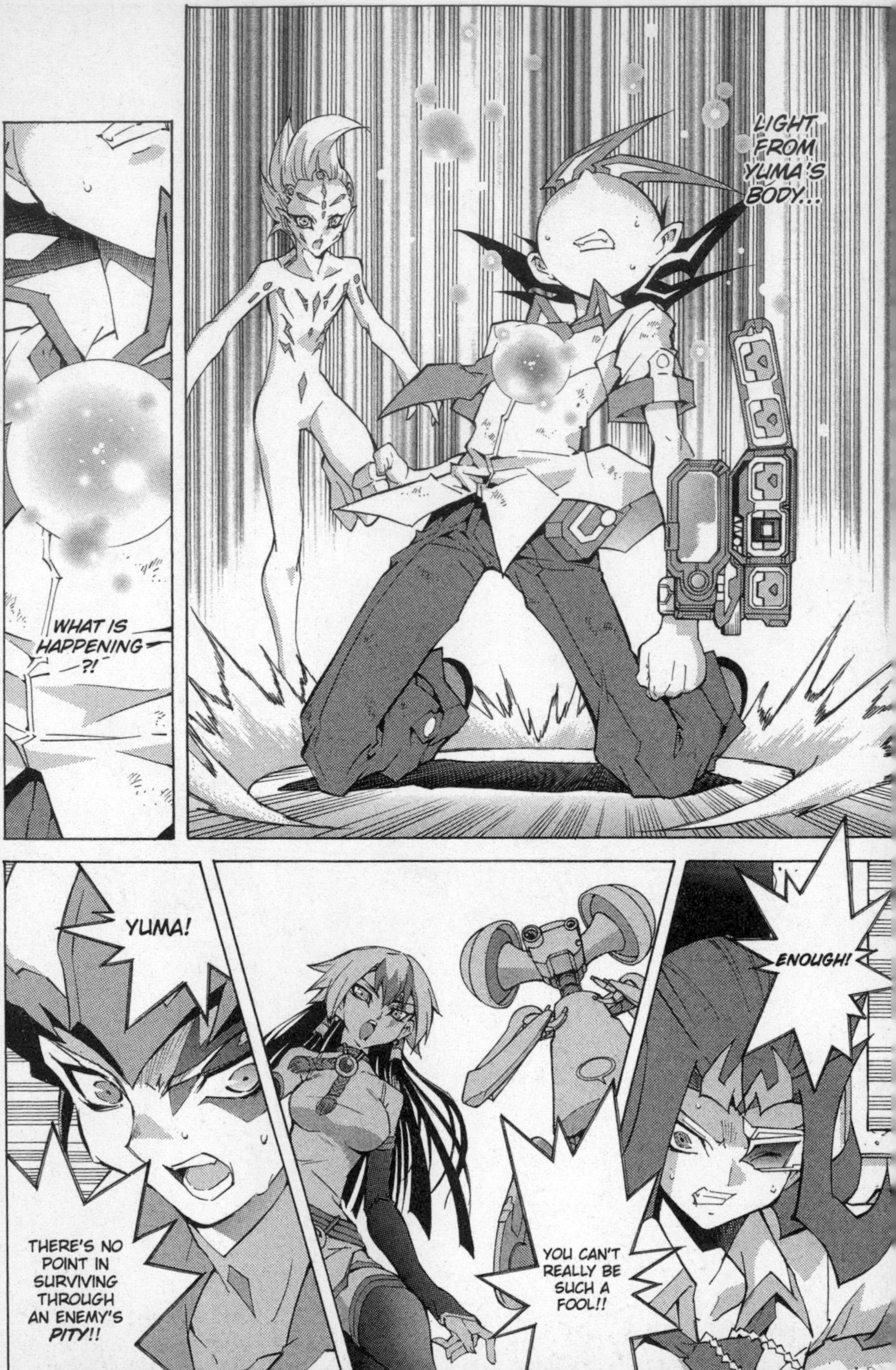

LIGHT FROM YUMA'S BODY...
WHAT IS HAPPENING?!
ENOUGH!
YOU CAN'T REALLY BE SUCH A FOOL!!
YUMA!
THERE'S NO POINT IN SURVIVING THROUGH AN ENEMY'S PITY!!

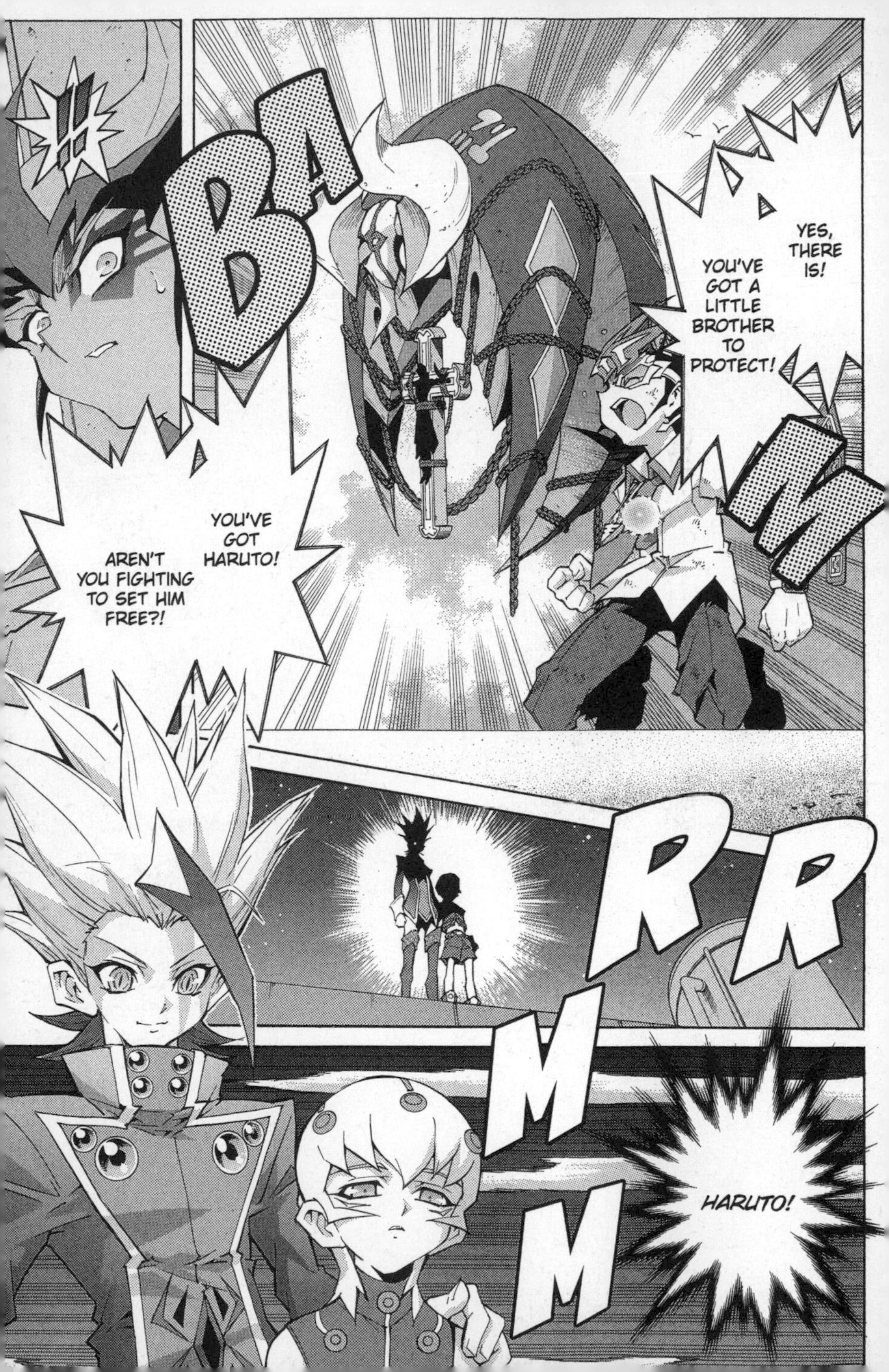
YES, THERE IS!
YOU'VE GOT A LITTLE BROTHER TO PROTECT!
BAM
!!
YOU'VE GOT HARUTO!
AREN'T YOU FIGHTING TO SET HIM FREE?!
RRMM
HARUTO!

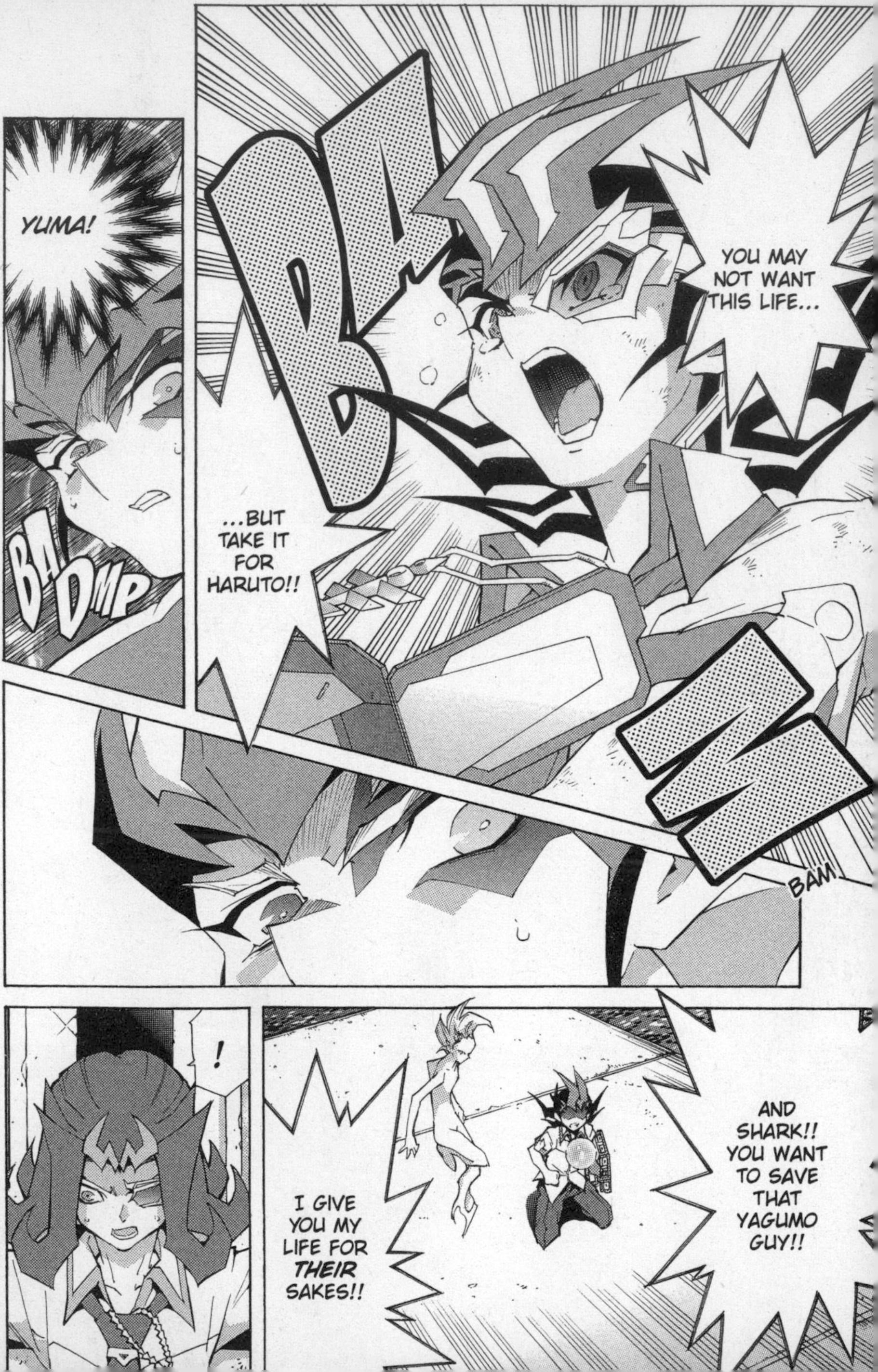
YOU MAY NOT WANT THIS LIFE...
...BUT TAKE IT FOR HARUTO!!
YUMA!
BADMP
BAM
AND SHARK!! YOU WANT TO SAVE THAT YAGUMO GUY!!
I GIVE YOU MY LIFE FOR *THEIR* SAKES!!
!

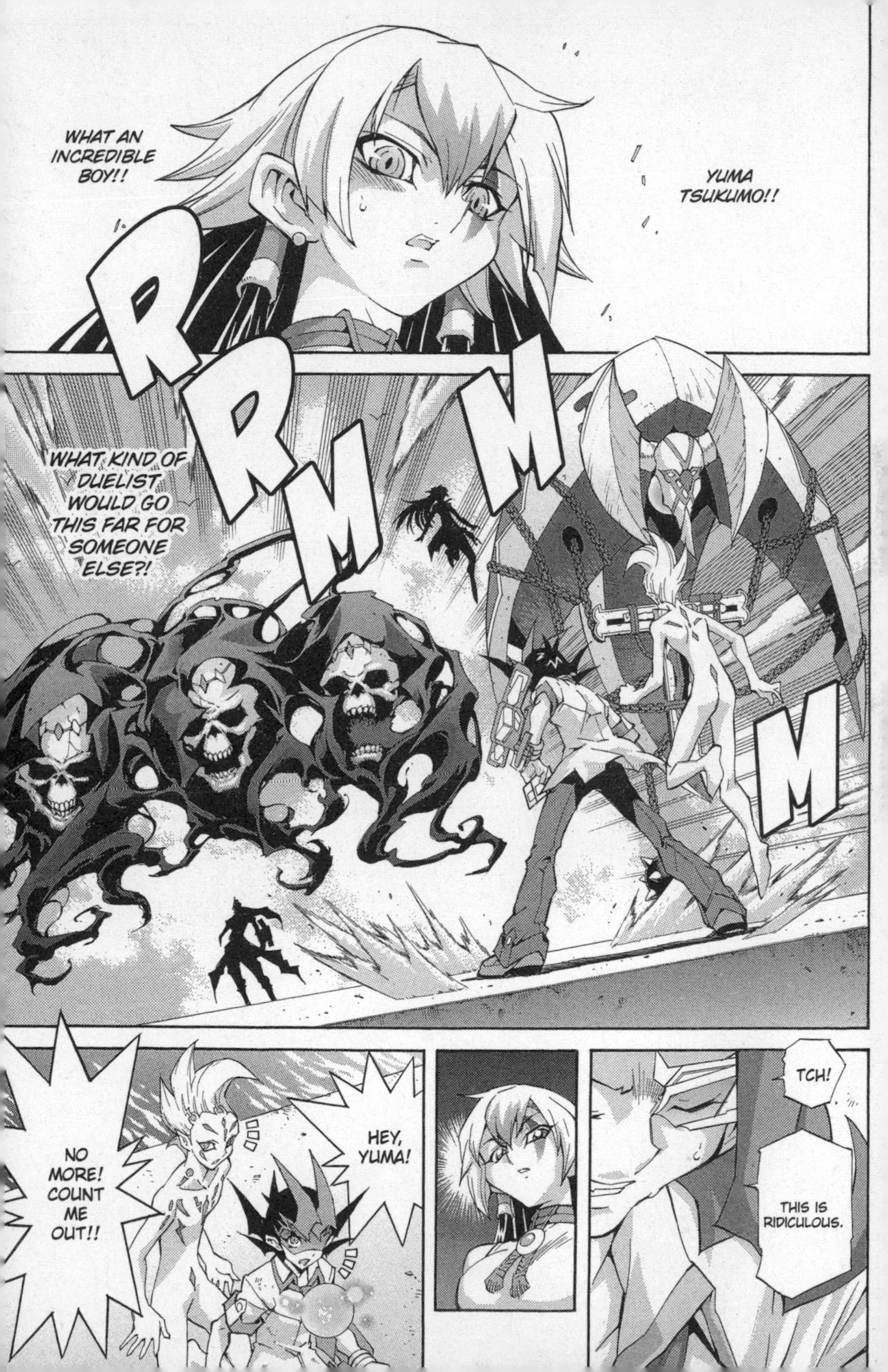

YUMA TSUKUMO!!
WHAT AN INCREDIBLE BOY!!
RRMMMMM
WHAT KIND OF DUELIST WOULD GO THIS FAR FOR SOMEONE ELSE?!
TCH!
THIS IS RIDICULOUS.
HEY, YUMA!
NO MORE! COUNT ME OUT!!

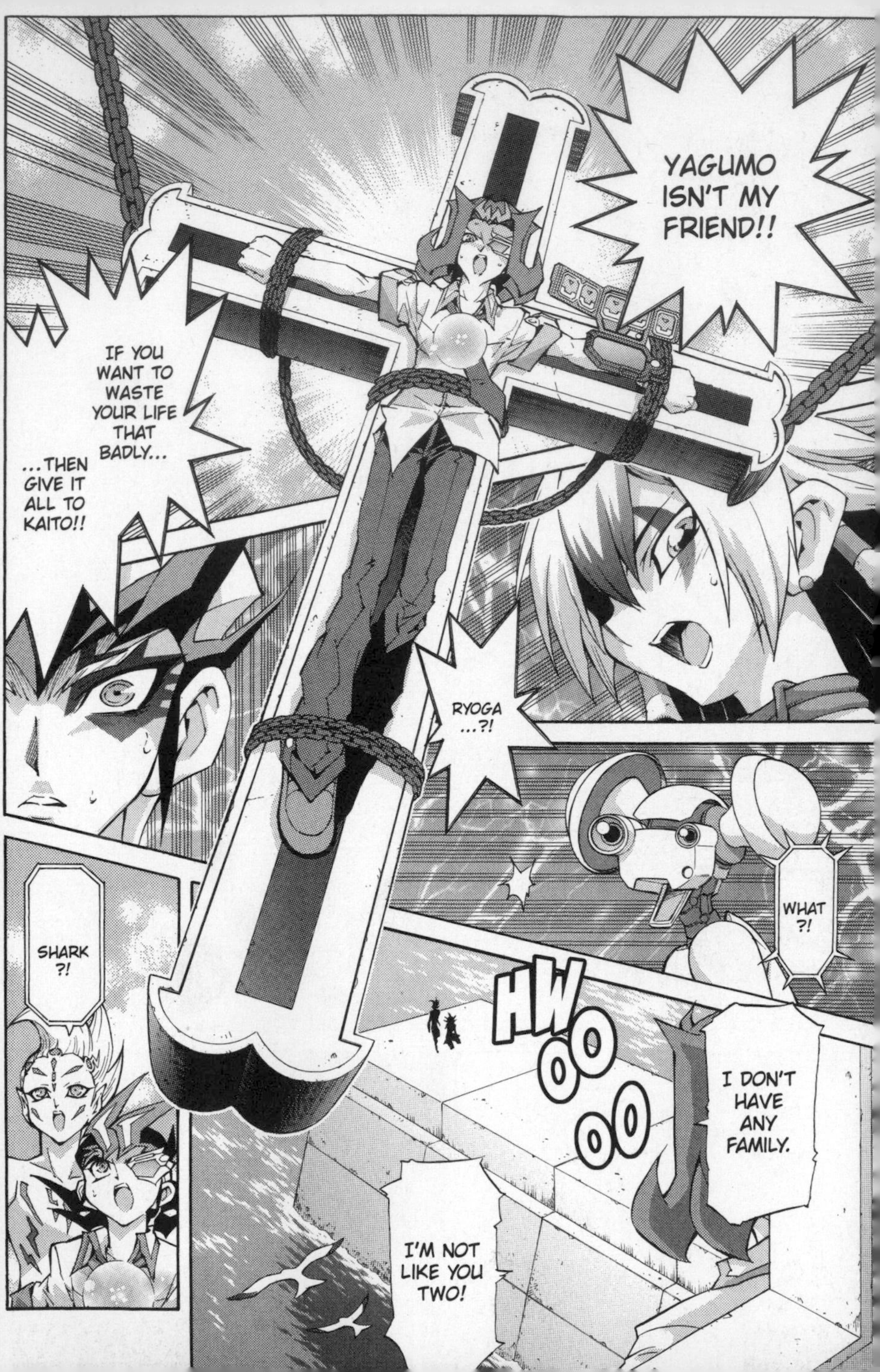
YAGUMO ISN'T MY FRIEND!!
IF YOU WANT TO WASTE YOUR LIFE THAT BADLY...
...THEN GIVE IT ALL TO KAITO!!
RYOGA ...?!
WHAT ?!
HWOOOO
I DON'T HAVE ANY FAMILY.
I'M NOT LIKE YOU TWO!
SHARK ?!

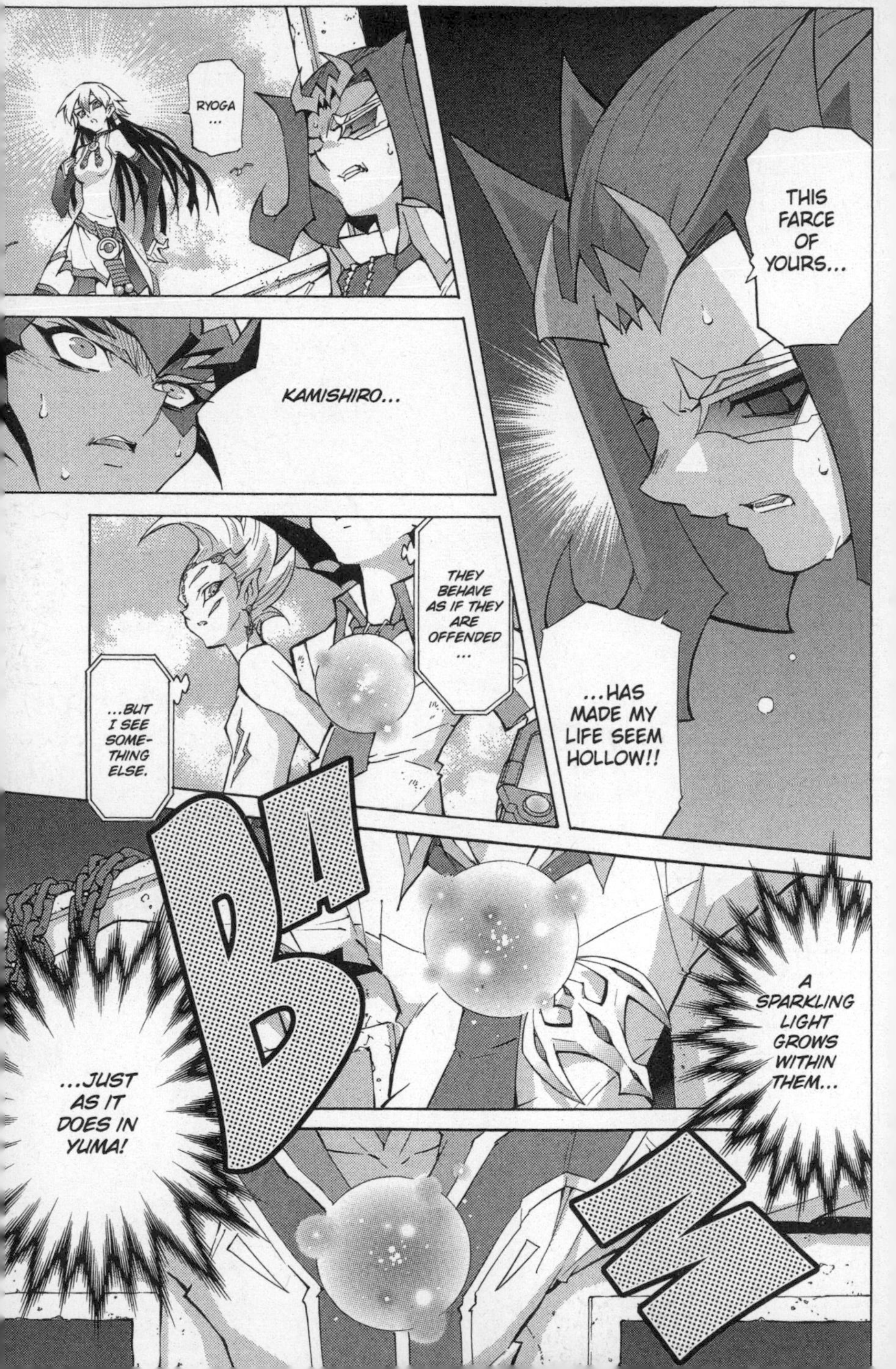
THIS FARCE OF YOURS...
...HAS MADE MY LIFE SEEM HOLLOW!!
RYOGA...
KAMISHIRO...
THEY BEHAVE AS IF THEY ARE OFFENDED...
...BUT I SEE SOMETHING ELSE.
A SPARKLING LIGHT GROWS WITHIN THEM...
...JUST AS IT DOES IN YUMA!
BAM

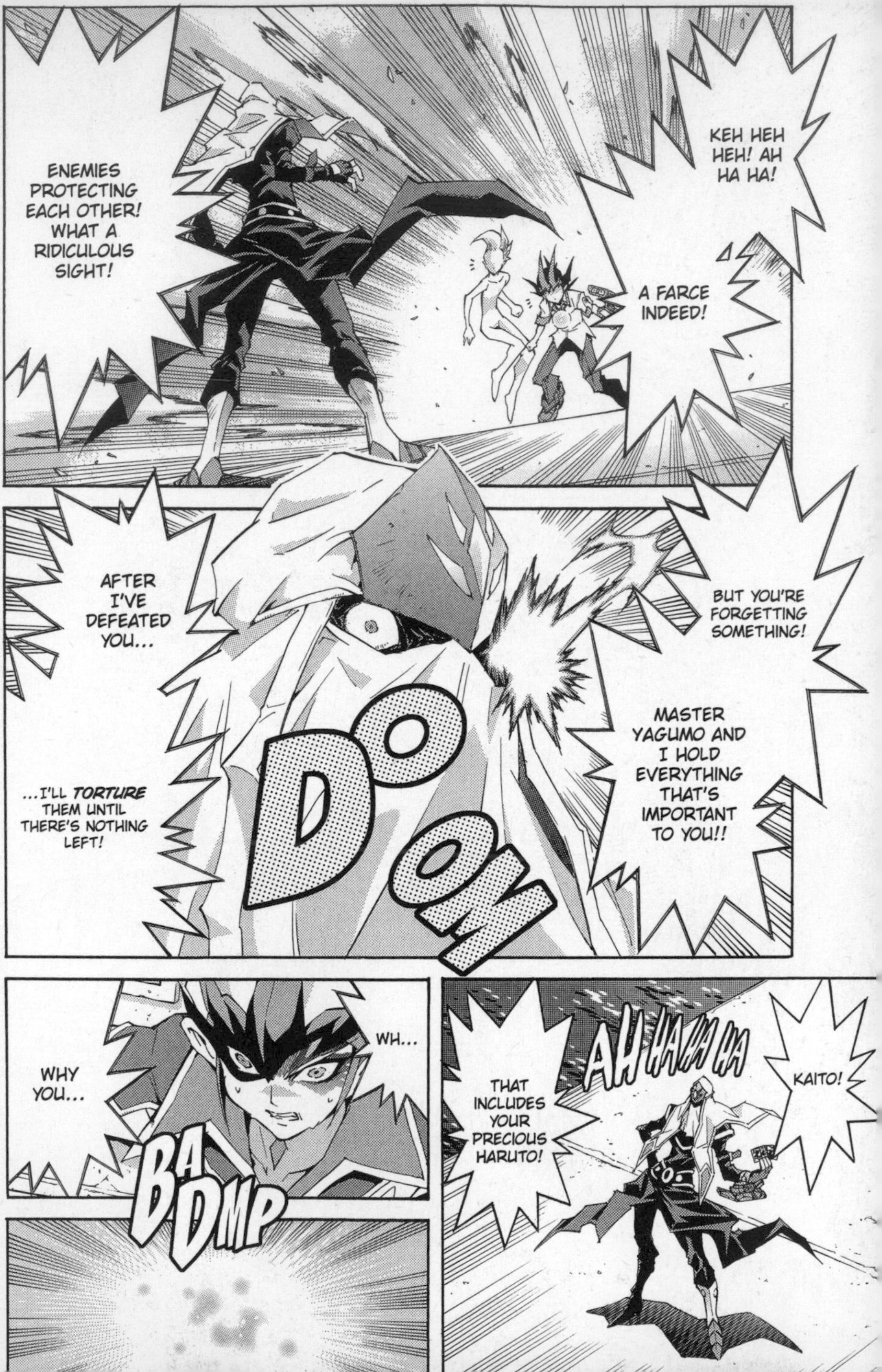
KEH HEH HEH! AH HA HA!
A FARCE INDEED!
ENEMIES PROTECTING EACH OTHER! WHAT A RIDICULOUS SIGHT!
BUT YOU'RE FORGETTING SOMETHING!
MASTER YAGUMO AND I HOLD EVERYTHING THAT'S IMPORTANT TO YOU!!
DOOM
AFTER I'VE DEFEATED YOU...
...I'LL *TORTURE* THEM UNTIL THERE'S NOTHING LEFT!
KAITO!
AH HA HA HA HA
THAT INCLUDES YOUR PRECIOUS HARUTO!
WH...
WHY YOU...
BA DMP

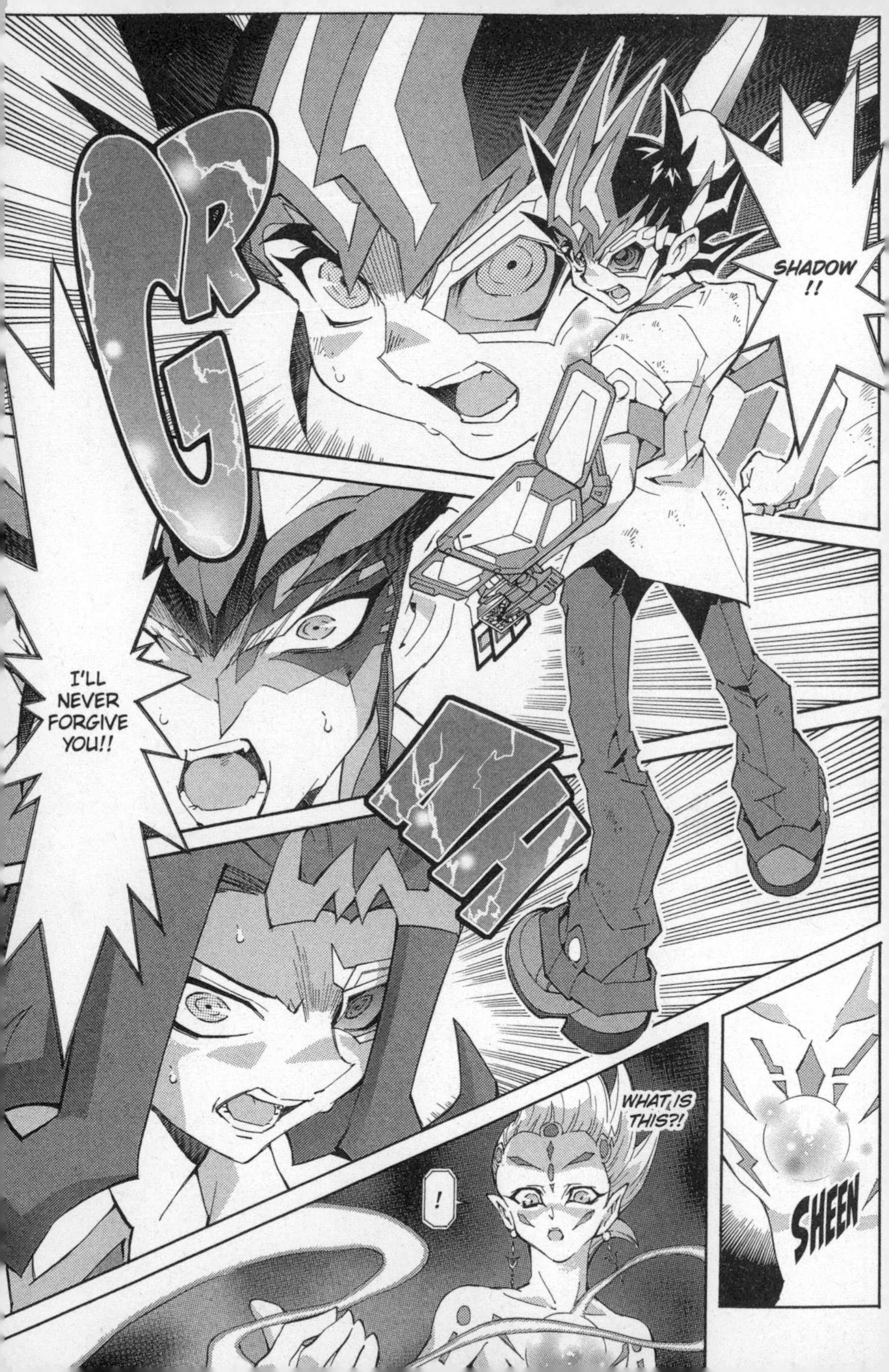
SHADOW!!
CRG
I'LL NEVER FORGIVE YOU!!
SHEEN
WHAT IS THIS?!
!

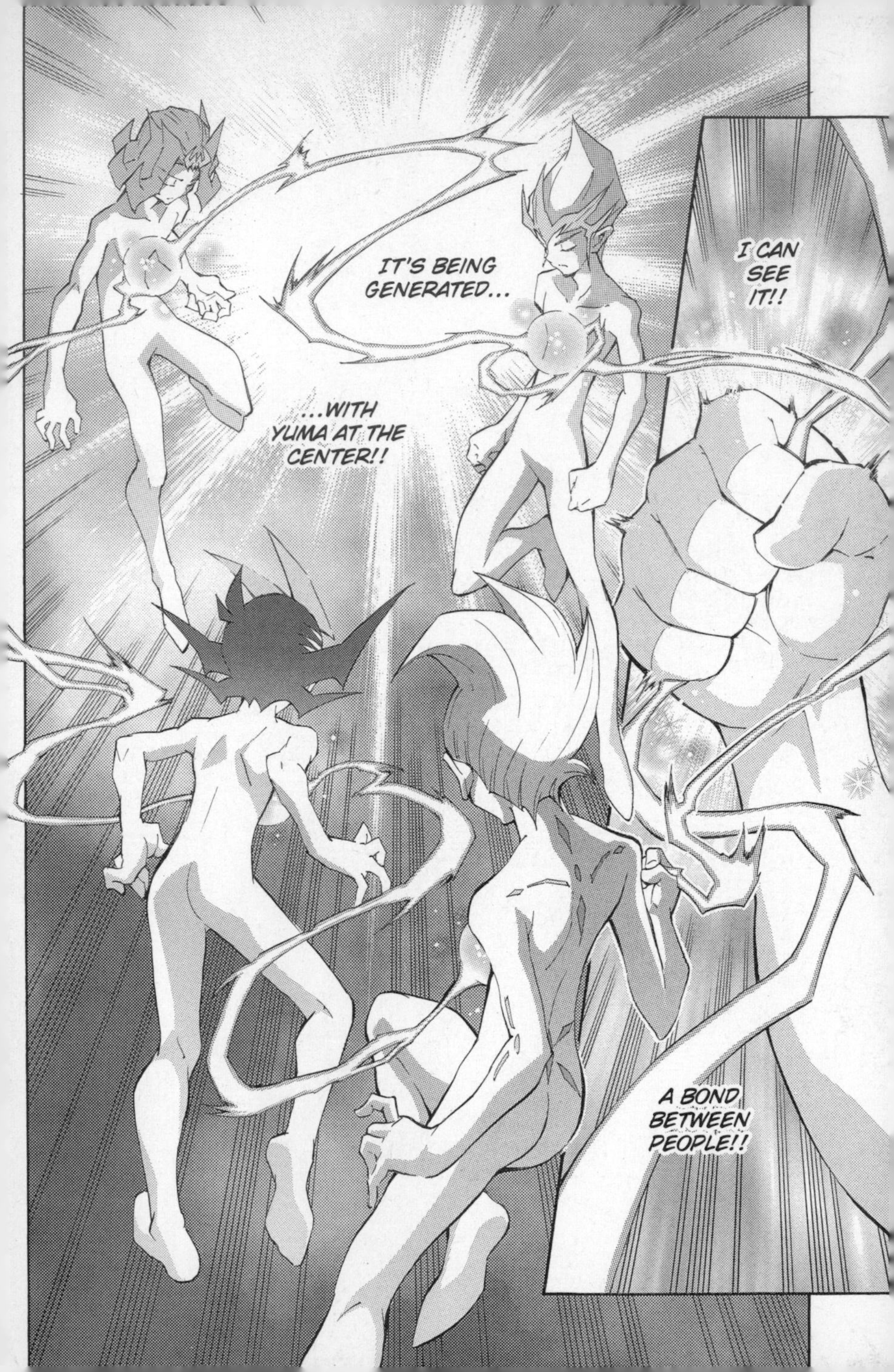

IT'S BEING GENERATED...
...WITH YUMA AT THE CENTER!!
I CAN SEE IT!!
A BOND BETWEEN PEOPLE!!

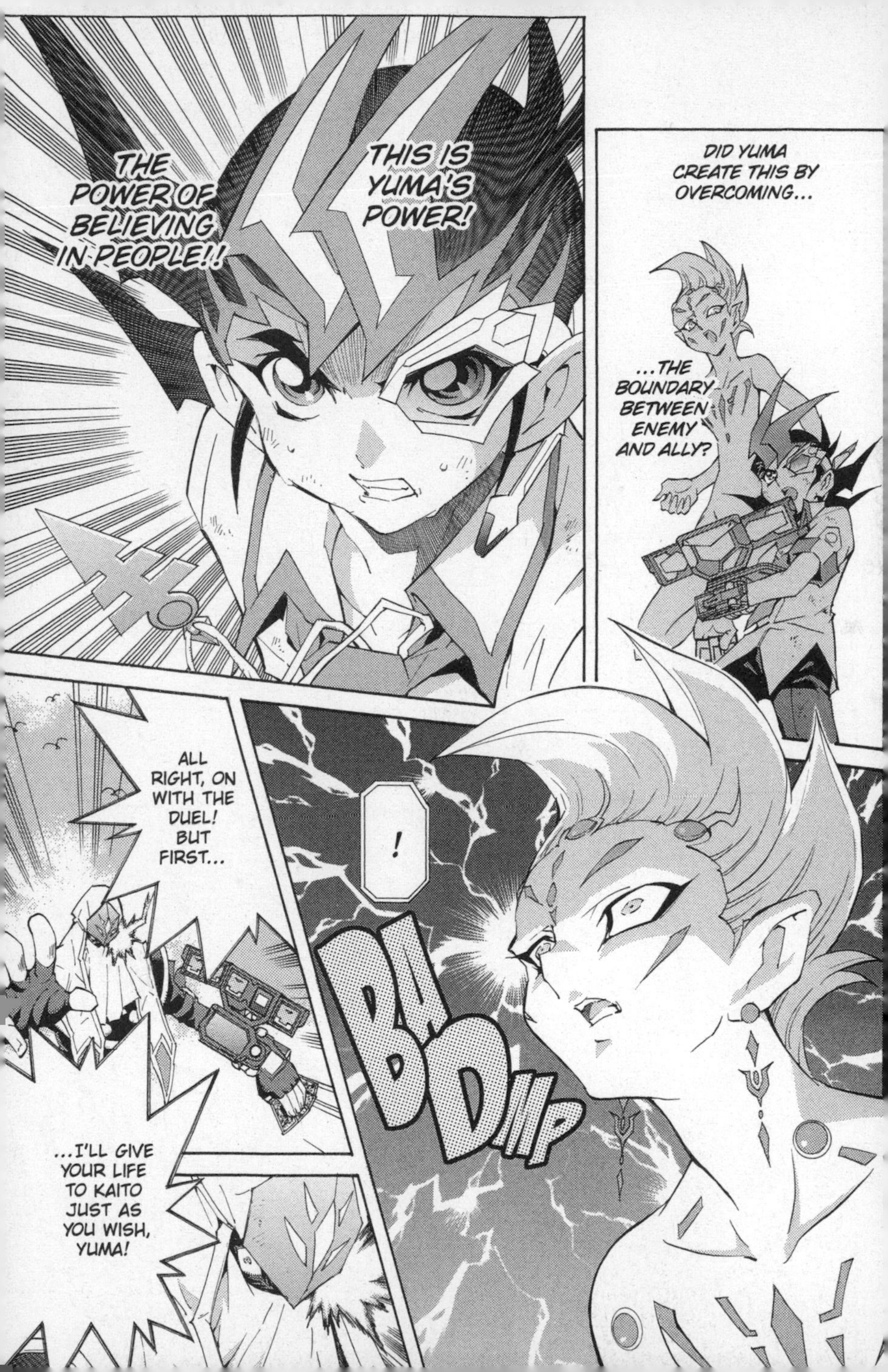
DID YUMA CREATE THIS BY OVERCOMING...
...THE BOUNDARY BETWEEN ENEMY AND ALLY?
THIS IS YUMA'S POWER!
THE POWER OF BELIEVING IN PEOPLE!!
!
BA BDUMP
ALL RIGHT, ON WITH THE DUEL! BUT FIRST...
...I'LL GIVE YOUR LIFE TO KAITO JUST AS YOU WISH, YUMA!

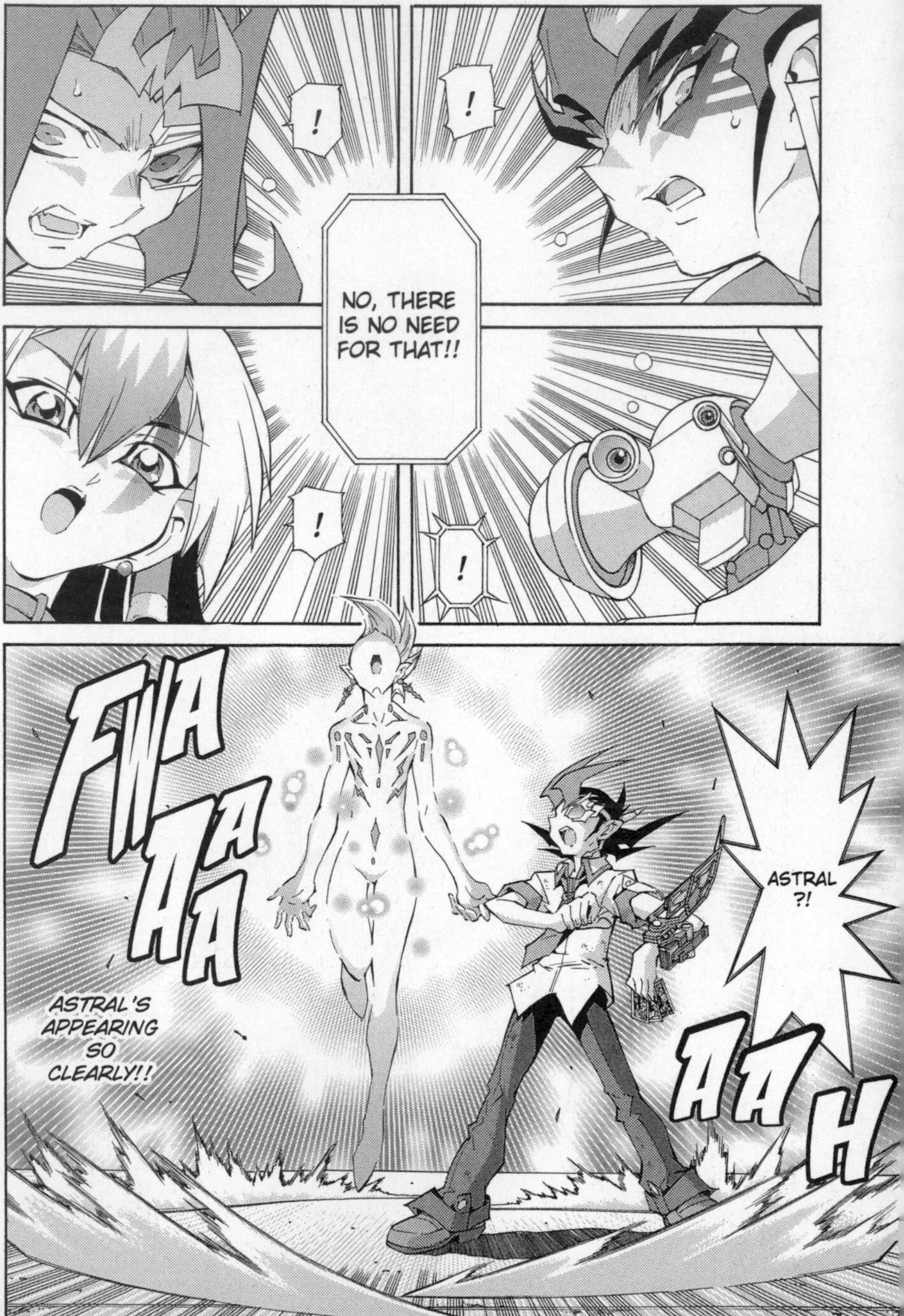
!
!
NO, THERE IS NO NEED FOR THAT!!
!
!
ASTRAL ?!
FWAAAA
AAH
ASTRAL'S APPEARING SO CLEARLY!!

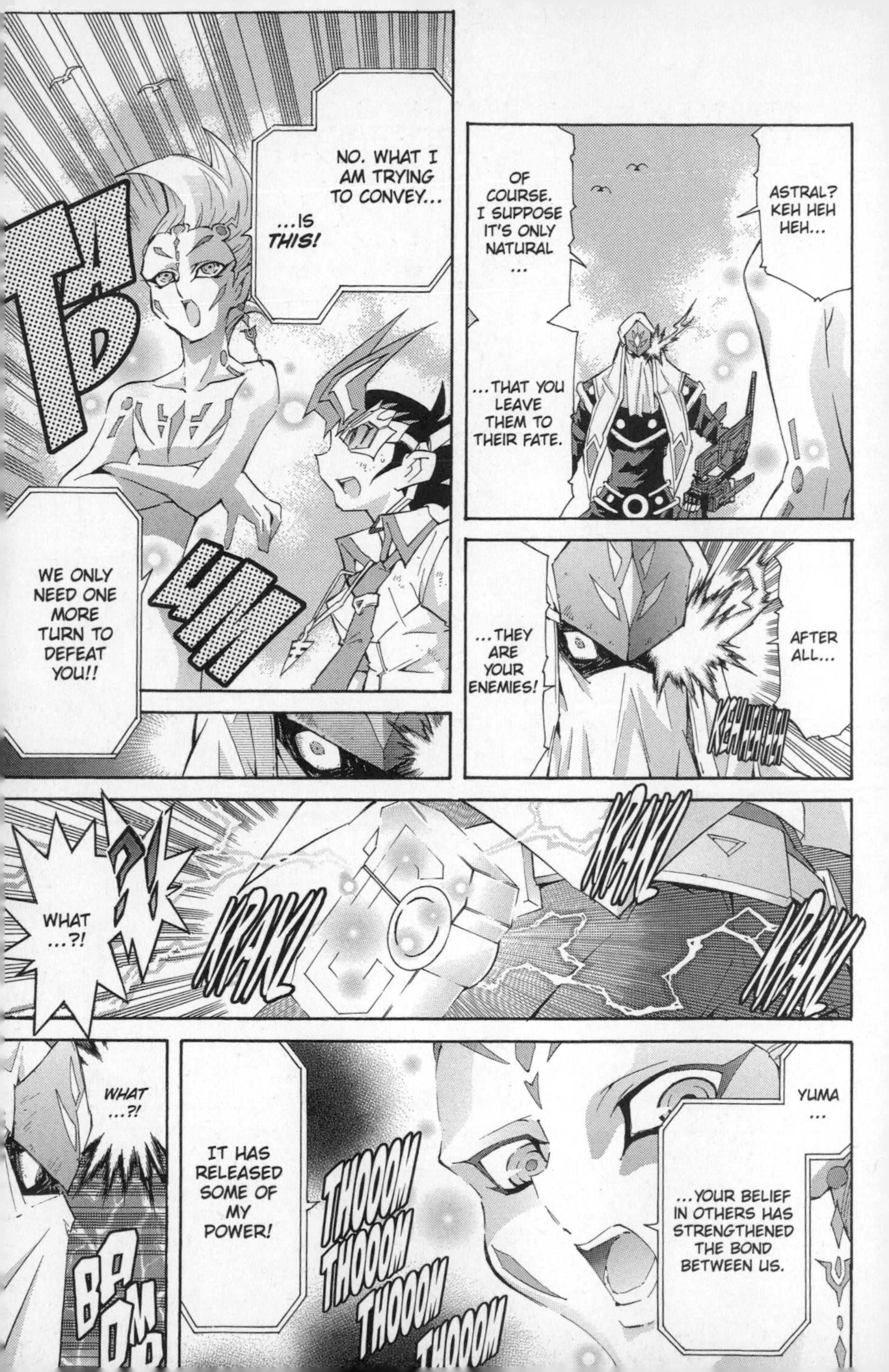
ASTRAL? KEH HEH HEH...
OF COURSE. I SUPPOSE IT'S ONLY NATURAL ...
...THAT YOU LEAVE THEM TO THEIR FATE.
AFTER ALL...
...THEY ARE YOUR ENEMIES!
NO. WHAT I AM TRYING TO CONVEY...
...IS *THIS!*
WE ONLY NEED ONE MORE TURN TO DEFEAT YOU!!
WHAT ...?!
YUMA ...
...YOUR BELIEF IN OTHERS HAS STRENGTHENED THE BOND BETWEEN US.
IT HAS RELEASED SOME OF MY POWER!
THOOOM THOOOM THOOOM THOOOM
WHAT ...?!

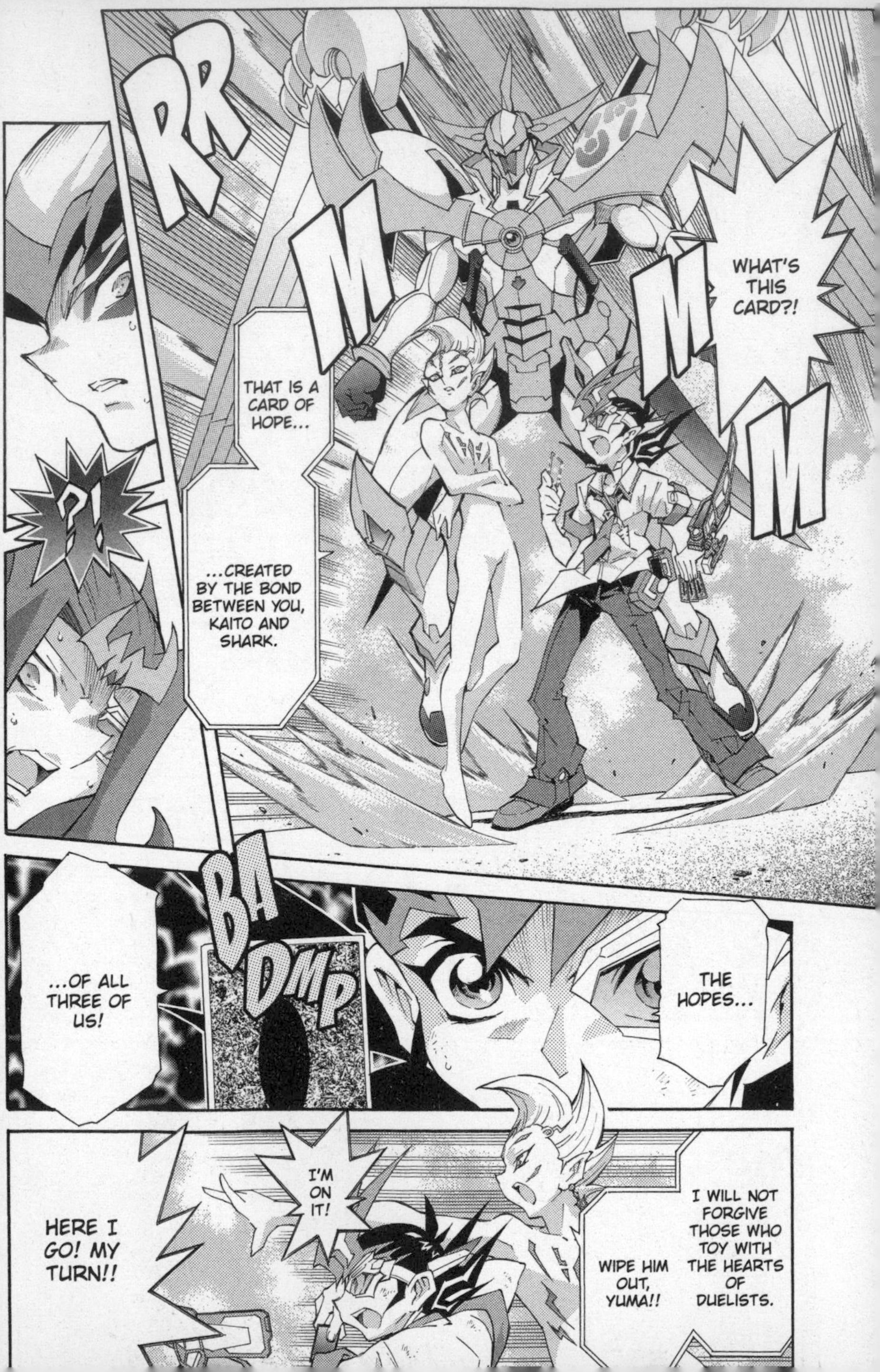
WHAT'S THIS CARD?!
RRMMMM
THAT IS A CARD OF HOPE...
...CREATED BY THE BOND BETWEEN YOU, KAITO AND SHARK.
?!
THE HOPES...
BADMP
...OF ALL THREE OF US!
I WILL NOT FORGIVE THOSE WHO TOY WITH THE HEARTS OF DUELISTS.
WIPE HIM OUT, YUMA!!
I'M ON IT!
HERE I GO! MY TURN!!

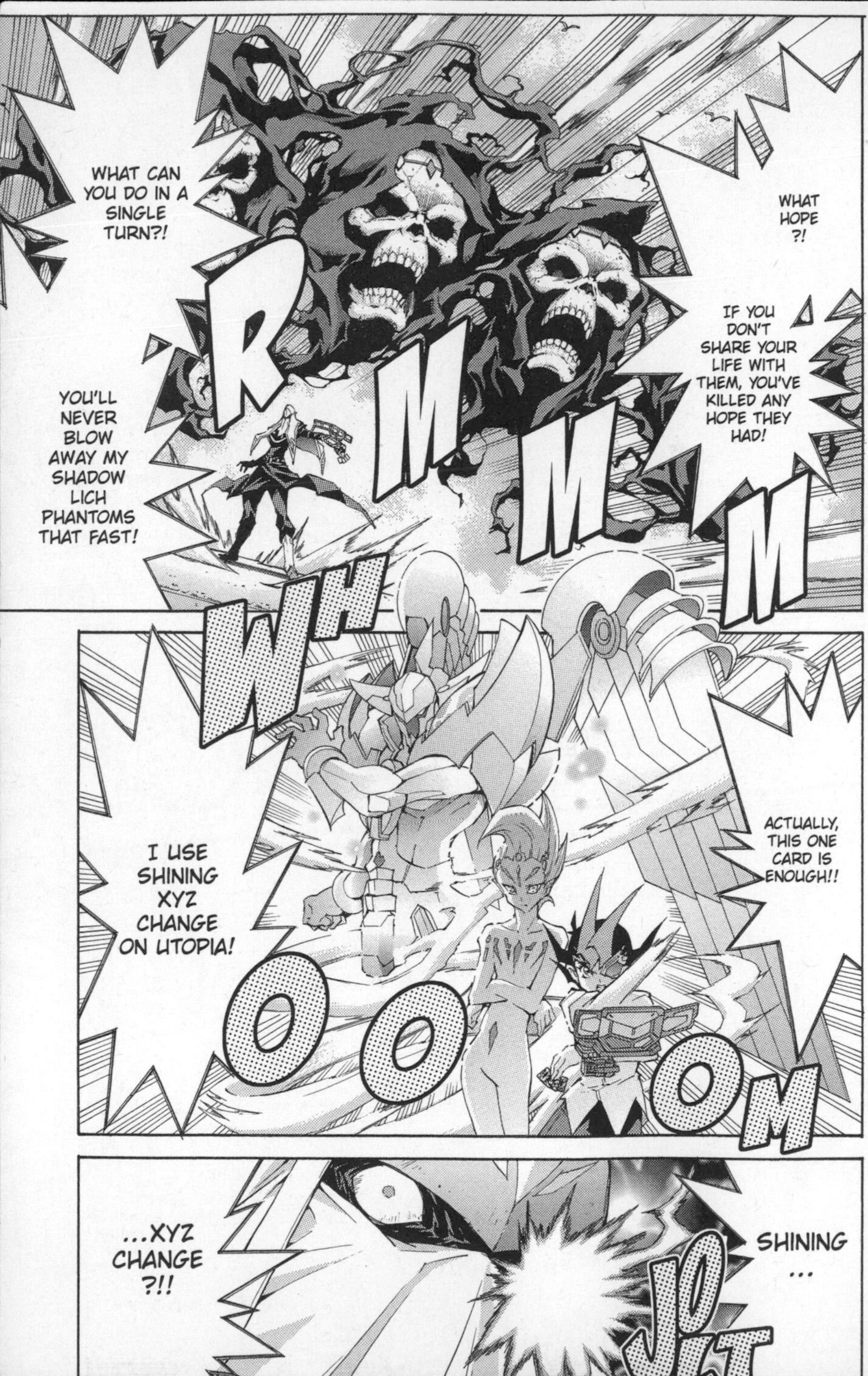
WHAT HOPE ?!
IF YOU DON'T SHARE YOUR LIFE WITH THEM, YOU'VE KILLED ANY HOPE THEY HAD!
WHAT CAN YOU DO IN A SINGLE TURN?!
YOU'LL NEVER BLOW AWAY MY SHADOW LICH PHANTOMS THAT FAST!
RMMMM
WHOOOM
ACTUALLY, THIS ONE CARD IS ENOUGH!!
I USE SHINING XYZ CHANGE ON UTOPIA!
SHINING ...
...XYZ CHANGE ?!!
JOLT

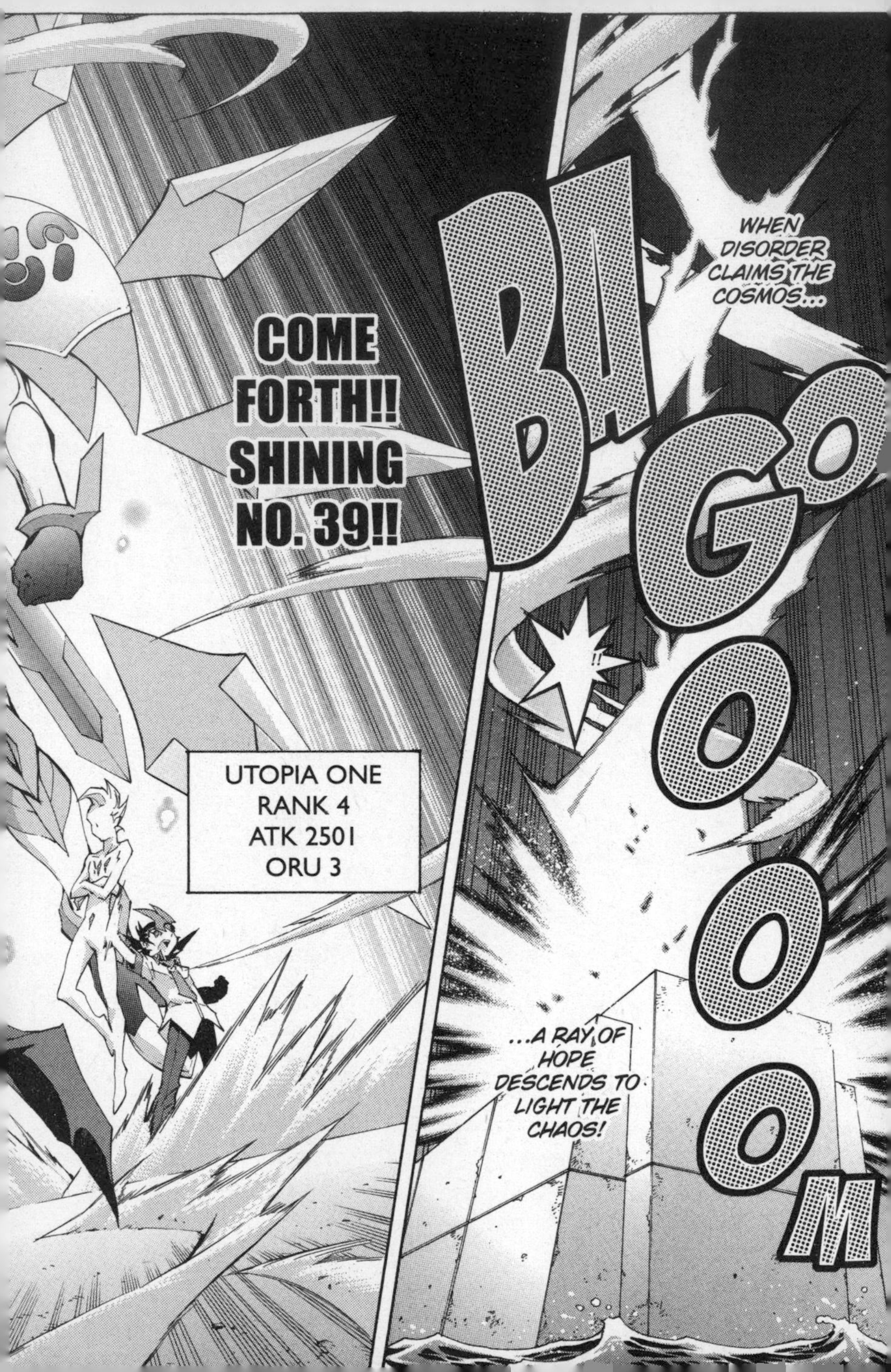
WHEN DISORDER CLAIMS THE COSMOS...
BAGOOOOM
!!
...A RAY OF HOPE DESCENDS TO LIGHT THE CHAOS!
COME FORTH!! SHINING NO. 39!!
UTOPIA ONE
RANK 4
ATK 2501
ORU 3

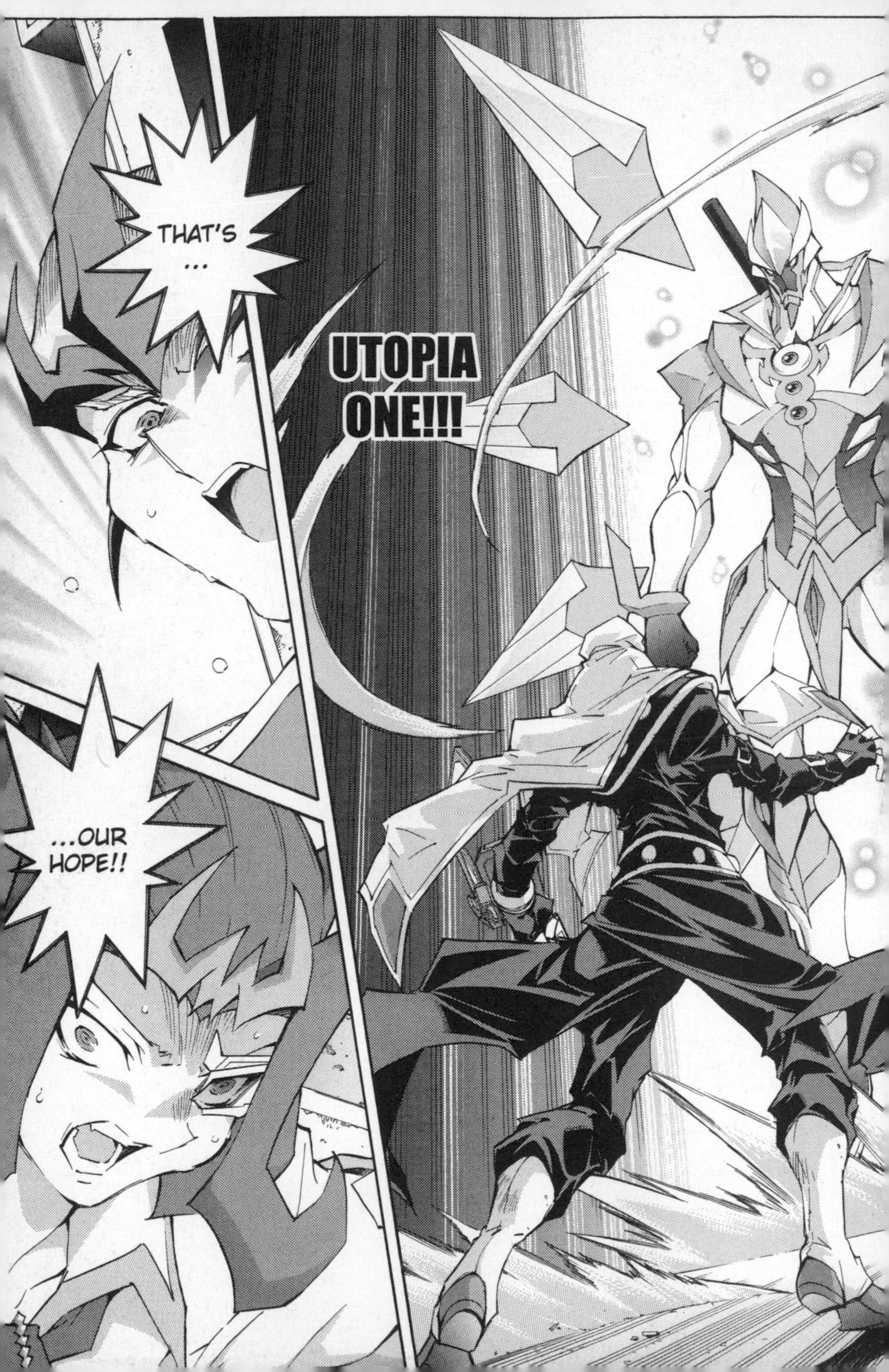
UTOPIA ONE!!!
THAT'S ...
...OUR HOPE!!

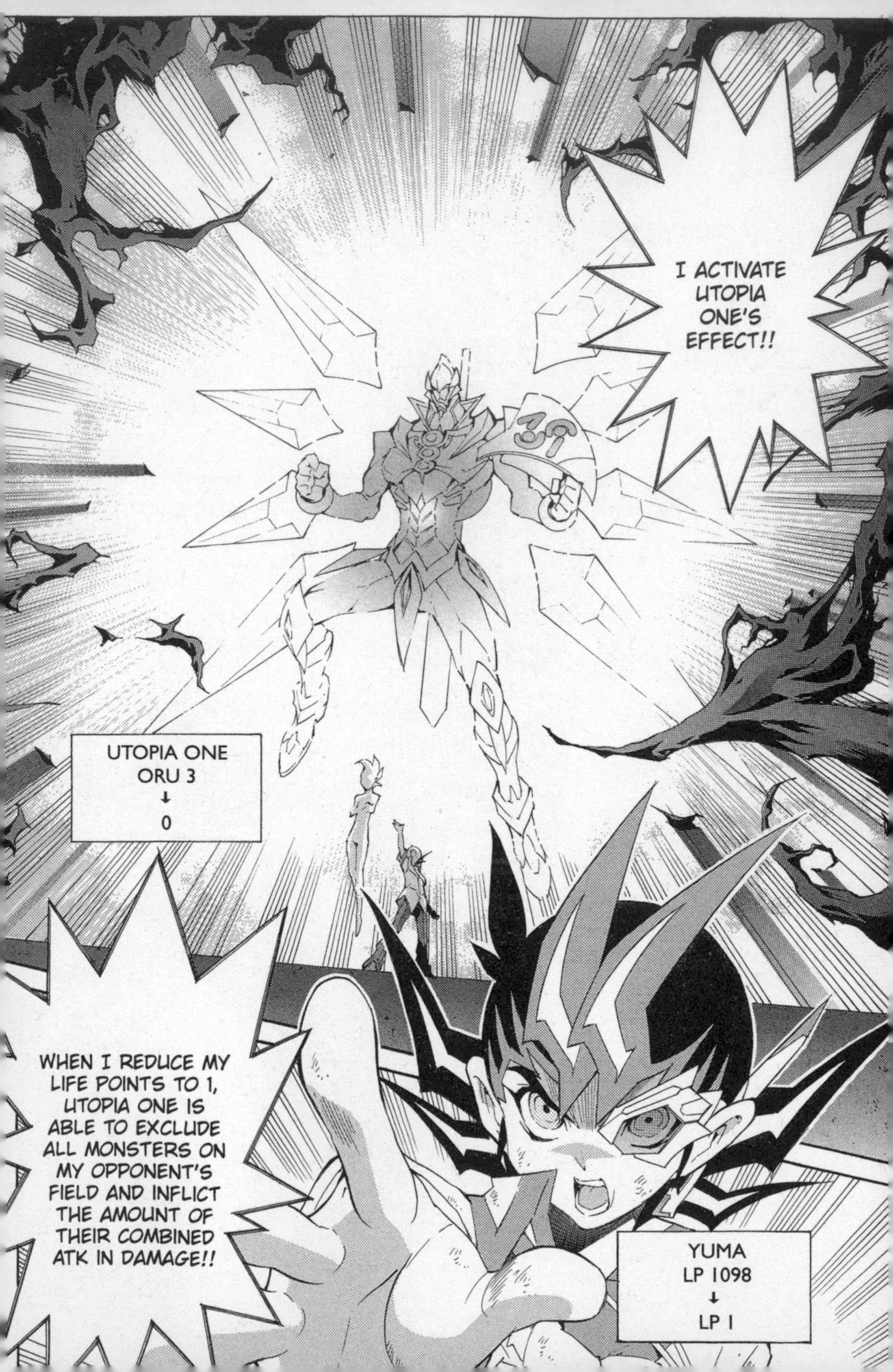
I ACTIVATE UTOPIA ONE'S EFFECT!!
UTOPIA ONE ORU 3 ↓ 0
YUMA LP 1098 ↓ LP 1
WHEN I REDUCE MY LIFE POINTS TO 1, UTOPIA ONE IS ABLE TO EXCLUDE ALL MONSTERS ON MY OPPONENT'S FIELD AND INFLICT THE AMOUNT OF THEIR COMBINED ATK IN DAMAGE!!

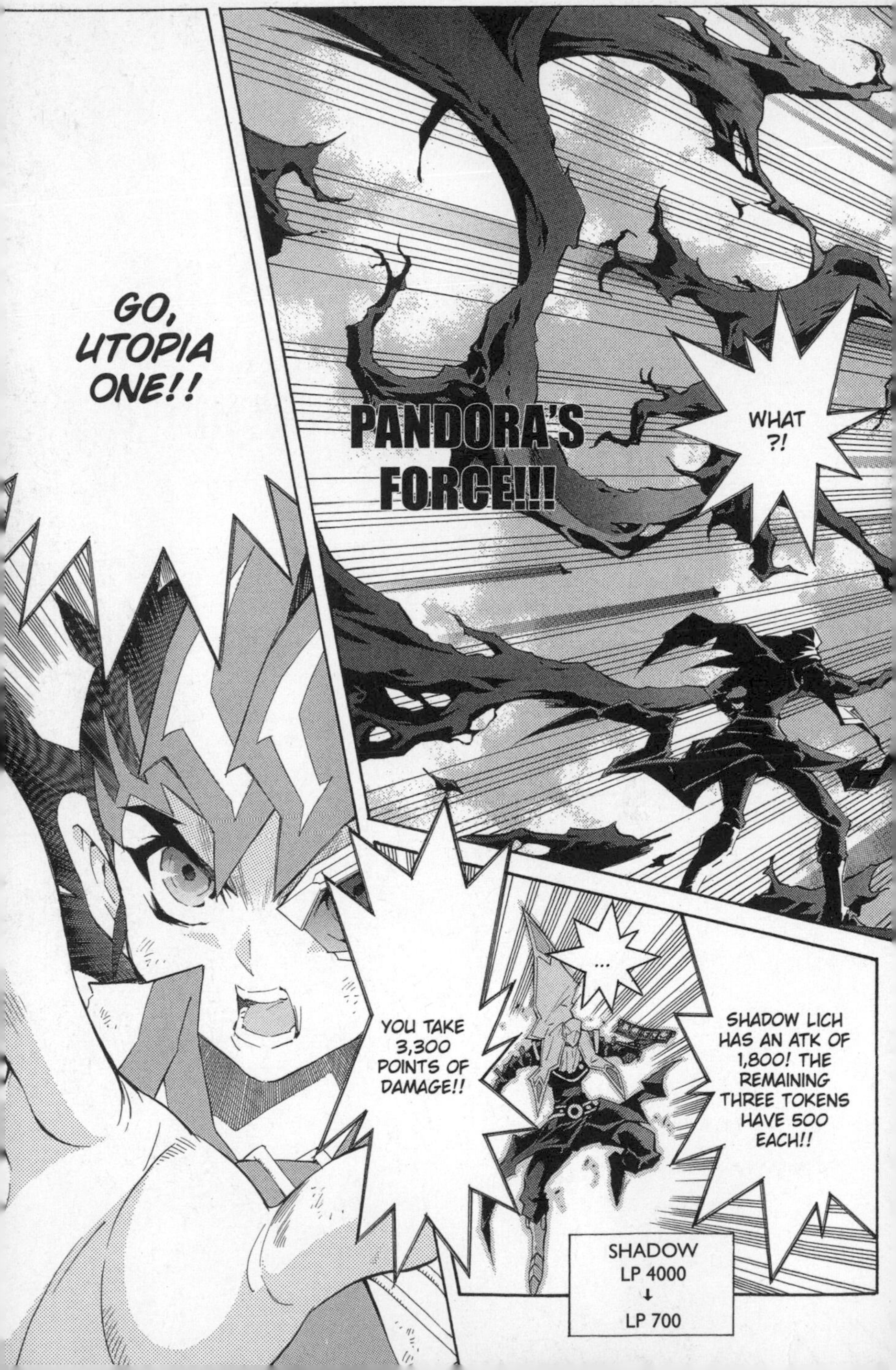
WHAT ?!
PANDORA'S FORCE!!!
...
SHADOW LICH HAS AN ATK OF 1,800! THE REMAINING THREE TOKENS HAVE 500 EACH!!
YOU TAKE 3,300 POINTS OF DAMAGE!!
SHADOW LP 4000 ↓ LP 700
GO, UTOPIA ONE!!

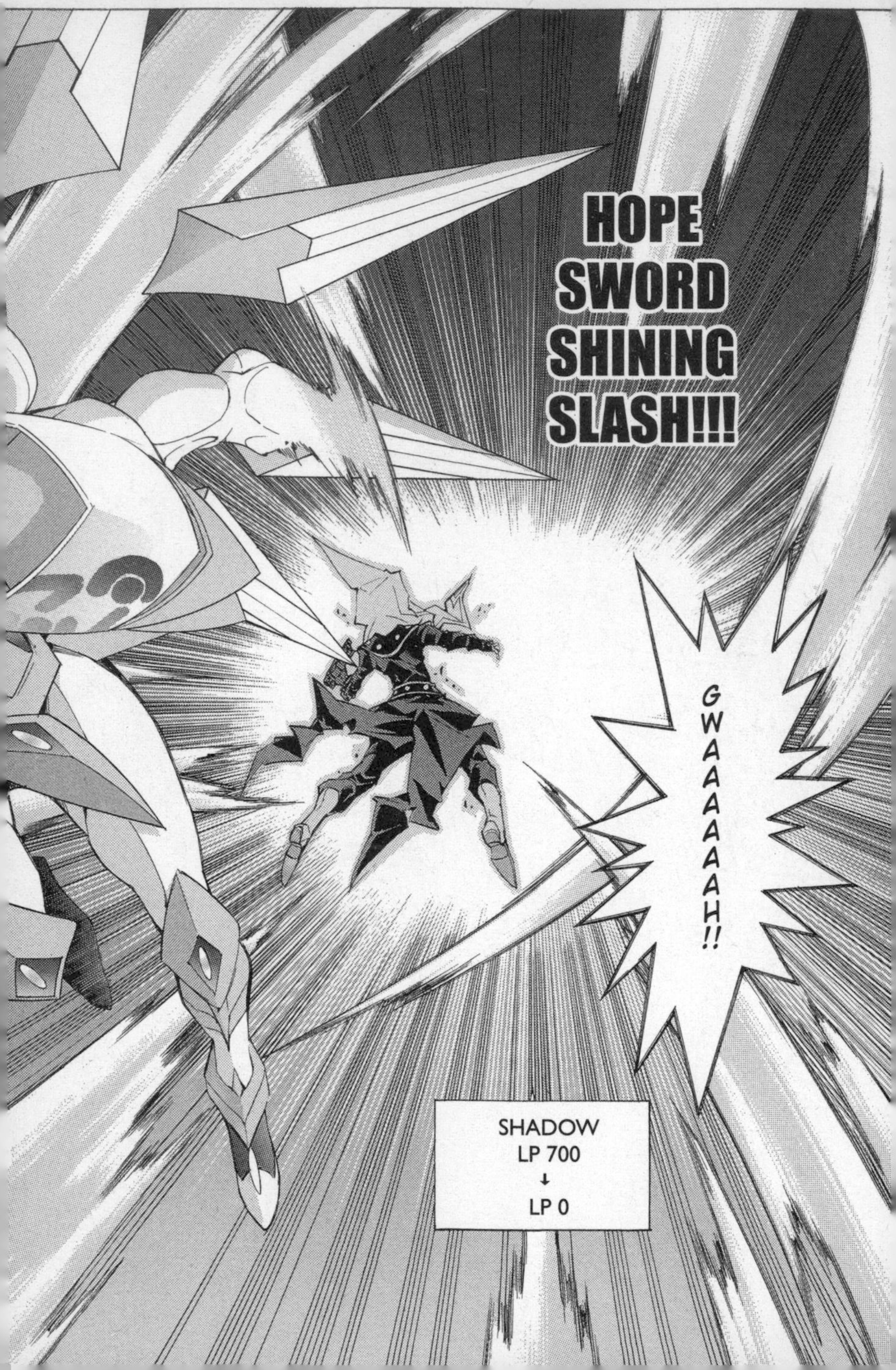

HOPE SWORD SHINING SLASH!!!
GWAAAAAAAAH!!
SHADOW
LP 700
↓
LP 0

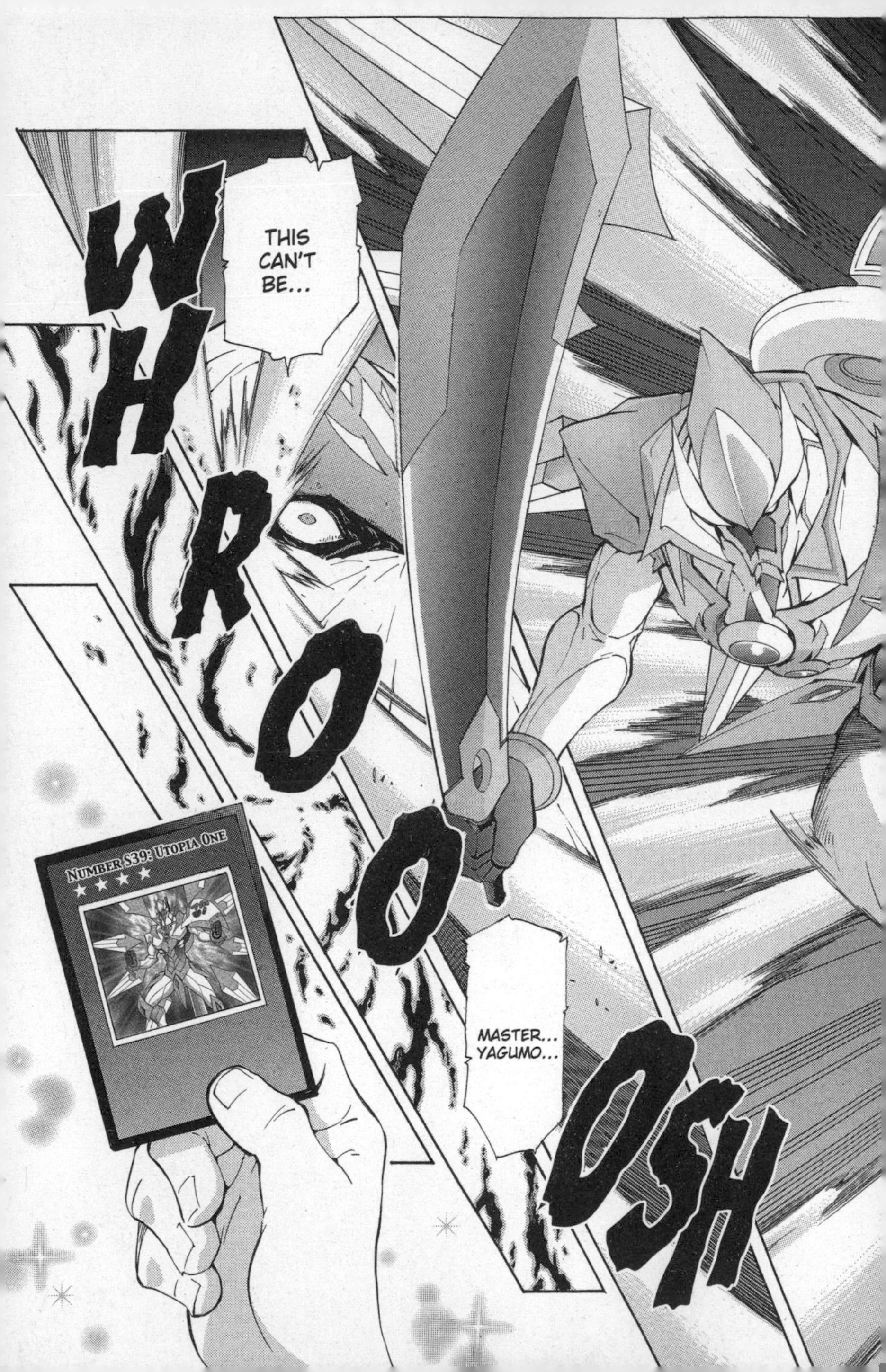
THIS CAN'T BE...
WHROOOSH
MASTER... YAGUMO...
NUMBER S39: UTOPIA ONE

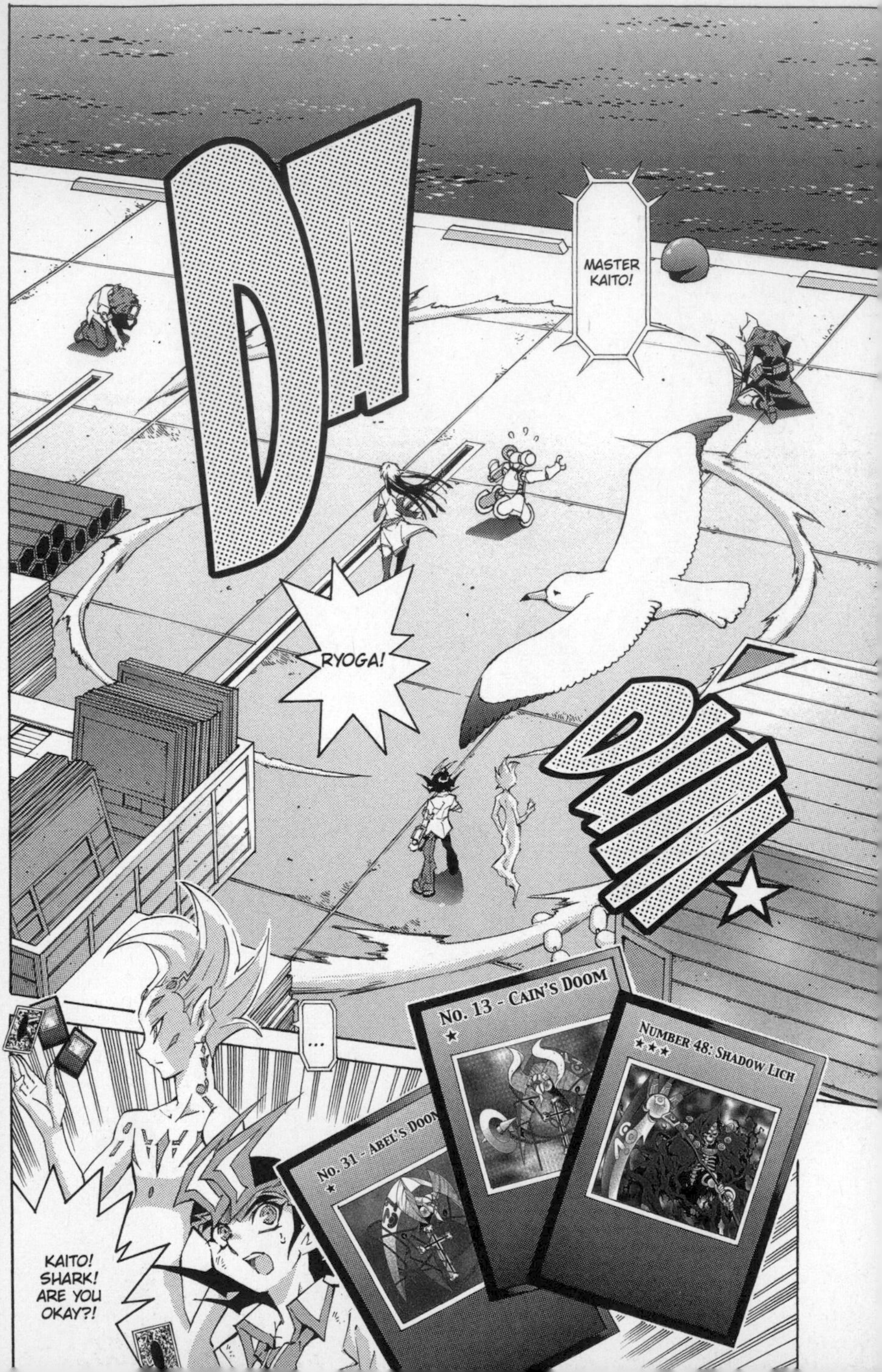
MASTER KAITO!
DA!
RYOGA!
NUMBER 48: SHADOW LICH
No. 13 - CAIN'S DOOM
No. 31 - ABEL'S DOOM
...
KAITO! SHARK! ARE YOU OKAY?!

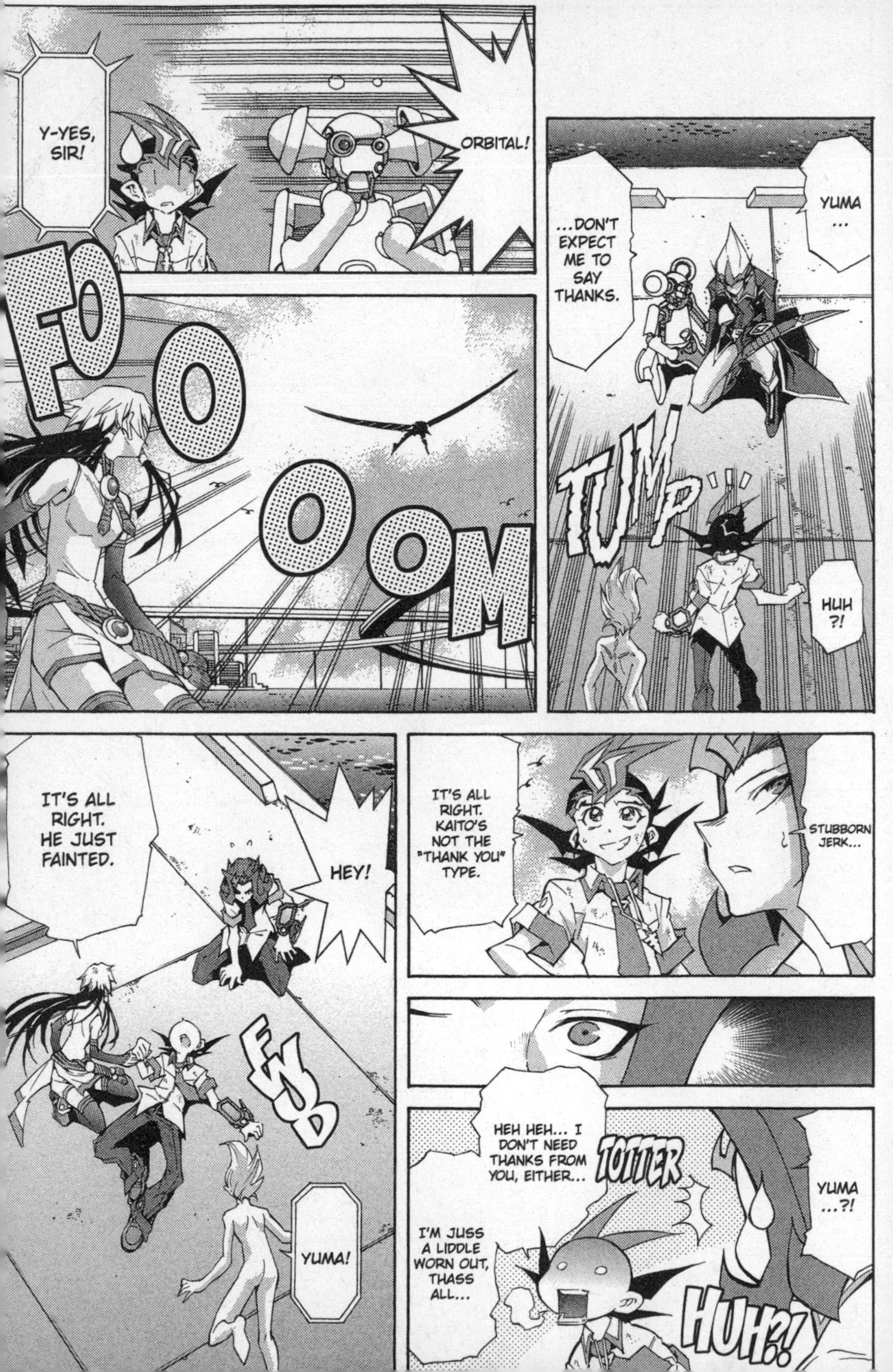
YUMA...
...DON'T EXPECT ME TO SAY THANKS.
TUMP
HUH?!
ORBITAL!
Y-YES, SIR!
FOOOOM
STUBBORN JERK...
IT'S ALL RIGHT. KAITO'S NOT THE "THANK YOU" TYPE.
YUMA...?!
HEH HEH... I DON'T NEED THANKS FROM YOU, EITHER...
TOTTER
I'M JUSS A LIDDLE WORN OUT, THASS ALL...
HUH?!
HEY!
IT'S ALL RIGHT. HE JUST FAINTED.
FWUD
YUMA!

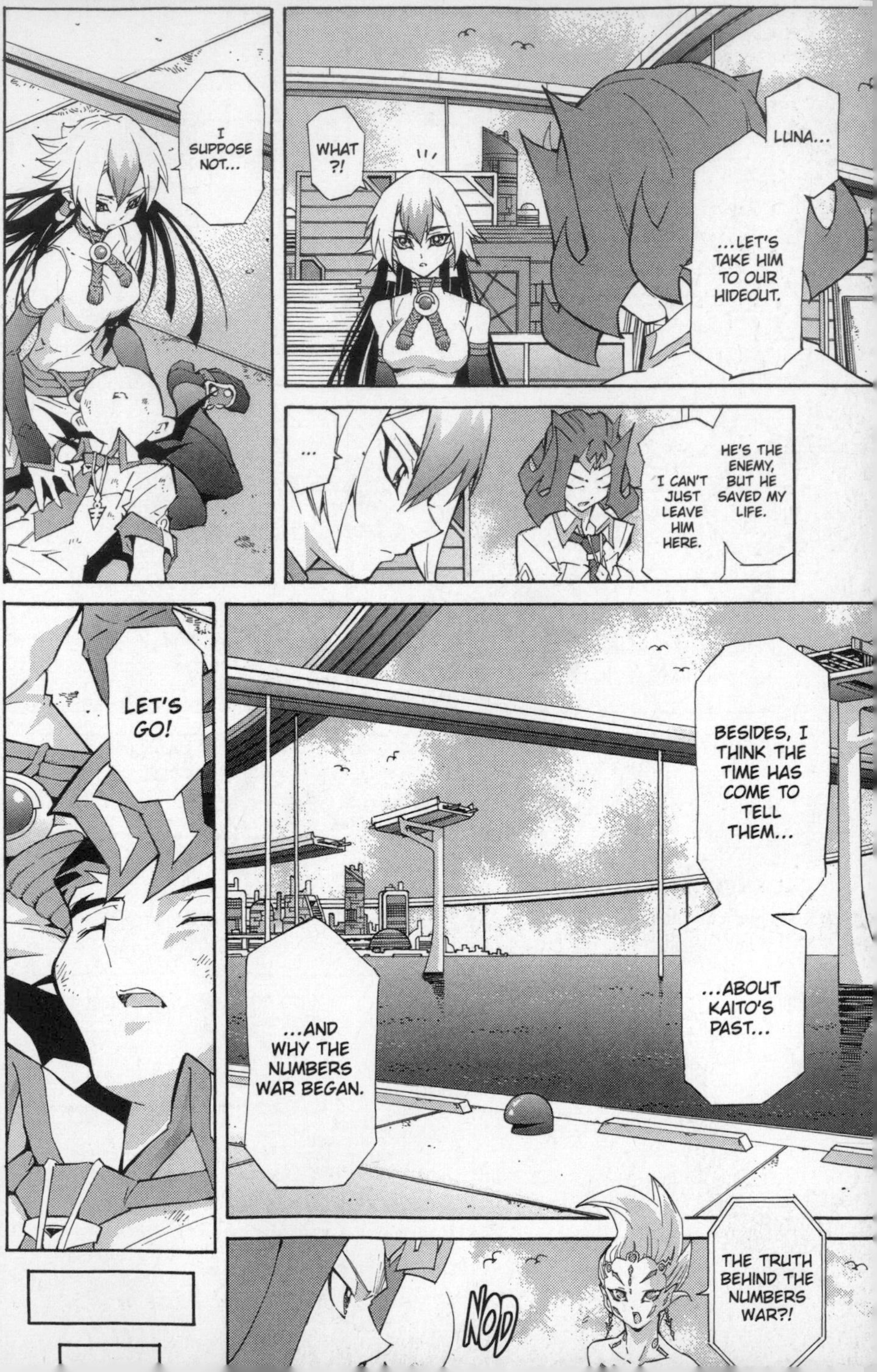
LUNA...
...LET'S TAKE HIM TO OUR HIDEOUT.
WHAT ?!
HE'S THE ENEMY, BUT HE SAVED MY LIFE.
I CAN'T JUST LEAVE HIM HERE.
...
I SUPPOSE NOT...
BESIDES, I THINK THE TIME HAS COME TO TELL THEM...
...ABOUT KAITO'S PAST...
...AND WHY THE NUMBERS WAR BEGAN.
THE TRUTH BEHIND THE NUMBERS WAR?!
NOD
LET'S GO!

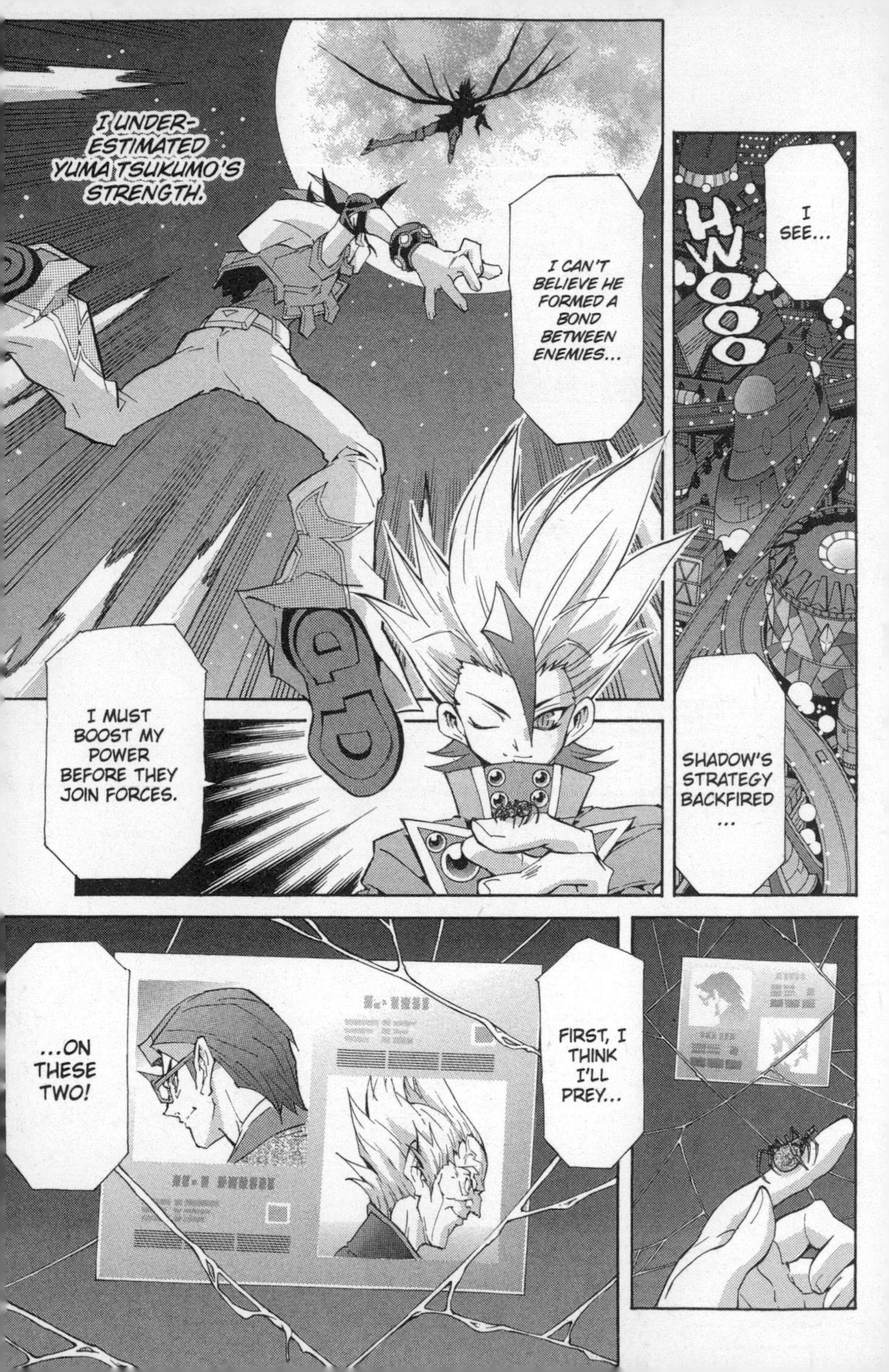
I SEE...
HWOOO
SHADOW'S STRATEGY BACKFIRED...
I UNDER-ESTIMATED YUMA TSUKUMO'S STRENGTH.
I CAN'T BELIEVE HE FORMED A BOND BETWEEN ENEMIES...
I MUST BOOST MY POWER BEFORE THEY JOIN FORCES.
FIRST, I THINK I'LL PREY...
...ON THESE TWO!

astral's
Journal
#9

2010: MIYOSHI'S FIRST YEAR-END YU-GI-OH! PARTY.
AT THE STATION WHERE HE WAS MEETING THE OTHERS.
MIYOSHI WAS NERVOUS AND SHOWED UP EARLY WHEN A DOG OUT FOR A WALK...
!
PANT PANT
...TOOK A SHINE TO HIM.
*HEY POOCH! DO YOU LIKE THIS GUY?
TEE HEE HEE
HOLD HIM! GO ON!
JUST THEN, MIYOSHI FELT A GAZE UPON HIM...
*I FORGOT THE DOG'S NAME.
A YOUNG MAN WAS LOOKING AT HIM AND GRINN-ING.
HEH HEH
NEITHER KNEW THE OTHER WORKED ON YU-GI-OH... HM?! WHO WAS IT, YOU ASK?!
IT WAS SAITO SENSEI! (LOL)

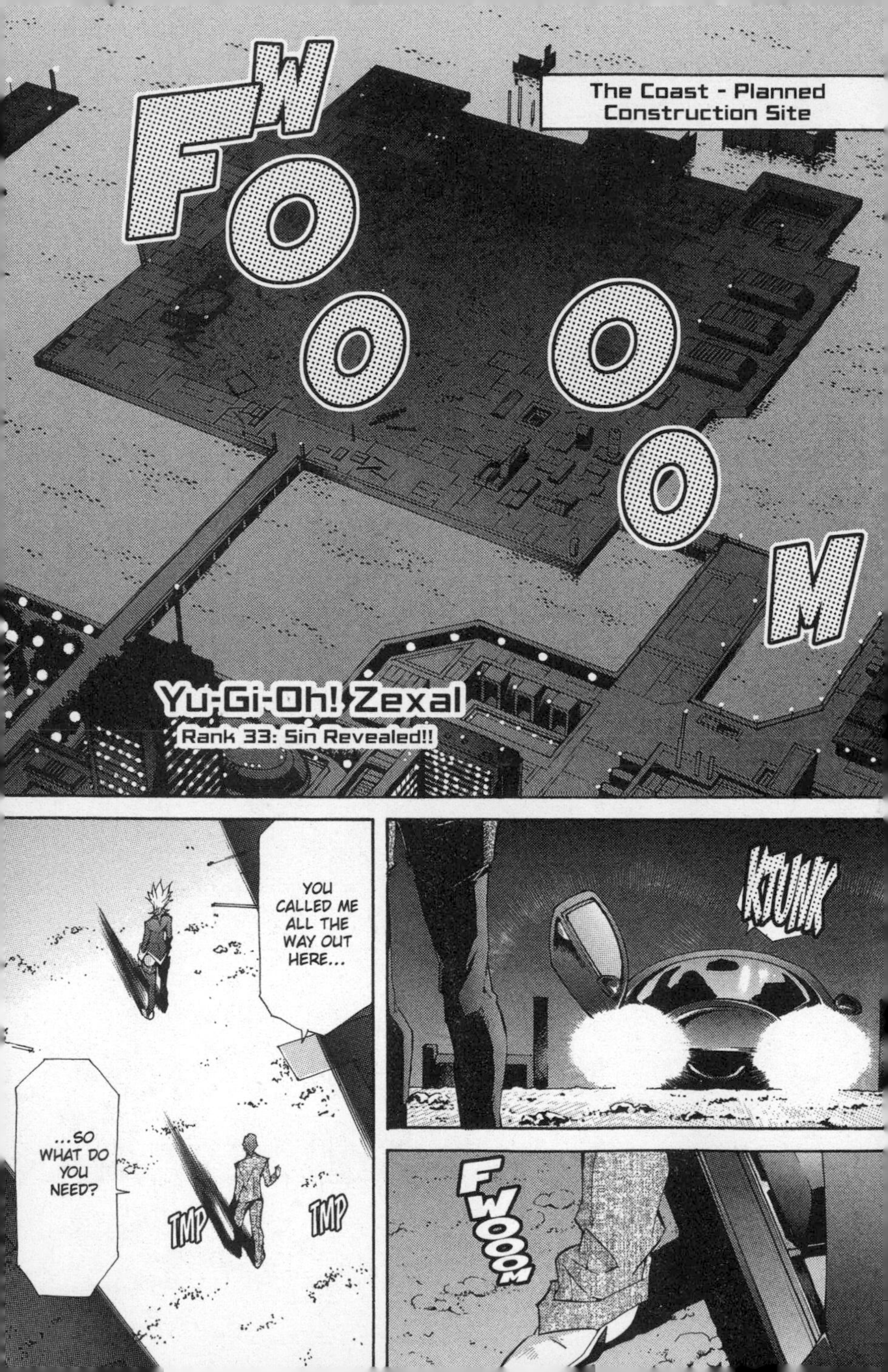
The Coast - Planned Construction Site
FWOOOOM
Yu-Gi-Oh! Zexal
Rank 33: Sin Revealed!!
KTUNK
FWOOOM
YOU CALLED ME ALL THE WAY OUT HERE...
...SO WHAT DO YOU NEED?
TMP
TMP

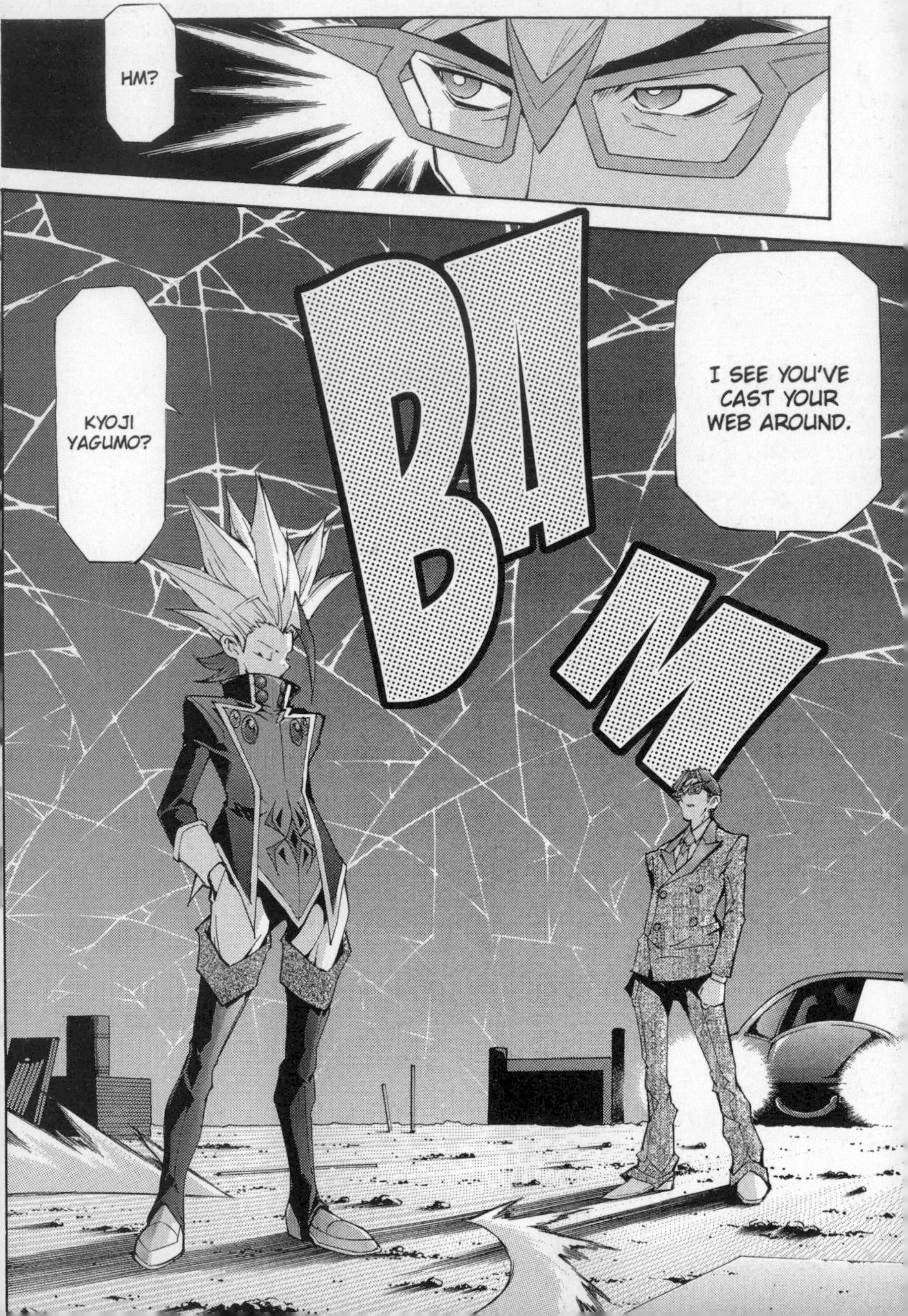
HM?
I SEE YOU'VE CAST YOUR WEB AROUND.
BAM
KYOJI YAGUMO?

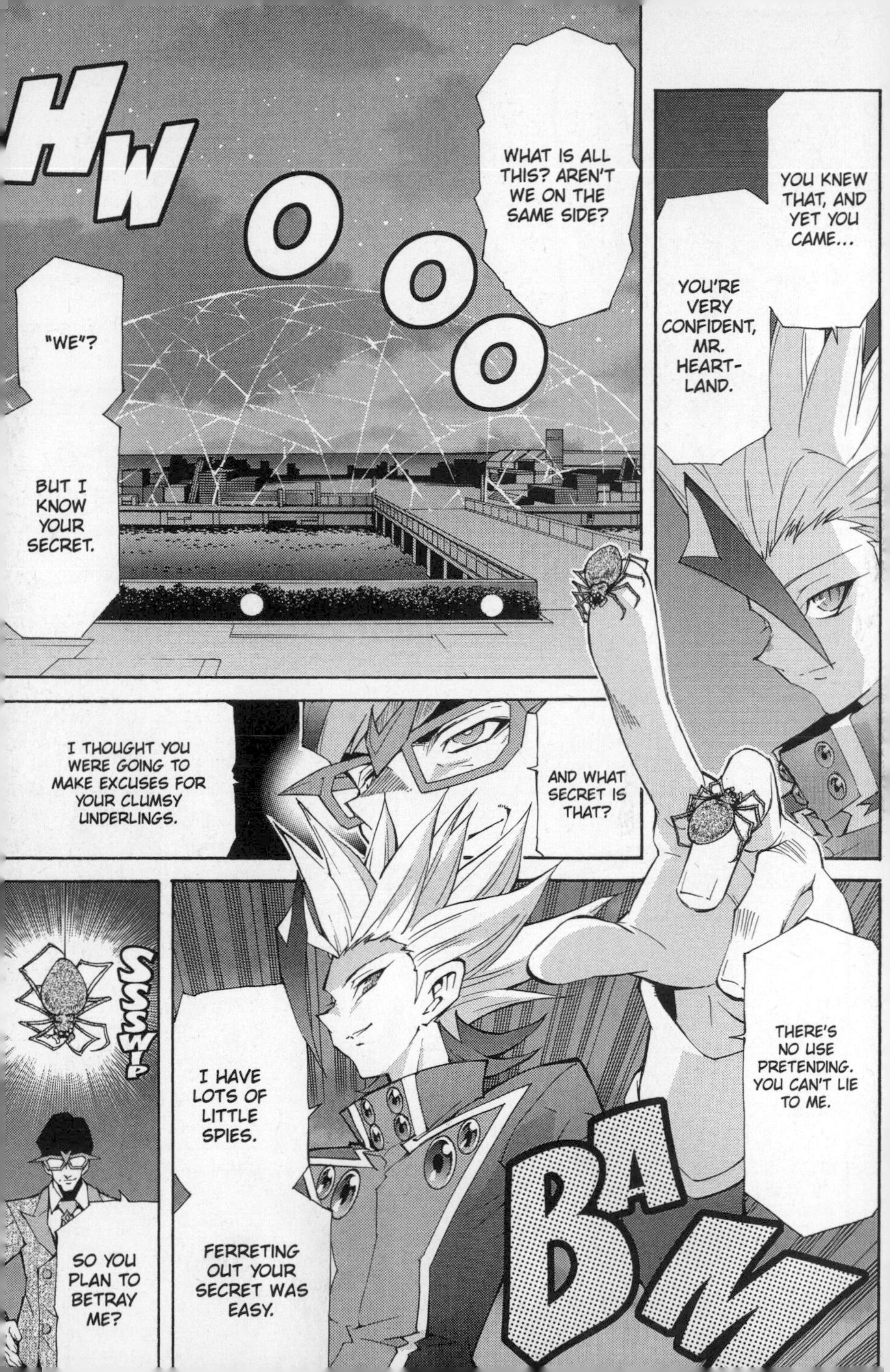

YOU KNEW THAT, AND YET YOU CAME...
YOU'RE VERY CONFIDENT, MR. HEART-LAND.
WHAT IS ALL THIS? AREN'T WE ON THE SAME SIDE?
HWOOOO
"WE"?
BUT I KNOW YOUR SECRET.
AND WHAT SECRET IS THAT?
I THOUGHT YOU WERE GOING TO MAKE EXCUSES FOR YOUR CLUMSY UNDERLINGS.
THERE'S NO USE PRETENDING. YOU CAN'T LIE TO ME.
BAM
I HAVE LOTS OF LITTLE SPIES.
FERRETING OUT YOUR SECRET WAS EASY.
SSSWIP
SO YOU PLAN TO BETRAY ME?

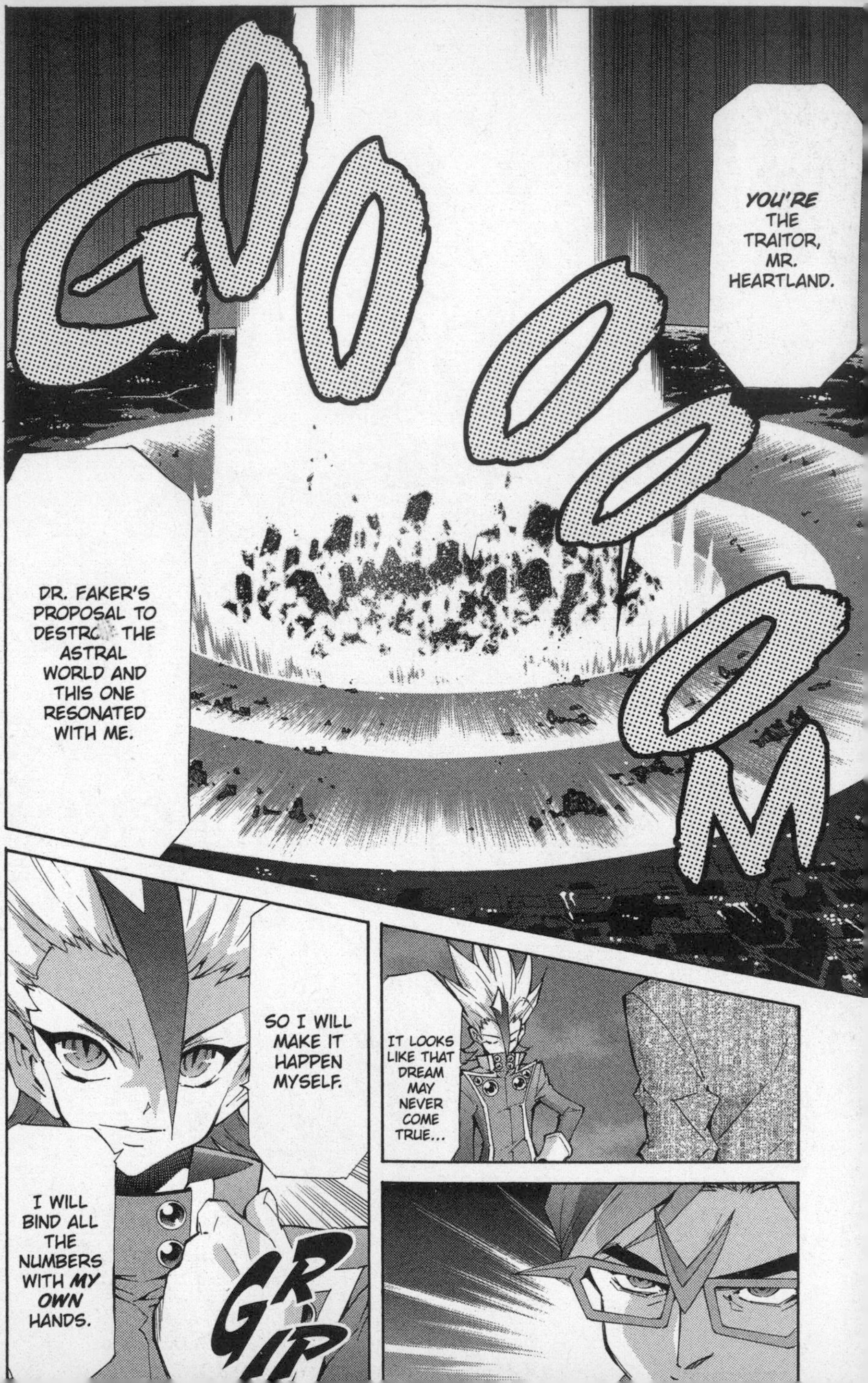
YOU'RE THE TRAITOR, MR. HEARTLAND.
GOOOOOOOM
DR. FAKER'S PROPOSAL TO DESTROY THE ASTRAL WORLD AND THIS ONE RESONATED WITH ME.
IT LOOKS LIKE THAT DREAM MAY NEVER COME TRUE...
SO I WILL MAKE IT HAPPEN MYSELF.
I WILL BIND ALL THE NUMBERS WITH *MY OWN* HANDS.
GRIP

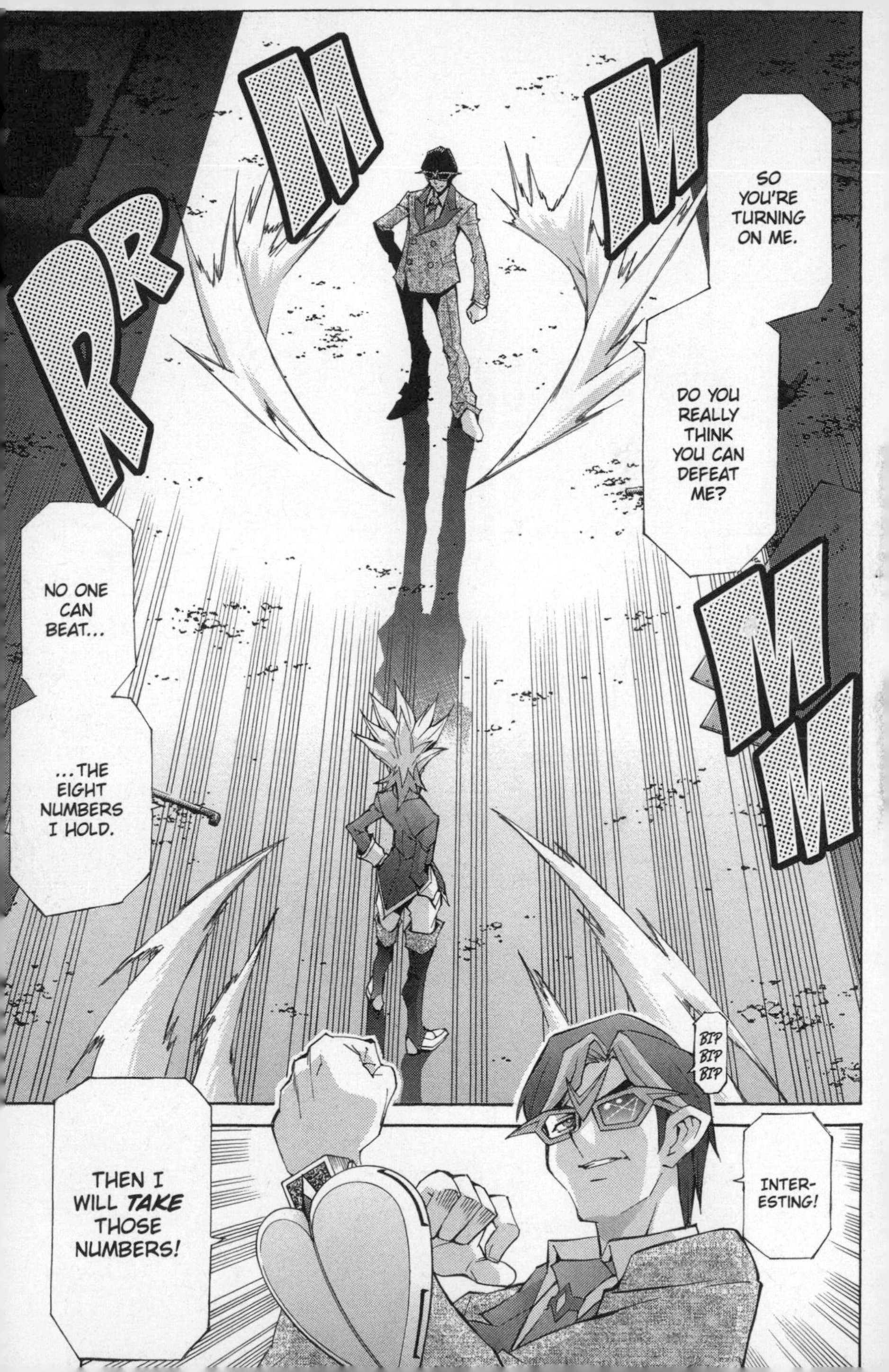
SO YOU'RE TURNING ON ME.
DO YOU REALLY THINK YOU CAN DEFEAT ME?
PRMMMM
NO ONE CAN BEAT...
...THE EIGHT NUMBERS I HOLD.
BIP BIP BIP
INTER-ESTING!
THEN I WILL *TAKE* THOSE NUMBERS!

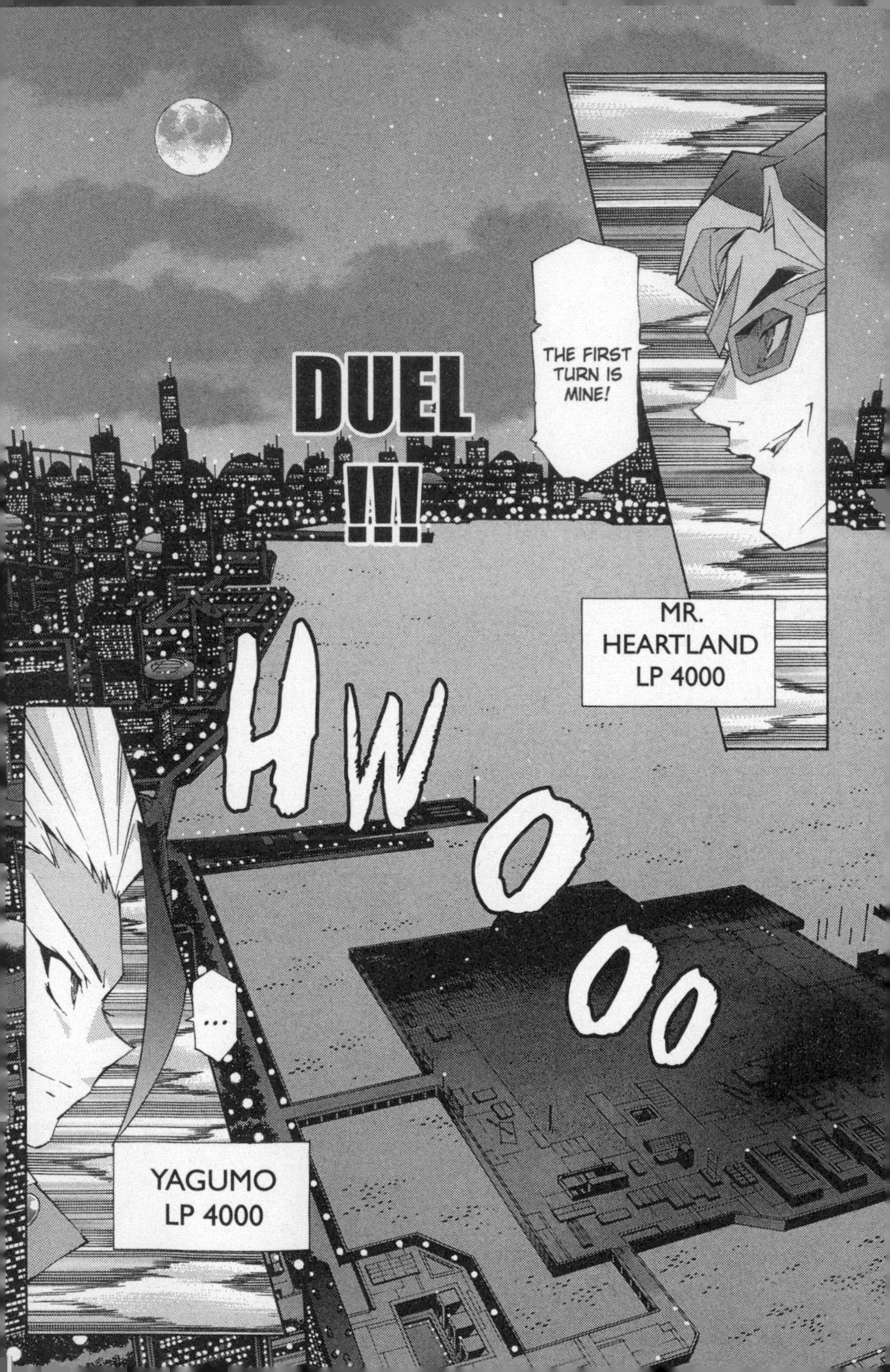
THE FIRST TURN IS MINE!
MR. HEARTLAND LP 4000
DUEL!!!
HWOOOO
...
YAGUMO LP 4000

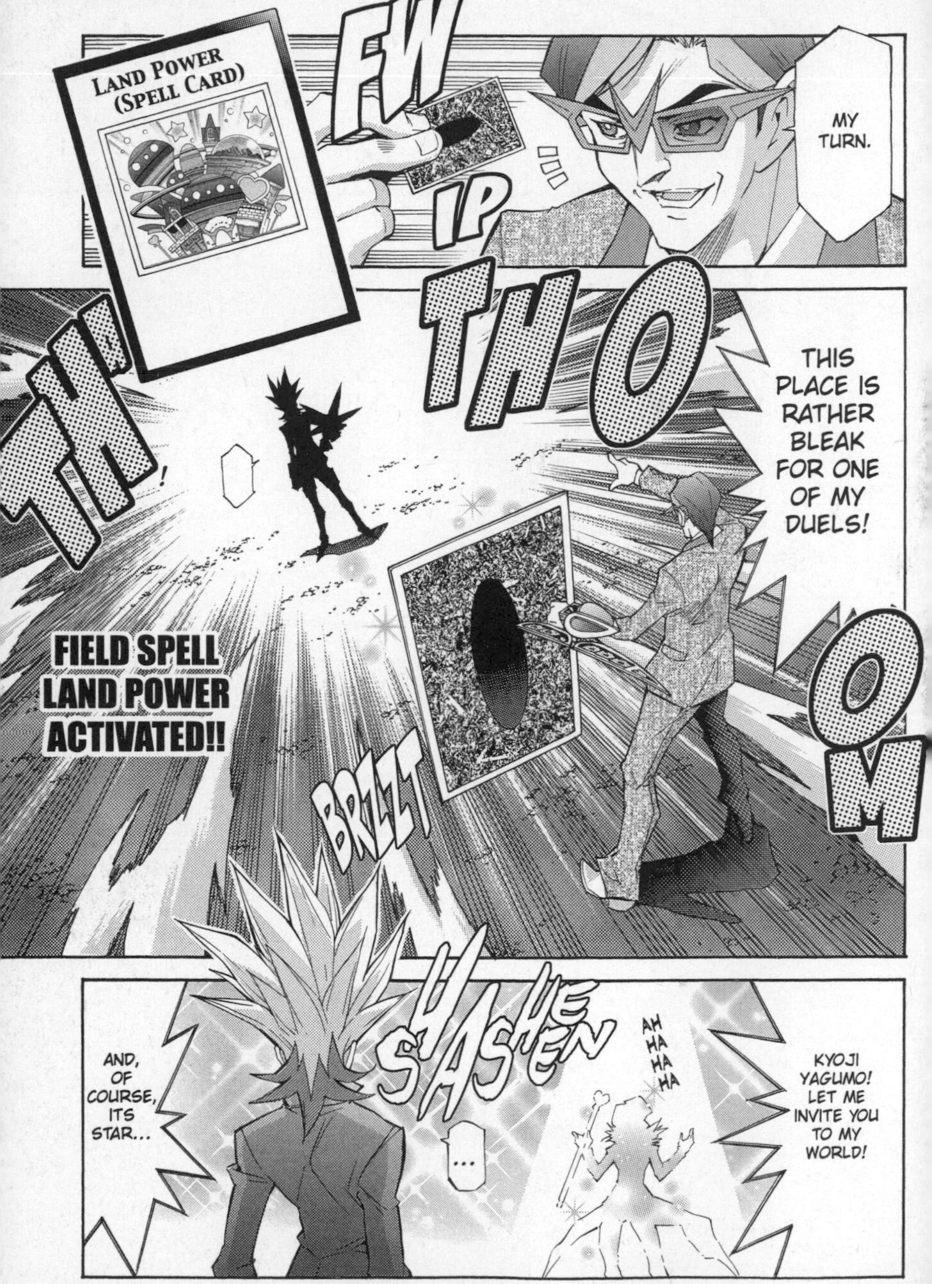
MY TURN.
FWIP
LAND POWER (SPELL CARD)
THOOM
THIS PLACE IS RATHER BLEAK FOR ONE OF MY DUELS!
FIELD SPELL LAND POWER ACTIVATED!!
BRZZT
THH!
KYOJI YAGUMO! LET ME INVITE YOU TO MY WORLD!
AH HA HA HA
...
AND, OF COURSE, ITS STAR...

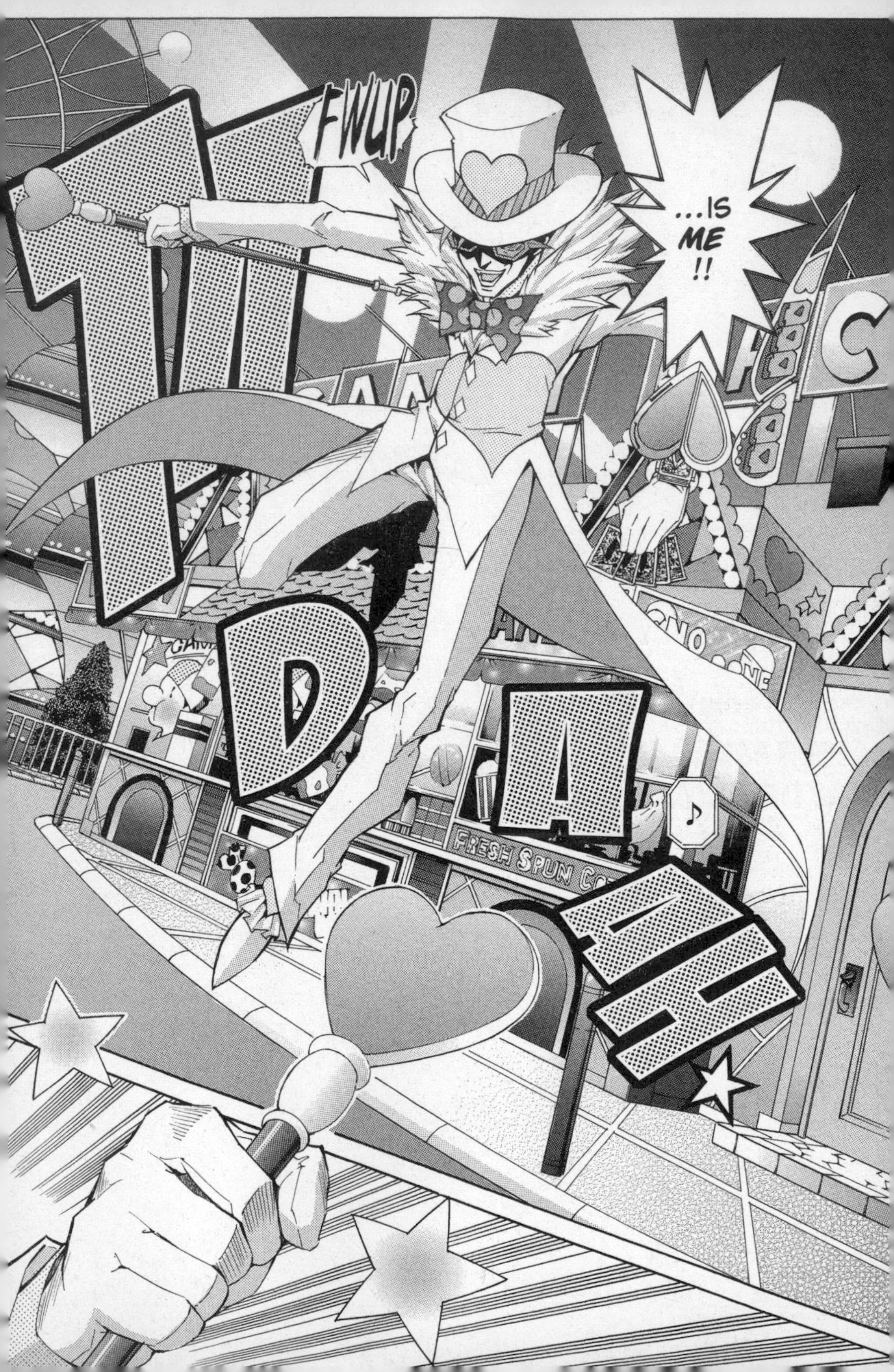
FWUP
...IS ME !!
T D A H
FRESH SPUN

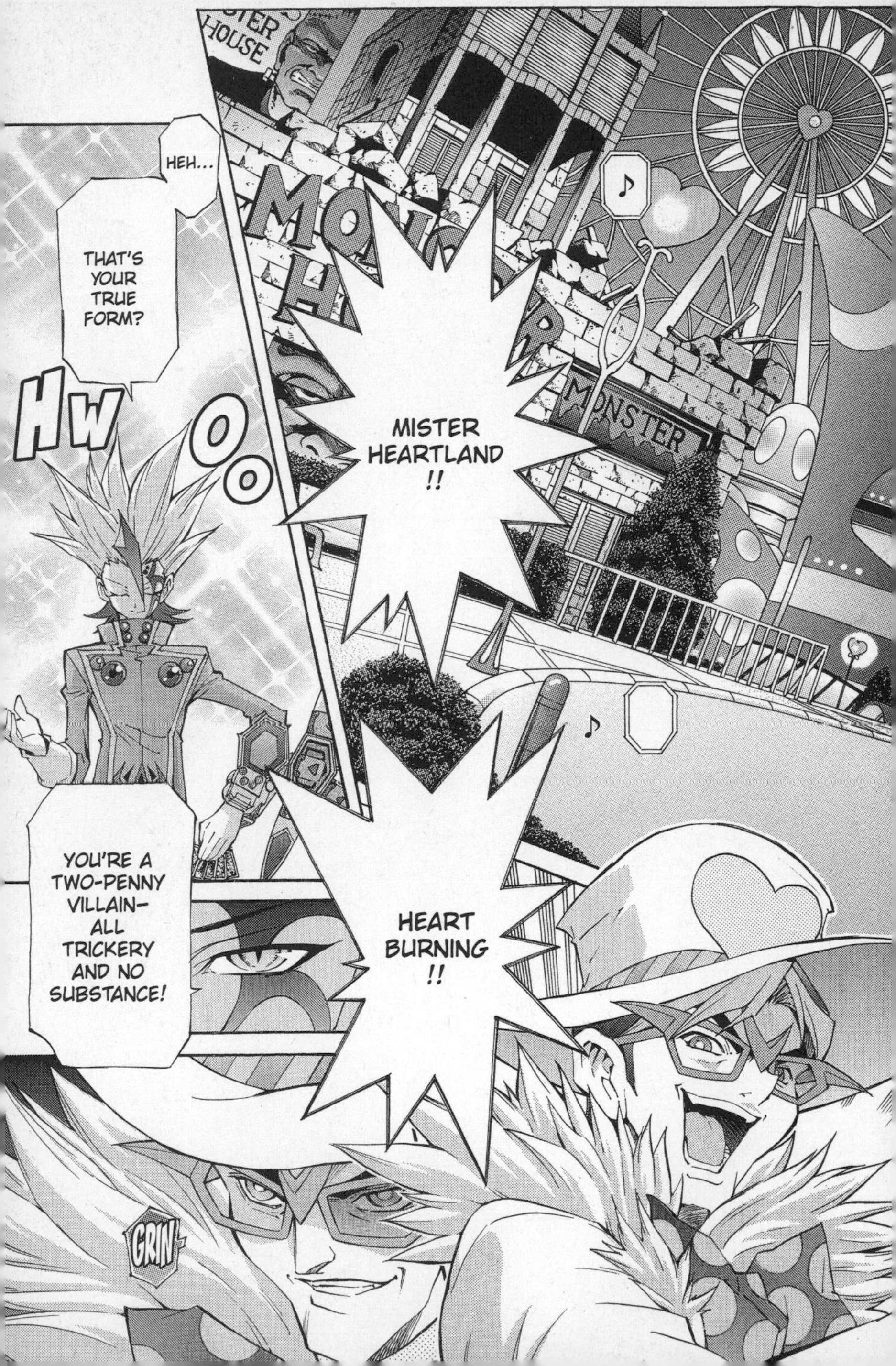
STER HOUSE
MONSTER
♪
MISTER HEARTLAND!!
HEH...
THAT'S YOUR TRUE FORM?
HWOO
HEART BURNING!!
YOU'RE A TWO-PENNY VILLAIN—ALL TRICKERY AND NO SUBSTANCE!
GRIN

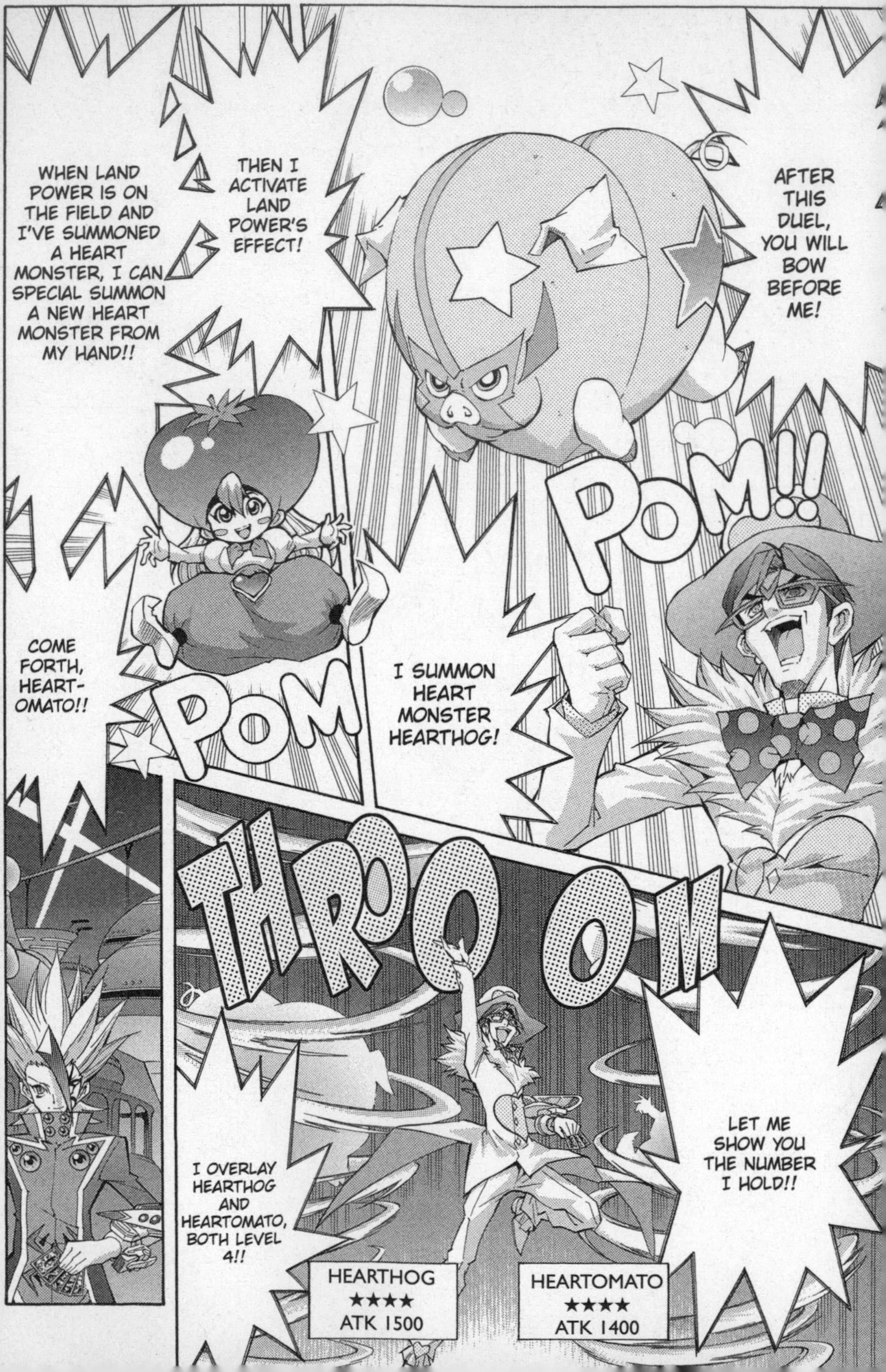
AFTER THIS DUEL, YOU WILL BOW BEFORE ME!
POM!!
I SUMMON HEART MONSTER HEARTHOG!
THEN I ACTIVATE LAND POWER'S EFFECT!
WHEN LAND POWER IS ON THE FIELD AND I'VE SUMMONED A HEART MONSTER, I CAN SPECIAL SUMMON A NEW HEART MONSTER FROM MY HAND!!
POM
COME FORTH, HEARTOMATO!!
THROOOM
LET ME SHOW YOU THE NUMBER I HOLD!!
I OVERLAY HEARTHOG AND HEARTOMATO, BOTH LEVEL 4!!
HEARTOMATO ★★★★ ATK 1400
HEARTHOG ★★★★ ATK 1500

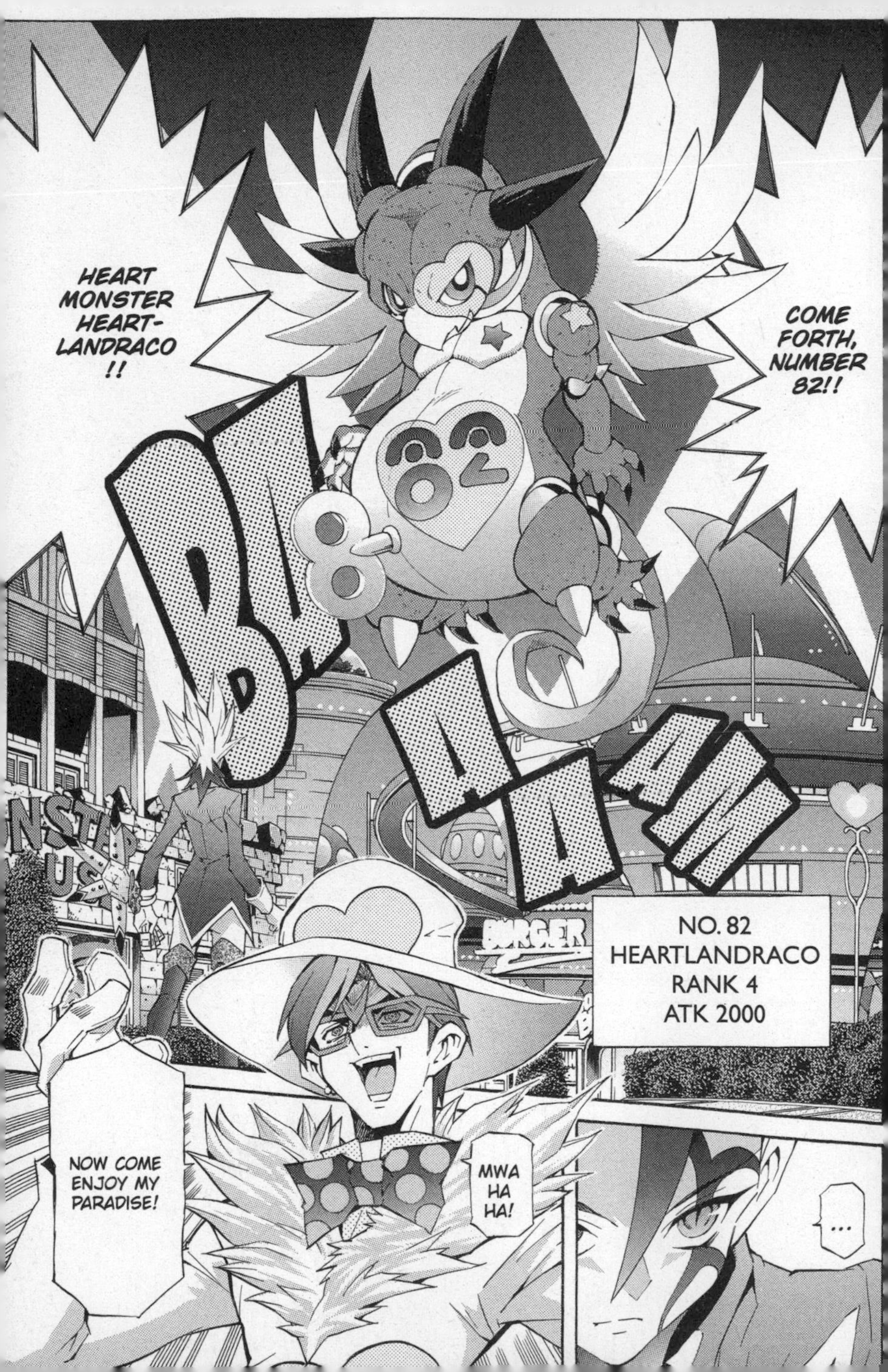
COME FORTH, NUMBER 82!!
HEART MONSTER HEART-LANDRACO!!
BAAAM
NO. 82 HEARTLANDRACO RANK 4 ATK 2000
BURGER
...
MWA HA HA!
NOW COME ENJOY MY PARADISE!

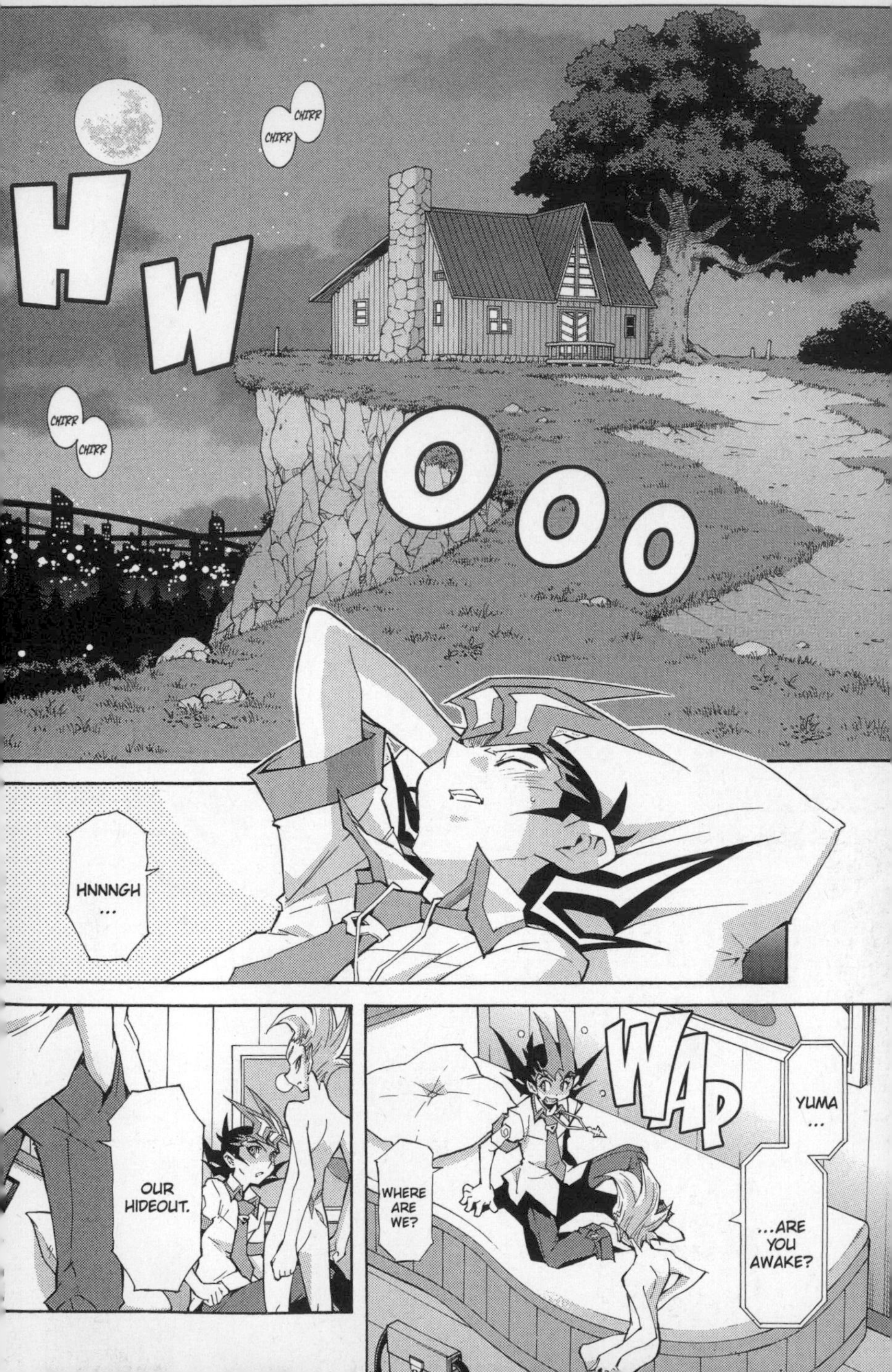
CHIRR CHIRR
HWOOO
CHIRR CHIRR
HNNNGH ...
YUMA ...
...ARE YOU AWAKE?
WAP
WHERE ARE WE?
OUR HIDEOUT.

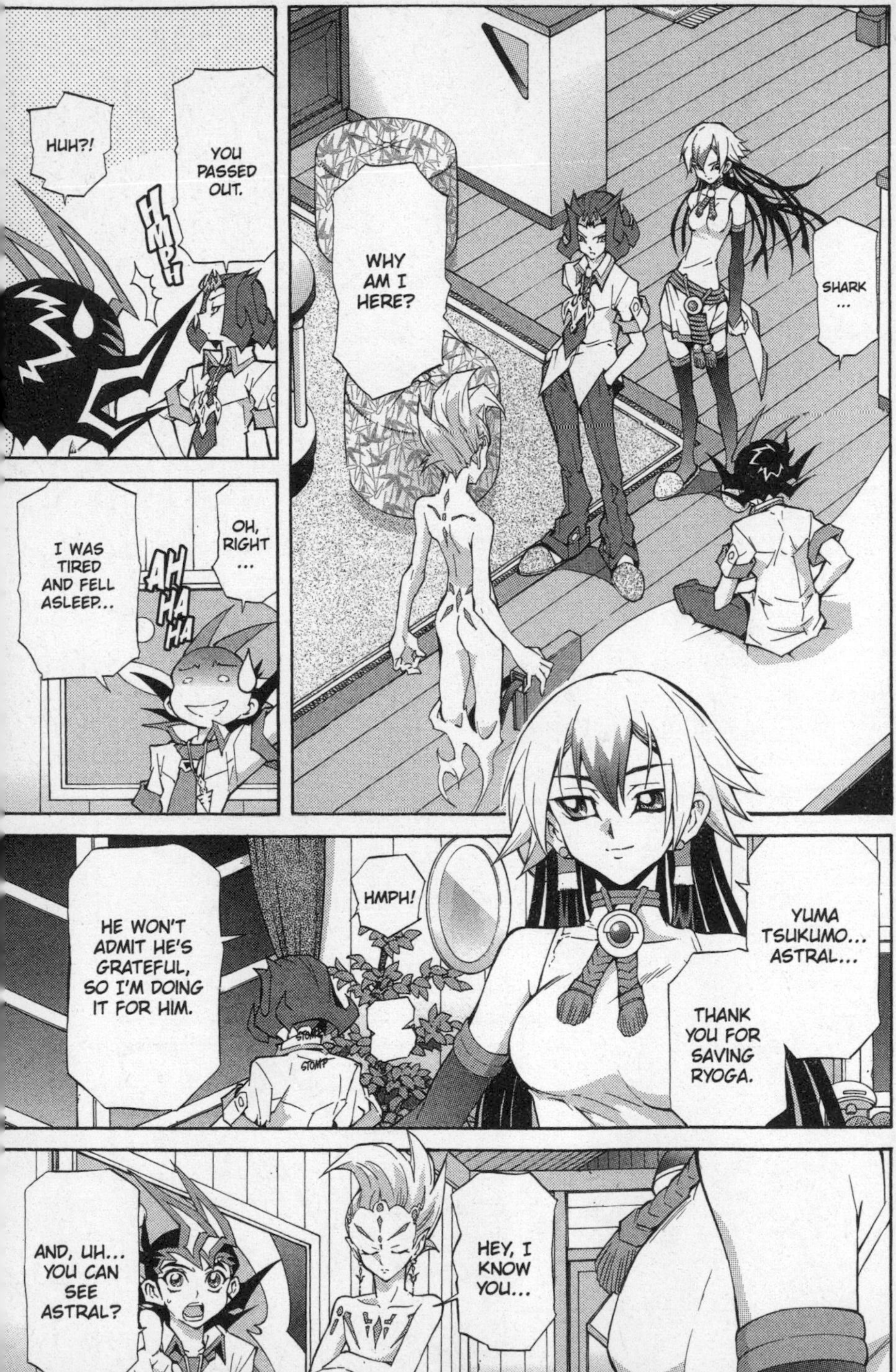
SHARK...
WHY AM I HERE?
YOU PASSED OUT.
HMPH
HUH?!
OH, RIGHT...
AH HA HA
I WAS TIRED AND FELL ASLEEP...
YUMA TSUKUMO... ASTRAL...
THANK YOU FOR SAVING RYOGA.
HMPH!
STOMP
STOMP
HE WON'T ADMIT HE'S GRATEFUL, SO I'M DOING IT FOR HIM.
HEY, I KNOW YOU...
AND, UH... YOU CAN SEE ASTRAL?

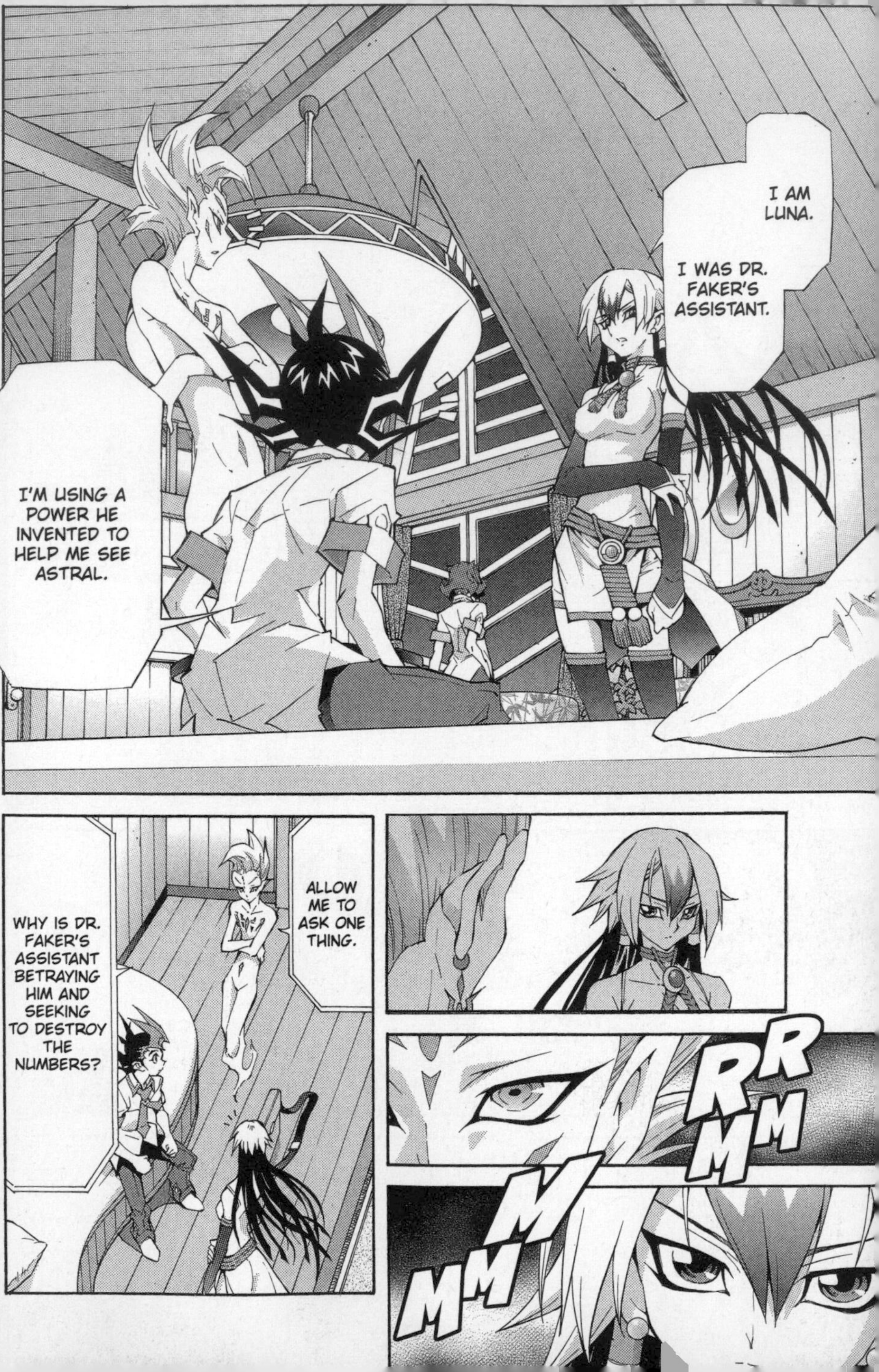

I AM LUNA.
I WAS DR. FAKER'S ASSISTANT.
I'M USING A POWER HE INVENTED TO HELP ME SEE ASTRAL.
RRMMM
MMMM
ALLOW ME TO ASK ONE THING.
WHY IS DR. FAKER'S ASSISTANT BETRAYING HIM AND SEEKING TO DESTROY THE NUMBERS?

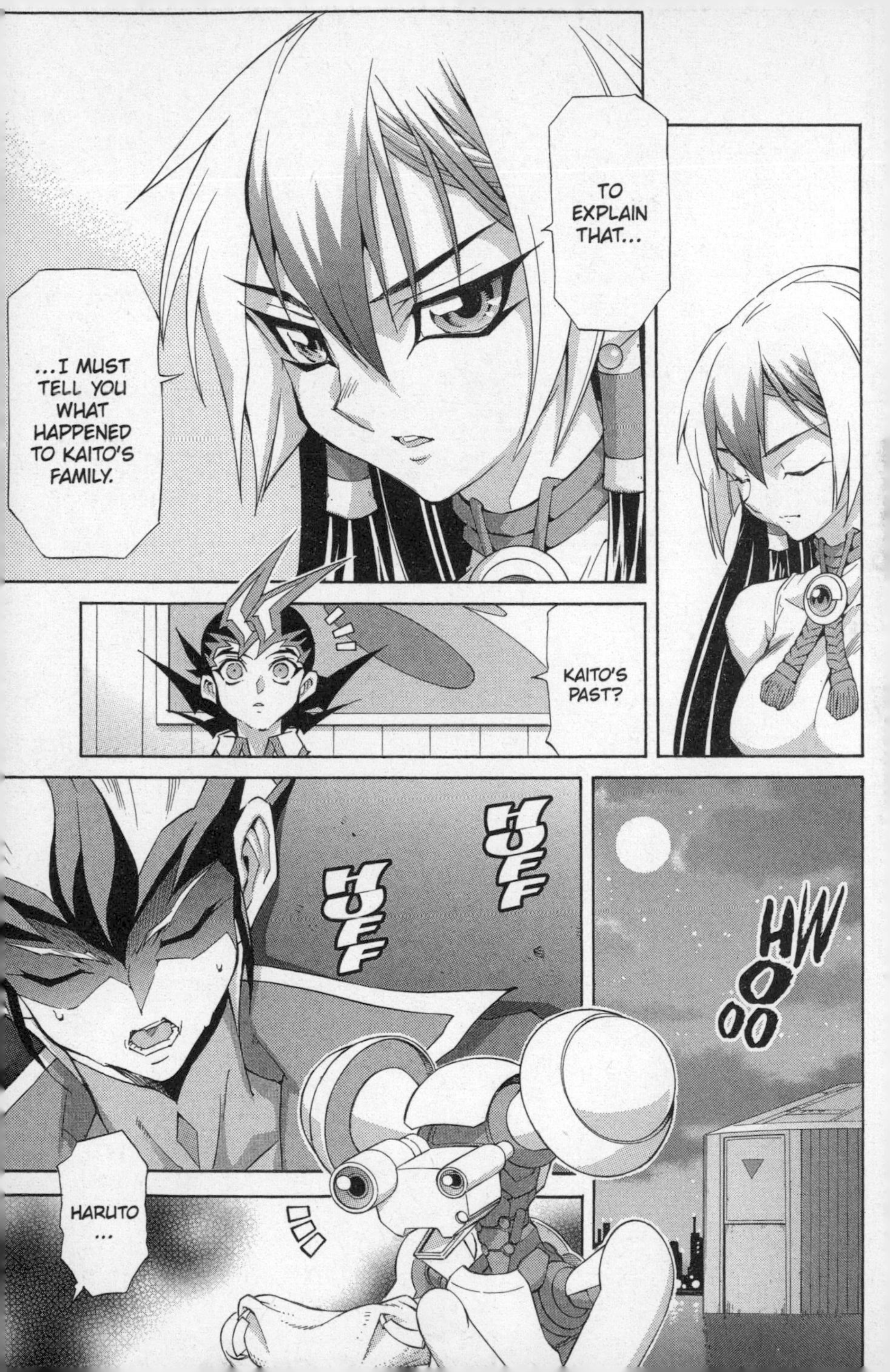
TO EXPLAIN THAT...
...I MUST TELL YOU WHAT HAPPENED TO KAITO'S FAMILY.
KAITO'S PAST?
HWOOO
HUFF
HUFF
HARUTO ...

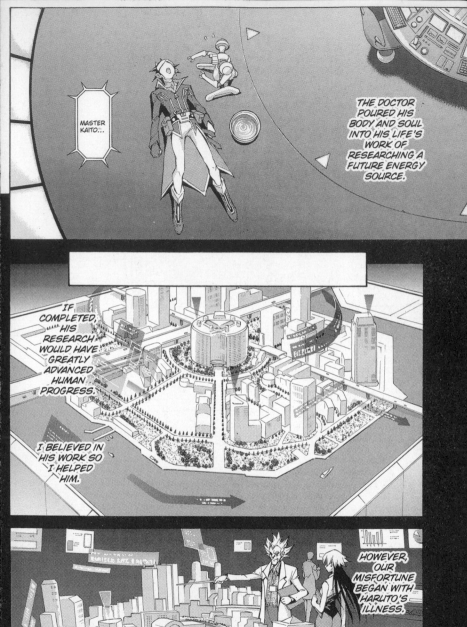

MASTER KAITO...

THE DOCTOR POURED HIS BODY AND SOUL INTO HIS LIFE'S WORK OF RESEARCHING A FUTURE ENERGY SOURCE.

IF COMPLETED, HIS RESEARCH WOULD HAVE GREATLY ADVANCED HUMAN PROGRESS.

I BELIEVED IN HIS WORK SO I HELPED HIM.

HOWEVER, OUR MISFORTUNE BEGAN WITH HARUTO'S ILLNESS.

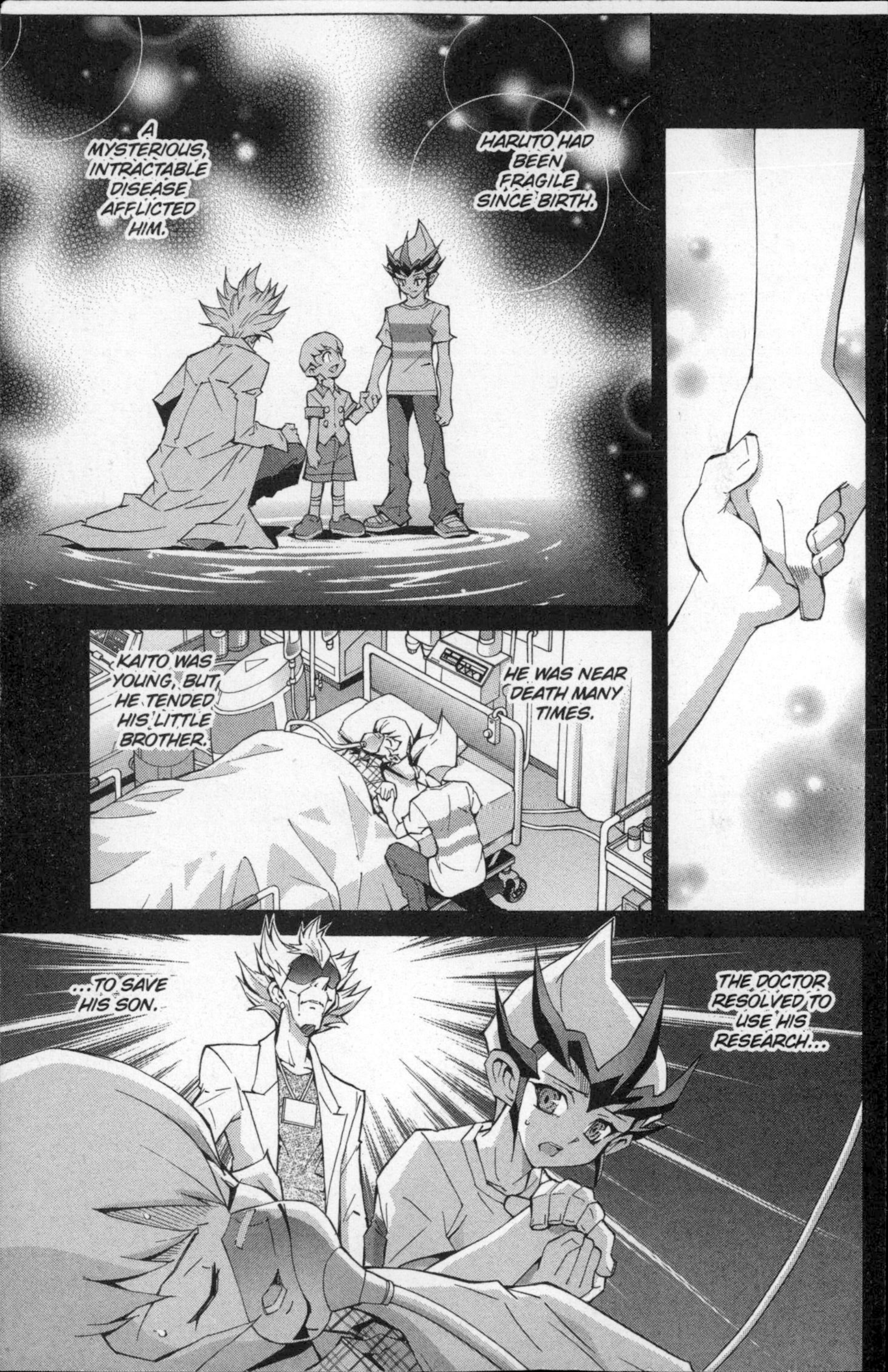
HARUTO HAD BEEN FRAGILE SINCE BIRTH.
A MYSTERIOUS, INTRACTABLE DISEASE AFFLICTED HIM.
HE WAS NEAR DEATH MANY TIMES.
KAITO WAS YOUNG, BUT HE TENDED HIS LITTLE BROTHER.
THE DOCTOR RESOLVED TO USE HIS RESEARCH...
...TO SAVE HIS SON.

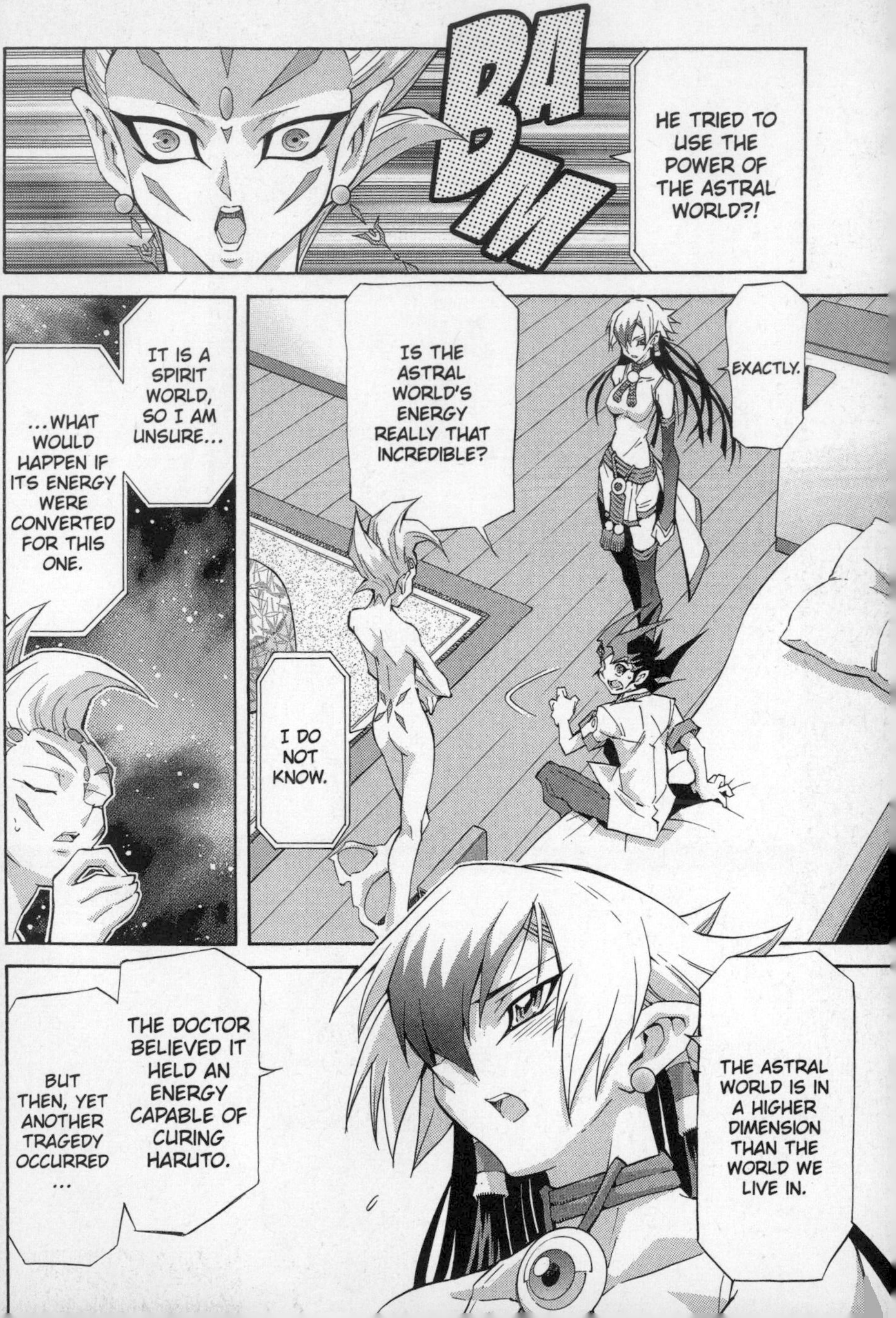
BAM
HE TRIED TO USE THE POWER OF THE ASTRAL WORLD?!
EXACTLY.
IS THE ASTRAL WORLD'S ENERGY REALLY THAT INCREDIBLE?
I DO NOT KNOW.
IT IS A SPIRIT WORLD, SO I AM UNSURE...
...WHAT WOULD HAPPEN IF ITS ENERGY WERE CONVERTED FOR THIS ONE.
THE ASTRAL WORLD IS IN A HIGHER DIMENSION THAN THE WORLD WE LIVE IN.
THE DOCTOR BELIEVED IT HELD AN ENERGY CAPABLE OF CURING HARUTO.
BUT THEN, YET ANOTHER TRAGEDY OCCURRED...

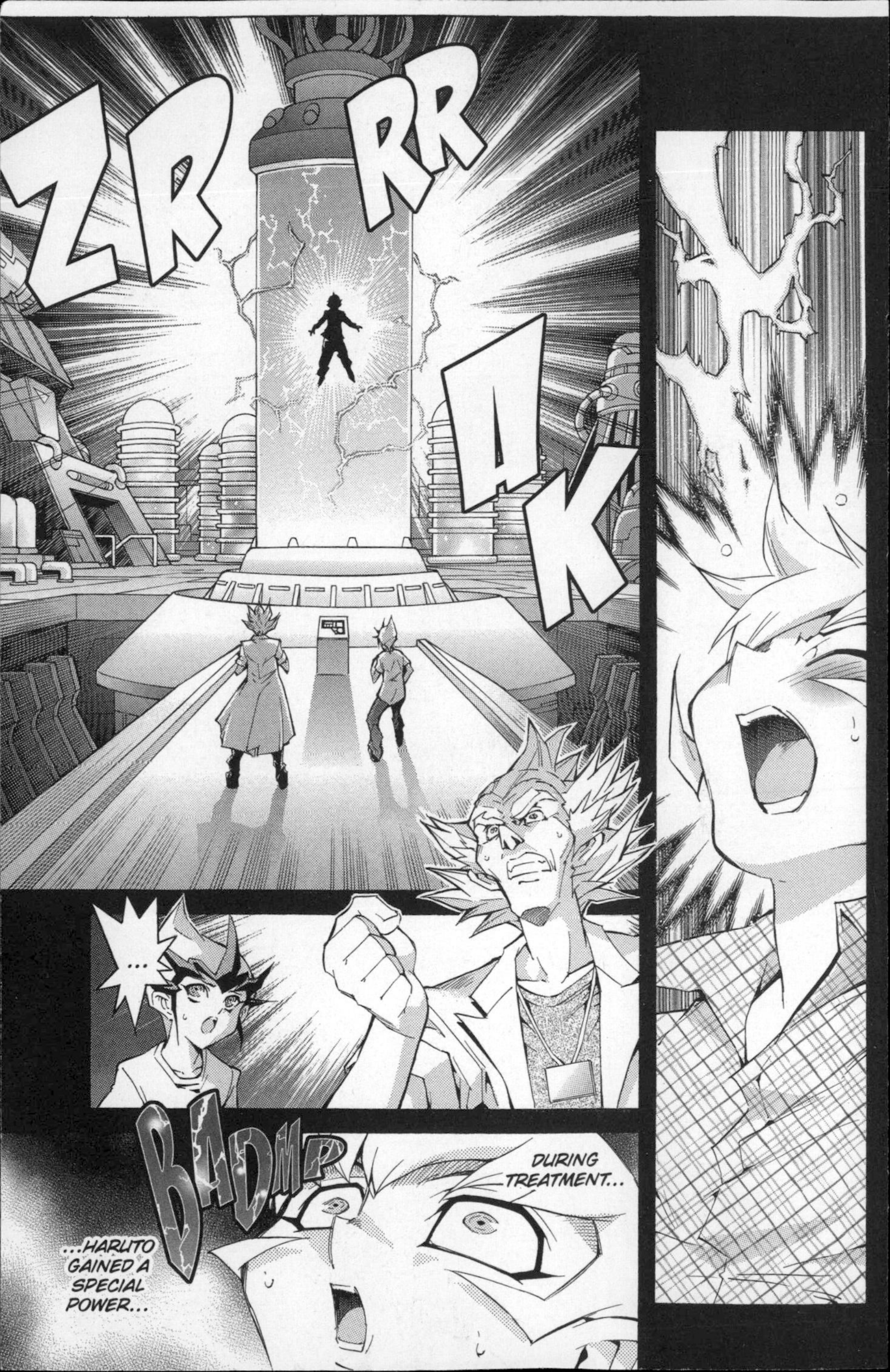
ZRRRAK
...
DURING TREATMENT...
BADMP
...HARUTO GAINED A SPECIAL POWER...

AAAAA
...BUT HIS SOUL...
...WAS PULLED INTO THE ASTRAL WORLD.
AAAH
CHIRR
CHIRR
CHIRR
CHIRR

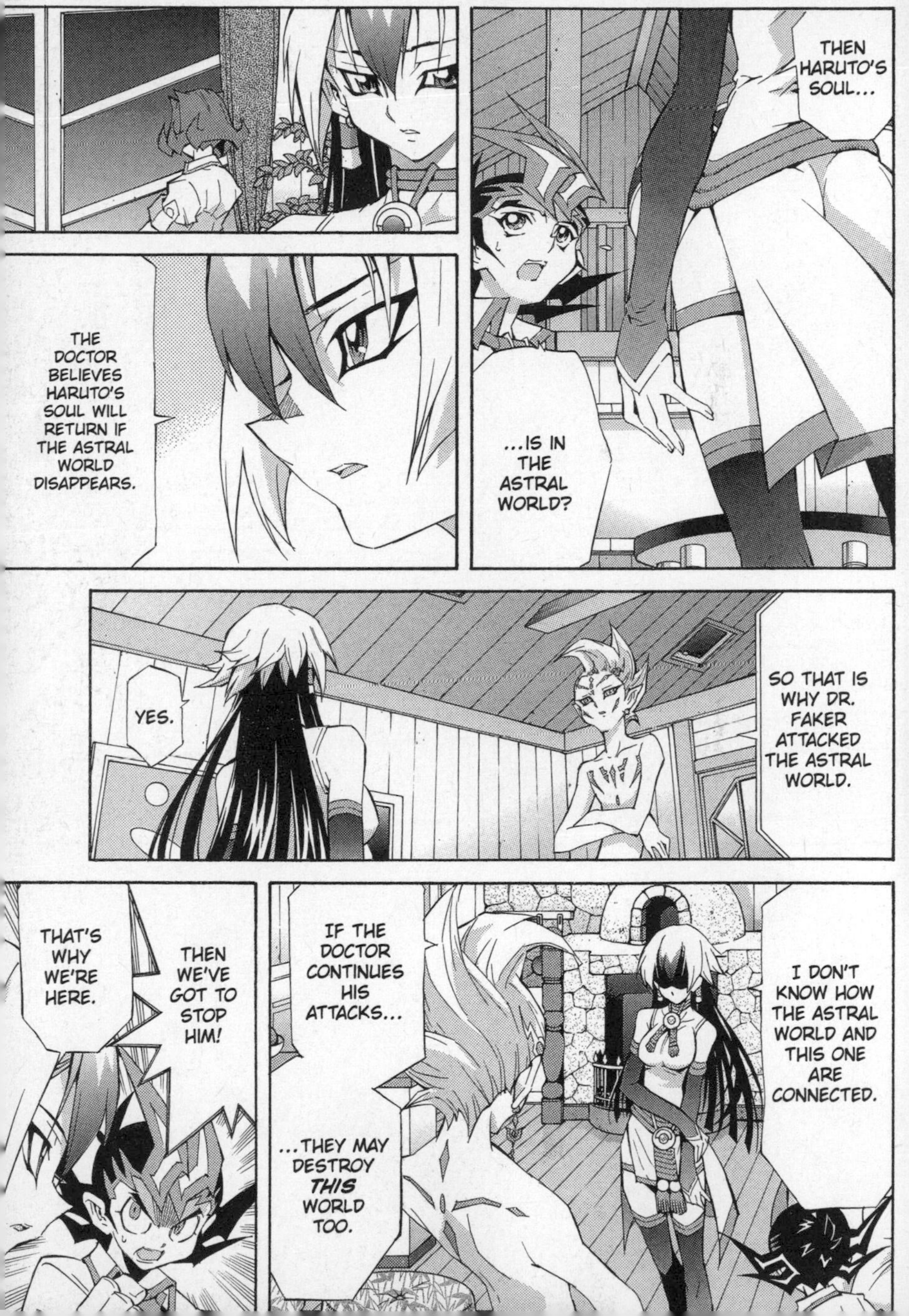
THEN HARUTO'S SOUL...
...IS IN THE ASTRAL WORLD?
THE DOCTOR BELIEVES HARUTO'S SOUL WILL RETURN IF THE ASTRAL WORLD DISAPPEARS.
SO THAT IS WHY DR. FAKER ATTACKED THE ASTRAL WORLD.
YES.
I DON'T KNOW HOW THE ASTRAL WORLD AND THIS ONE ARE CONNECTED.
IF THE DOCTOR CONTINUES HIS ATTACKS...
...THEY MAY DESTROY *THIS* WORLD TOO.
THEN WE'VE GOT TO STOP HIM!
THAT'S WHY WE'RE HERE.

I WON'T LET HIM USE MY ASSISTANCE TO DESTROY THE WORLD.

YES. I AM A SCIENTIST TOO.

AFTER DEFEATING THE DOCTOR, WE WILL DESTROY ALL THE NUMBERS!

...AND PROVIDED A WEAPON TO USE AGAINST THE DOCTOR.

ASTRAL, THAT WAS WHEN YOUR NUMBERS APPEARED....

THAT IS YOUR PHILO-SOPHY?

FIGHT FIRE WITH FIRE....

ASTRAL LOOKS WEIRD, BUT HE'S NOT ALL BAD!

YOU DON'T KNOW THAT!

...

THE NUMBERS TRANSFORM DESIRE INTO CARD POWER.

THAT'S TOO MUCH POWER FOR ONE PERSON. IF THEY EXIST, THEY WILL SOMEDAY DESTROY THIS WORLD.

BUT WHAT ABOUT THIS GUY'S MEMORIES?

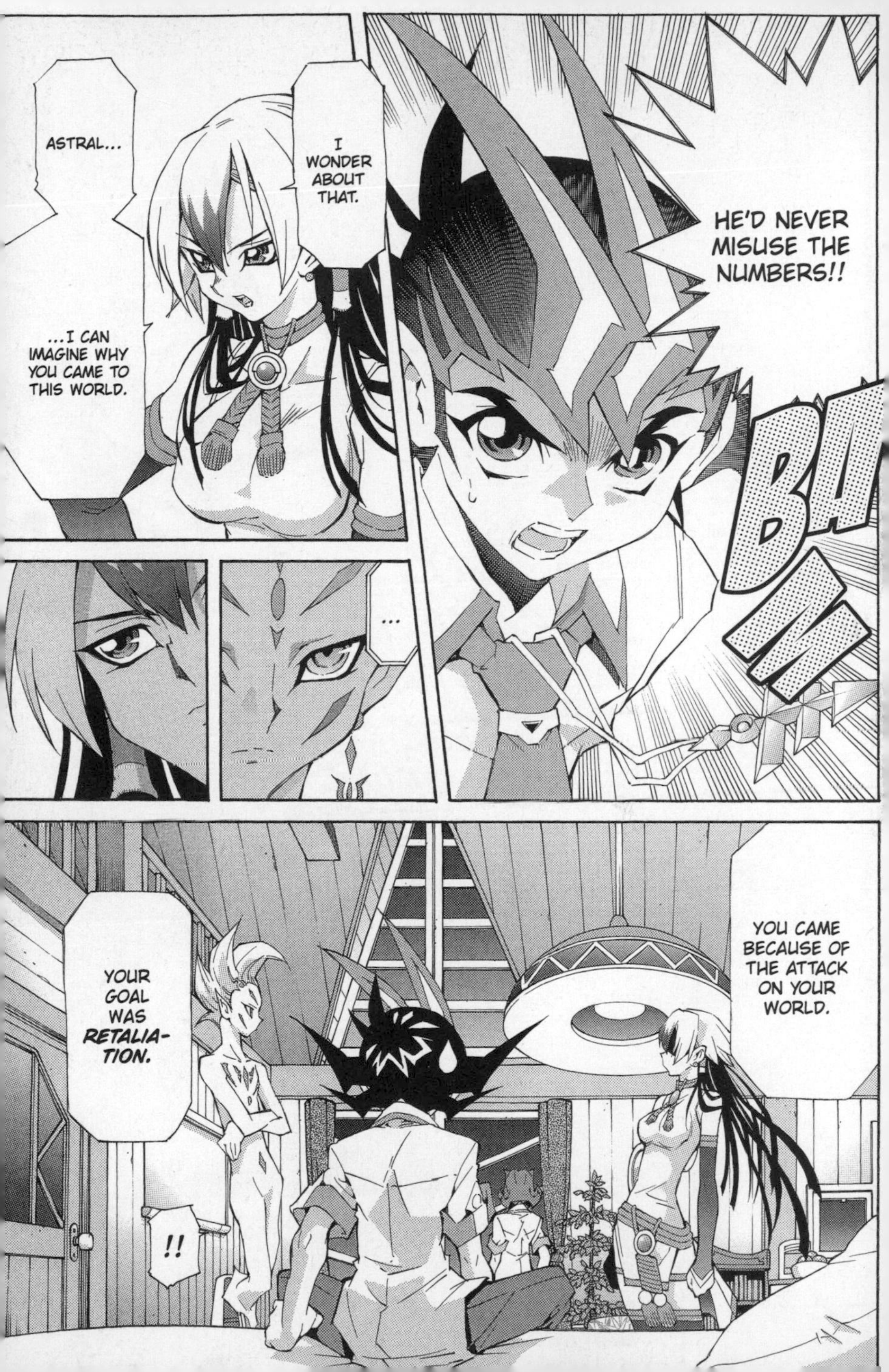
HE'D NEVER MISUSE THE NUMBERS!!
BAM
I WONDER ABOUT THAT.
ASTRAL...
...I CAN IMAGINE WHY YOU CAME TO THIS WORLD.
...
YOU CAME BECAUSE OF THE ATTACK ON YOUR WORLD.
YOUR GOAL WAS *RETALIATION.*
!!

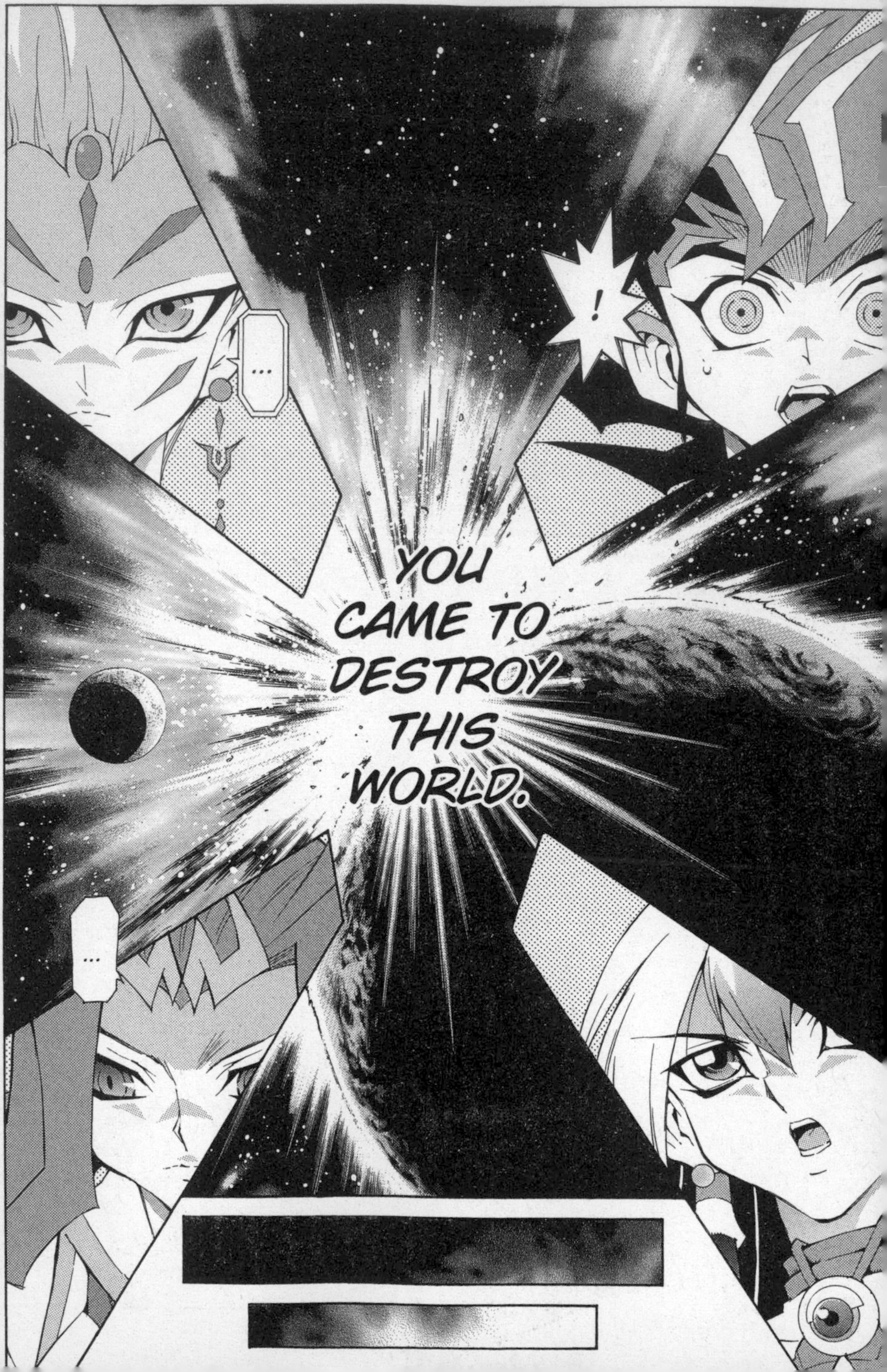
!
...
YOU CAME TO DESTROY THIS WORLD.
...

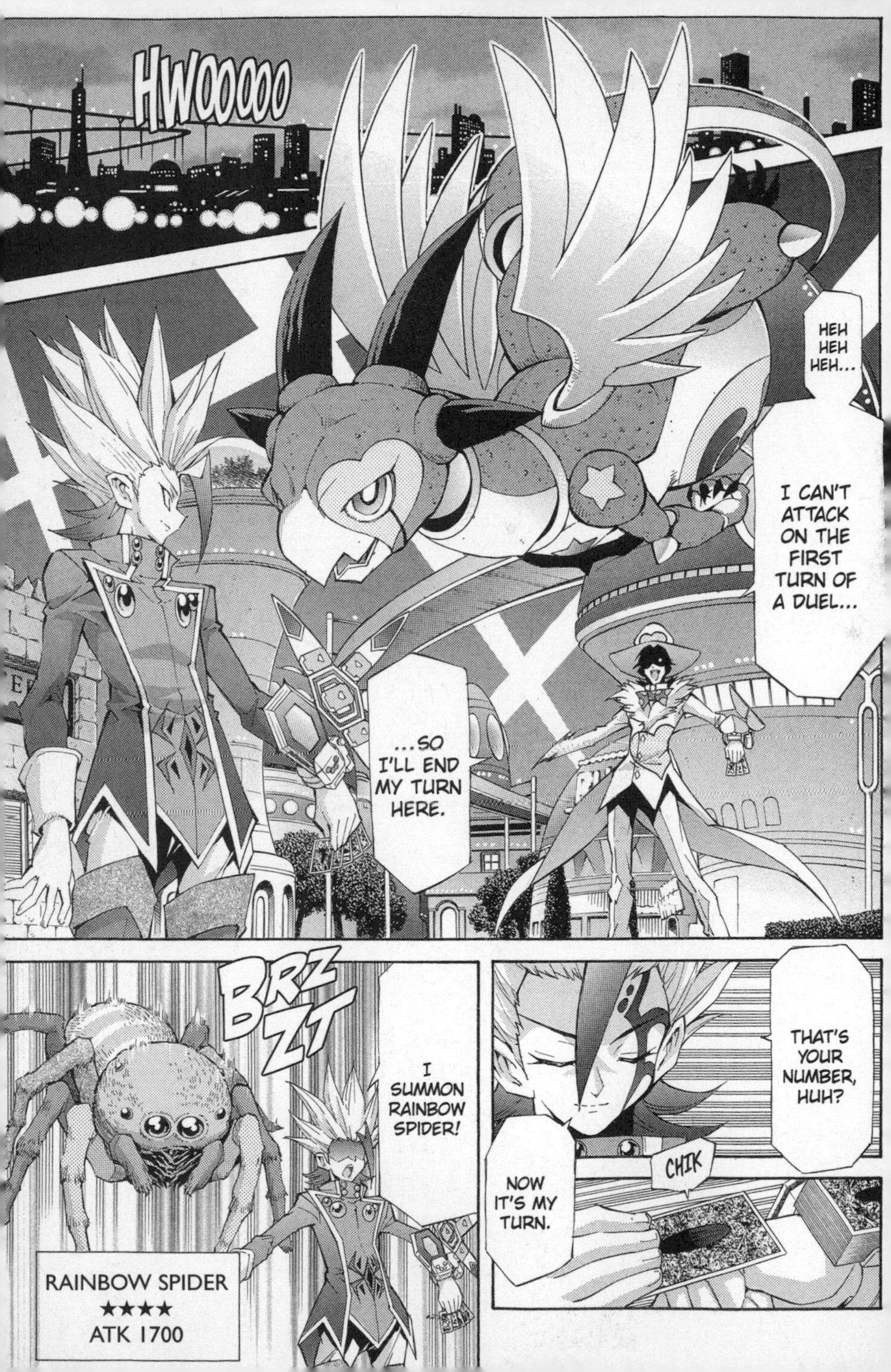
HWOOOOO
HEH HEH HEH...
I CAN'T ATTACK ON THE FIRST TURN OF A DUEL...
...SO I'LL END MY TURN HERE.
THAT'S YOUR NUMBER, HUH?
CHIK
NOW IT'S MY TURN.
BRZ ZT
I SUMMON RAINBOW SPIDER!
RAINBOW SPIDER
★★★★
ATK 1700

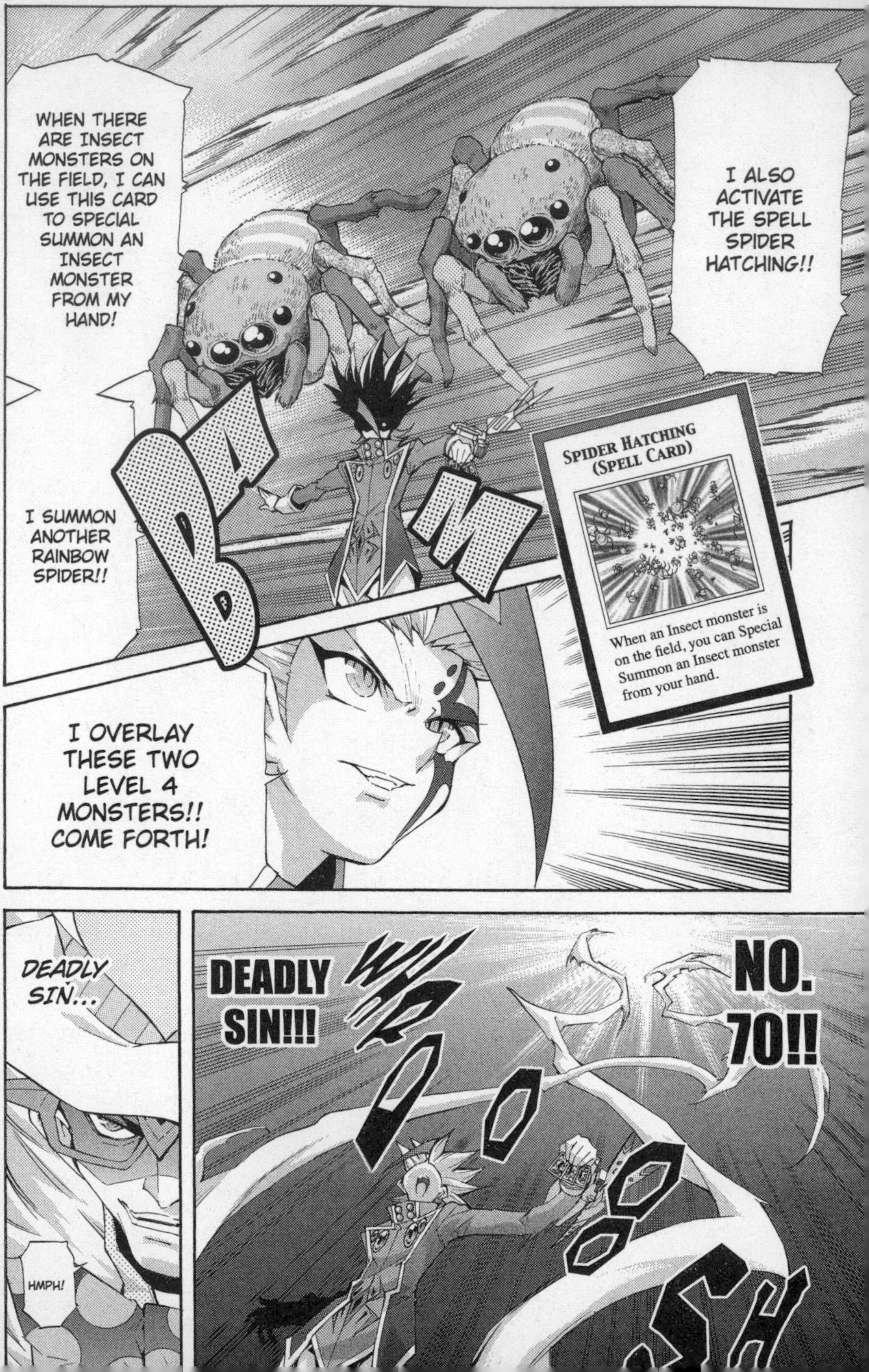

I ALSO ACTIVATE THE SPELL SPIDER HATCHING!!
SPIDER HATCHING (SPELL CARD)
When an Insect monster is on the field, you can Special Summon an Insect monster from your hand.
WHEN THERE ARE INSECT MONSTERS ON THE FIELD, I CAN USE THIS CARD TO SPECIAL SUMMON AN INSECT MONSTER FROM MY HAND!
BAM
I SUMMON ANOTHER RAINBOW SPIDER!!
I OVERLAY THESE TWO LEVEL 4 MONSTERS!! COME FORTH!
NO. 70!!
DEADLY SIN!!!
DEADLY SIN...
HMPH!

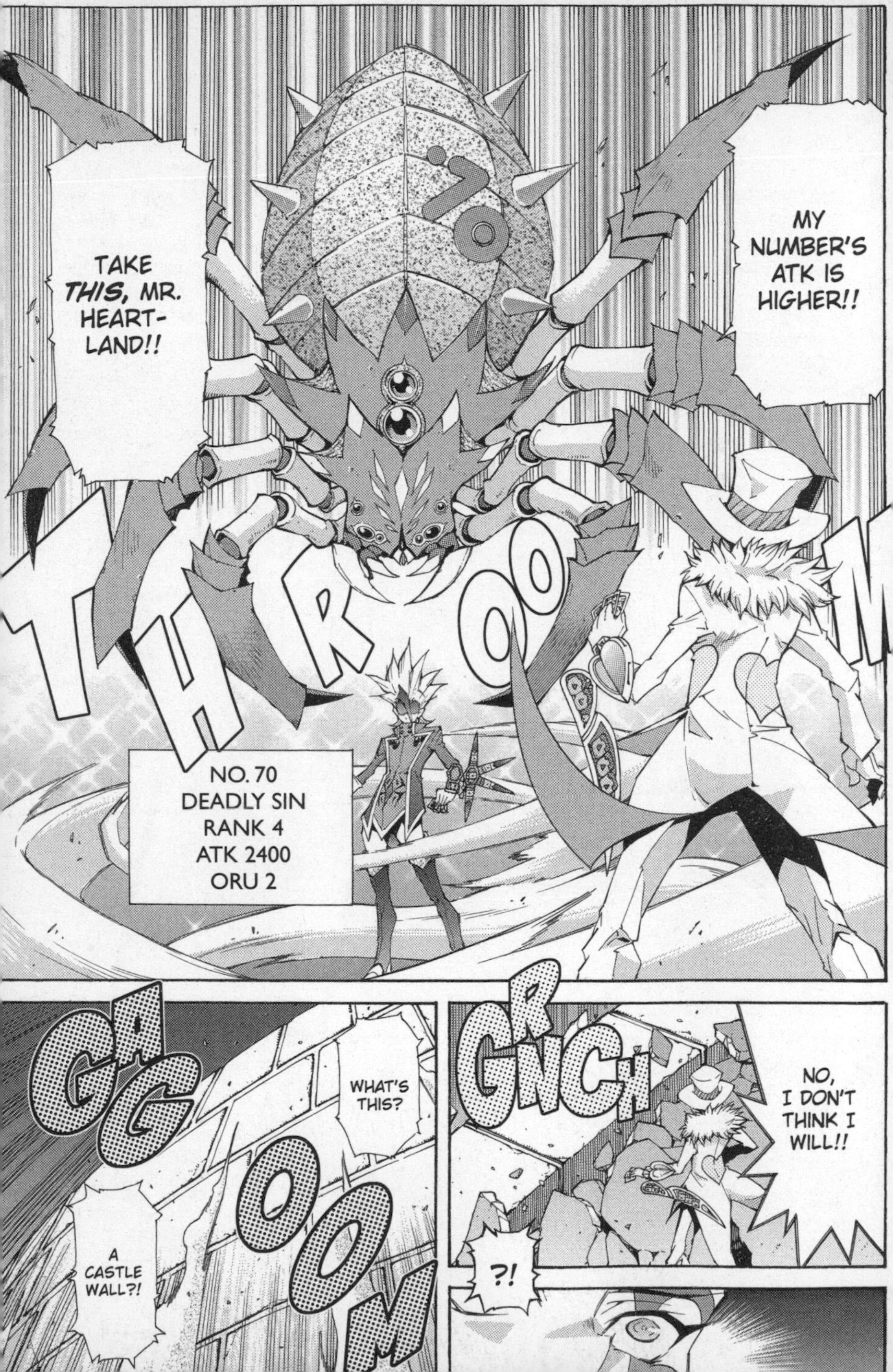
MY NUMBER'S ATK IS HIGHER!!
TAKE *THIS,* MR. HEART-LAND!!
THROOOM
NO. 70 DEADLY SIN RANK 4 ATK 2400 ORU 2
GRNCH
NO, I DON'T THINK I WILL!!
?!
WHAT'S THIS?
A CASTLE WALL?!
GAGOOOM

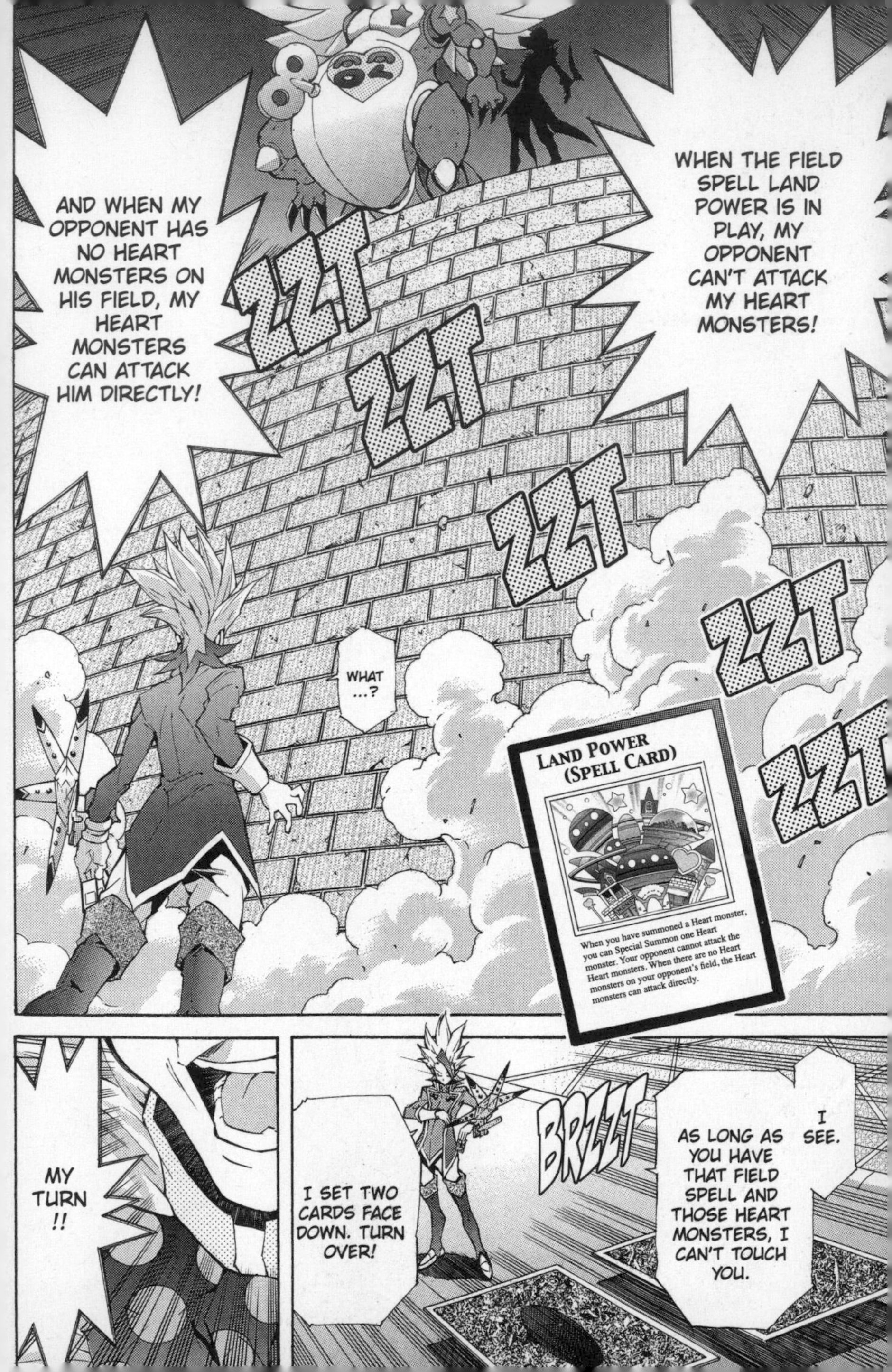
WHEN THE FIELD SPELL LAND POWER IS IN PLAY, MY OPPONENT CAN'T ATTACK MY HEART MONSTERS!
AND WHEN MY OPPONENT HAS NO HEART MONSTERS ON HIS FIELD, MY HEART MONSTERS CAN ATTACK HIM DIRECTLY!
ZZT
ZZT
ZZT
ZZT
ZZT
WHAT ...?
LAND POWER (SPELL CARD)
When you have summoned a Heart monster, you can Special Summon one Heart monster. Your opponent cannot attack the Heart monsters. When there are no Heart monsters on your opponent's field, the Heart monsters can attack directly.
I SEE.
AS LONG AS YOU HAVE THAT FIELD SPELL AND THOSE HEART MONSTERS, I CAN'T TOUCH YOU.
BRZZT
I SET TWO CARDS FACE DOWN. TURN OVER!
MY TURN !!

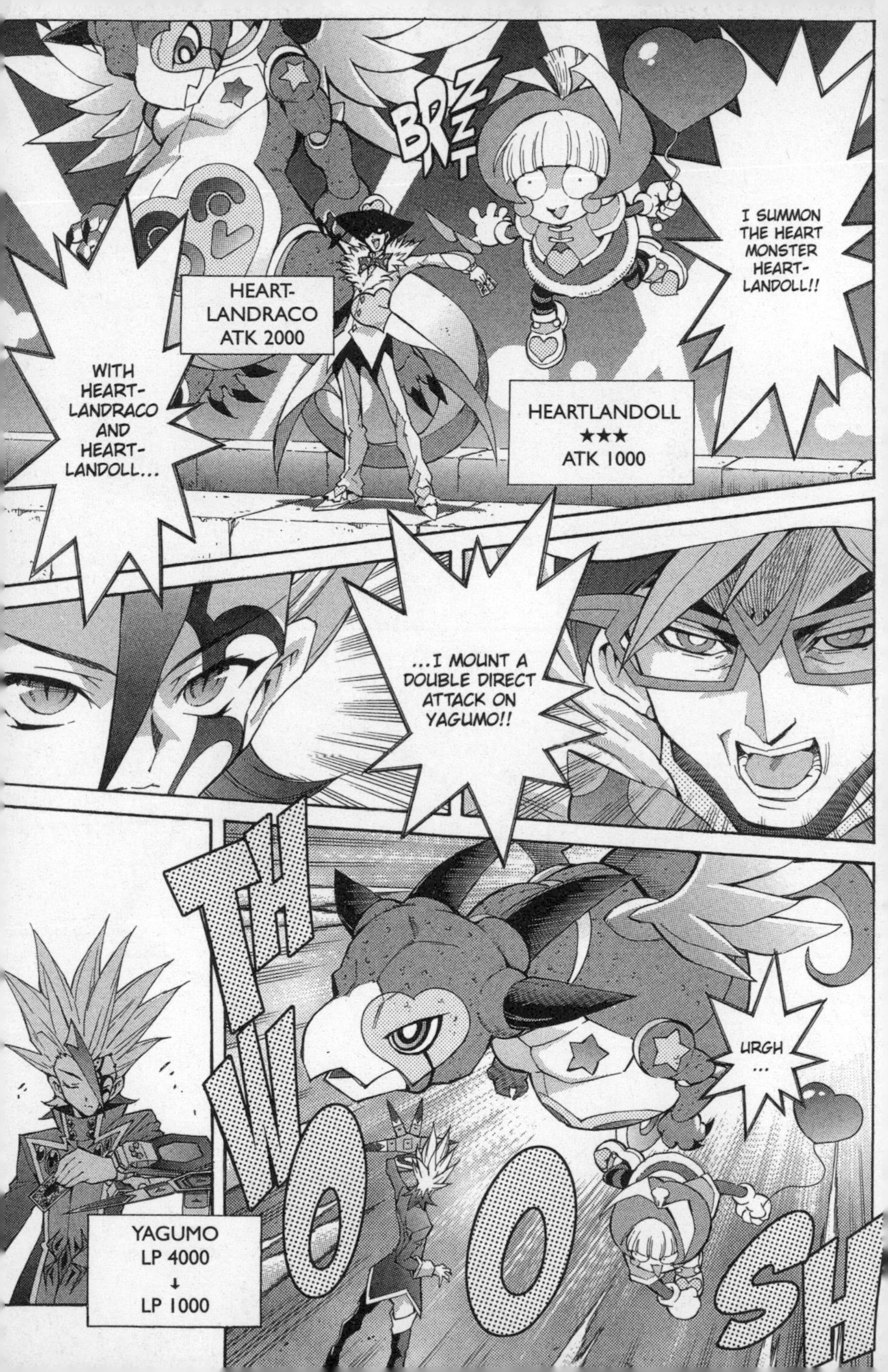
I SUMMON THE HEART MONSTER HEART-LANDOLL!!
HEARTLANDOLL ★★★ ATK 1000
BRZZT
HEART-LANDRACO ATK 2000
WITH HEART-LANDRACO AND HEART-LANDOLL...
...I MOUNT A DOUBLE DIRECT ATTACK ON YAGUMO!!
URGH ...
THWOOOSH
YAGUMO LP 4000 ↓ LP 1000

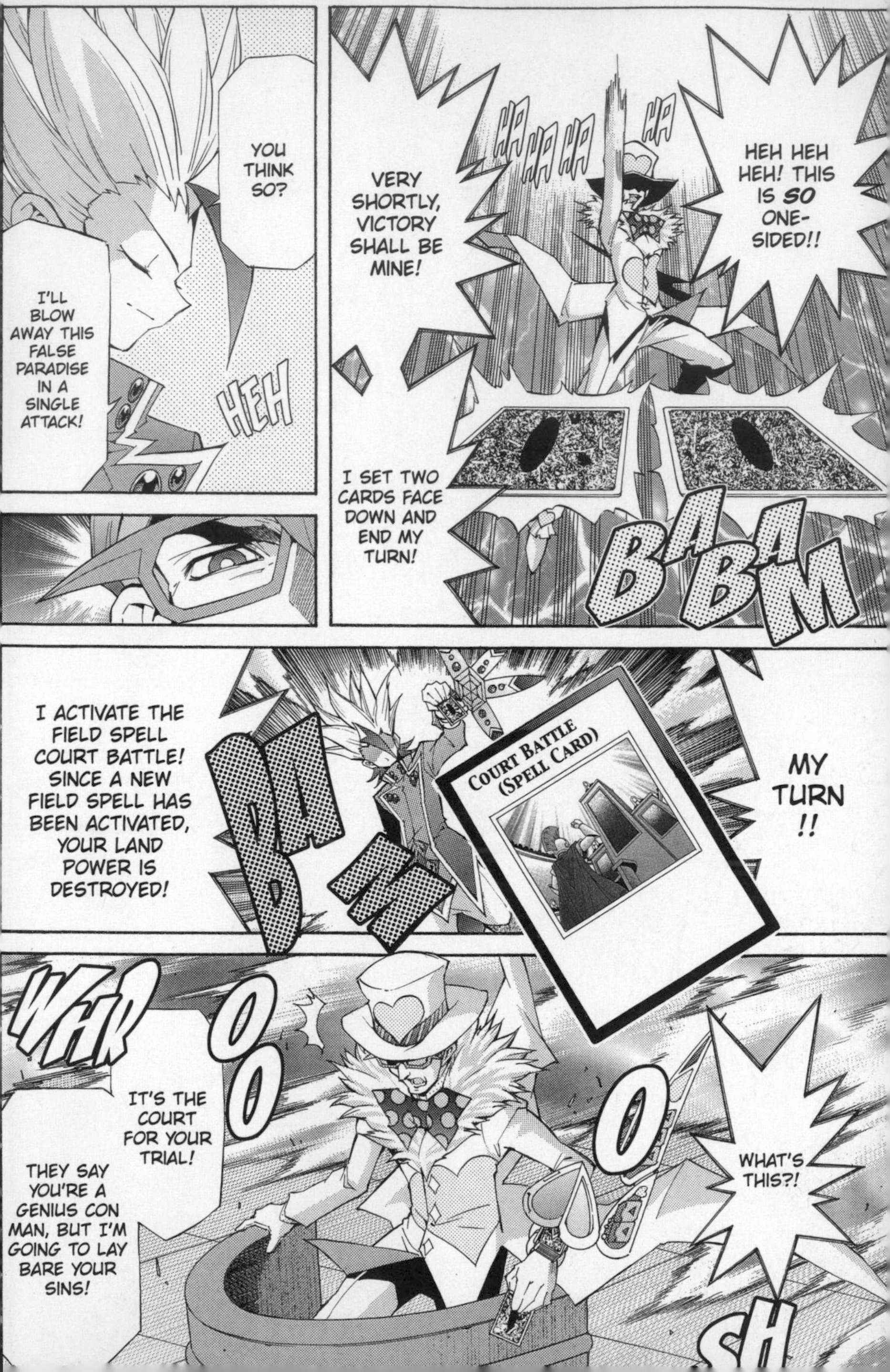
HA HA HA HA HA
HEH HEH HEH! THIS IS *SO* ONE-SIDED!!
VERY SHORTLY, VICTORY SHALL BE MINE!
I SET TWO CARDS FACE DOWN AND END MY TURN!
BABAM
YOU THINK SO?
I'LL BLOW AWAY THIS FALSE PARADISE IN A SINGLE ATTACK!
HEH
MY TURN!!
COURT BATTLE (SPELL CARD)
I ACTIVATE THE FIELD SPELL COURT BATTLE! SINCE A NEW FIELD SPELL HAS BEEN ACTIVATED, YOUR LAND POWER IS DESTROYED!
WHAT'S THIS?!
IT'S THE COURT FOR YOUR TRIAL!
THEY SAY YOU'RE A GENIUS CON MAN, BUT I'M GOING TO LAY BARE YOUR SINS!
SH

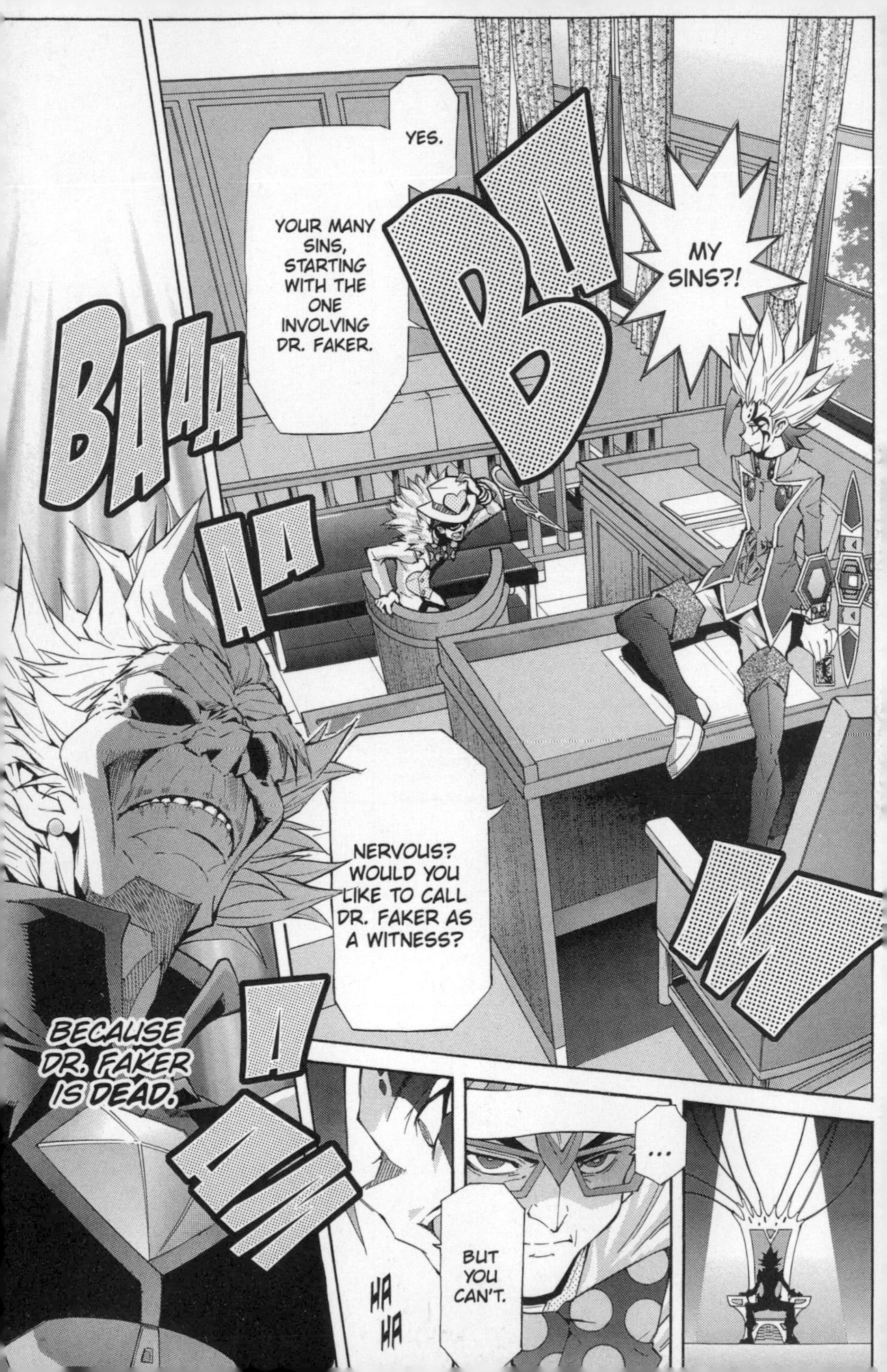

MY SINS?!
YES.
YOUR MANY SINS, STARTING WITH THE ONE INVOLVING DR. FAKER.
BAM
NERVOUS? WOULD YOU LIKE TO CALL DR. FAKER AS A WITNESS?
...
BUT YOU CAN'T.
HA HA
BECAUSE DR. FAKER IS DEAD.
BAAAAAAAA

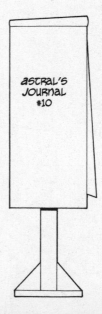

astral's Journal #10

I GOT A 3DS!!
TADAH
HEH HEH HEH
YU-GI-OH! ZEXAL CLASH! DUEL CARNIVAL!
NOW I CAN DUEL AS MUCH AS I WANT!
HE CHOSE AKARI AS HIS FIRST OPPONENT.
HE WONDERED IF SHE WOULD RESCIND THE BAN ON DUELING IF YUMA WON, BUT...
MAN... SHE'S REALLY TOUGH...
YUMA'S VOICE
WOW, SIS... YOU'RE GOOD...
HE LOST EVERY DUEL!!
TRMBL TRMBL

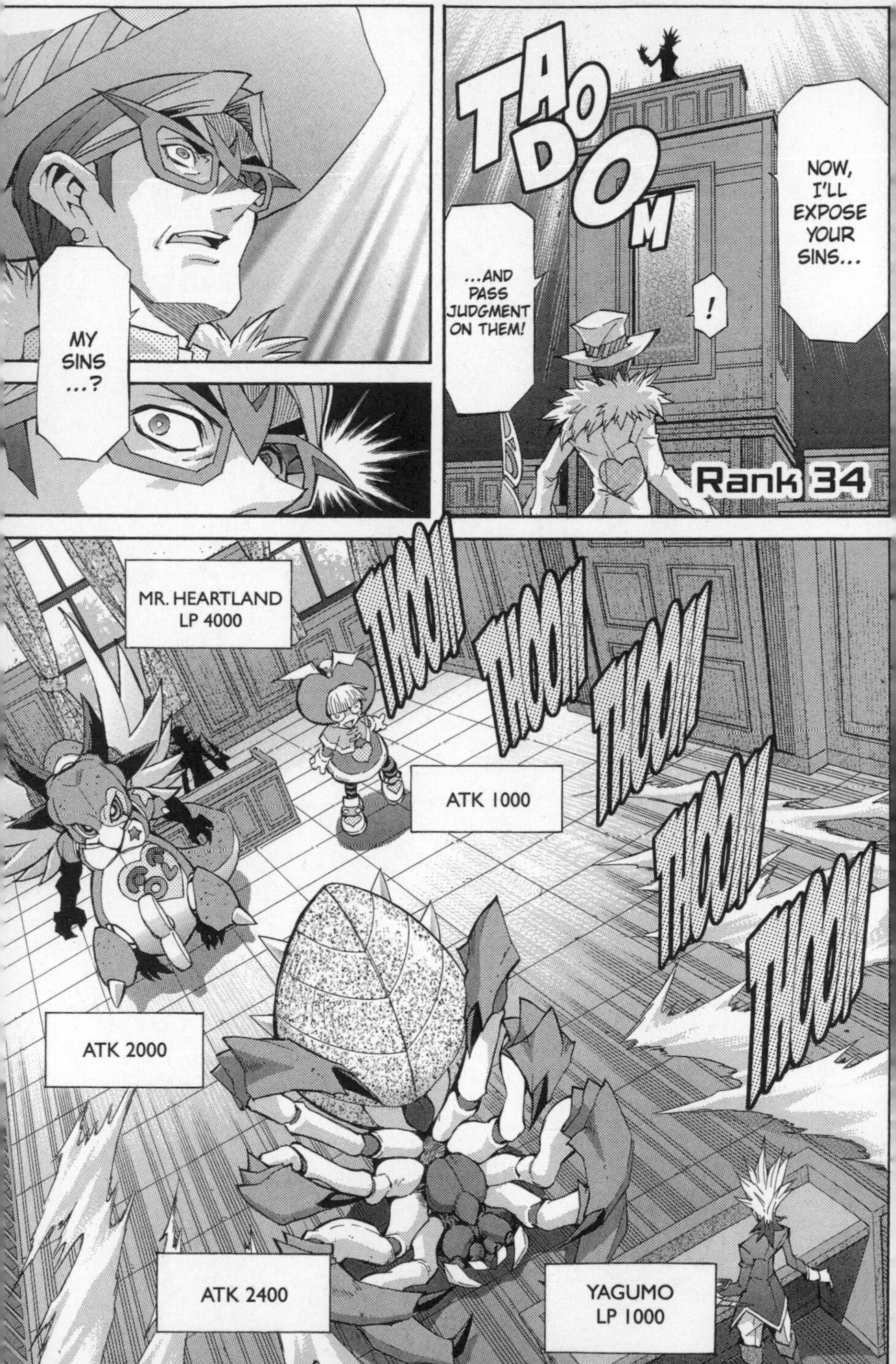
TADOOM
NOW, I'LL EXPOSE YOUR SINS...
!
...AND PASS JUDGMENT ON THEM!
Rank 34
MY SINS ...?
THOOM THOOM THOOM THOOM THOOM THOOM
MR. HEARTLAND LP 4000
ATK 1000
ATK 2000
YAGUMO LP 1000
ATK 2400

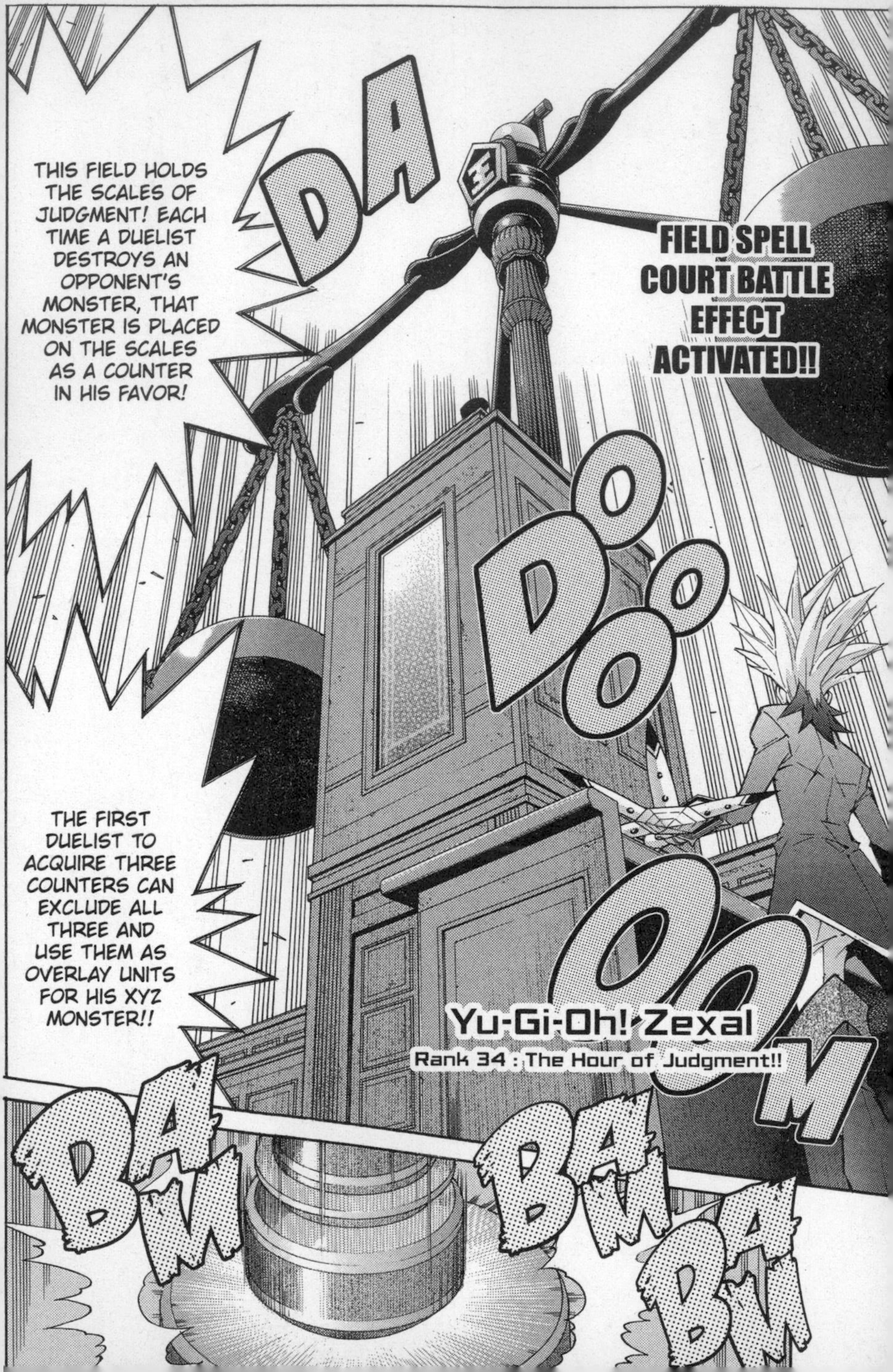
FIELD SPELL COURT BATTLE EFFECT ACTIVATED!!
DA
THIS FIELD HOLDS THE SCALES OF JUDGMENT! EACH TIME A DUELIST DESTROYS AN OPPONENT'S MONSTER, THAT MONSTER IS PLACED ON THE SCALES AS A COUNTER IN HIS FAVOR!
DOOOOOM
THE FIRST DUELIST TO ACQUIRE THREE COUNTERS CAN EXCLUDE ALL THREE AND USE THEM AS OVERLAY UNITS FOR HIS XYZ MONSTER!!
Yu-Gi-Oh! Zexal
Rank 34 : The Hour of Judgment!!
BAM
BAM
BAM

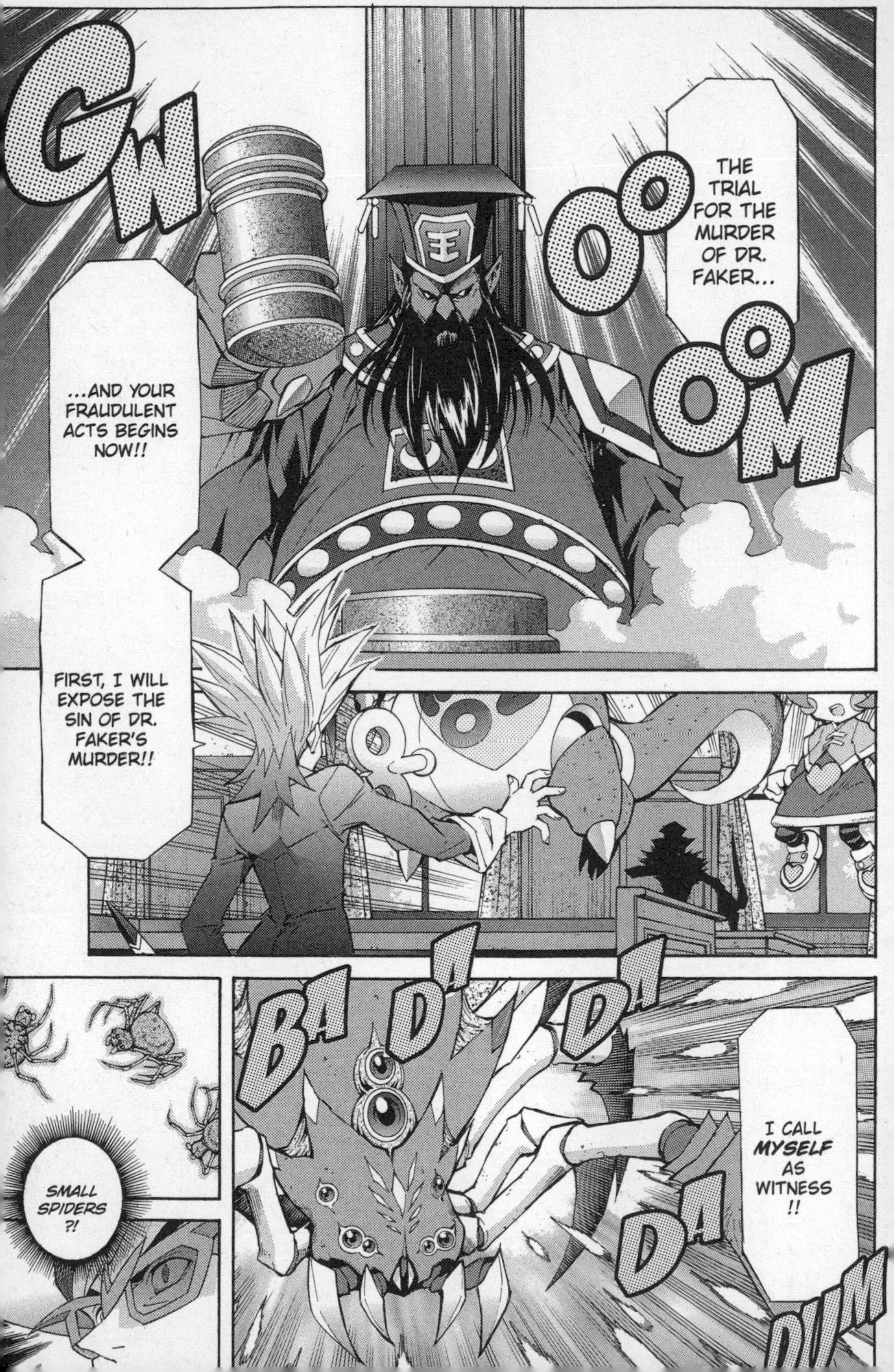
GWOOOOOM
THE TRIAL FOR THE MURDER OF DR. FAKER...
...AND YOUR FRAUDULENT ACTS BEGINS NOW!!
FIRST, I WILL EXPOSE THE SIN OF DR. FAKER'S MURDER!!
BA DA DA DA
I CALL ***MYSELF*** AS WITNESS!!
DUM
SMALL SPIDERS?!

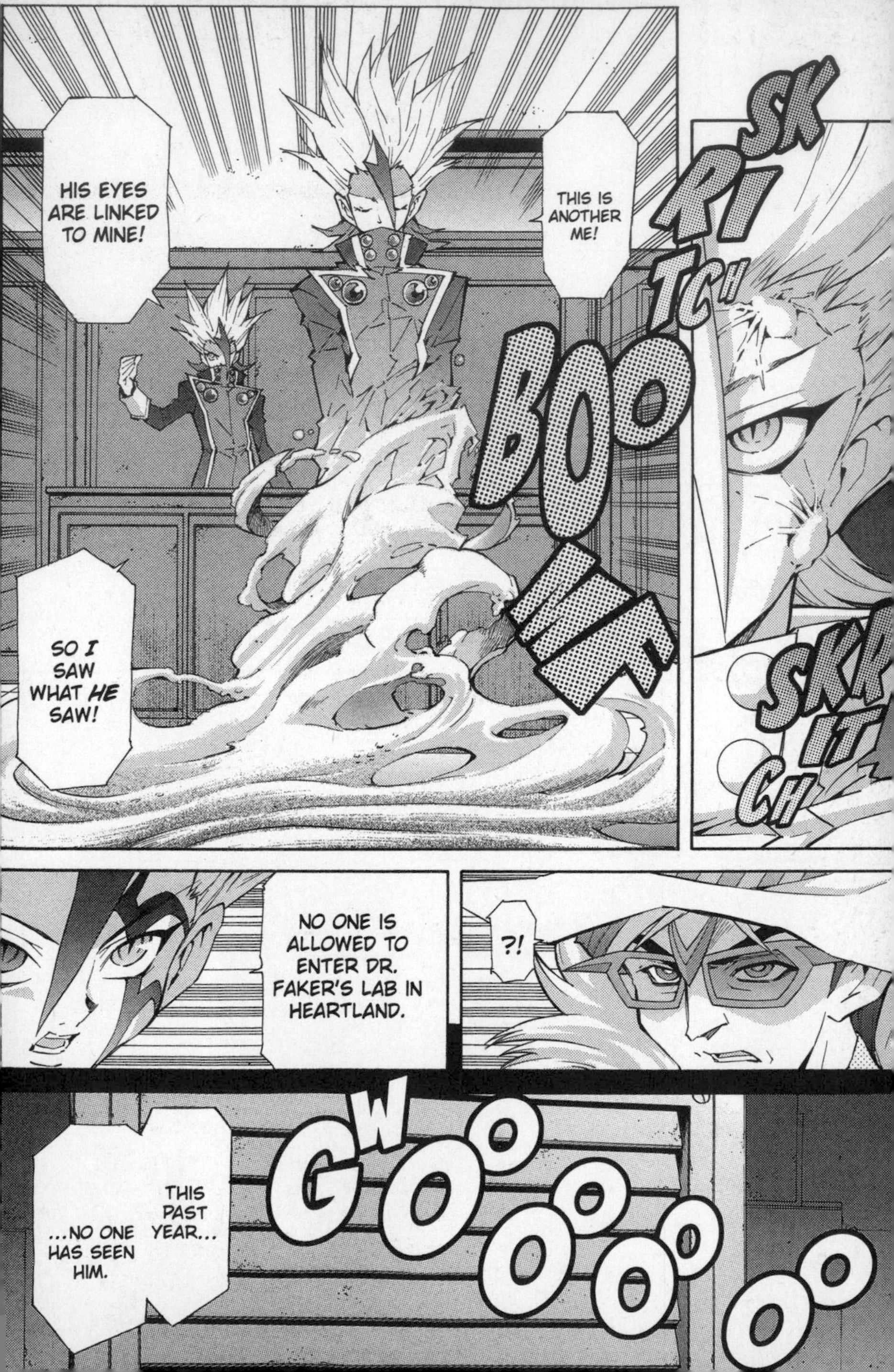
SK
RI
TCH
SKK
IT
CH
THIS IS ANOTHER ME!
HIS EYES ARE LINKED TO MINE!
BOOO
SO I SAW WHAT HE SAW!
?!
NO ONE IS ALLOWED TO ENTER DR. FAKER'S LAB IN HEARTLAND.
GWOOOOOOOOO
THIS PAST YEAR...
...NO ONE HAS SEEN HIM.

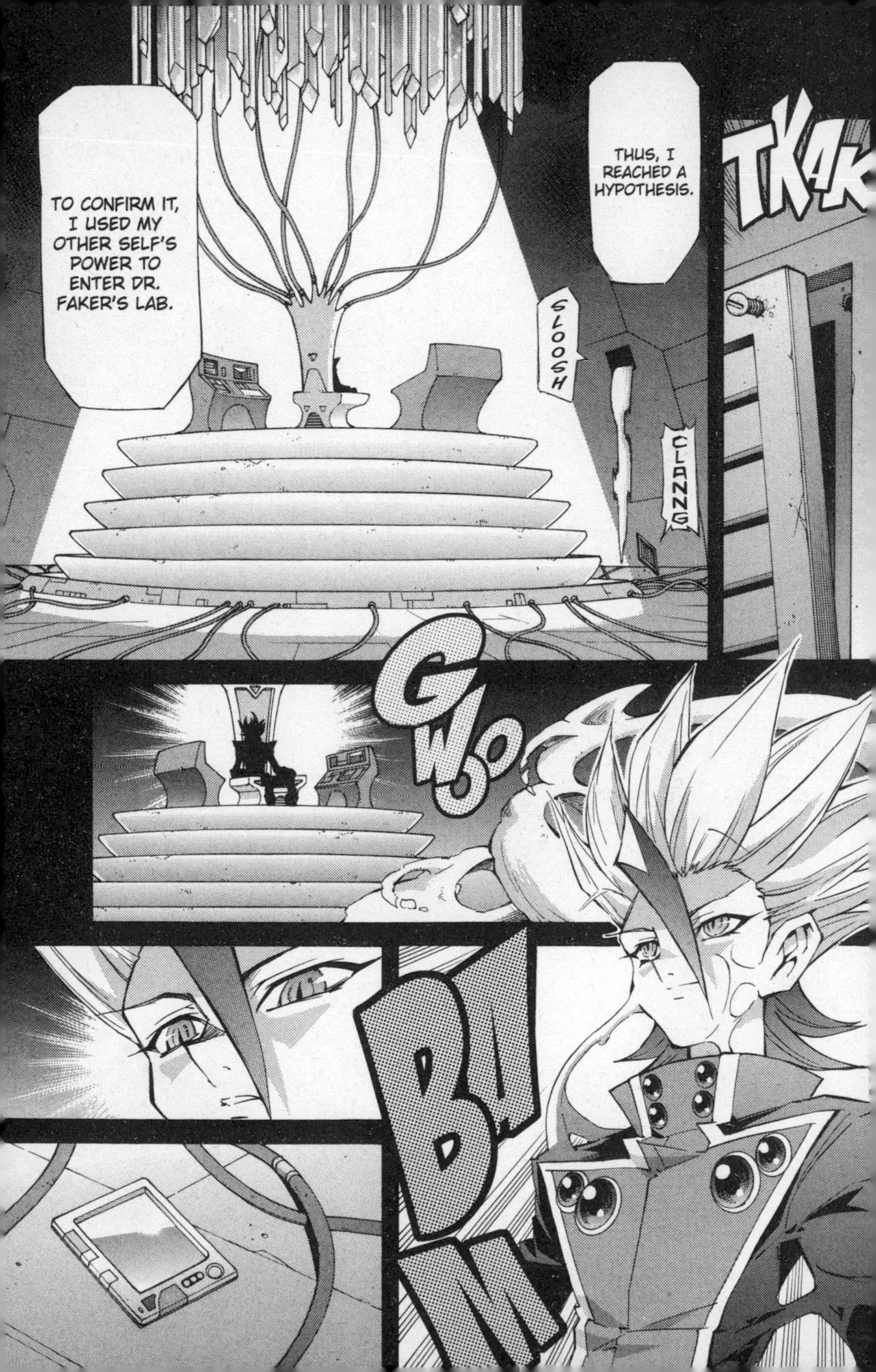
TKAK
THUS, I REACHED A HYPOTHESIS.
TO CONFIRM IT, I USED MY OTHER SELF'S POWER TO ENTER DR. FAKER'S LAB.
CLANNG
SLOOSH
GWOO
BAM

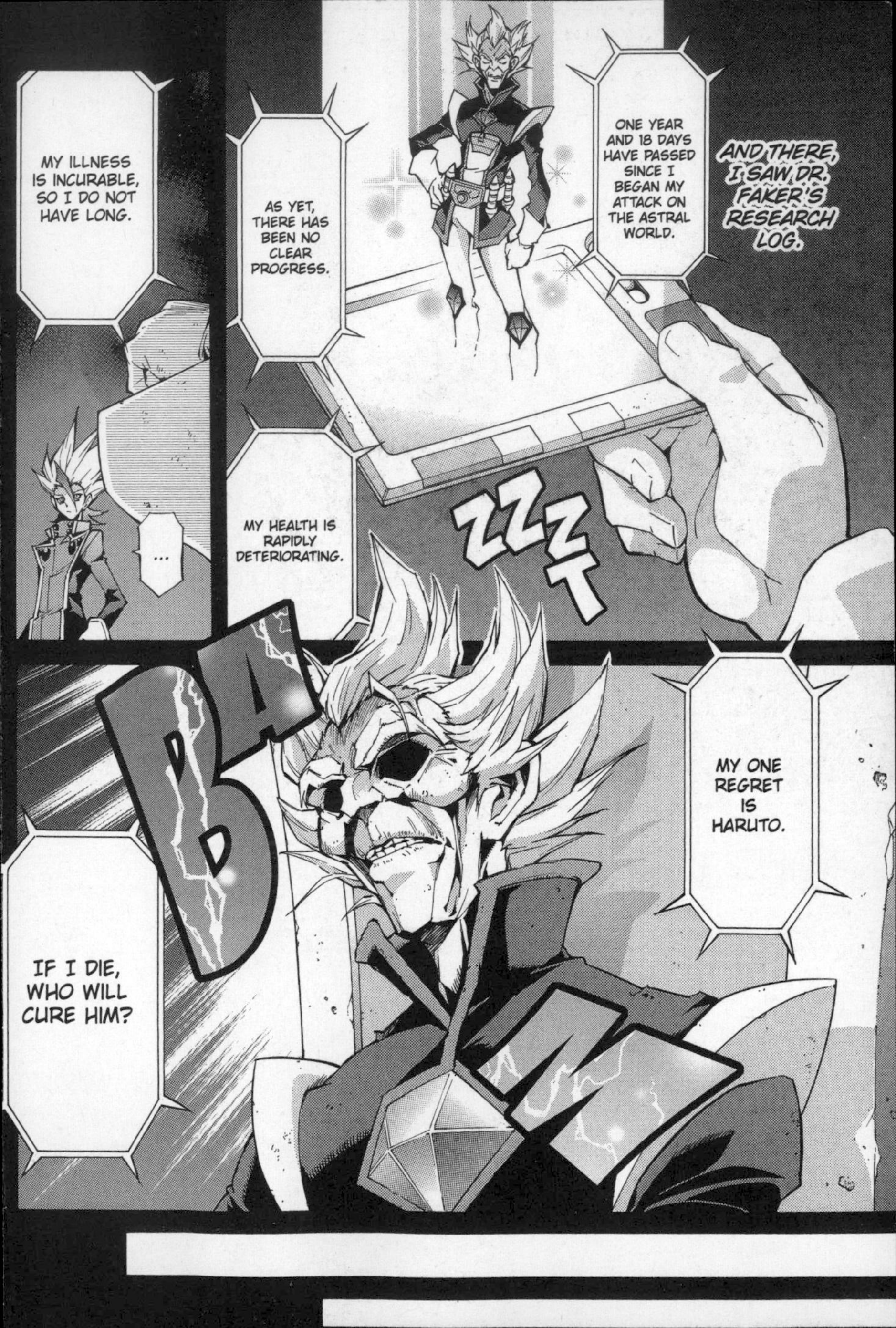
AND THERE, I SAW DR. FAKER'S RESEARCH LOG.
ONE YEAR AND 18 DAYS HAVE PASSED SINCE I BEGAN MY ATTACK ON THE ASTRAL WORLD.
AS YET, THERE HAS BEEN NO CLEAR PROGRESS.
MY HEALTH IS RAPIDLY DETERIORATING.
ZZZT
MY ILLNESS IS INCURABLE, SO I DO NOT HAVE LONG.
...
MY ONE REGRET IS HARUTO.
BAM
IF I DIE, WHO WILL CURE HIM?

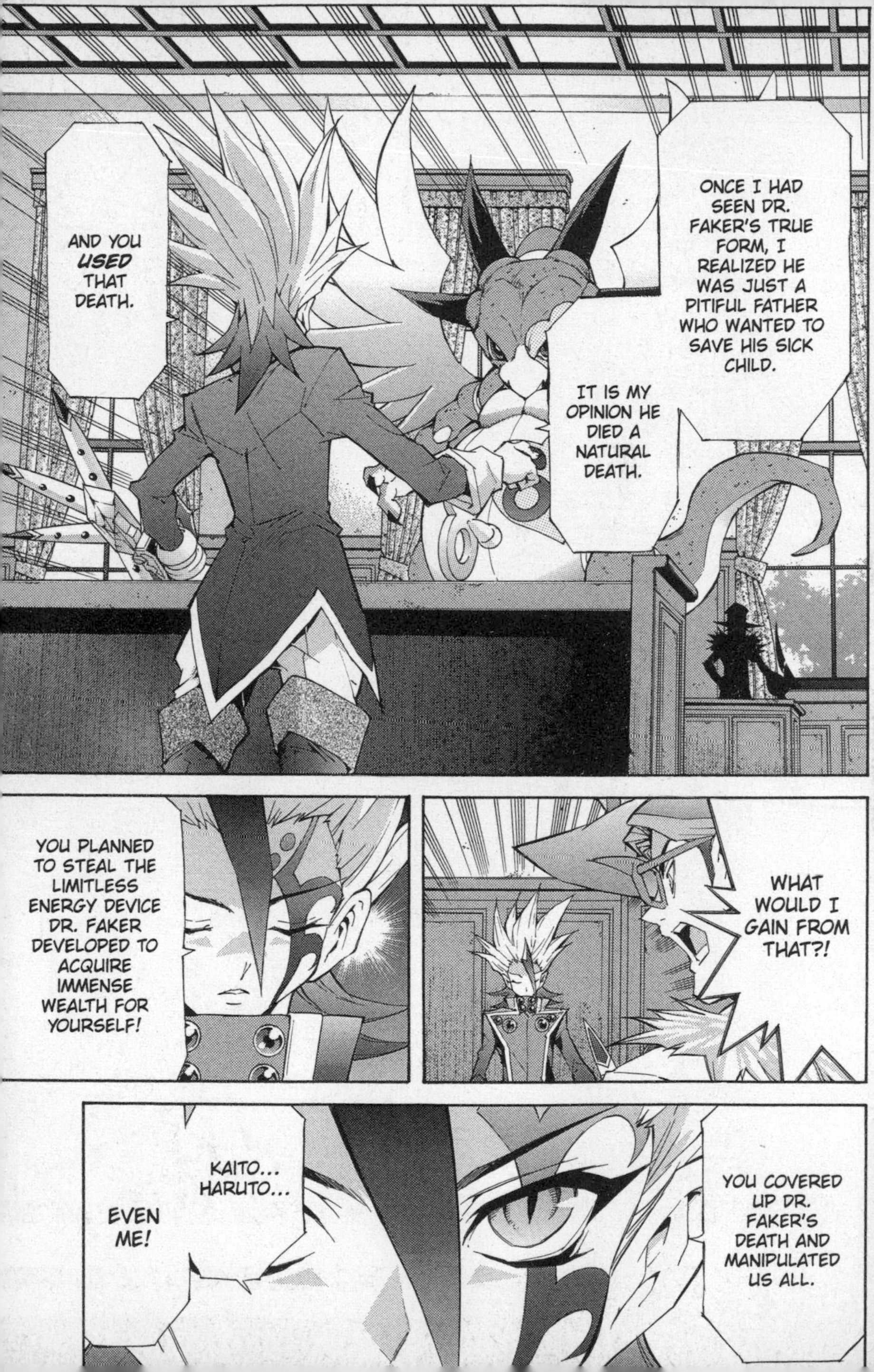
ONCE I HAD SEEN DR. FAKER'S TRUE FORM, I REALIZED HE WAS JUST A PITIFUL FATHER WHO WANTED TO SAVE HIS SICK CHILD.
IT IS MY OPINION HE DIED A NATURAL DEATH.
AND YOU *USED* THAT DEATH.
WHAT WOULD I GAIN FROM THAT?!
YOU PLANNED TO STEAL THE LIMITLESS ENERGY DEVICE DR. FAKER DEVELOPED TO ACQUIRE IMMENSE WEALTH FOR YOURSELF!
YOU COVERED UP DR. FAKER'S DEATH AND MANIPULATED US ALL.
KAITO... HARUTO...
EVEN ME!

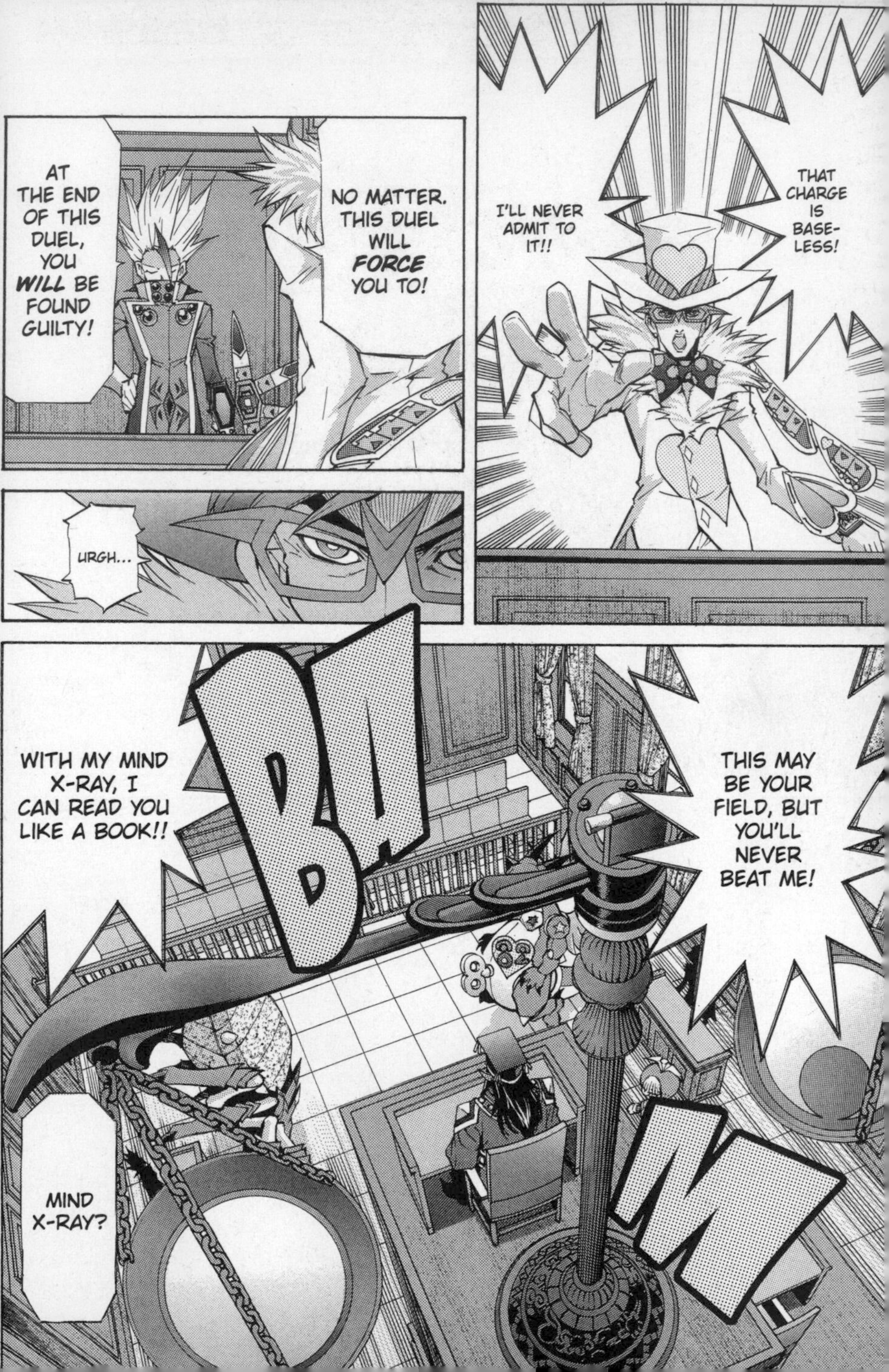
THAT CHARGE IS BASELESS!
I'LL NEVER ADMIT TO IT!!
NO MATTER. THIS DUEL WILL *FORCE* YOU TO!
AT THE END OF THIS DUEL, YOU *WILL* BE FOUND GUILTY!
URGH...
THIS MAY BE YOUR FIELD, BUT YOU'LL NEVER BEAT ME!
BA
M
WITH MY MIND X-RAY, I CAN READ YOU LIKE A BOOK!!
MIND X-RAY?

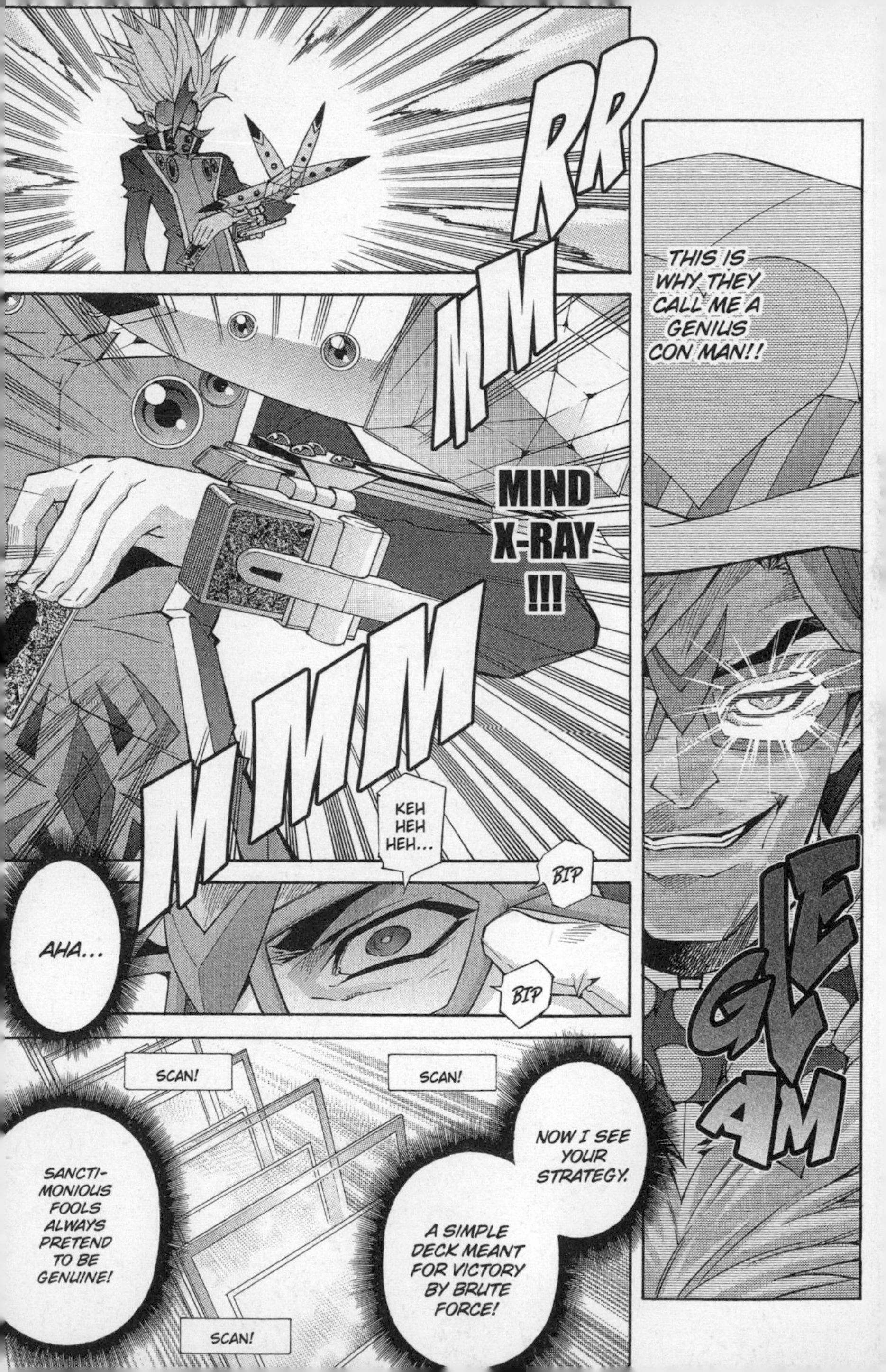
THIS IS WHY THEY CALL ME A GENIUS CON MAN!!
GLEAM
RR
MM
MIND X-RAY!!!
MMMM
KEH HEH HEH...
BIP
BIP
AHA...
SCAN!
SCAN!
NOW I SEE YOUR STRATEGY.
A SIMPLE DECK MEANT FOR VICTORY BY BRUTE FORCE!
SANCTI-MONIOUS FOOLS ALWAYS PRETEND TO BE GENUINE!
SCAN!

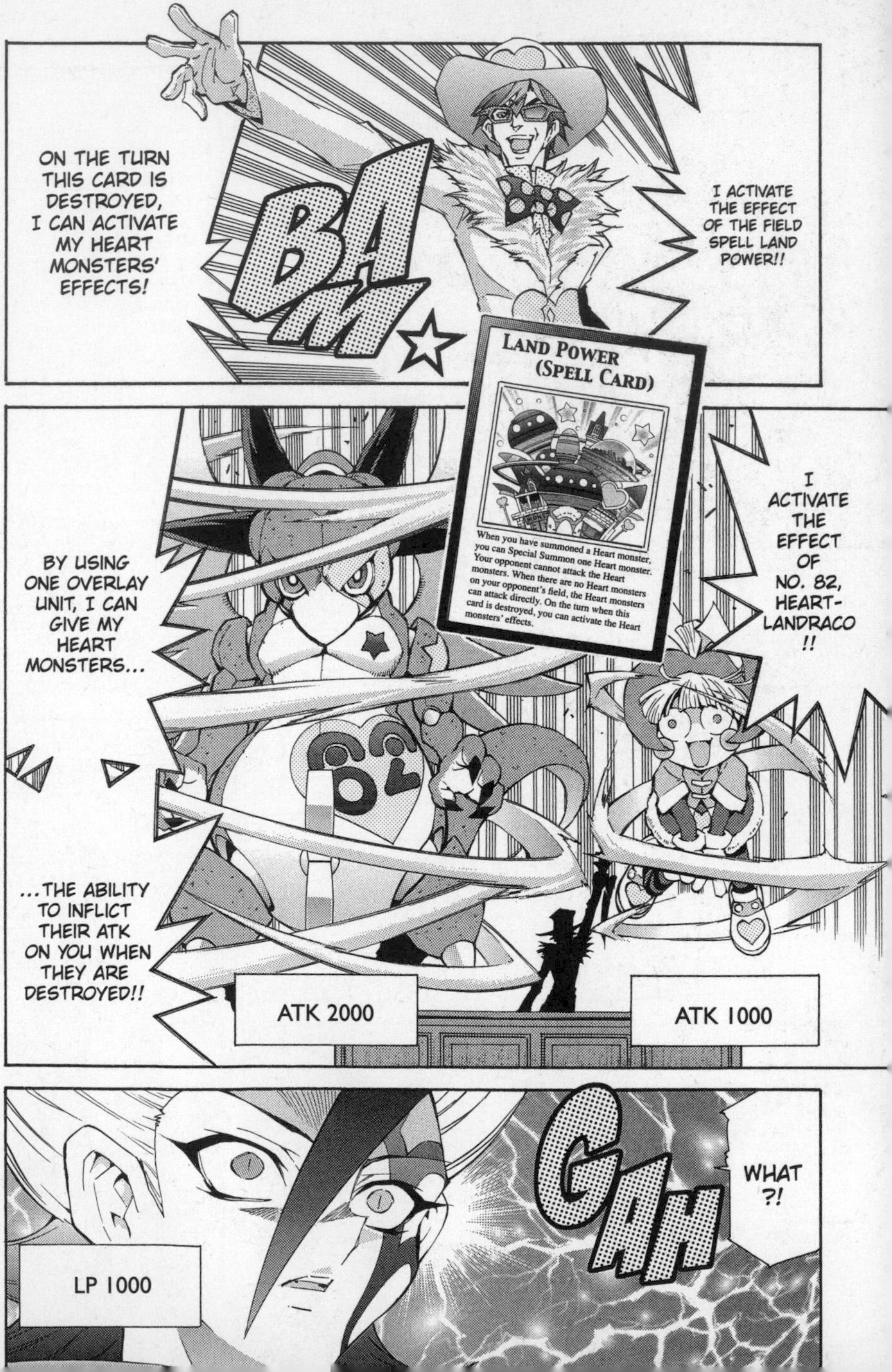
I ACTIVATE THE EFFECT OF THE FIELD SPELL LAND POWER!!
BAM
ON THE TURN THIS CARD IS DESTROYED, I CAN ACTIVATE MY HEART MONSTERS' EFFECTS!
LAND POWER (SPELL CARD)
When you have summoned a Heart monster, you can Special Summon one Heart monster. Your opponent cannot attack the Heart monsters. When there are no Heart monsters on your opponent's field, the Heart monsters can attack directly. On the turn when this card is destroyed, you can activate the Heart monsters' effects.
I ACTIVATE THE EFFECT OF NO. 82, HEART-LANDRACO!!
BY USING ONE OVERLAY UNIT, I CAN GIVE MY HEART MONSTERS...
...THE ABILITY TO INFLICT THEIR ATK ON YOU WHEN THEY ARE DESTROYED!!
ATK 1000
ATK 2000
WHAT?!
GAH
LP 1000

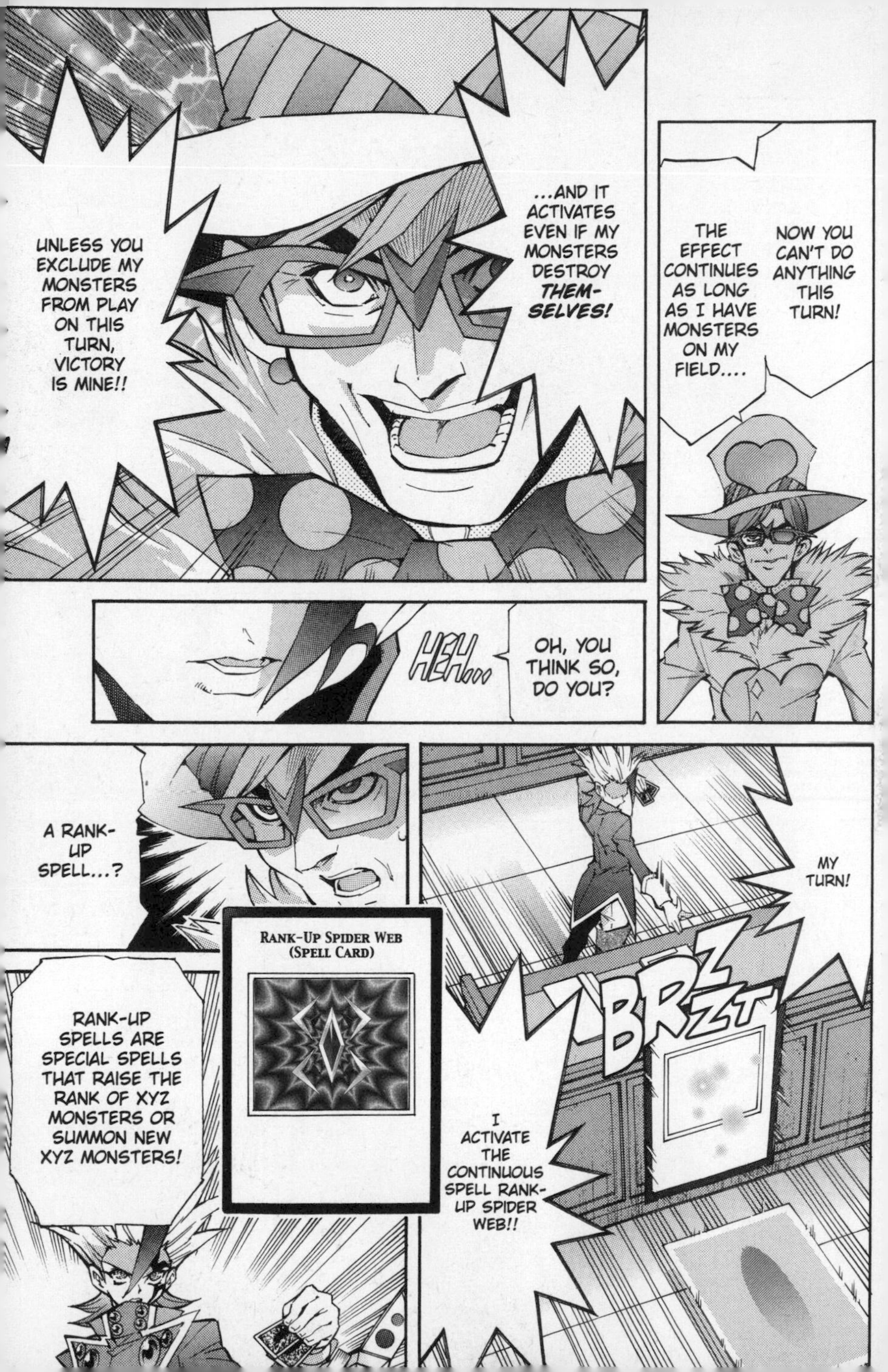
NOW YOU CAN'T DO ANYTHING THIS TURN!
THE EFFECT CONTINUES AS LONG AS I HAVE MONSTERS ON MY FIELD....
...AND IT ACTIVATES EVEN IF MY MONSTERS DESTROY THEMSELVES!
UNLESS YOU EXCLUDE MY MONSTERS FROM PLAY ON THIS TURN, VICTORY IS MINE!!
OH, YOU THINK SO, DO YOU?
HEH...
MY TURN!
BRZZT
I ACTIVATE THE CONTINUOUS SPELL RANK-UP SPIDER WEB!!
A RANK-UP SPELL...?
RANK-UP SPIDER WEB (SPELL CARD)
RANK-UP SPELLS ARE SPECIAL SPELLS THAT RAISE THE RANK OF XYZ MONSTERS OR SUMMON NEW XYZ MONSTERS!

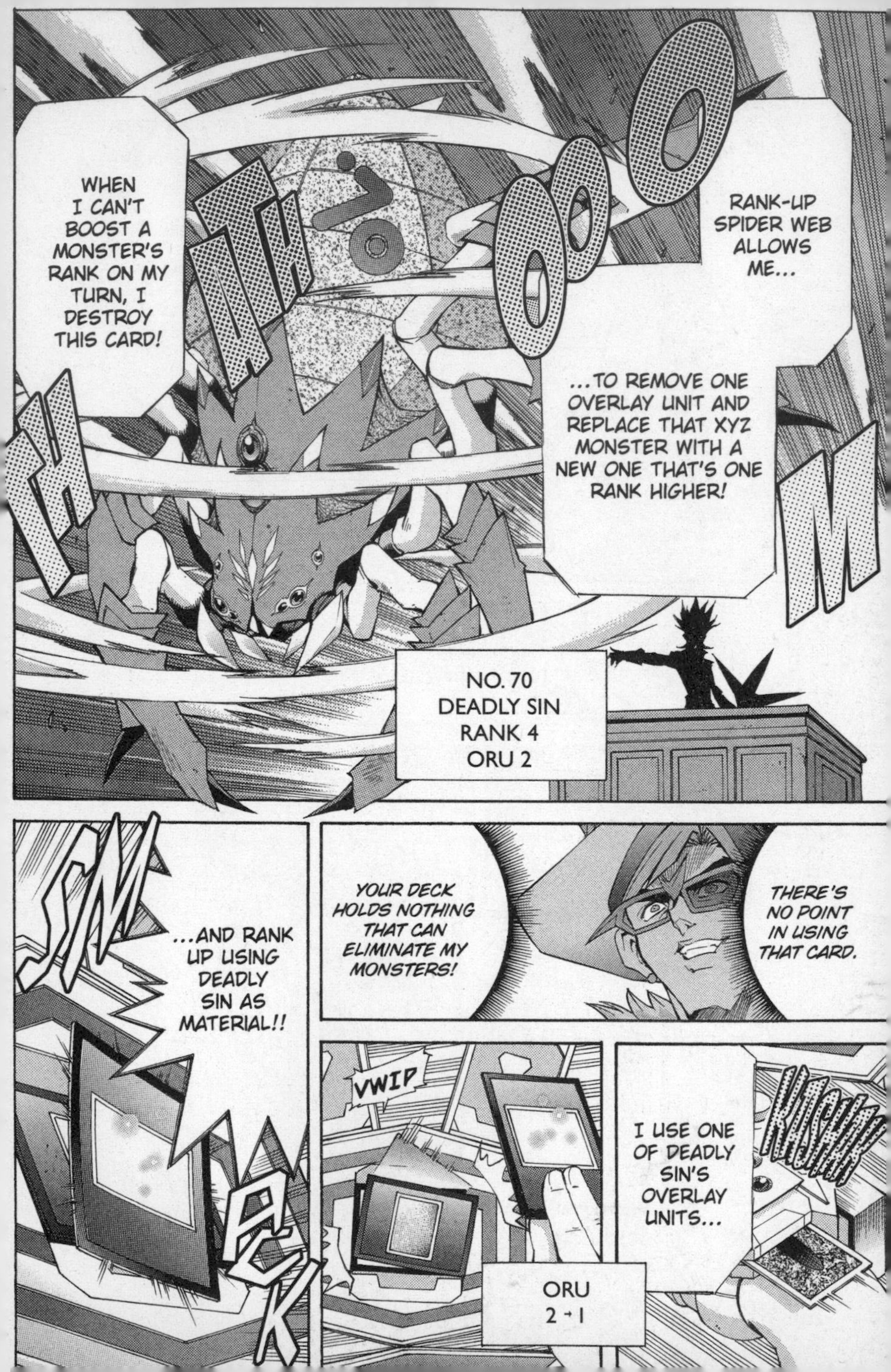

RANK-UP SPIDER WEB ALLOWS ME...
...TO REMOVE ONE OVERLAY UNIT AND REPLACE THAT XYZ MONSTER WITH A NEW ONE THAT'S ONE RANK HIGHER!
WHEN I CAN'T BOOST A MONSTER'S RANK ON MY TURN, I DESTROY THIS CARD!
NO. 70 DEADLY SIN RANK 4 ORU 2
THERE'S NO POINT IN USING THAT CARD.
YOUR DECK HOLDS NOTHING THAT CAN ELIMINATE MY MONSTERS!
I USE ONE OF DEADLY SIN'S OVERLAY UNITS...
ORU 2→1
VWIP
...AND RANK UP USING DEADLY SIN AS MATERIAL!!

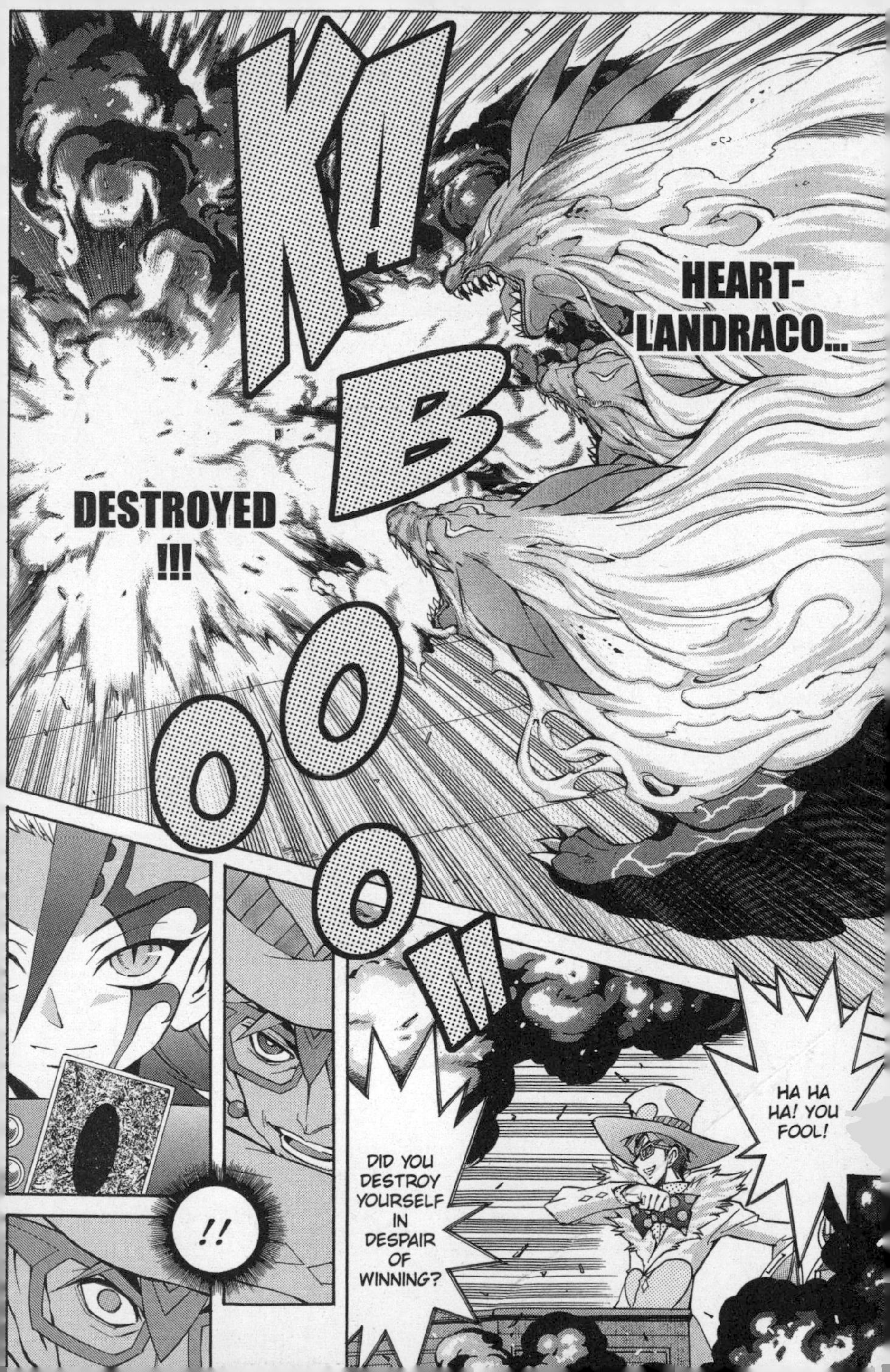
HEART-LANDRACO...
KA
BOOOOM
DESTROYED!!!
HA HA HA! YOU FOOL!
DID YOU DESTROY YOURSELF IN DESPAIR OF WINNING?
!!

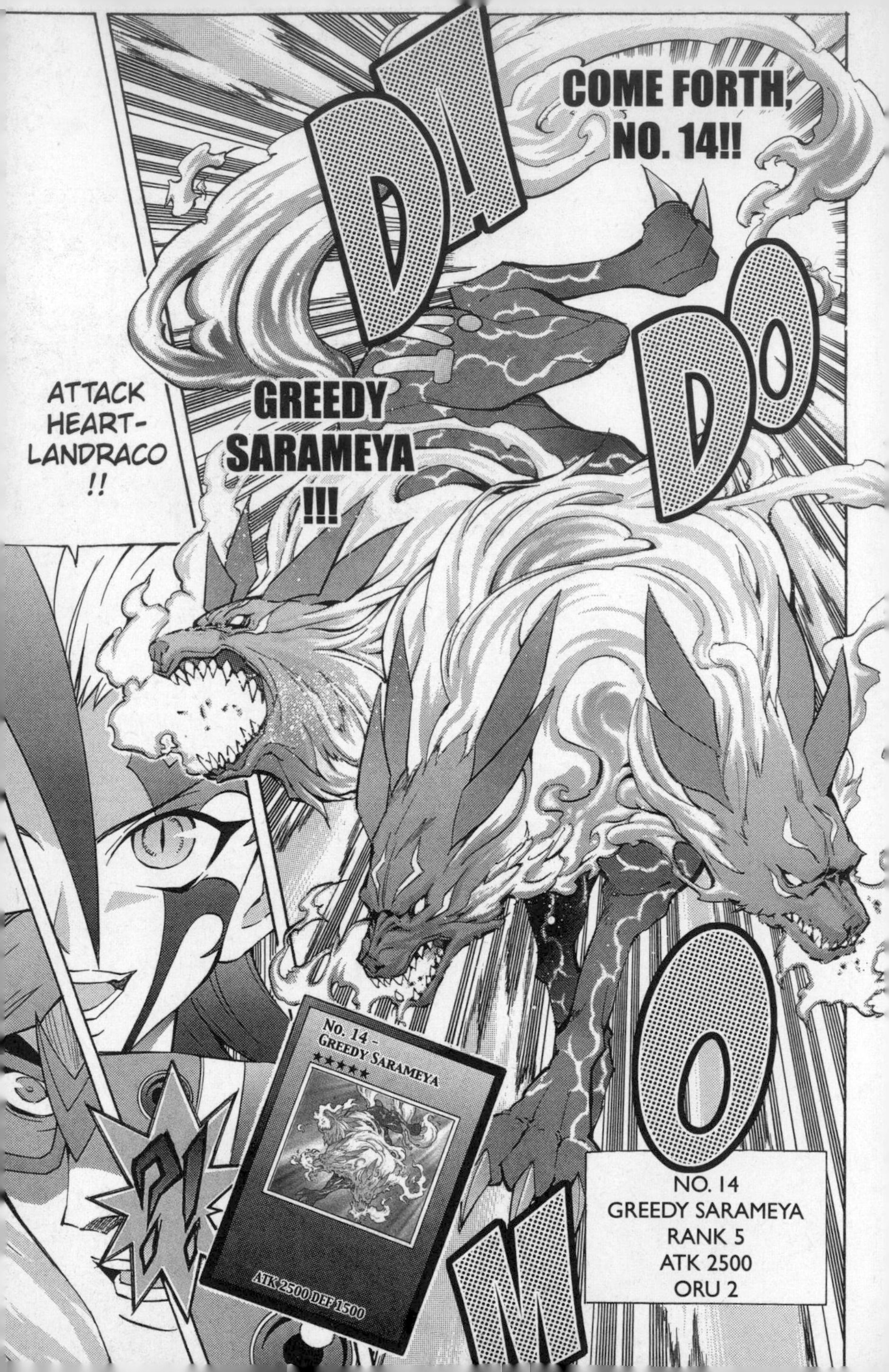
COME FORTH, NO. 14!!
DA
GREEDY SARAMEYA!!!
DODO
ATTACK HEART-LANDRACO!!
OOM
NO. 14
GREEDY SARAMEYA
RANK 5
ATK 2500
ORU 2
No. 14 - Greedy Sarameya
ATK 2500 DEF 1500
?!

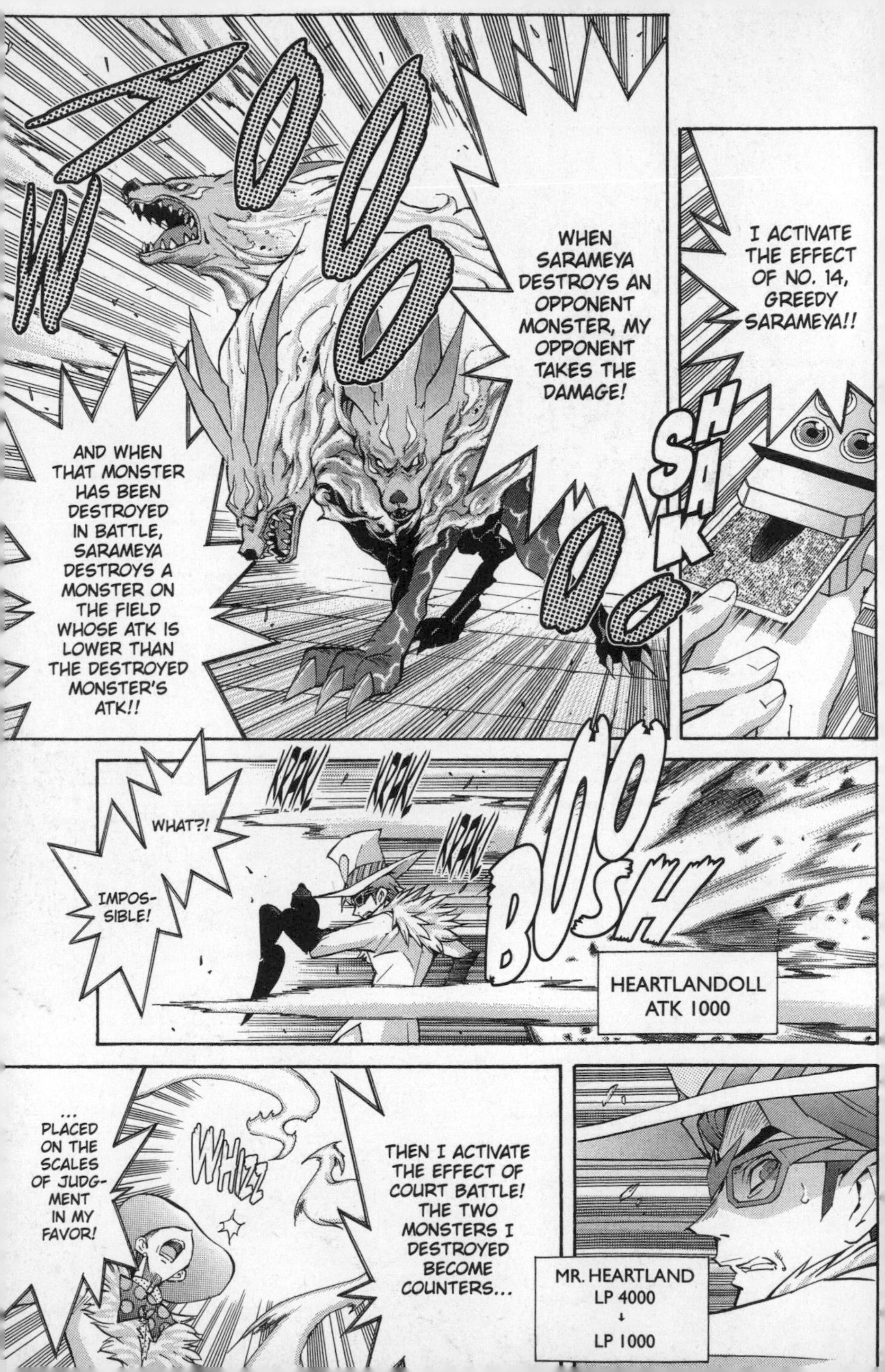
I ACTIVATE THE EFFECT OF NO. 14, GREEDY SARAMEYA!!
SHAKOOO
WOOOOO
WHEN SARAMEYA DESTROYS AN OPPONENT MONSTER, MY OPPONENT TAKES THE DAMAGE!
AND WHEN THAT MONSTER HAS BEEN DESTROYED IN BATTLE, SARAMEYA DESTROYS A MONSTER ON THE FIELD WHOSE ATK IS LOWER THAN THE DESTROYED MONSTER'S ATK!!
BOOSH
HEARTLANDOLL ATK 1000
WHAT?!
IMPOS-SIBLE!
MR. HEARTLAND LP 4000 ↓ LP 1000
THEN I ACTIVATE THE EFFECT OF COURT BATTLE! THE TWO MONSTERS I DESTROYED BECOME COUNTERS...
WHIZZ
... PLACED ON THE SCALES OF JUDG-MENT IN MY FAVOR!

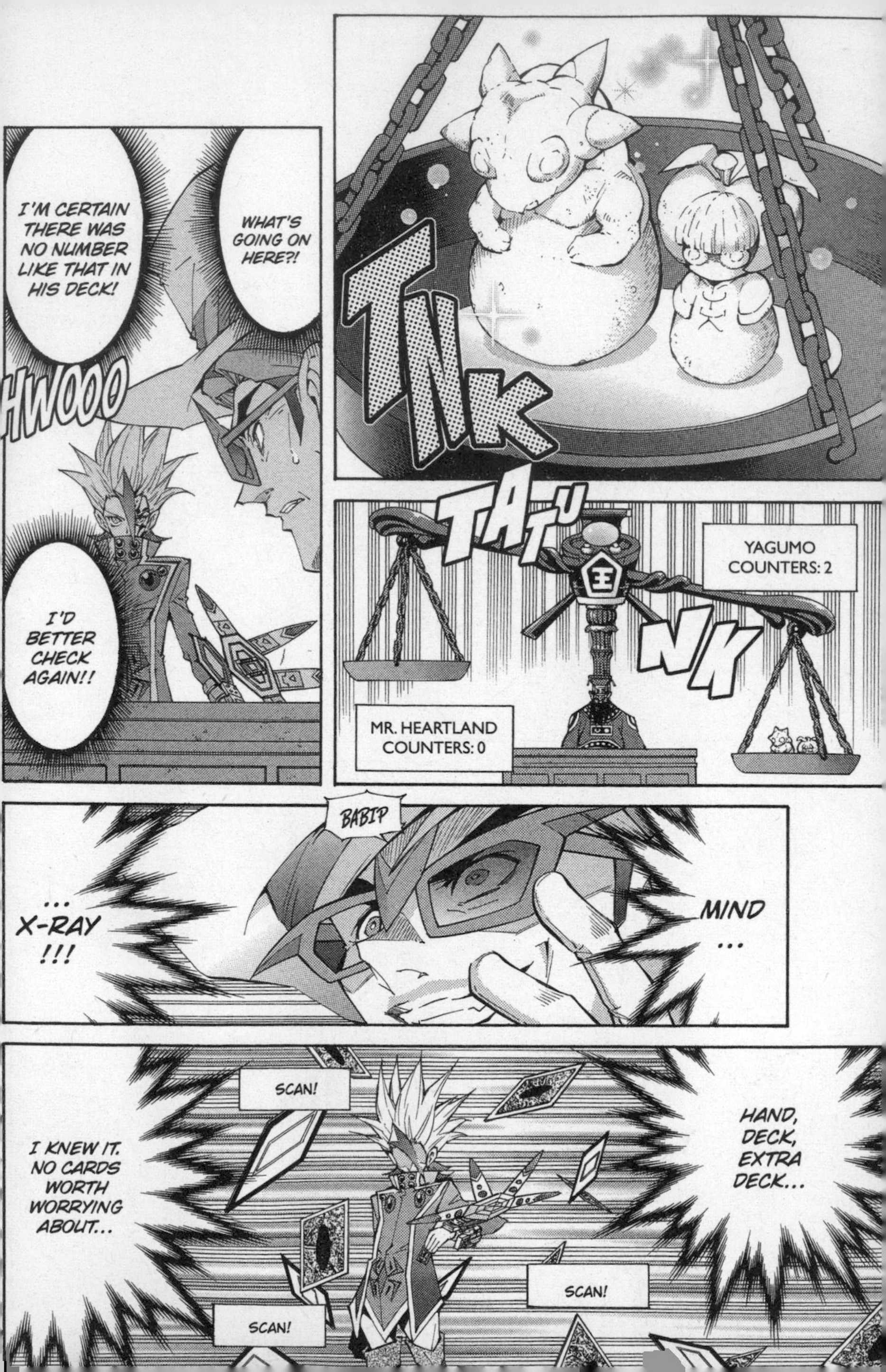
TINK
TATUNK
YAGUMO COUNTERS: 2
MR. HEARTLAND COUNTERS: 0
WHAT'S GOING ON HERE?!
I'M CERTAIN THERE WAS NO NUMBER LIKE THAT IN HIS DECK!
HWOOO
I'D BETTER CHECK AGAIN!!
BABIP
MIND...
...X-RAY!!!
SCAN!
HAND, DECK, EXTRA DECK...
I KNEW IT. NO CARDS WORTH WORRYING ABOUT...
SCAN!
SCAN!

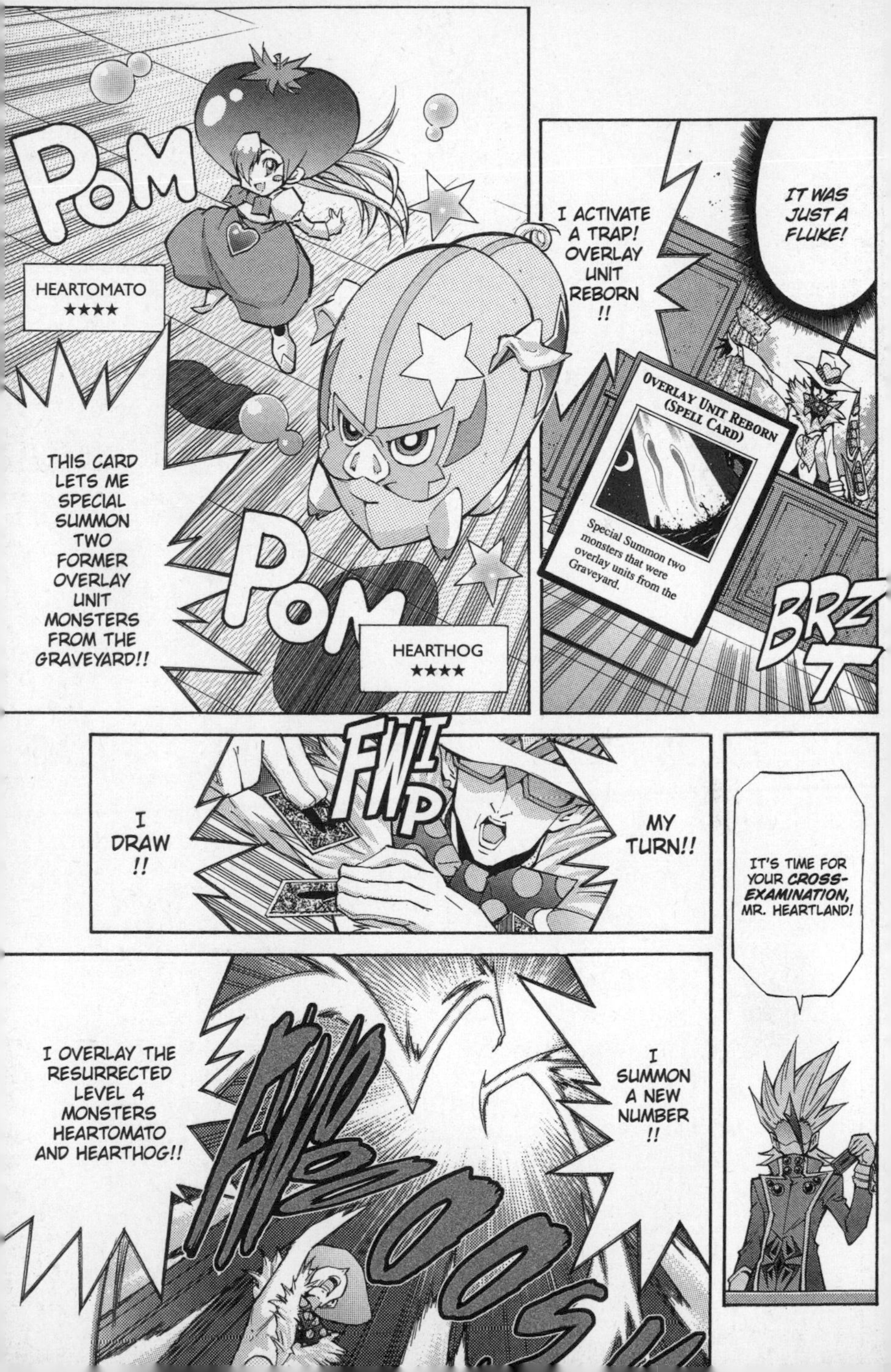
IT WAS JUST A FLUKE!
I ACTIVATE A TRAP! OVERLAY UNIT REBORN!!
OVERLAY UNIT REBORN (SPELL CARD)
Special Summon two monsters that were overlay units from the Graveyard.
BRZT
POM
HEARTOMATO ★★★★
THIS CARD LETS ME SPECIAL SUMMON TWO FORMER OVERLAY UNIT MONSTERS FROM THE GRAVEYARD!!
POM
HEARTHOG ★★★★
IT'S TIME FOR YOUR *CROSS-EXAMINATION,* MR. HEARTLAND!
MY TURN!!
FWIP
I DRAW!!
I SUMMON A NEW NUMBER!!
I OVERLAY THE RESURRECTED LEVEL 4 MONSTERS HEARTOMATO AND HEARTHOG!!

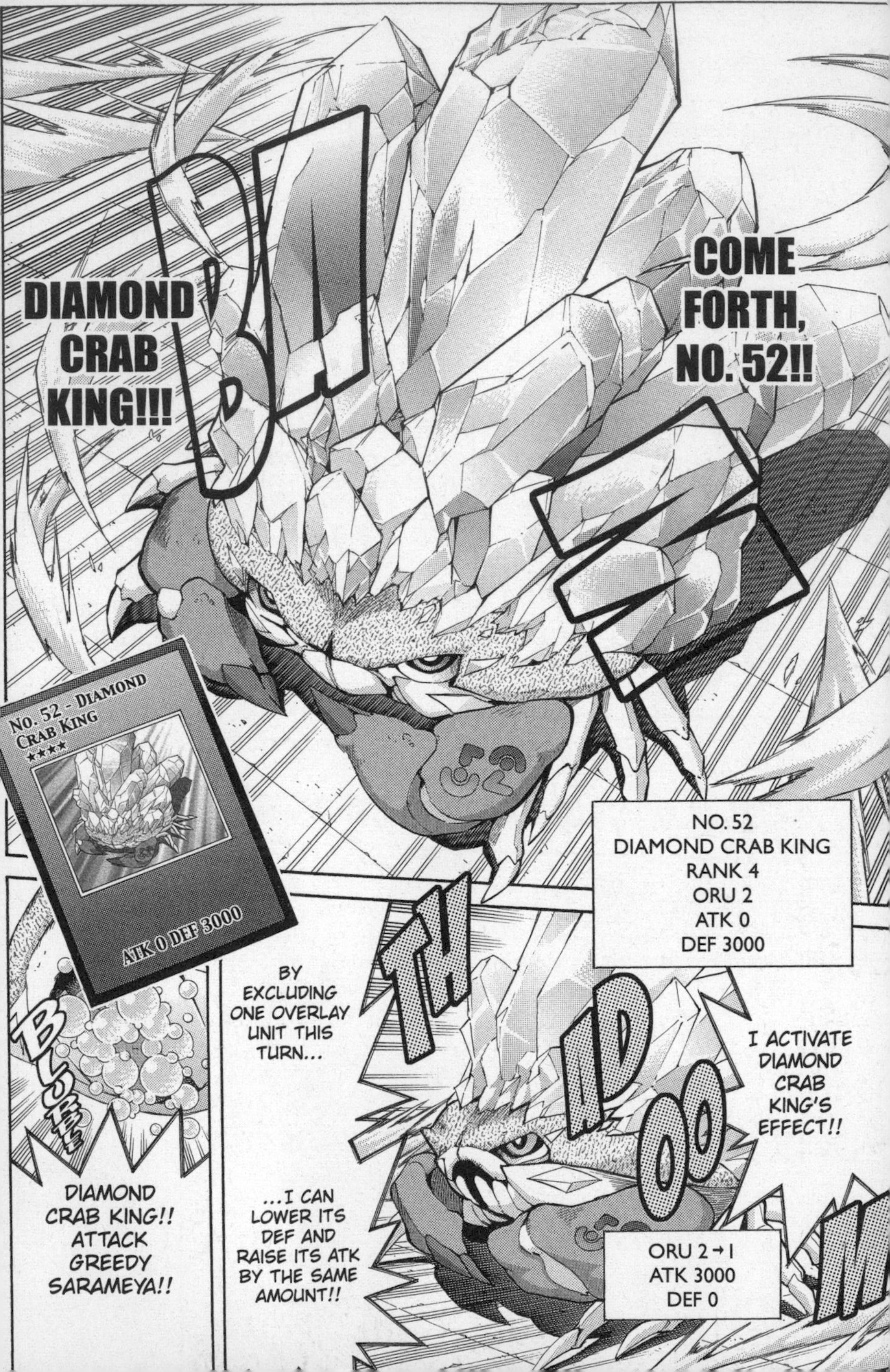
COME FORTH, NO. 52!!
DIAMOND CRAB KING!!!
NO. 52 - DIAMOND CRAB KING
★★★★
ATK 0 DEF 3000
NO. 52
DIAMOND CRAB KING
RANK 4
ORU 2
ATK 0
DEF 3000
I ACTIVATE DIAMOND CRAB KING'S EFFECT!!
ORU 2 → 1
ATK 3000
DEF 0
BY EXCLUDING ONE OVERLAY UNIT THIS TURN...
...I CAN LOWER ITS DEF AND RAISE ITS ATK BY THE SAME AMOUNT!!
DIAMOND CRAB KING!! ATTACK GREEDY SARAMEYA!!

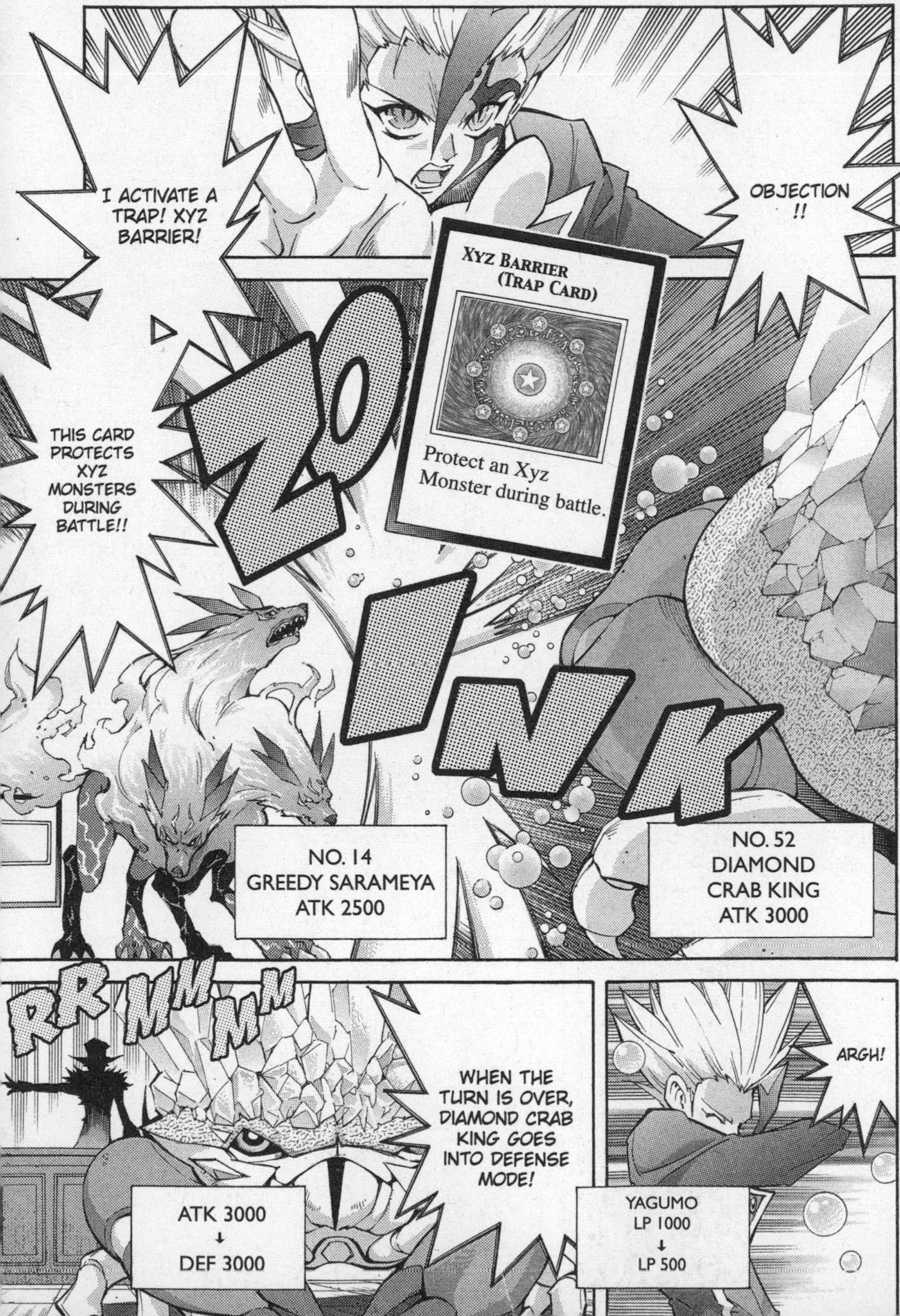
OBJECTION!!
I ACTIVATE A TRAP! XYZ BARRIER!
XYZ BARRIER (TRAP CARD)
Protect an Xyz Monster during battle.
THIS CARD PROTECTS XYZ MONSTERS DURING BATTLE!!
ZOINK
NO. 52 DIAMOND CRAB KING ATK 3000
NO. 14 GREEDY SARAMEYA ATK 2500
ARGH!
YAGUMO LP 1000 ↓ LP 500
RRMMMMM
WHEN THE TURN IS OVER, DIAMOND CRAB KING GOES INTO DEFENSE MODE!
ATK 3000 ↓ DEF 3000

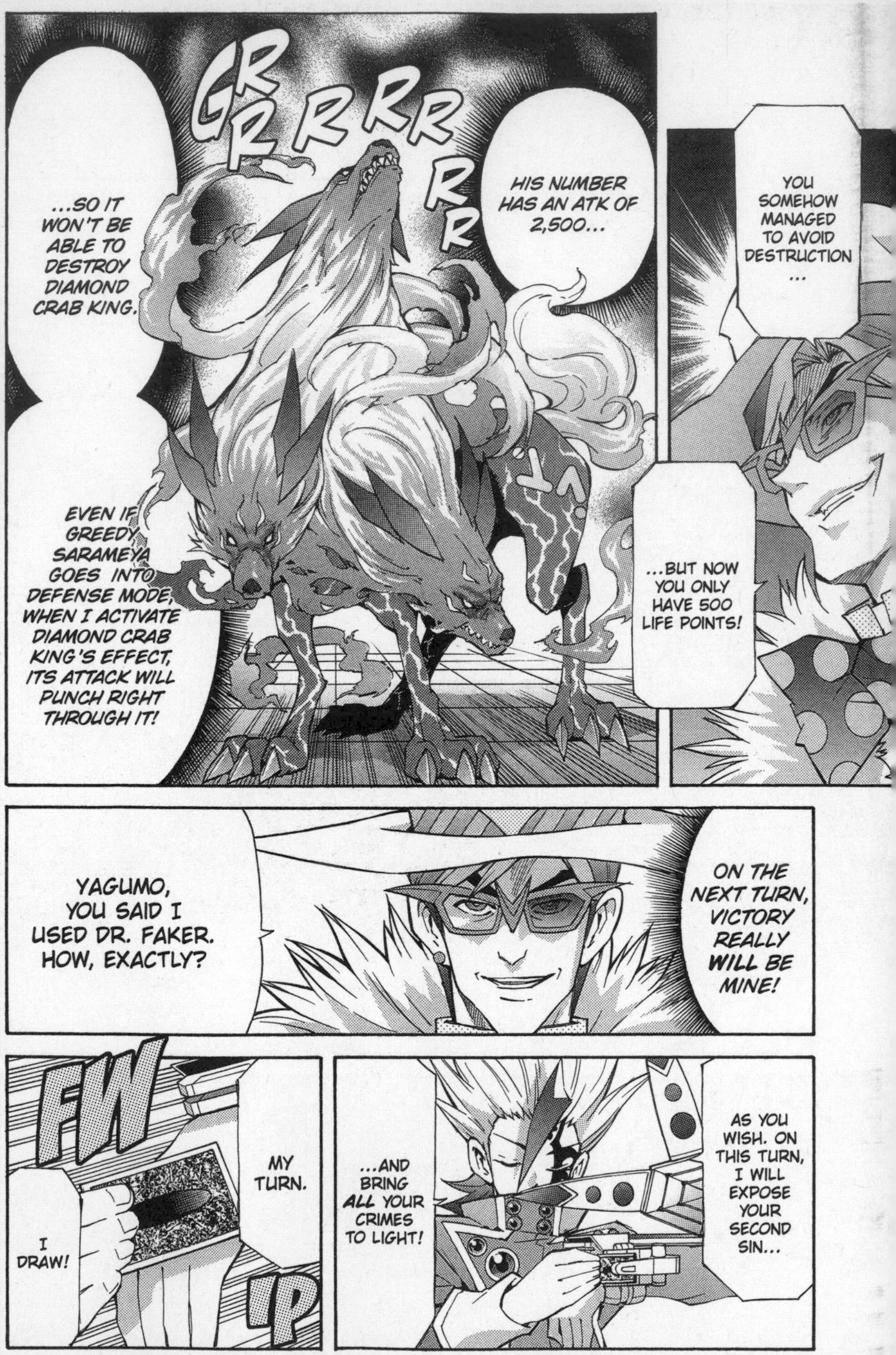
YOU SOMEHOW MANAGED TO AVOID DESTRUCTION...
...BUT NOW YOU ONLY HAVE 500 LIFE POINTS!
GRRRRRRR
HIS NUMBER HAS AN ATK OF 2,500...
...SO IT WON'T BE ABLE TO DESTROY DIAMOND CRAB KING.
EVEN IF GREEDY SARAMEYA GOES INTO DEFENSE MODE, WHEN I ACTIVATE DIAMOND CRAB KING'S EFFECT, ITS ATTACK WILL PUNCH RIGHT THROUGH IT!
ON THE NEXT TURN, VICTORY REALLY WILL BE MINE!
YAGUMO, YOU SAID I USED DR. FAKER. HOW, EXACTLY?
AS YOU WISH. ON THIS TURN, I WILL EXPOSE YOUR SECOND SIN...
...AND BRING ALL YOUR CRIMES TO LIGHT!
MY TURN.
FWIP
I DRAW!

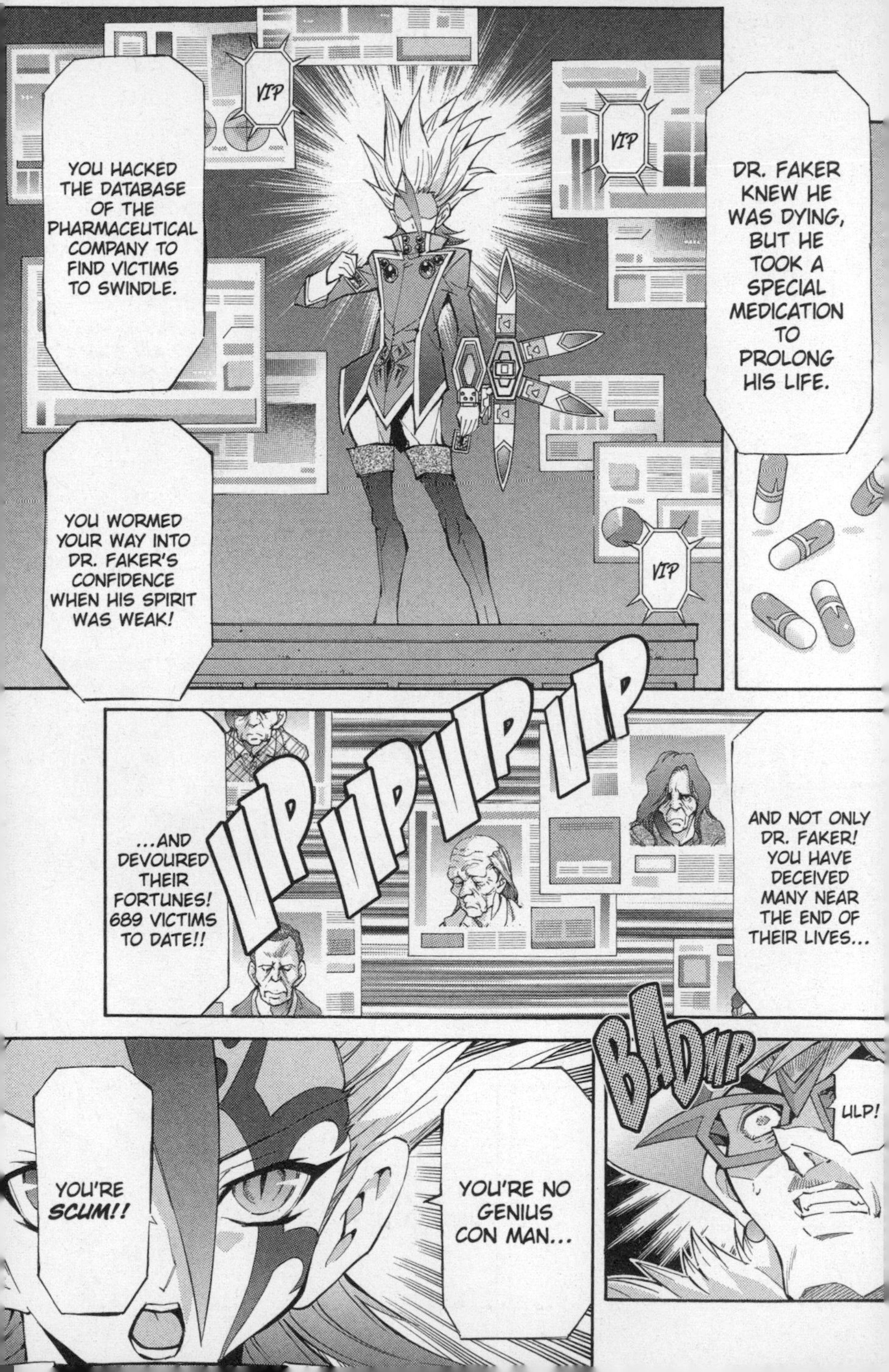
DR. FAKER KNEW HE WAS DYING, BUT HE TOOK A SPECIAL MEDICATION TO PROLONG HIS LIFE.
VIP
VIP
VIP
YOU HACKED THE DATABASE OF THE PHARMACEUTICAL COMPANY TO FIND VICTIMS TO SWINDLE.
YOU WORMED YOUR WAY INTO DR. FAKER'S CONFIDENCE WHEN HIS SPIRIT WAS WEAK!
AND NOT ONLY DR. FAKER! YOU HAVE DECEIVED MANY NEAR THE END OF THEIR LIVES...
VIP VIP VIP VIP
...AND DEVOURED THEIR FORTUNES! 689 VICTIMS TO DATE!!
BADUMP
ULP!
YOU'RE NO GENIUS CON MAN...
YOU'RE *SCUM!!*

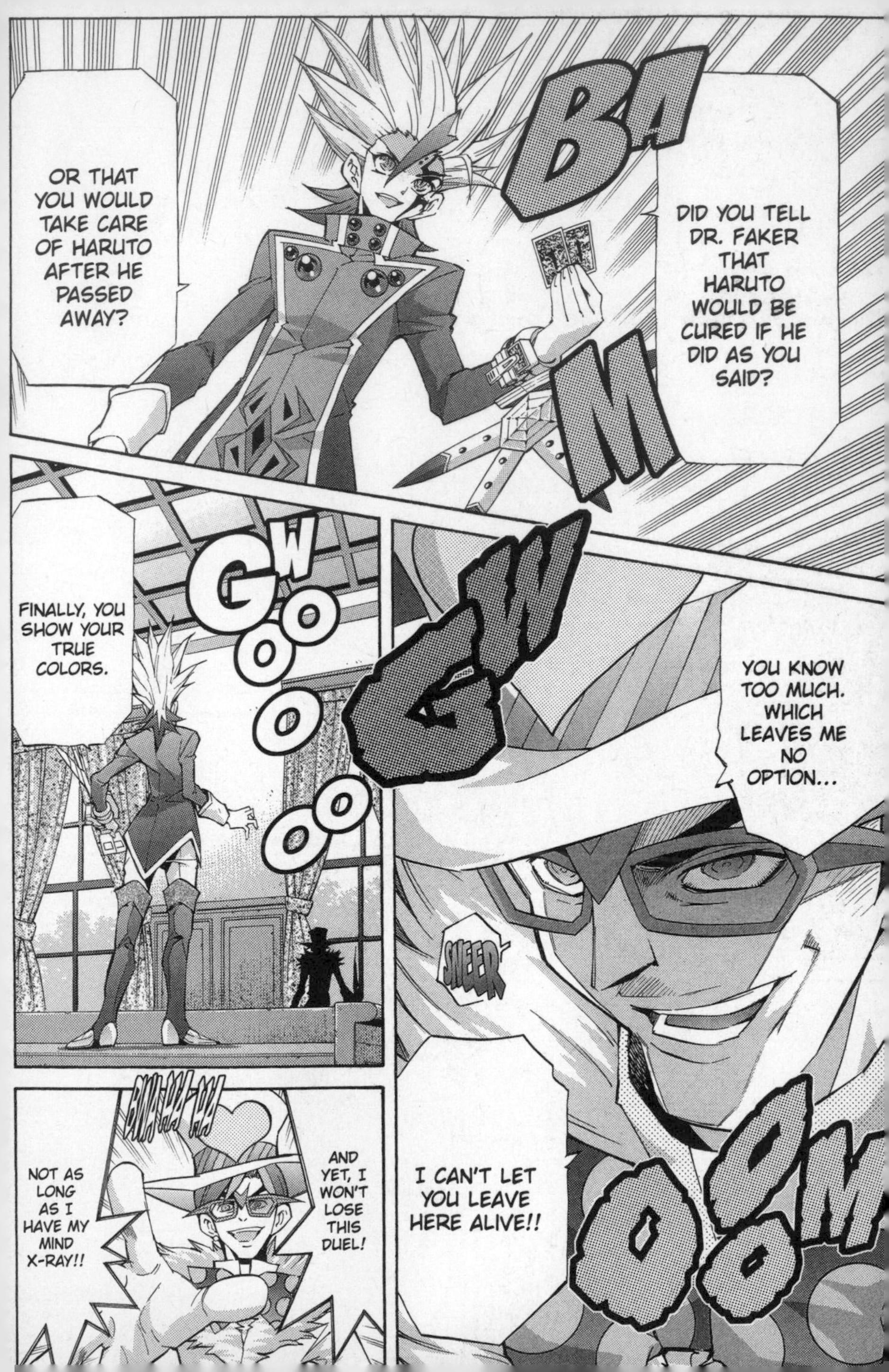
DID YOU TELL DR. FAKER THAT HARUTO WOULD BE CURED IF HE DID AS YOU SAID?
BAM
OR THAT YOU WOULD TAKE CARE OF HARUTO AFTER HE PASSED AWAY?
YOU KNOW TOO MUCH. WHICH LEAVES ME NO OPTION...
SNEER
GWOOOOOO
FINALLY, YOU SHOW YOUR TRUE COLORS.
I CAN'T LET YOU LEAVE HERE ALIVE!!
OOOM
AND YET, I WON'T LOSE THIS DUEL!
NOT AS LONG AS I HAVE MY MIND X-RAY!!

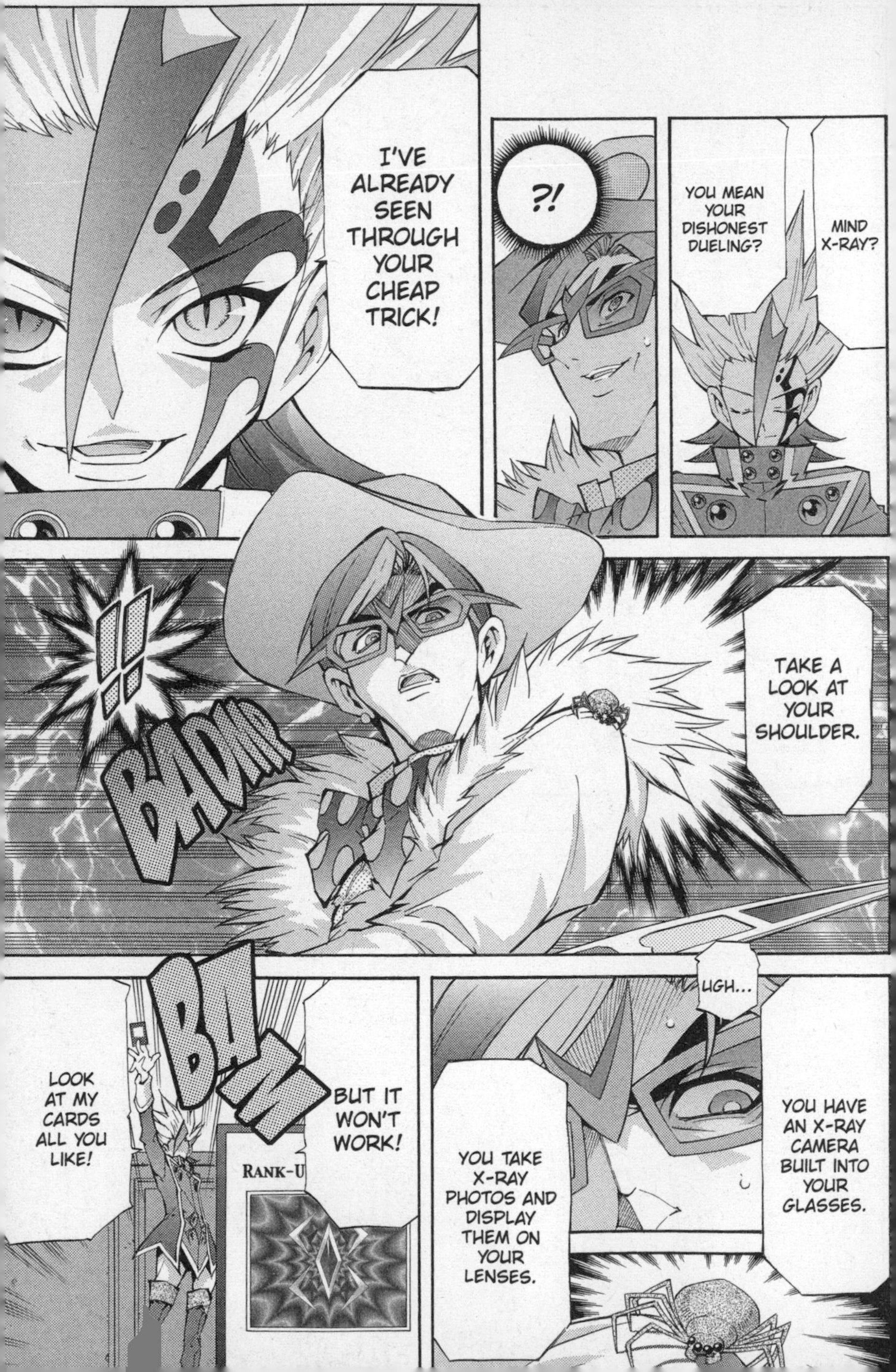
MIND X-RAY?
YOU MEAN YOUR DISHONEST DUELING?
?!
I'VE ALREADY SEEN THROUGH YOUR CHEAP TRICK!
TAKE A LOOK AT YOUR SHOULDER.
!!
BADMP
UGH...
YOU HAVE AN X-RAY CAMERA BUILT INTO YOUR GLASSES.
YOU TAKE X-RAY PHOTOS AND DISPLAY THEM ON YOUR LENSES.
BAM
BUT IT WON'T WORK!
LOOK AT MY CARDS ALL YOU LIKE!
RANK-U

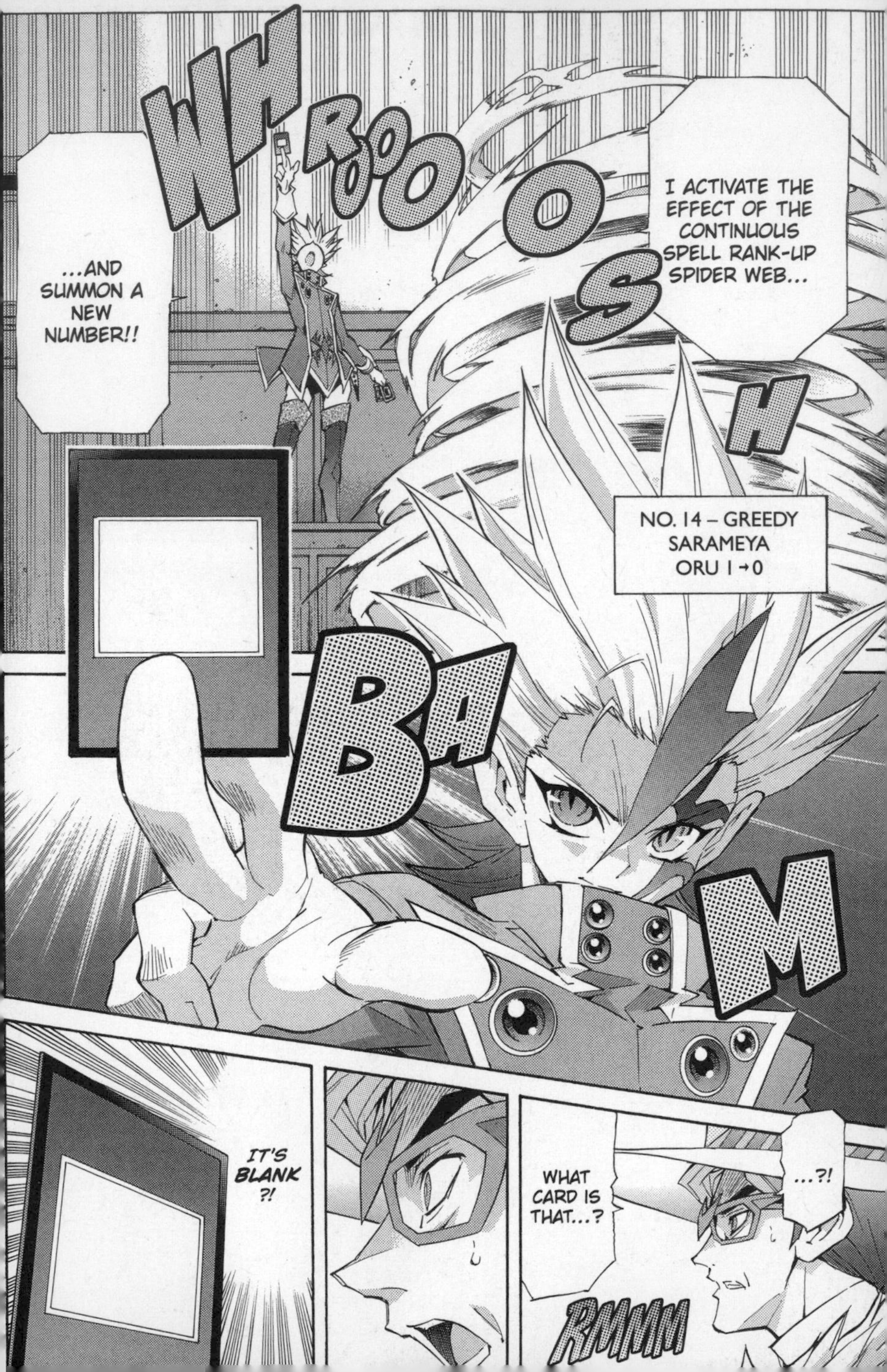
I ACTIVATE THE EFFECT OF THE CONTINUOUS SPELL RANK-UP SPIDER WEB...
...AND SUMMON A NEW NUMBER!!
WHROOOOOSH
NO. 14 – GREEDY SARAMEYA ORU 1→0
BAM
...?!
WHAT CARD IS THAT...?
RMMM
IT'S BLANK ?!

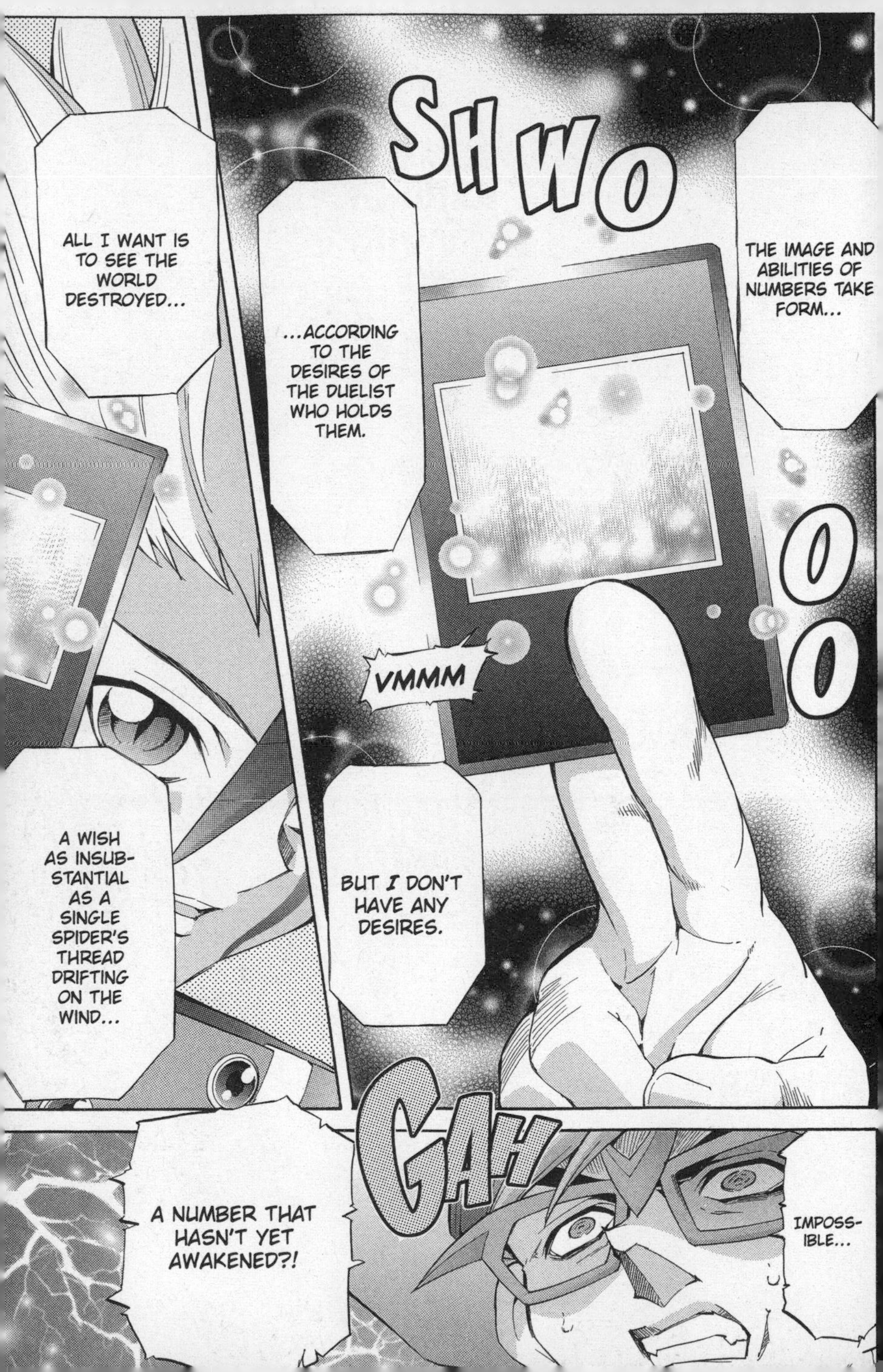
SHWOOO
THE IMAGE AND ABILITIES OF NUMBERS TAKE FORM...
...ACCORDING TO THE DESIRES OF THE DUELIST WHO HOLDS THEM.
VMMM
BUT I DON'T HAVE ANY DESIRES.
ALL I WANT IS TO SEE THE WORLD DESTROYED...
A WISH AS INSUB-STANTIAL AS A SINGLE SPIDER'S THREAD DRIFTING ON THE WIND...
GAH
IMPOSS-IBLE...
A NUMBER THAT HASN'T YET AWAKENED?!

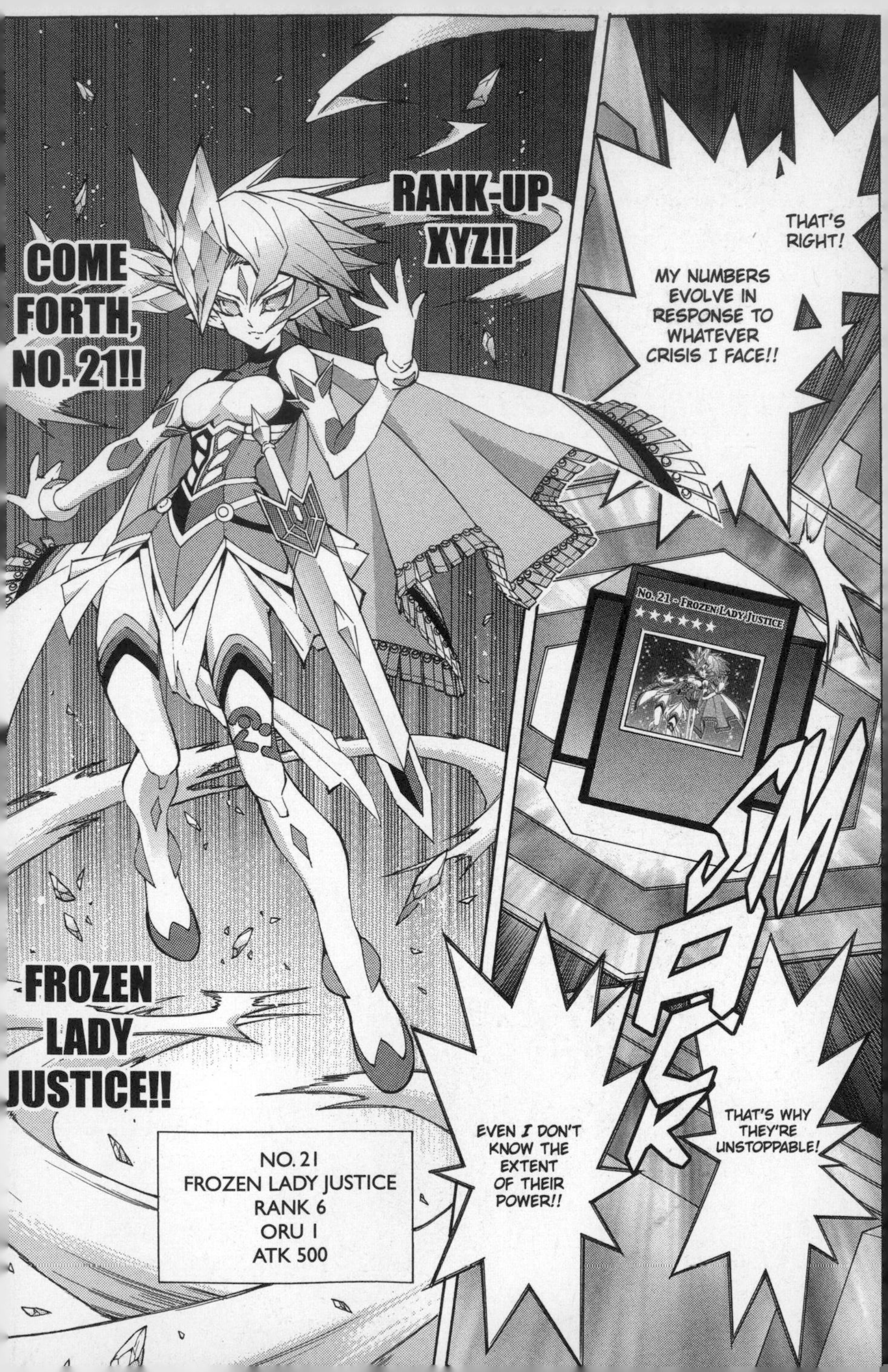
THAT'S RIGHT!
MY NUMBERS EVOLVE IN RESPONSE TO WHATEVER CRISIS I FACE!!
NO. 21 - FROZEN LADY JUSTICE
SNAP
EVEN I DON'T KNOW THE EXTENT OF THEIR POWER!!
THAT'S WHY THEY'RE UNSTOPPABLE!
RANK-UP XYZ!!
COME FORTH, NO. 21!!
FROZEN LADY JUSTICE!!
NO. 21
FROZEN LADY JUSTICE
RANK 6
ORU 1
ATK 500

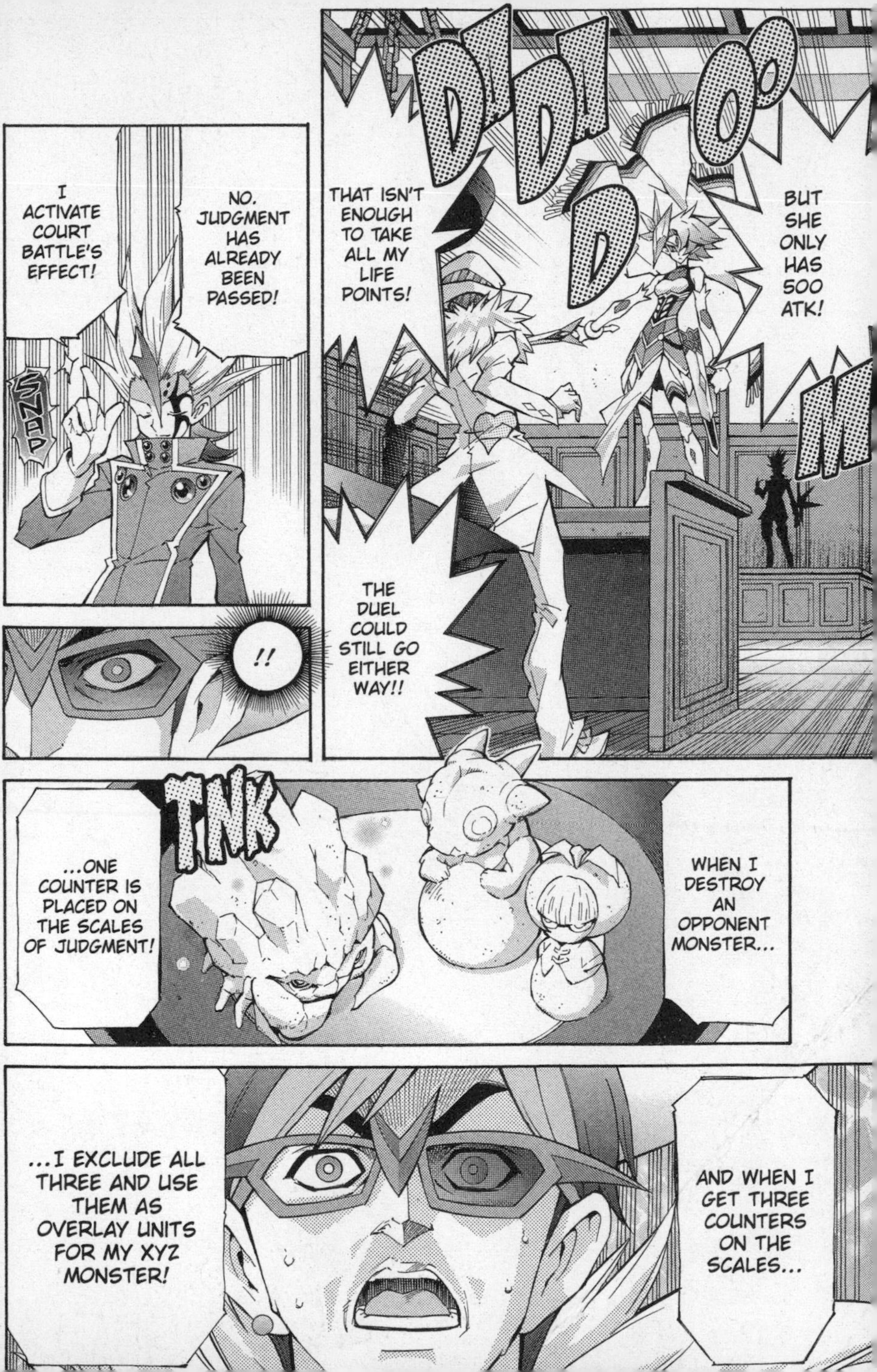
D! D! D O O O M
BUT SHE ONLY HAS 500 ATK!
THAT ISN'T ENOUGH TO TAKE ALL MY LIFE POINTS!
THE DUEL COULD STILL GO EITHER WAY!!
NO. JUDGMENT HAS ALREADY BEEN PASSED!
I ACTIVATE COURT BATTLE'S EFFECT!
SNAP
!!
TNK
WHEN I DESTROY AN OPPONENT MONSTER...
...ONE COUNTER IS PLACED ON THE SCALES OF JUDGMENT!
AND WHEN I GET THREE COUNTERS ON THE SCALES...
...I EXCLUDE ALL THREE AND USE THEM AS OVERLAY UNITS FOR MY XYZ MONSTER!

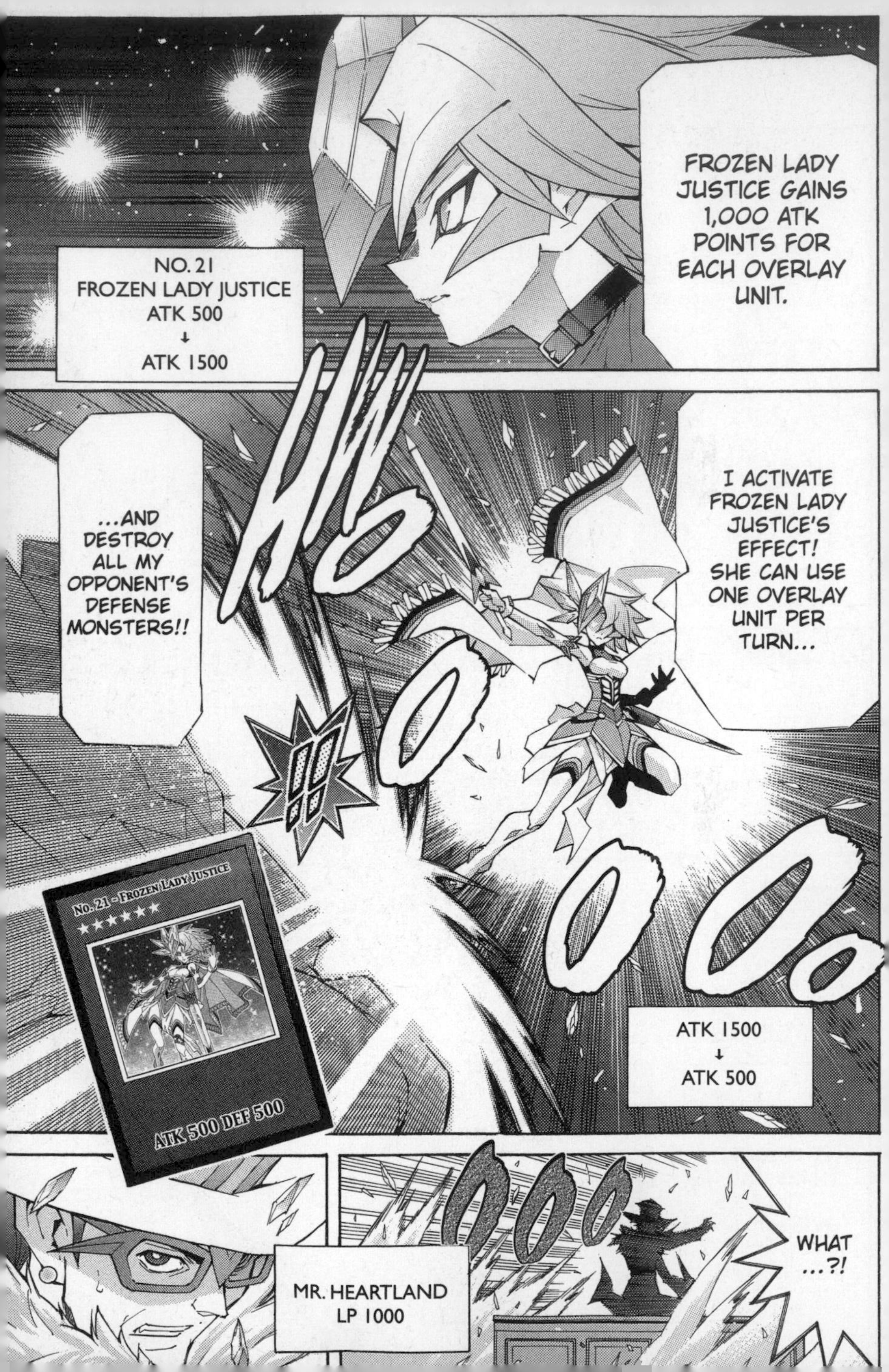
FROZEN LADY JUSTICE GAINS 1,000 ATK POINTS FOR EACH OVERLAY UNIT.
NO. 21 FROZEN LADY JUSTICE ATK 500 ↓ ATK 1500
I ACTIVATE FROZEN LADY JUSTICE'S EFFECT! SHE CAN USE ONE OVERLAY UNIT PER TURN...
...AND DESTROY ALL MY OPPONENT'S DEFENSE MONSTERS!!
!!
No. 21 - Frozen Lady Justice
ATK 500 DEF 500
ATK 1500 ↓ ATK 500
WHAT ...?!
MR. HEARTLAND LP 1000

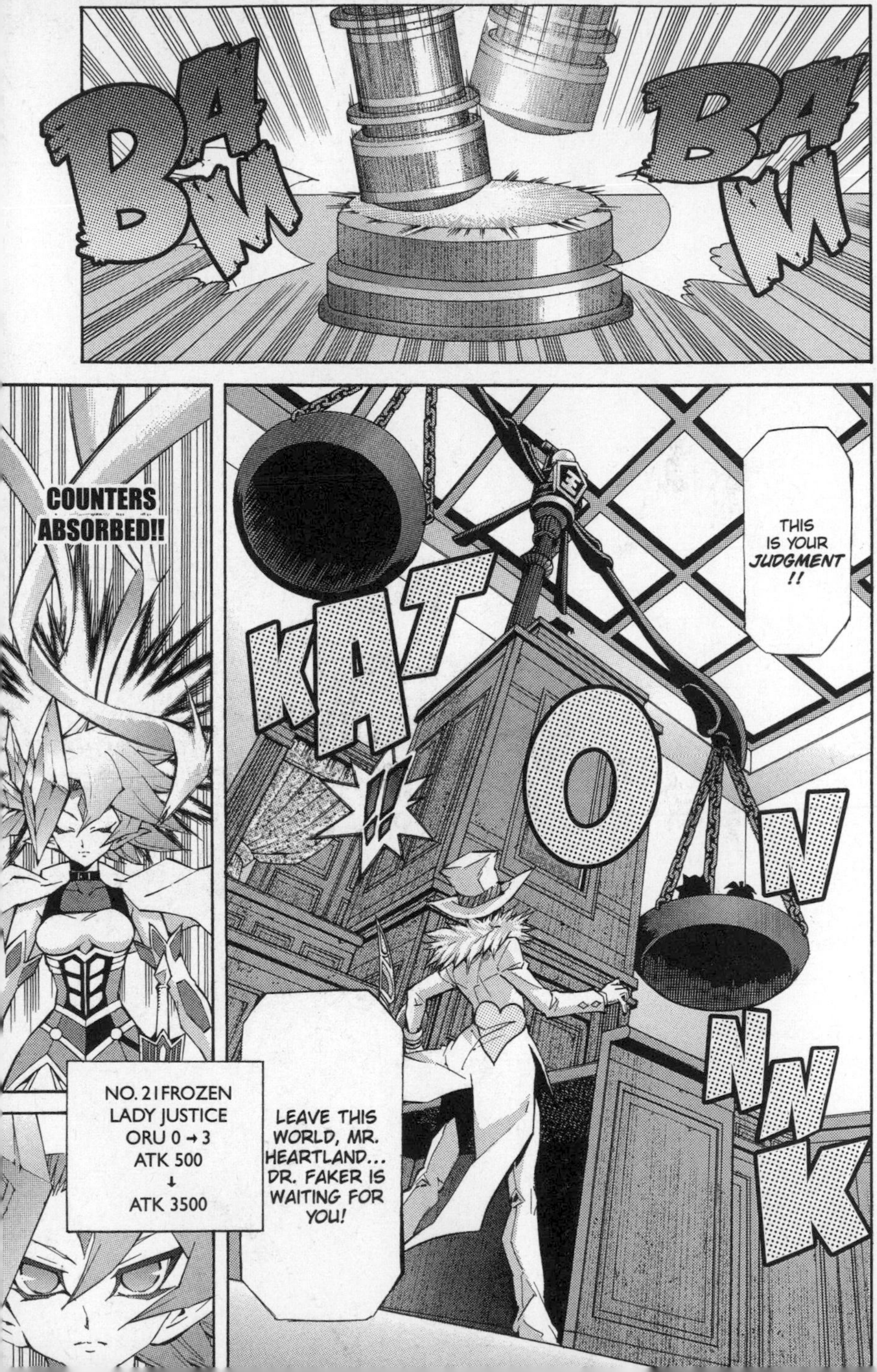
BAM
BAM
THIS IS YOUR JUDGMENT!!
KATOWNNNK
!!
LEAVE THIS WORLD, MR. HEARTLAND... DR. FAKER IS WAITING FOR YOU!
COUNTERS ABSORBED!!
NO. 21 FROZEN LADY JUSTICE ORU 0 → 3 ATK 500 ↓ ATK 3500

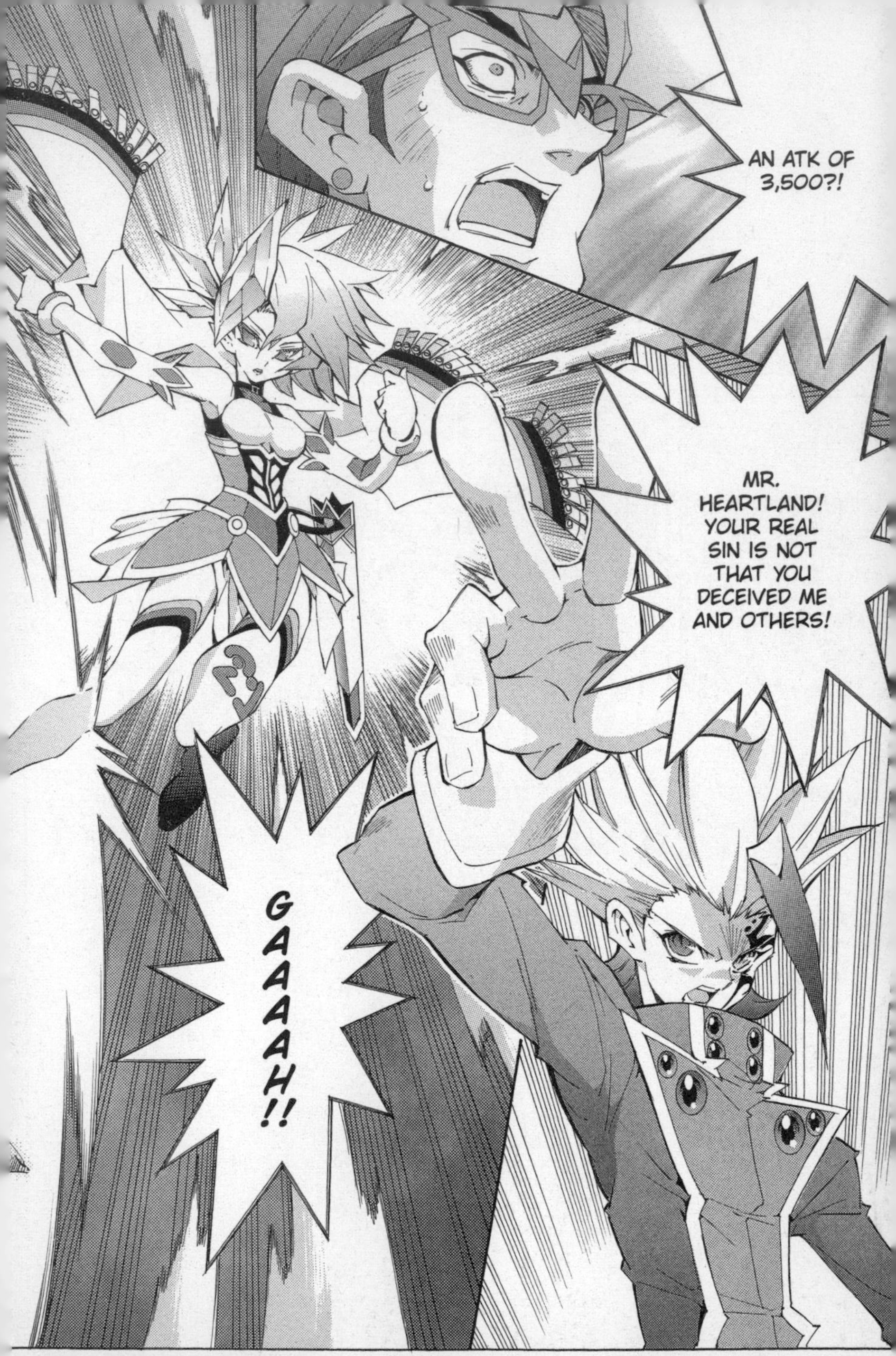
AN ATK OF 3,500?!
MR. HEARTLAND! YOUR REAL SIN IS NOT THAT YOU DECEIVED ME AND OTHERS!
GAAAAAH!!

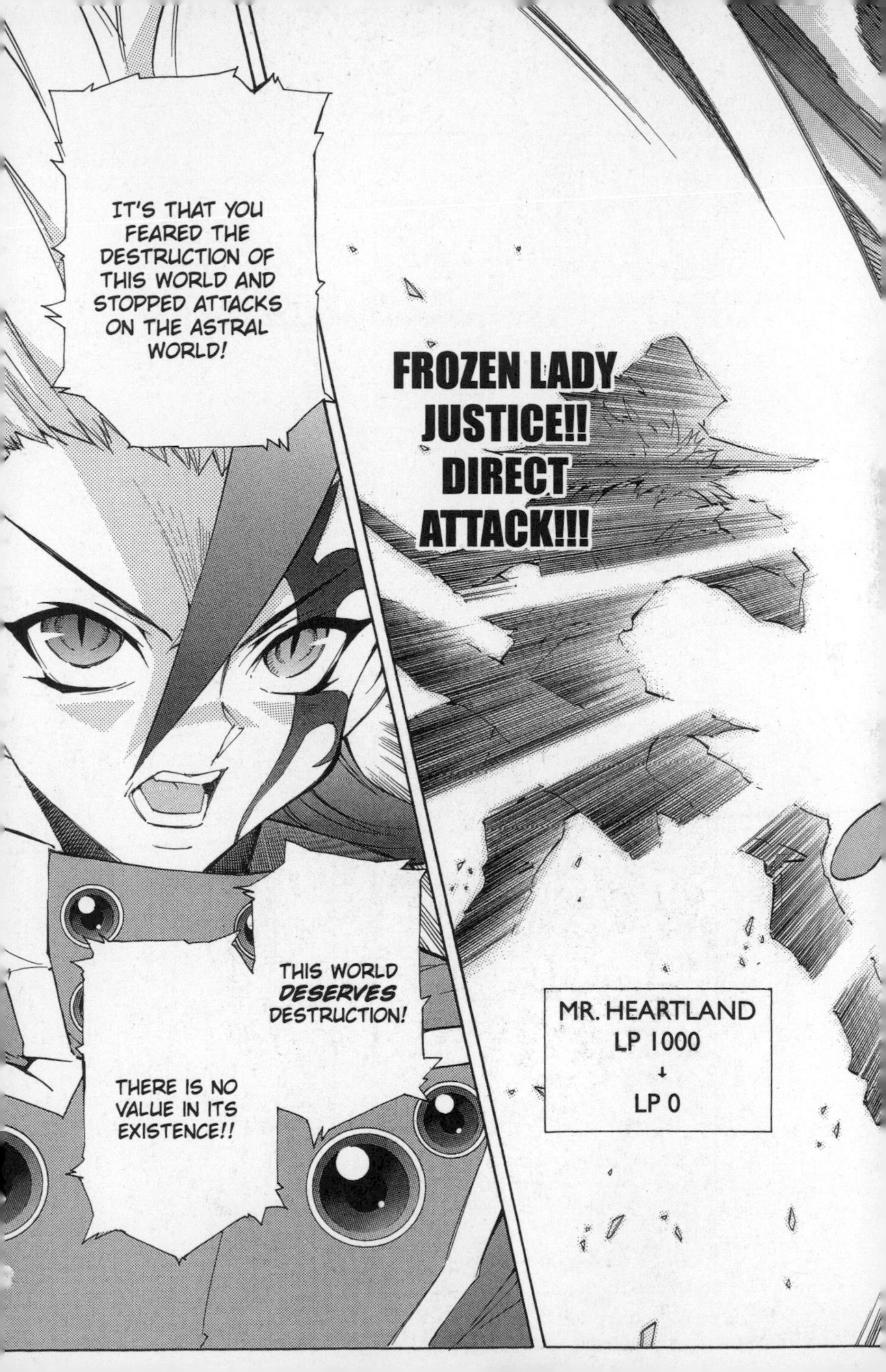
FROZEN LADY JUSTICE!!! DIRECT ATTACK!!!
MR. HEARTLAND LP 1000 ↓ LP 0
IT'S THAT YOU FEARED THE DESTRUCTION OF THIS WORLD AND STOPPED ATTACKS ON THE ASTRAL WORLD!
THIS WORLD *DESERVES* DESTRUCTION!
THERE IS NO VALUE IN ITS EXISTENCE!!

astral's
journal
#10

APPARENTLY, MONSTER DESIGN IS DIFFICULT.
MIYOSHI ALWAYS HAS TROUBLE.
ERASE ERASE
KEEP TRYING!
I THINK THAT DESIGN IS EXCEL-LENT!

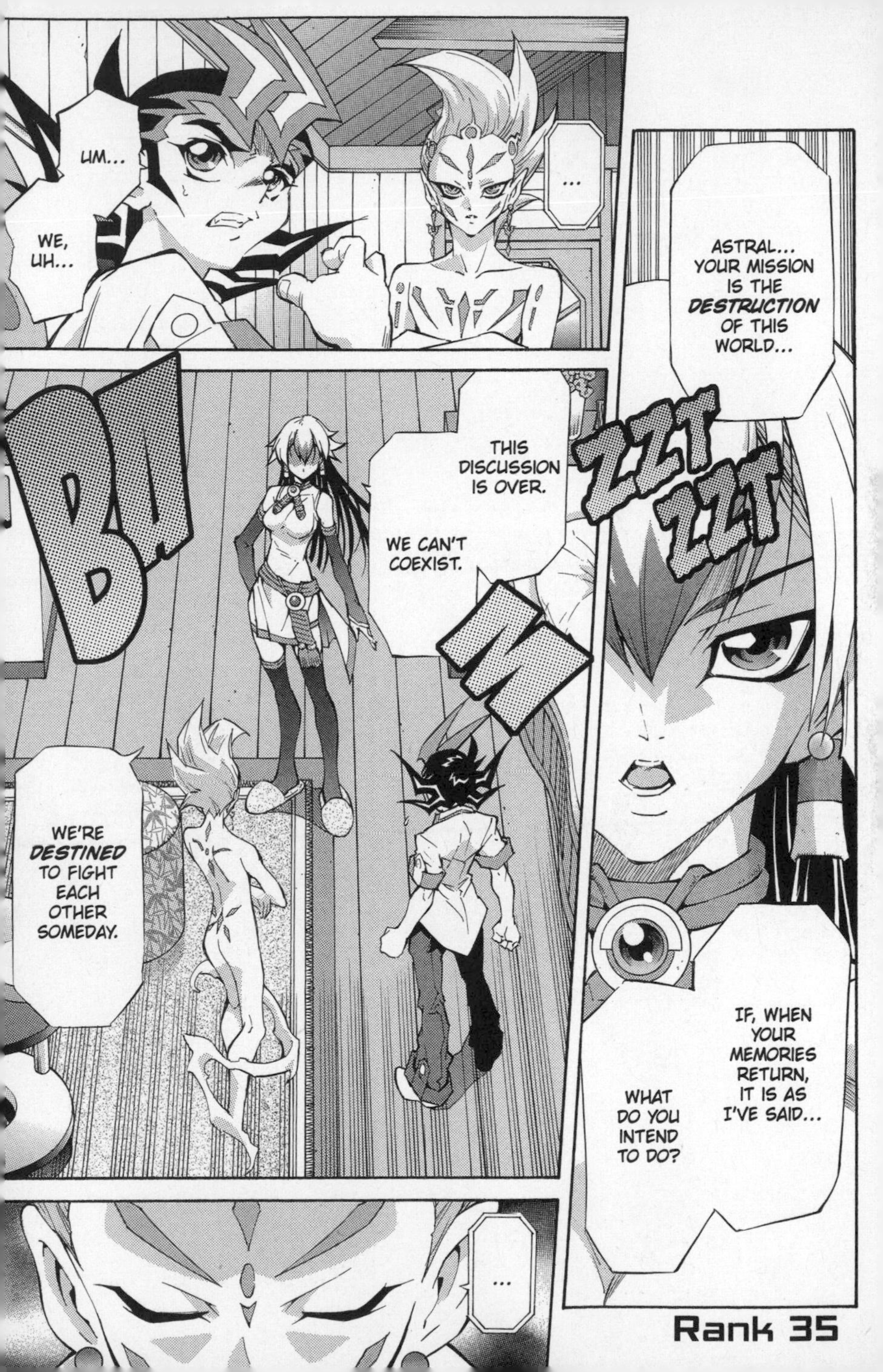
UM...
WE, UH...
...
ASTRAL... YOUR MISSION IS THE *DESTRUCTION* OF THIS WORLD...
ZZT ZZT
IF, WHEN YOUR MEMORIES RETURN, IT IS AS I'VE SAID...
WHAT DO YOU INTEND TO DO?
BAM
THIS DISCUSSION IS OVER.
WE CAN'T COEXIST.
WE'RE *DESTINED* TO FIGHT EACH OTHER SOMEDAY.
...

Rank 35

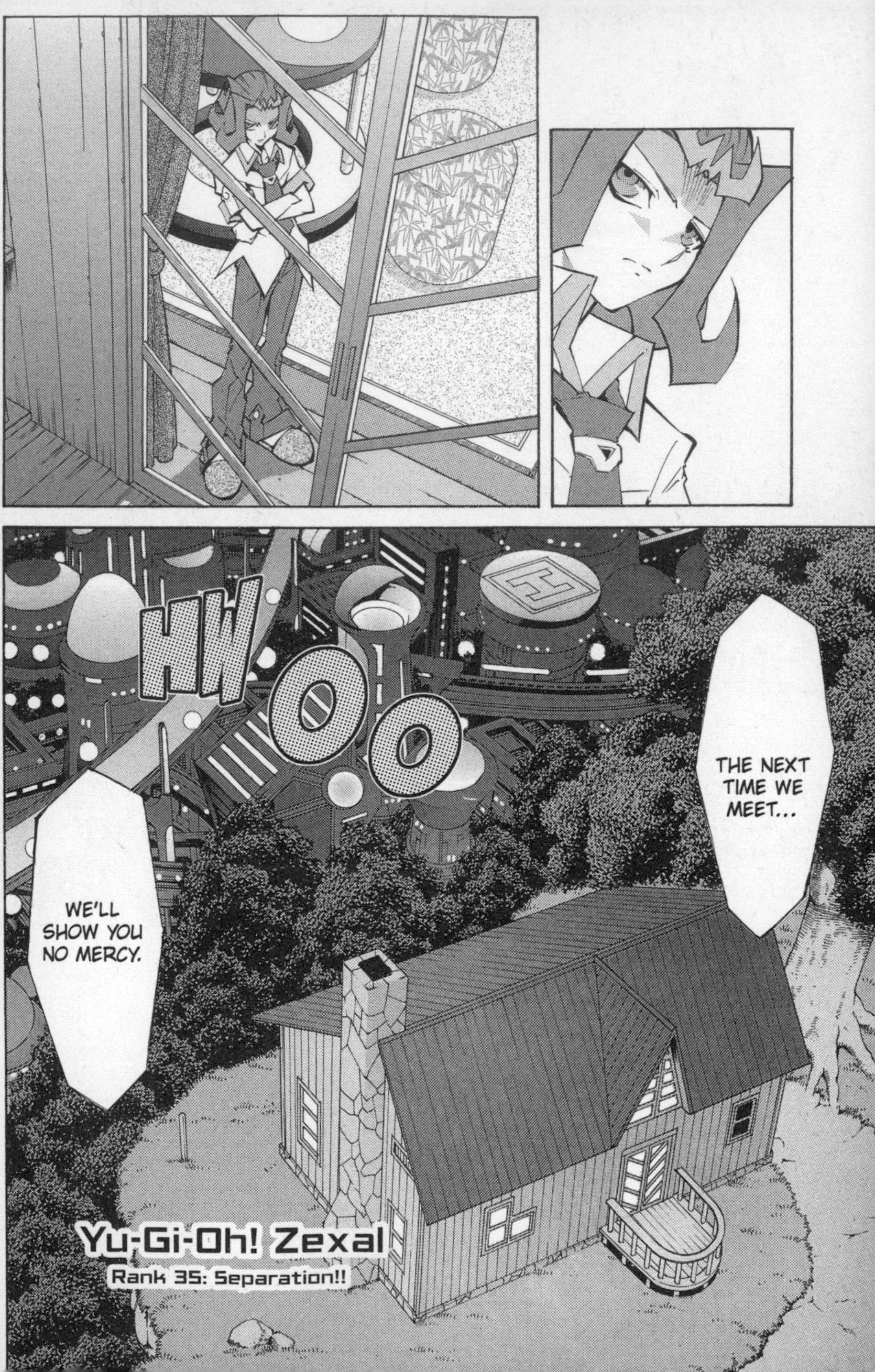
THE NEXT TIME WE MEET...
HWOO
WE'LL SHOW YOU NO MERCY.
Yu-Gi-Oh! Zexal
Rank 35: Separation!!

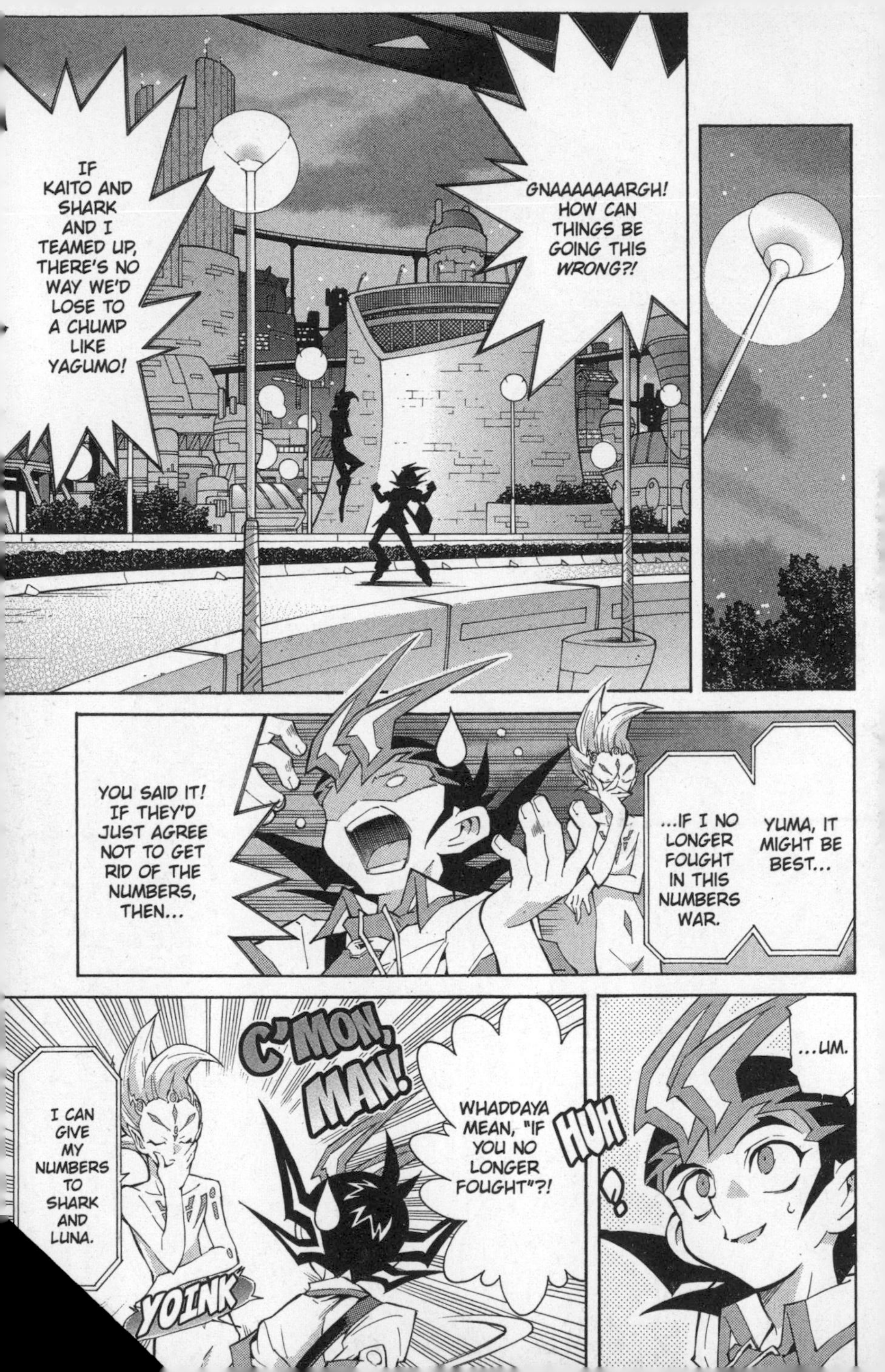
GNAAAAAAARGH! HOW CAN THINGS BE GOING THIS *WRONG*?!
IF KAITO AND SHARK AND I TEAMED UP, THERE'S NO WAY WE'D LOSE TO A CHUMP LIKE YAGUMO!
YUMA, IT MIGHT BE BEST...
...IF I NO LONGER FOUGHT IN THIS NUMBERS WAR.
YOU SAID IT! IF THEY'D JUST AGREE NOT TO GET RID OF THE NUMBERS, THEN...
...UM.
HUH
C'MON, MAN!
WHADDAYA MEAN, "IF YOU NO LONGER FOUGHT"?!
I CAN GIVE MY NUMBERS TO SHARK AND LUNA.
YOINK

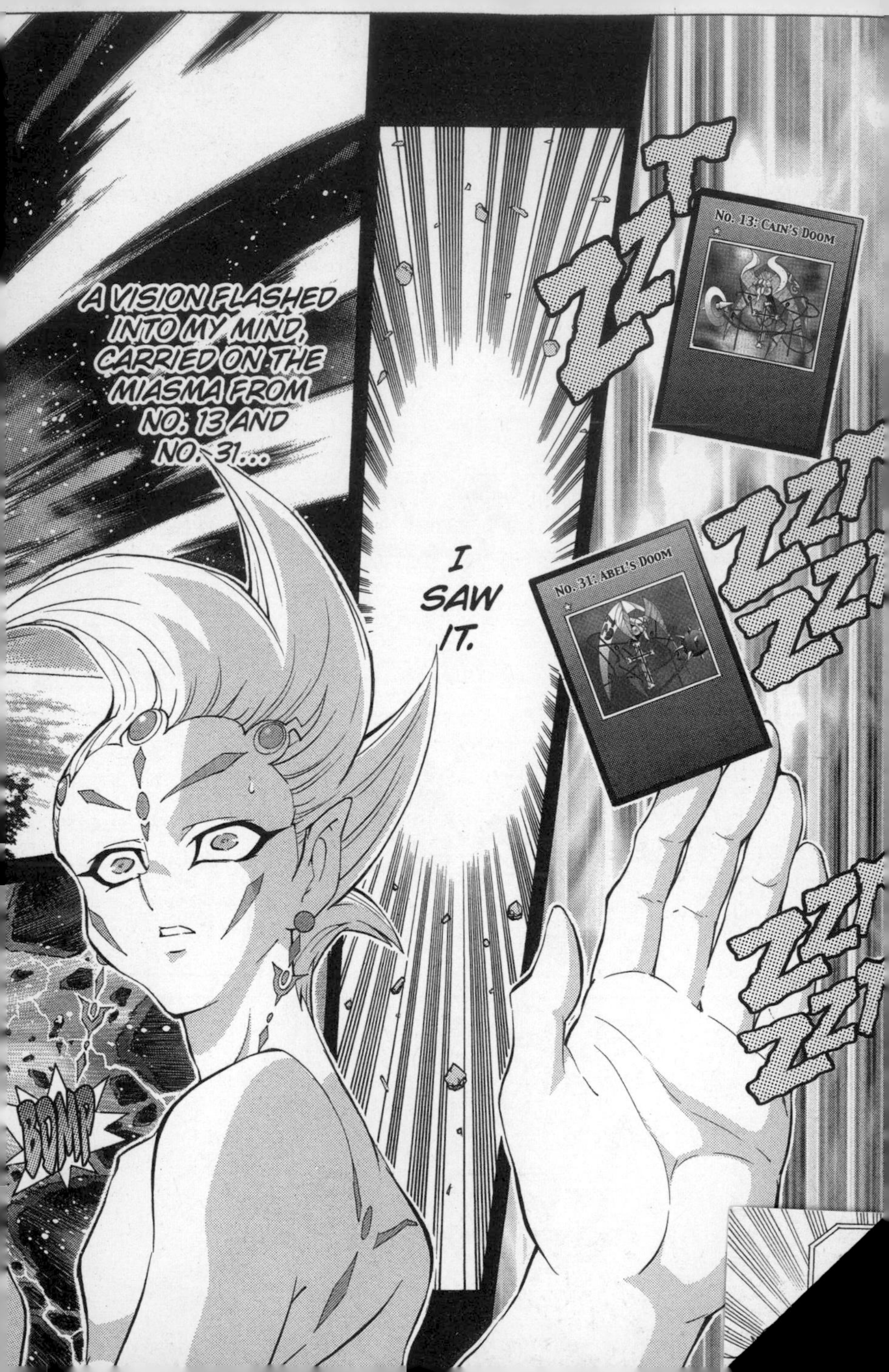
ZZT
No. 13: Cain's Doom
ZZZT
ZZZT
No. 31: Abel's Doom
ZZZT
ZZZT
I SAW IT.
A VISION FLASHED INTO MY MIND, CARRIED ON THE MIASMA FROM NO. 13 AND NO. 31...
BOMP

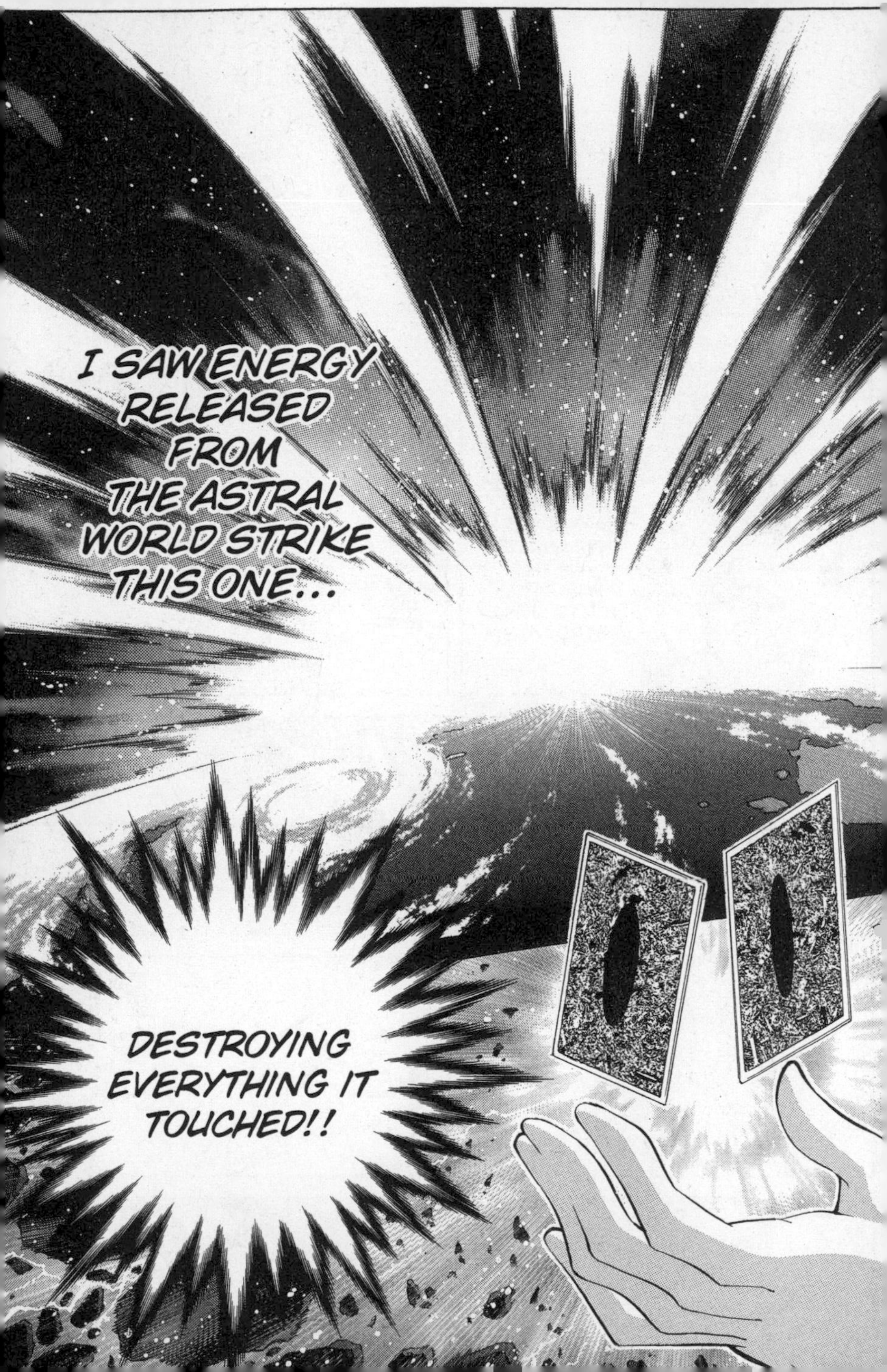
I SAW ENERGY RELEASED FROM THE ASTRAL WORLD STRIKE THIS ONE...
DESTROYING EVERYTHING IT TOUCHED!!

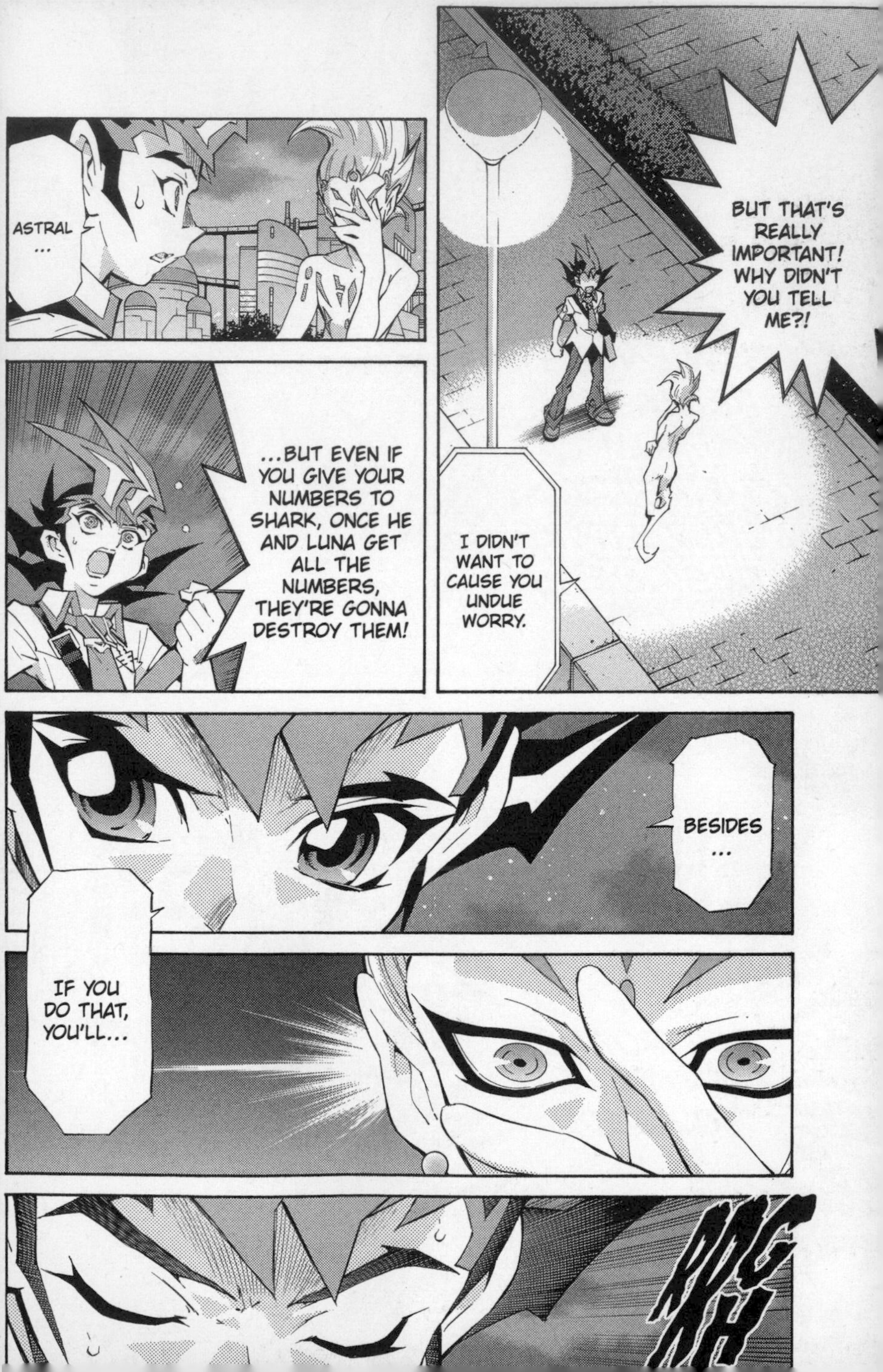
BUT THAT'S REALLY IMPORTANT! WHY DIDN'T YOU TELL ME?!
I DIDN'T WANT TO CAUSE YOU UNDUE WORRY.
ASTRAL ...
...BUT EVEN IF YOU GIVE YOUR NUMBERS TO SHARK, ONCE HE AND LUNA GET ALL THE NUMBERS, THEY'RE GONNA DESTROY THEM!
BESIDES ...
IF YOU DO THAT, YOU'LL...

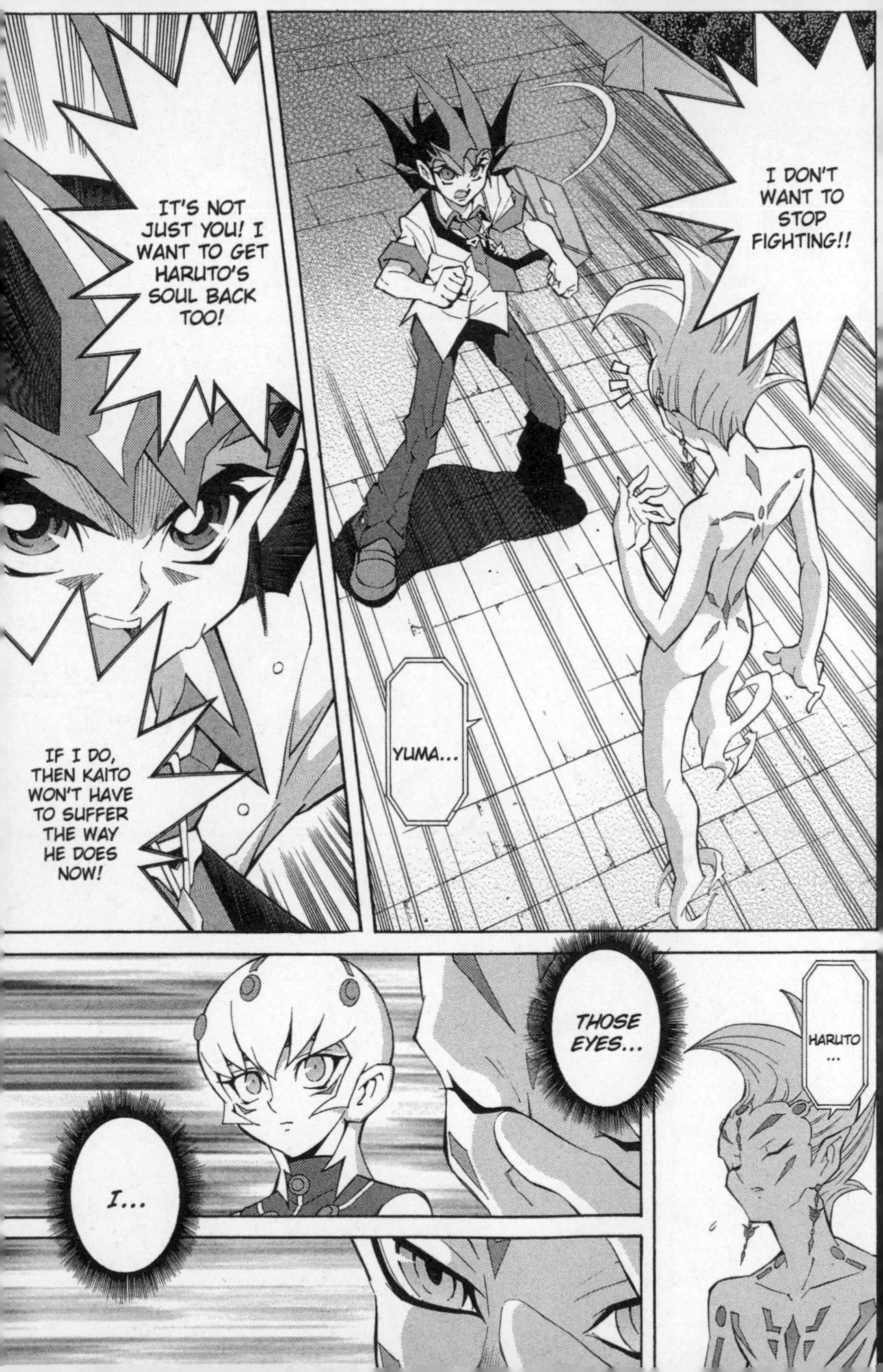
I DON'T WANT TO STOP FIGHTING!!
YUMA...
IT'S NOT JUST YOU! I WANT TO GET HARUTO'S SOUL BACK TOO!
IF I DO, THEN KAITO WON'T HAVE TO SUFFER THE WAY HE DOES NOW!
HARUTO ...
THOSE EYES...
I...

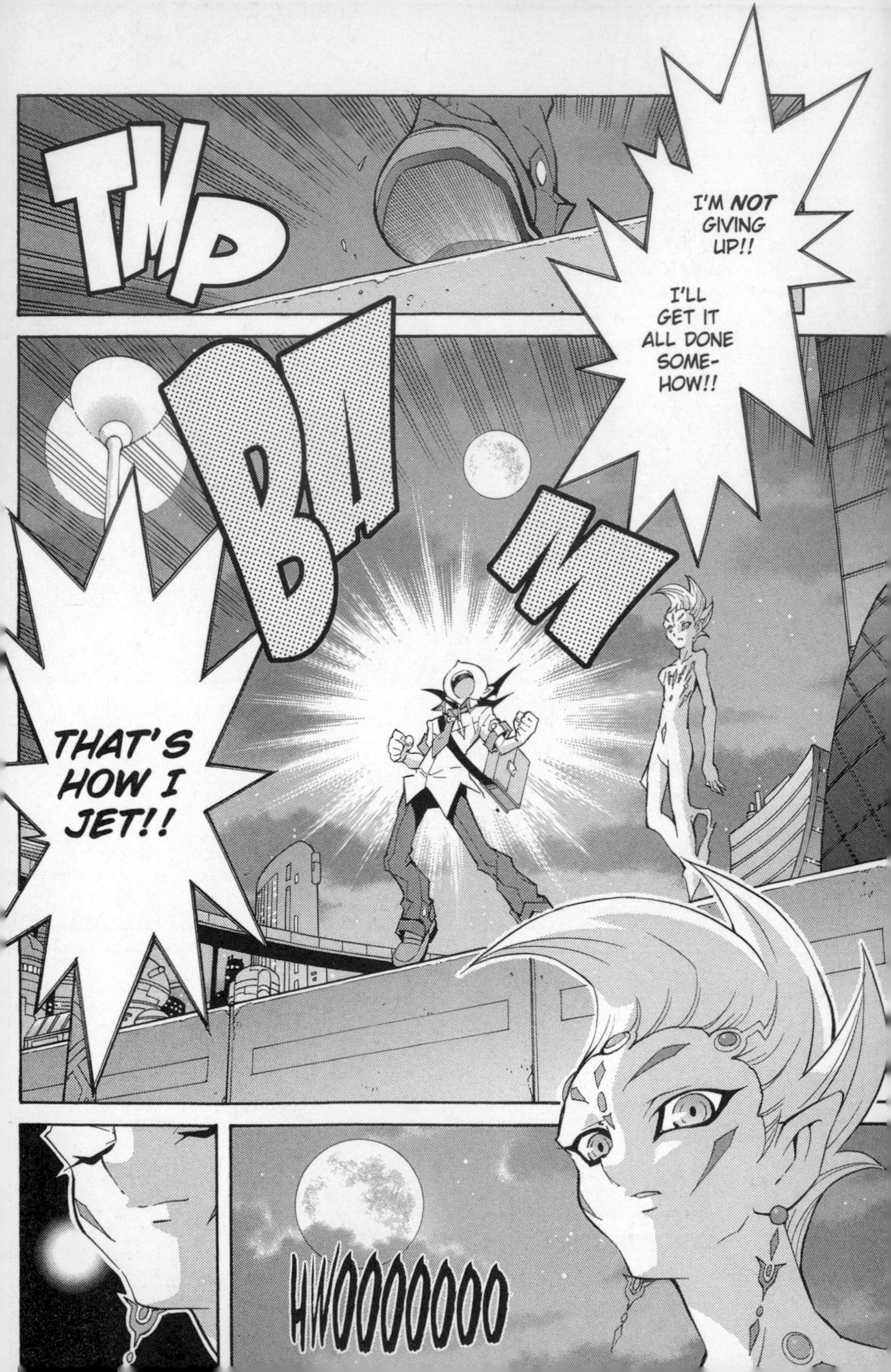
TMP
I'M NOT GIVING UP!!
I'LL GET IT ALL DONE SOME-HOW!!
BAM
THAT'S HOW I JET!!
HWOOOOOOO

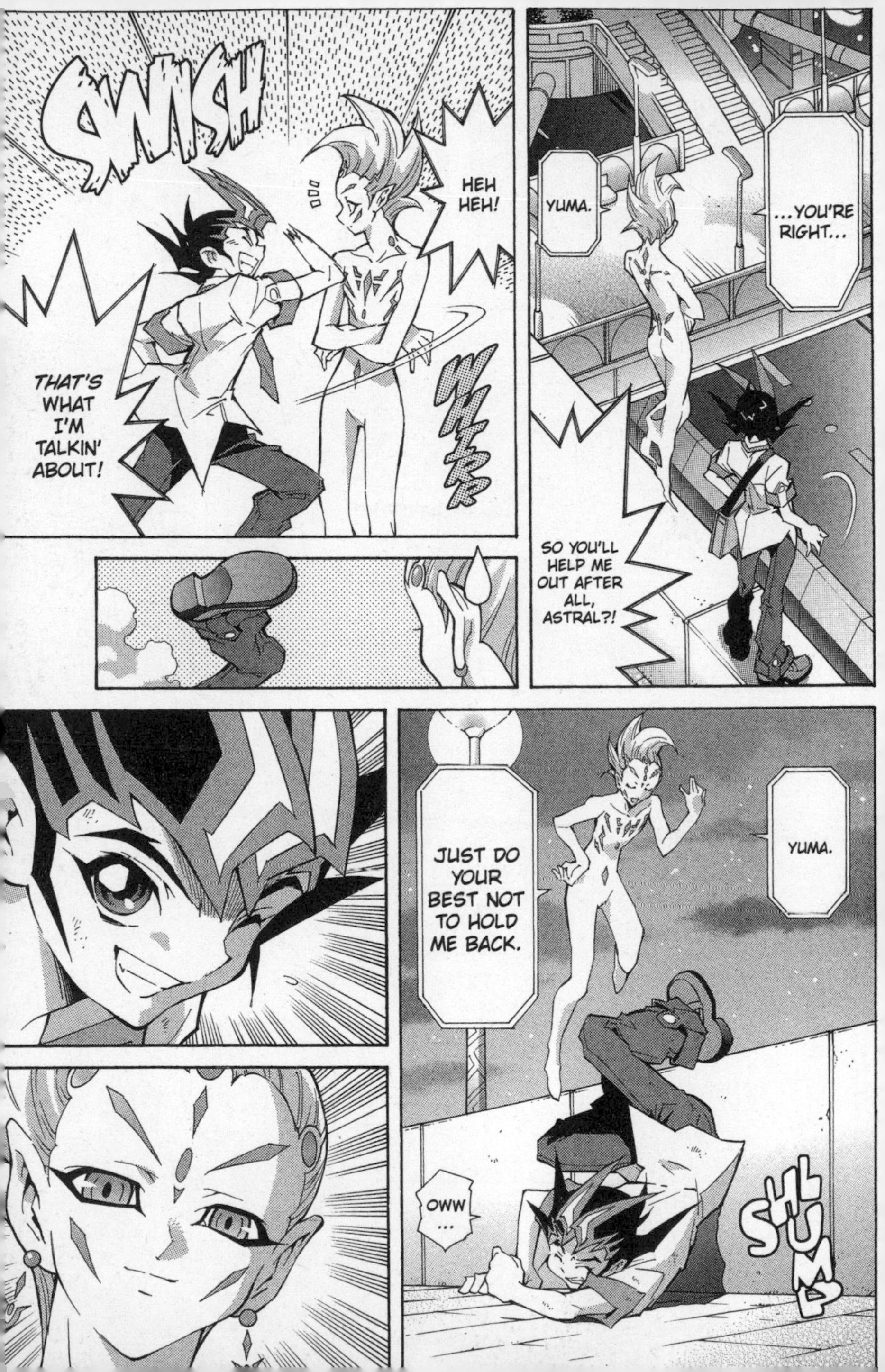
...YOU'RE RIGHT...
YUMA.
SO YOU'LL HELP ME OUT AFTER ALL, ASTRAL?!
HEH HEH!
WHIRR
SWISH
THAT'S WHAT I'M TALKIN' ABOUT!
YUMA.
JUST DO YOUR BEST NOT TO HOLD ME BACK.
SHLUMP
OWW...

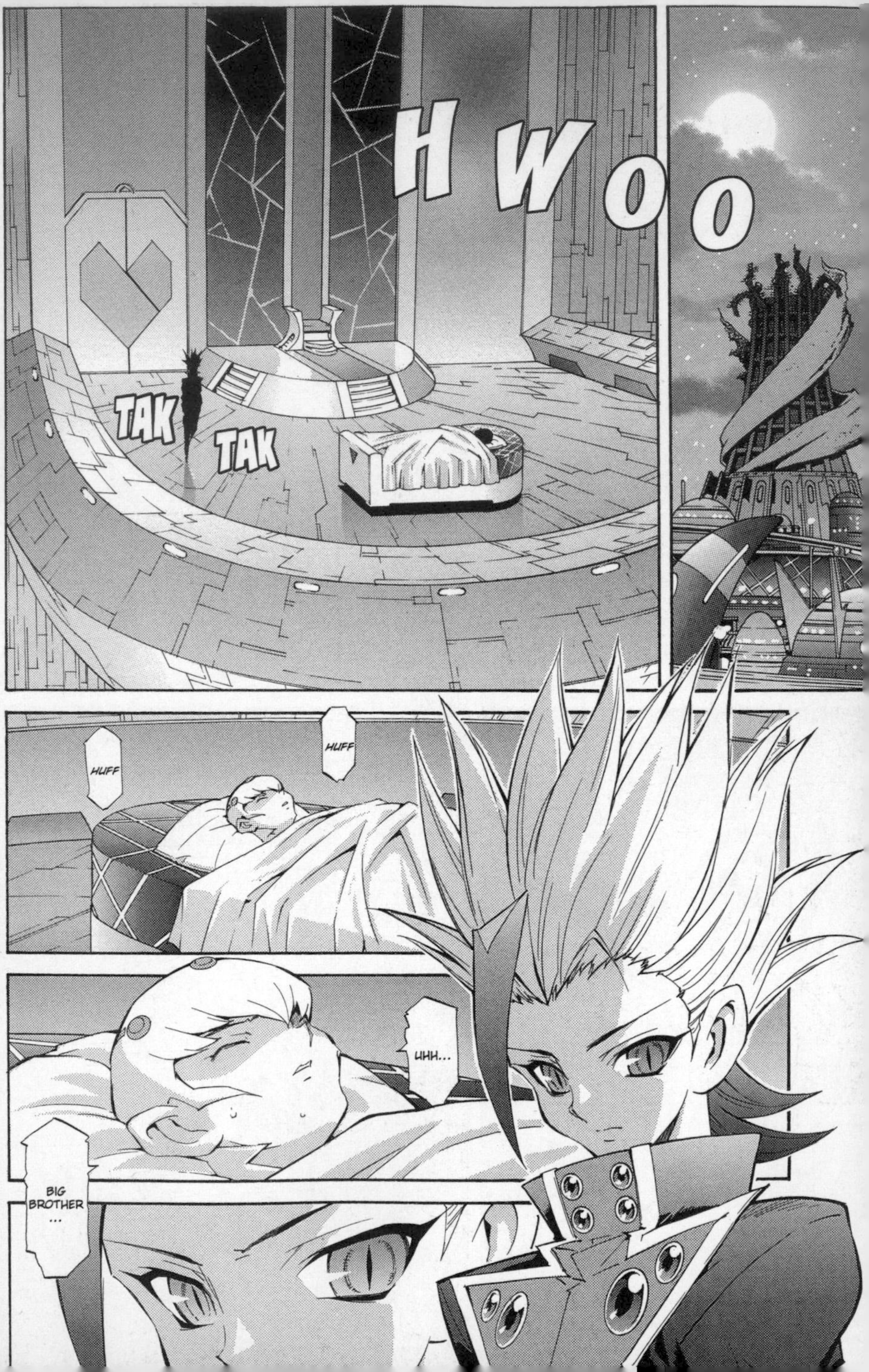
HWOOO
TAK
TAK
HUFF
HUFF
UHH...
BIG BROTHER...

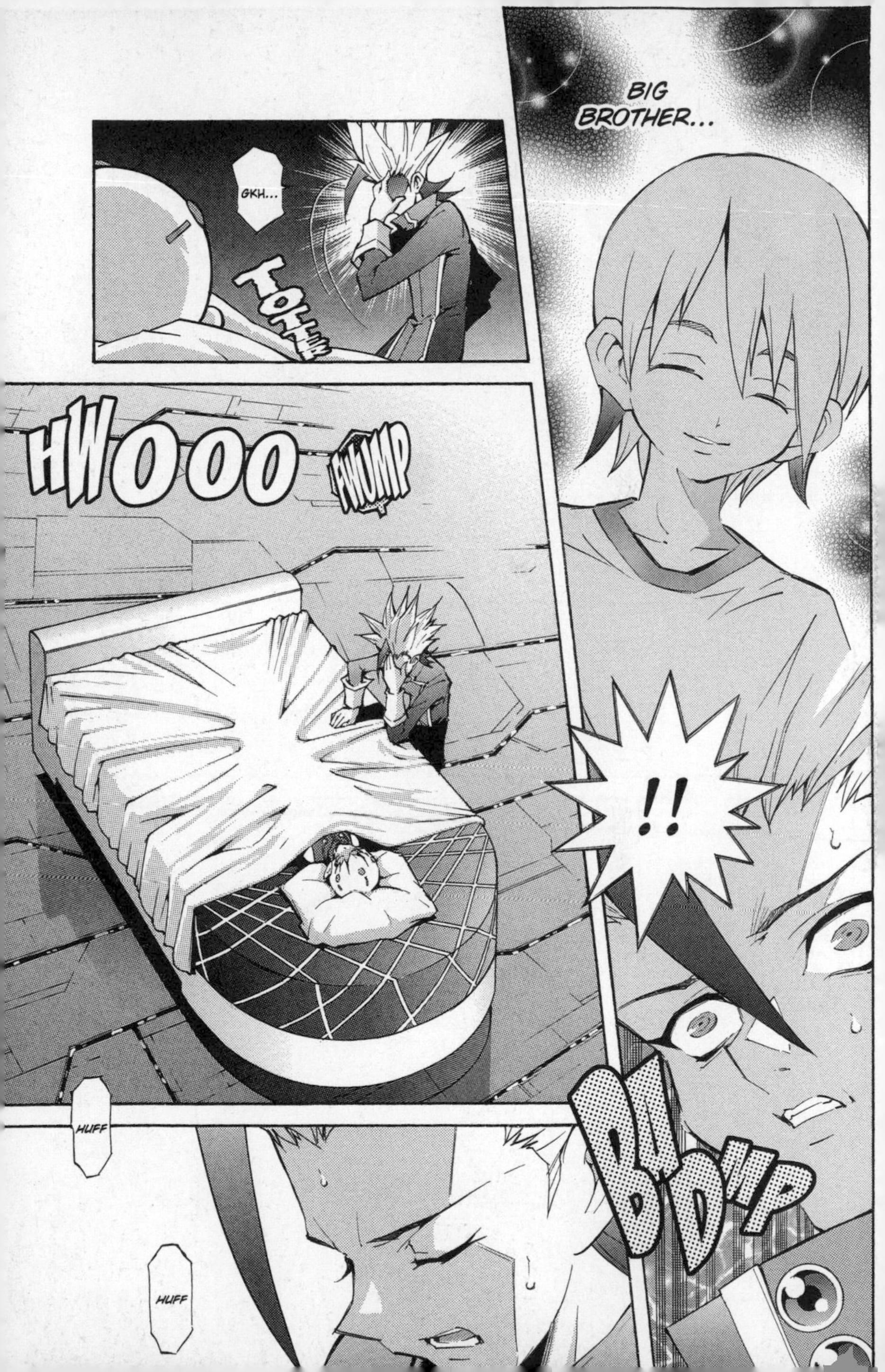
BIG BROTHER...
!!
GKH...
HWOOO
FWUMP
HUFF
HUFF

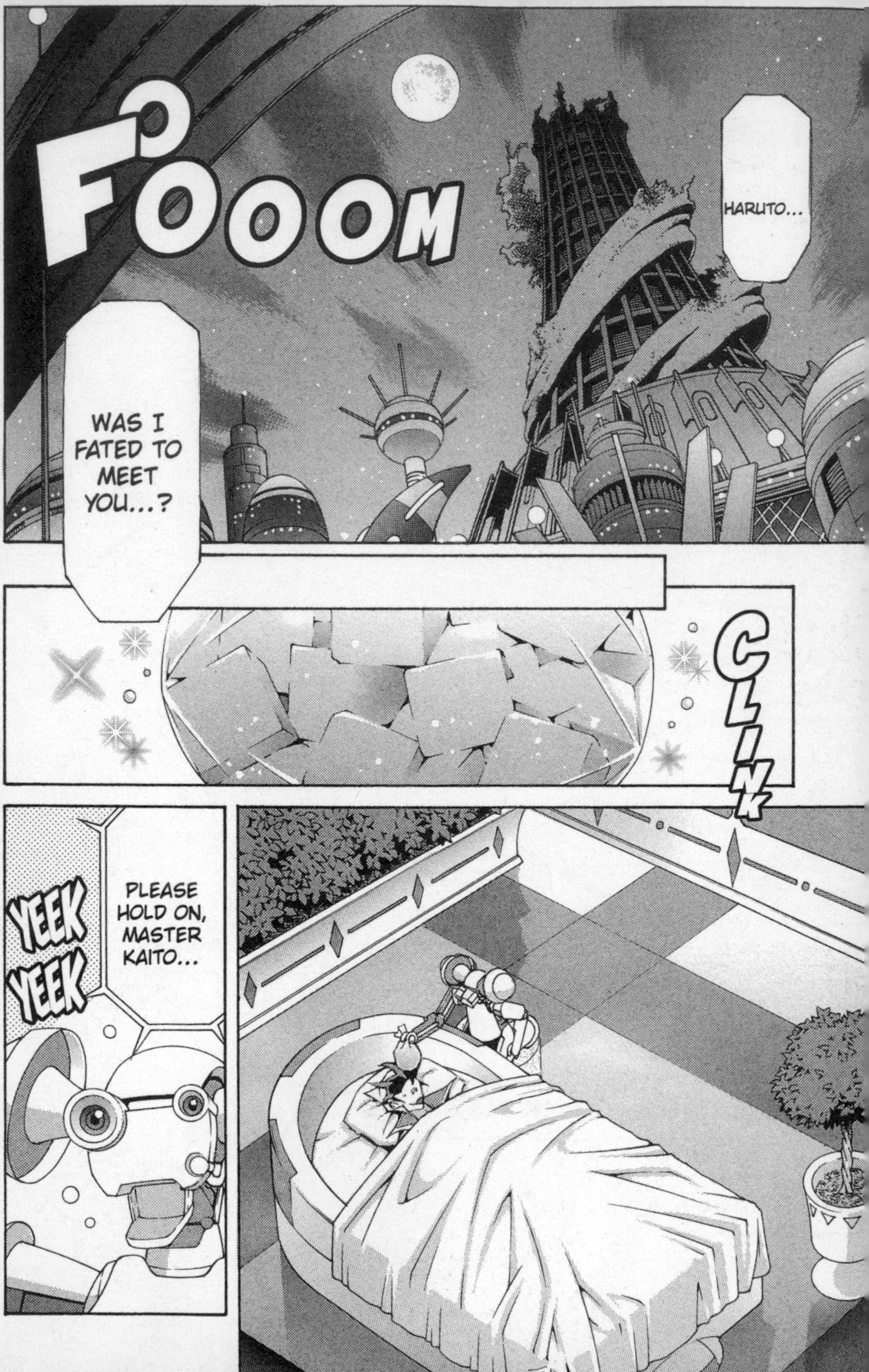
HARUTO...
FOOOM
WAS I FATED TO MEET YOU...?
CLINK
PLEASE HOLD ON, MASTER KAITO...
YEEK YEEK

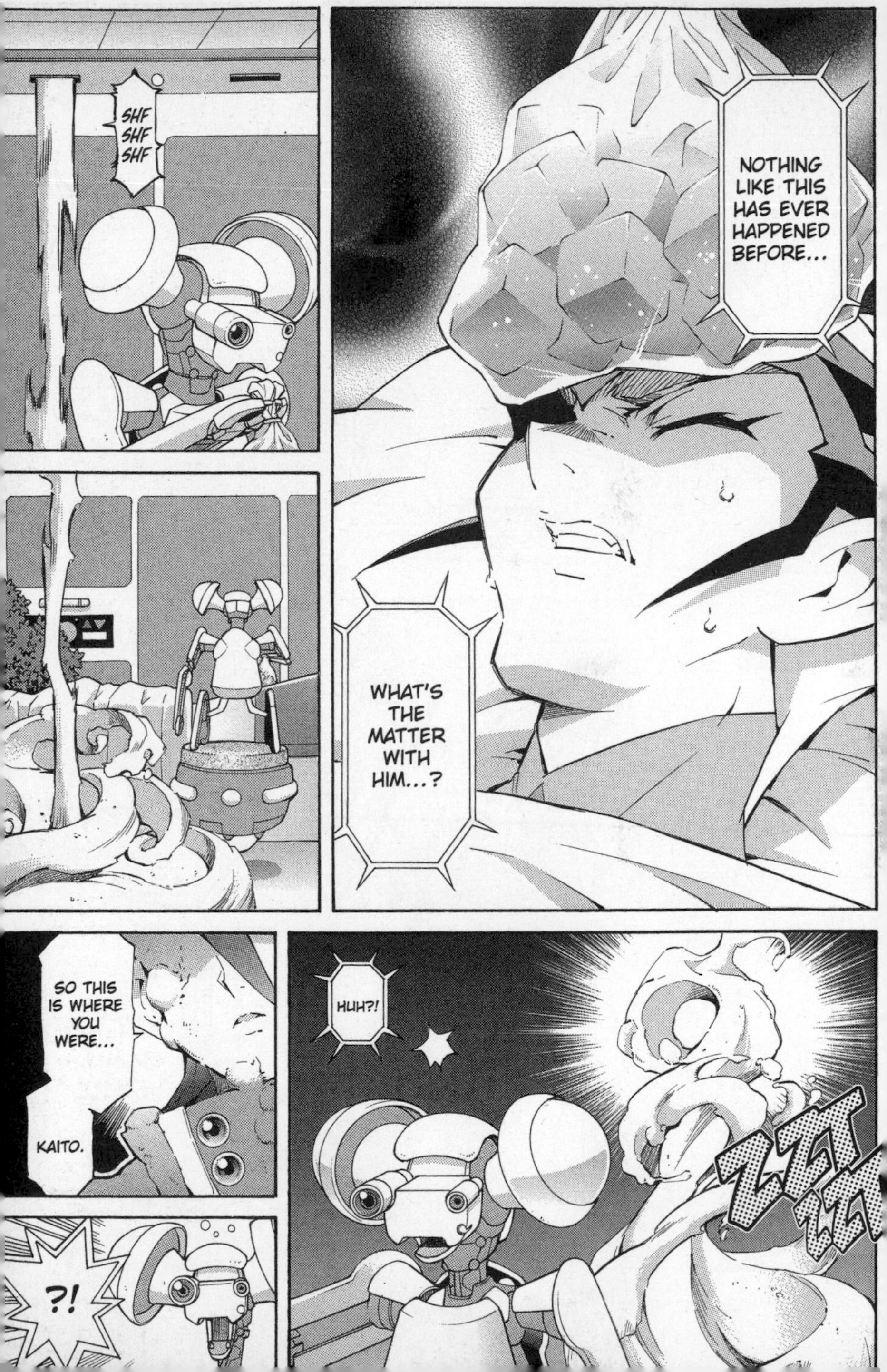
NOTHING LIKE THIS HAS EVER HAPPENED BEFORE...
WHAT'S THE MATTER WITH HIM...?
SHF SHF SHF
HUH?!
SO THIS IS WHERE YOU WERE...
KAITO.
?!

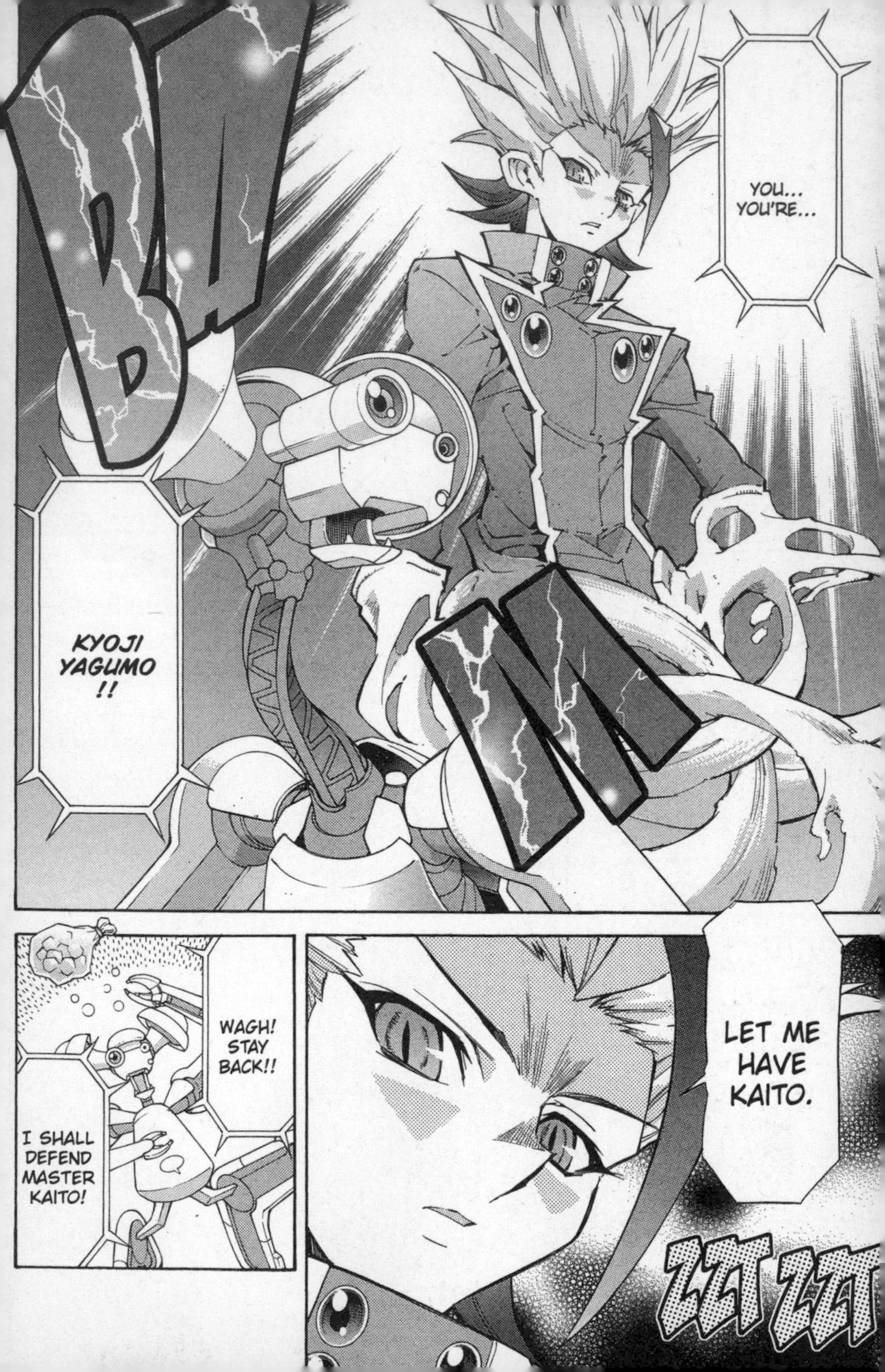
YOU... YOU'RE...
BAM
KYOJI YAGUMO!!
LET ME HAVE KAITO.
ZZT ZZT
WAGH! STAY BACK!!
I SHALL DEFEND MASTER KAITO!

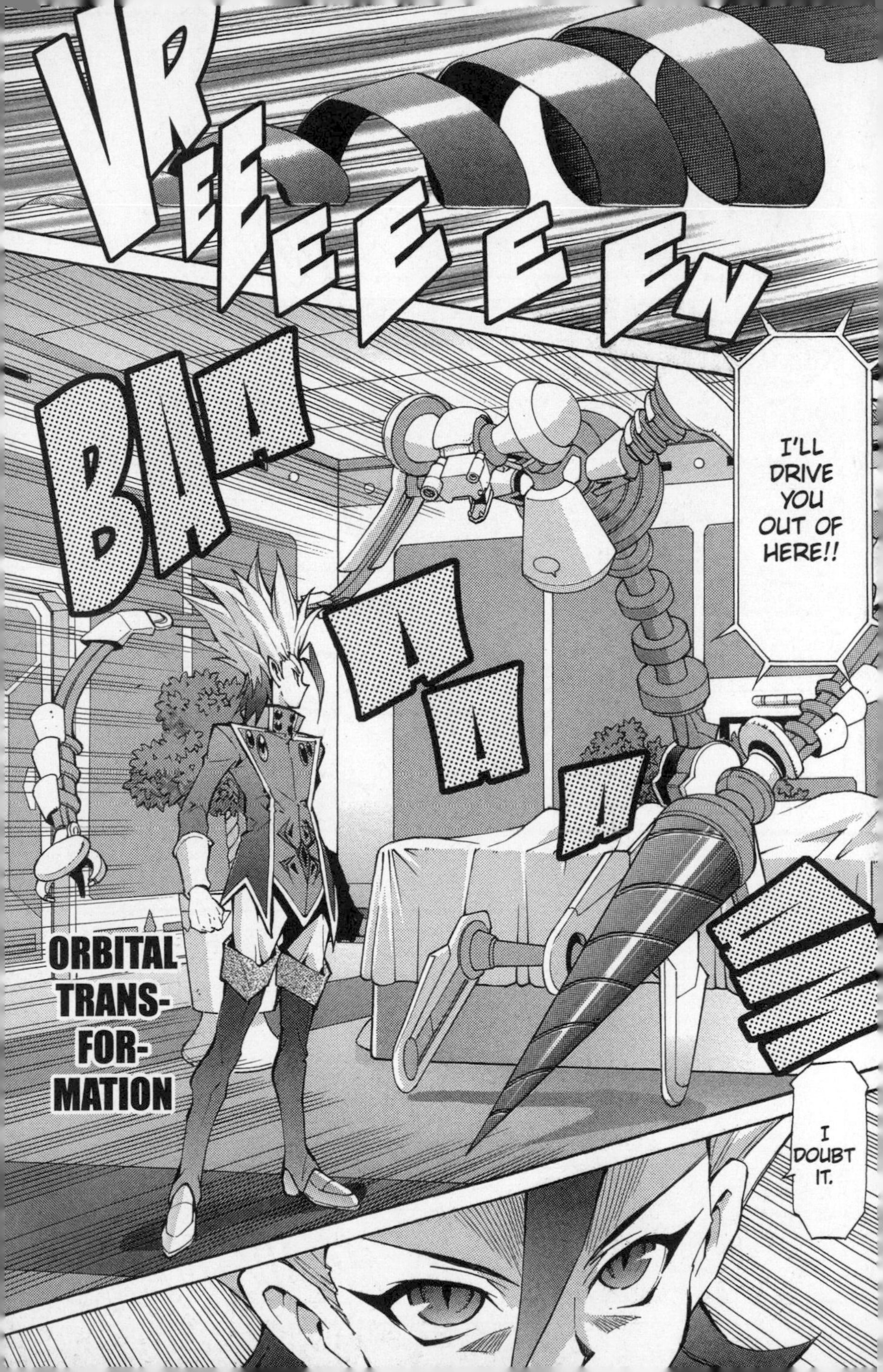
VREEEEEEN
I'LL DRIVE YOU OUT OF HERE!!
BAAAA
ORBITAL TRANS- FOR- MATION
I DOUBT IT.

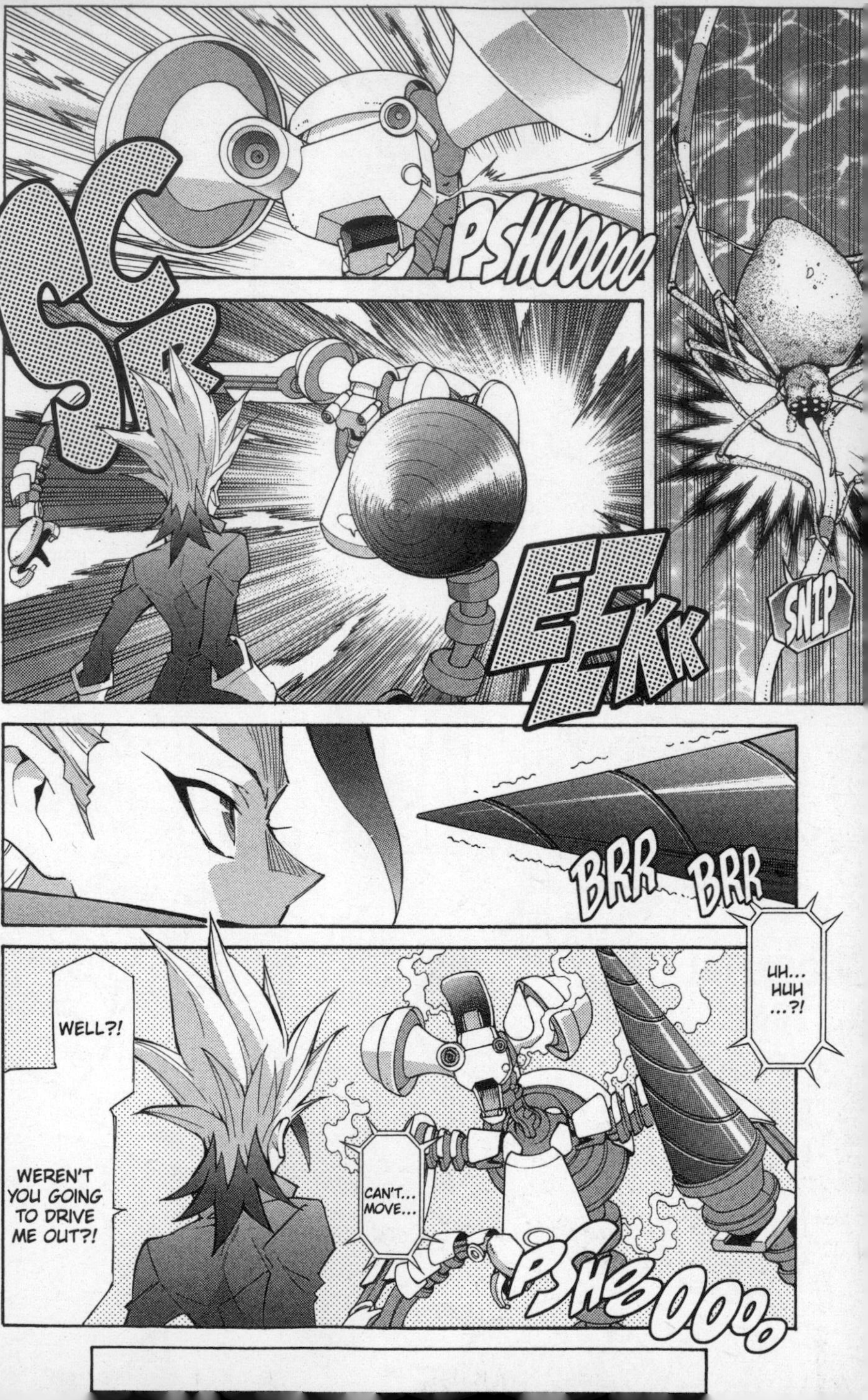
SNIP
PSHOOOOO
EEKK
BRR BRR
UH... HUH ...?!
WELL?!
CAN'T... MOVE...
WEREN'T YOU GOING TO DRIVE ME OUT?!
PSHOOOOO

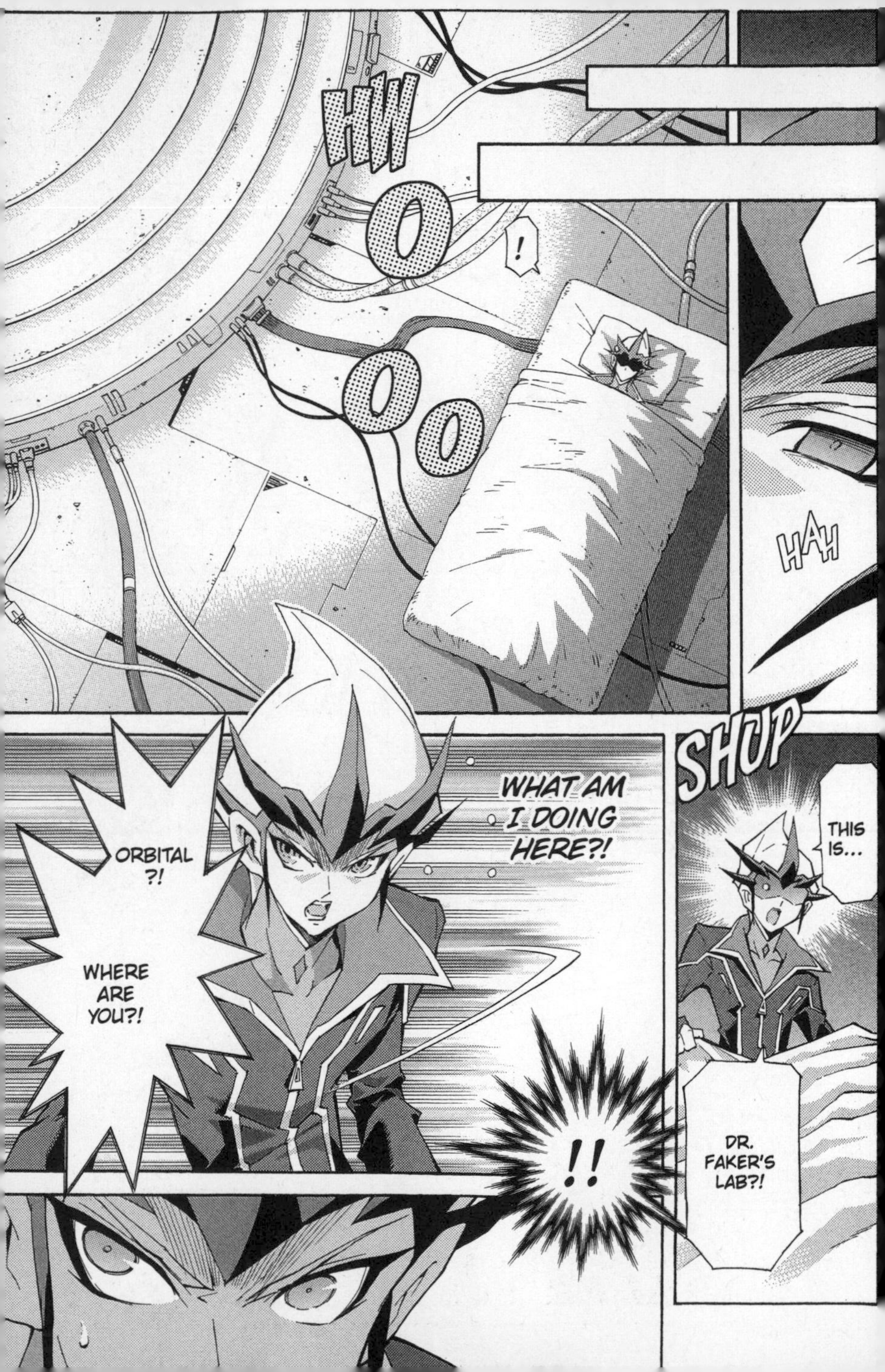
HAH
HWOOOO
!
SHUP
THIS IS...
DR. FAKER'S LAB?!
WHAT AM I DOING HERE?!
ORBITAL ?!
WHERE ARE YOU?!
!!

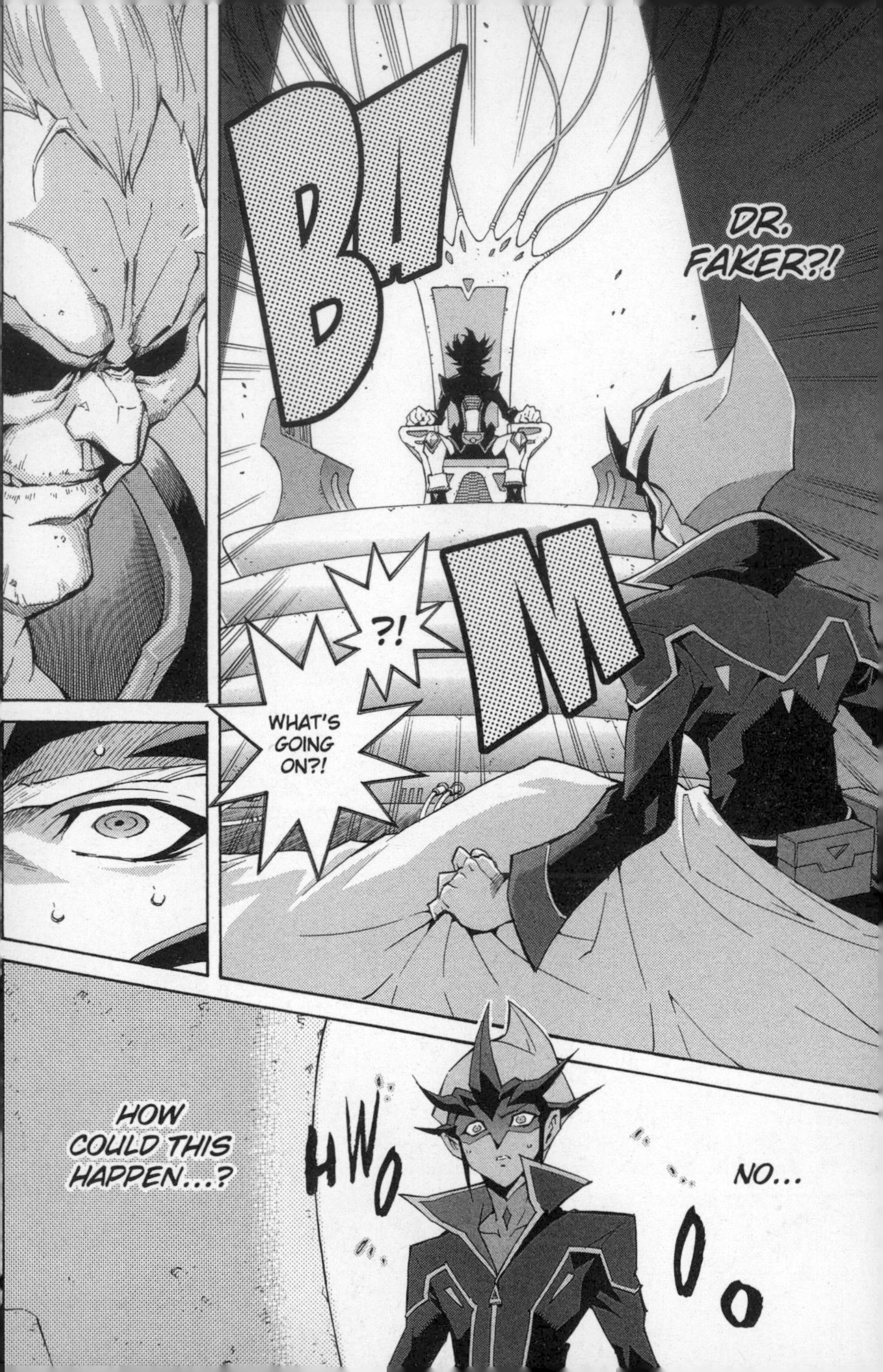
DR. FAKER?!
BAM
?!
WHAT'S GOING ON?!
NO...
HOW COULD THIS HAPPEN...?

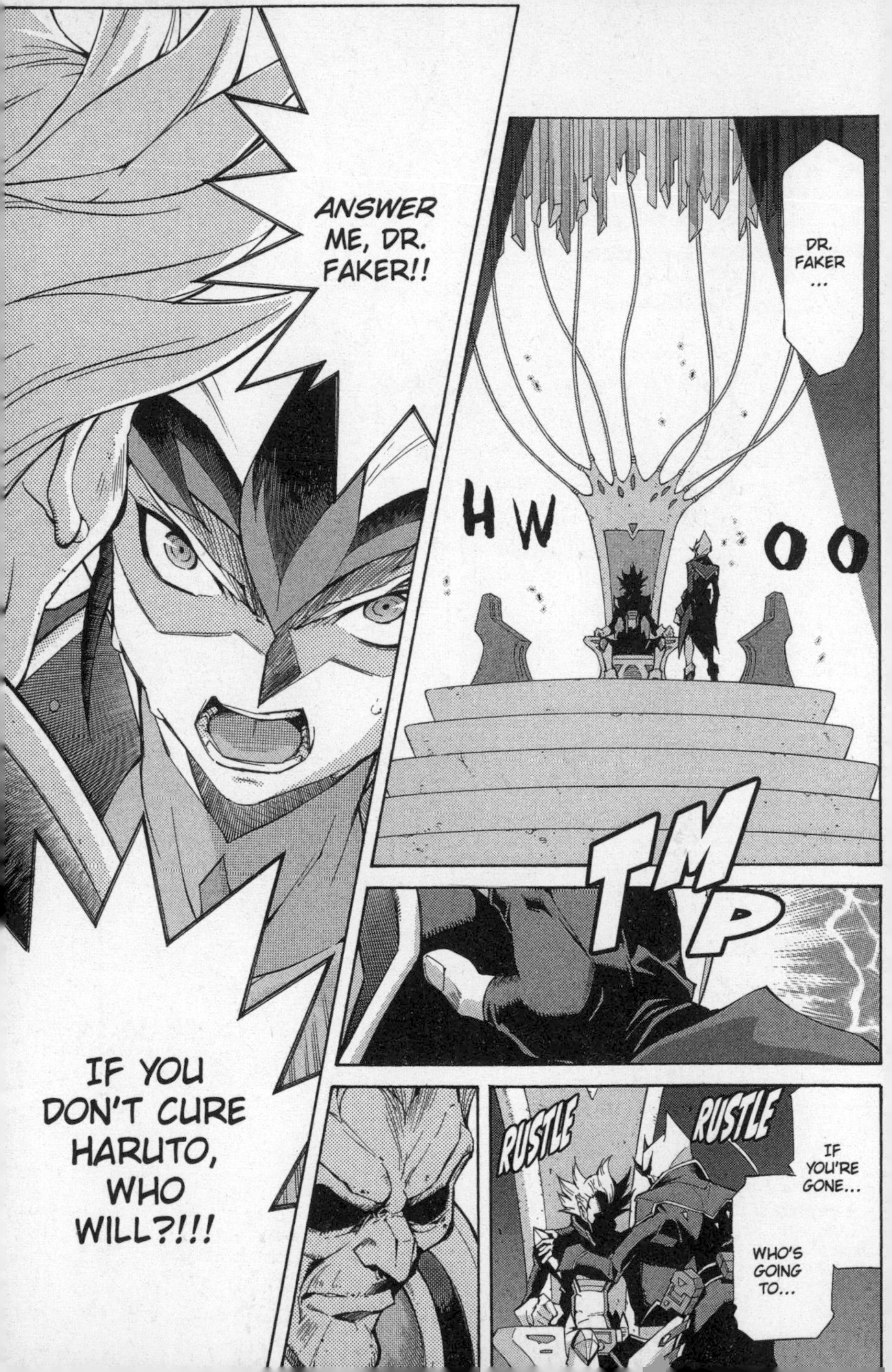
DR. FAKER...
HWOO
TMP
ANSWER ME, DR. FAKER!!
IF YOU DON'T CURE HARUTO, WHO WILL?!!!
RUSTLE
RUSTLE
IF YOU'RE GONE...
WHO'S GOING TO...

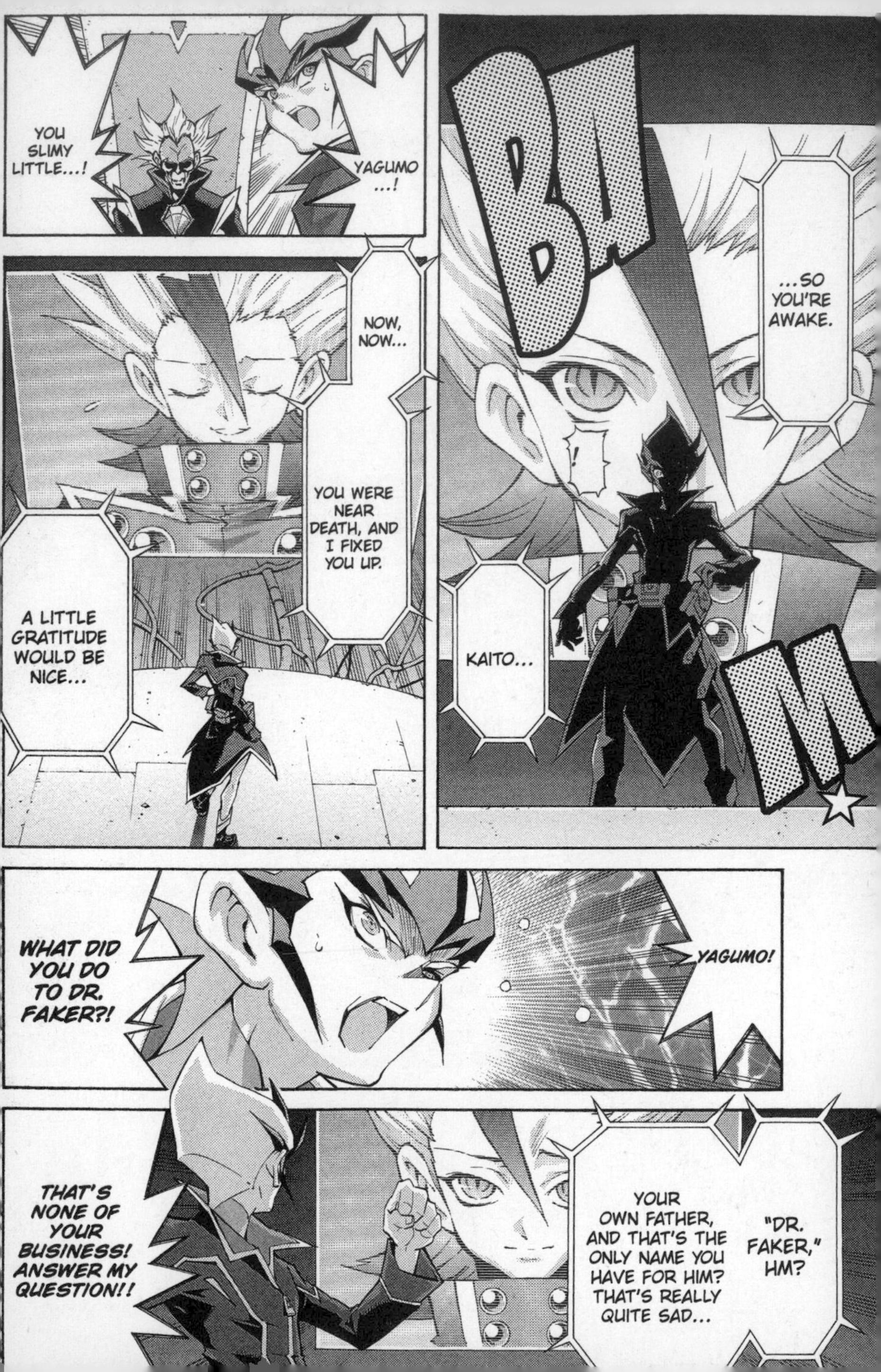
BA
...SO YOU'RE AWAKE.
!
KAITO...
M
YAGUMO ...!
YOU SLIMY LITTLE...!
NOW, NOW...
YOU WERE NEAR DEATH, AND I FIXED YOU UP.
A LITTLE GRATITUDE WOULD BE NICE...
YAGUMO!
WHAT DID YOU DO TO DR. FAKER?!
"DR. FAKER," HM?
YOUR OWN FATHER, AND THAT'S THE ONLY NAME YOU HAVE FOR HIM? THAT'S REALLY QUITE SAD...
THAT'S NONE OF YOUR BUSINESS! ANSWER MY QUESTION!!

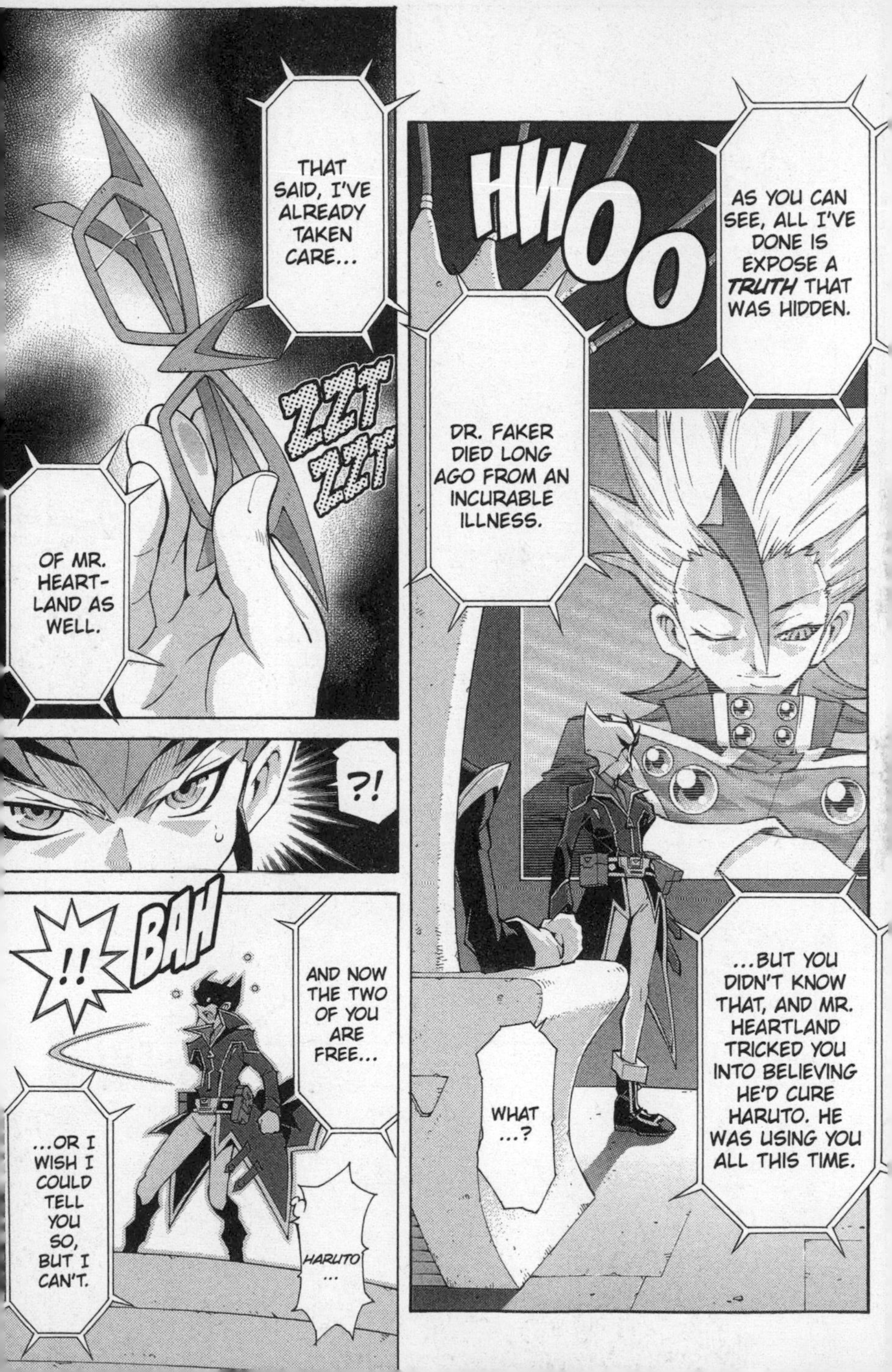
AS YOU CAN SEE, ALL I'VE DONE IS EXPOSE A *TRUTH* THAT WAS HIDDEN.
HWOO
DR. FAKER DIED LONG AGO FROM AN INCURABLE ILLNESS.
...BUT YOU DIDN'T KNOW THAT, AND MR. HEARTLAND TRICKED YOU INTO BELIEVING HE'D CURE HARUTO. HE WAS USING YOU ALL THIS TIME.
WHAT ...?
THAT SAID, I'VE ALREADY TAKEN CARE...
ZZZT ZZZT
OF MR. HEART-LAND AS WELL.
?!
AND NOW THE TWO OF YOU ARE FREE...
BAH
!!
...OR I WISH I COULD TELL YOU SO, BUT I CAN'T.
HARUTO ...

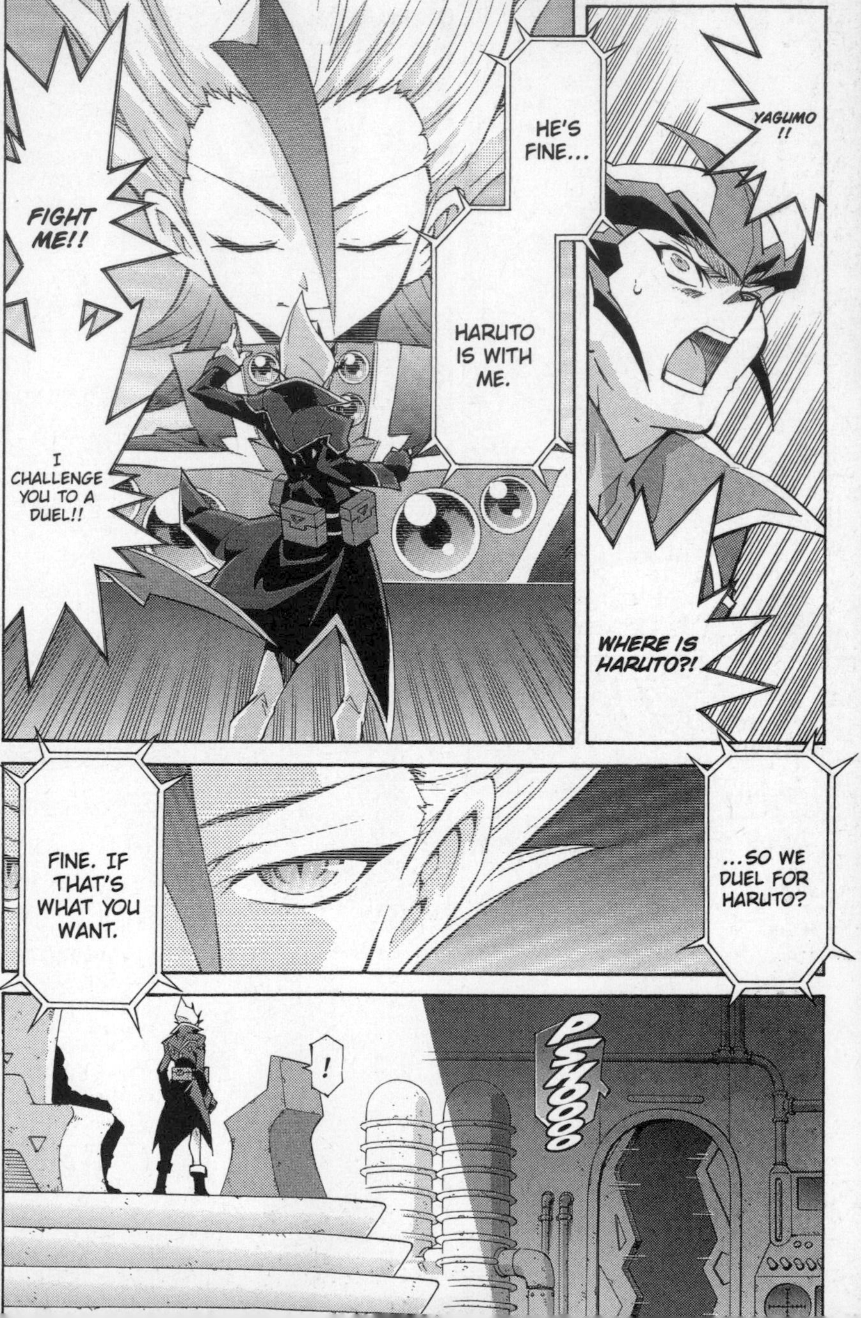
YAGUMO!!
WHERE IS HARUTO?!
HE'S FINE...
HARUTO IS WITH ME.
FIGHT ME!!
I CHALLENGE YOU TO A DUEL!!
...SO WE DUEL FOR HARUTO?
FINE. IF THAT'S WHAT YOU WANT.
PSHOOOO
!

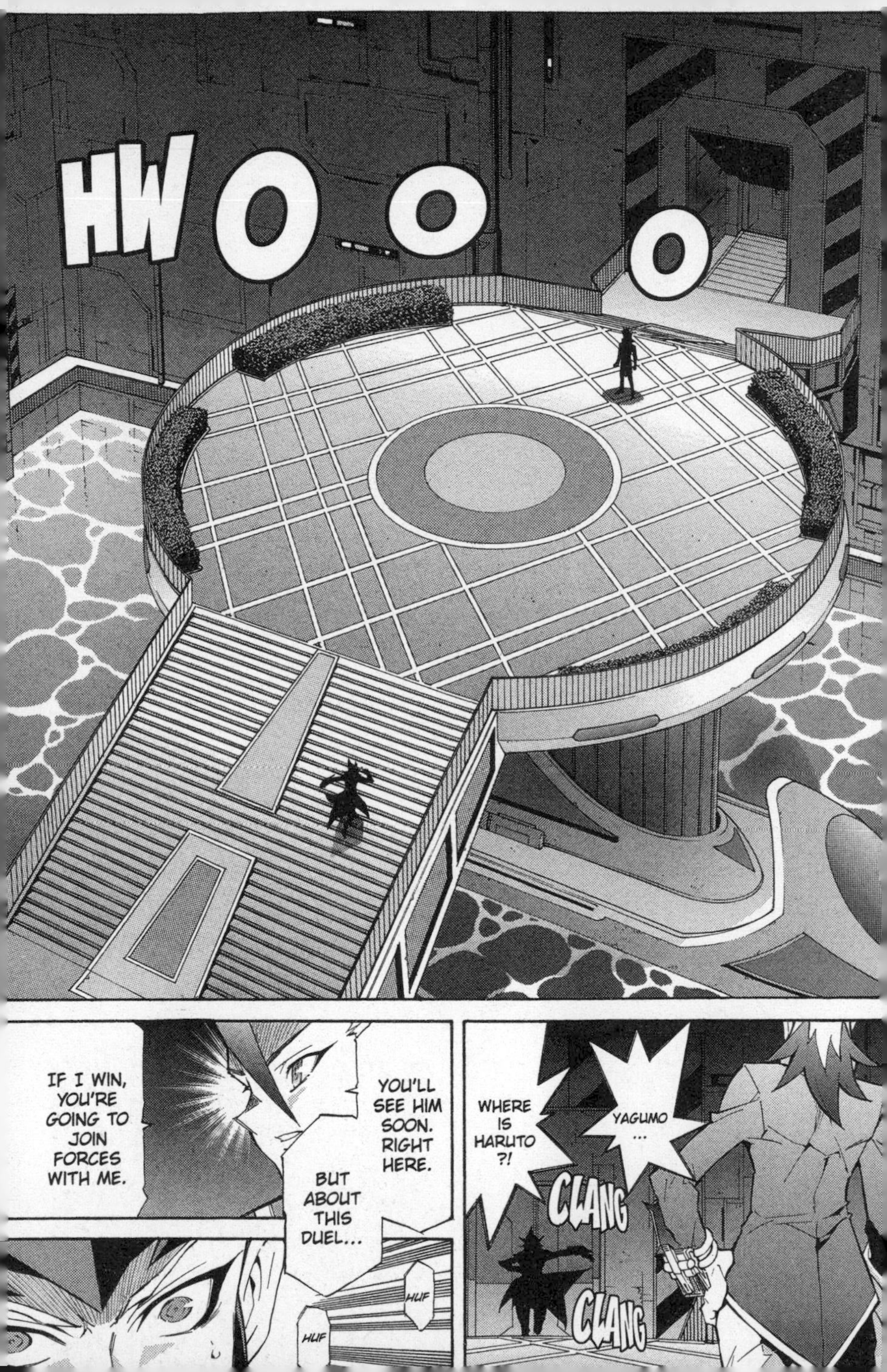
HWOOOO
YAGUMO...
WHERE IS HARUTO?!
CLANG
CLANG
YOU'LL SEE HIM SOON. RIGHT HERE.
BUT ABOUT THIS DUEL...
IF I WIN, YOU'RE GOING TO JOIN FORCES WITH ME.
HUF
HUF

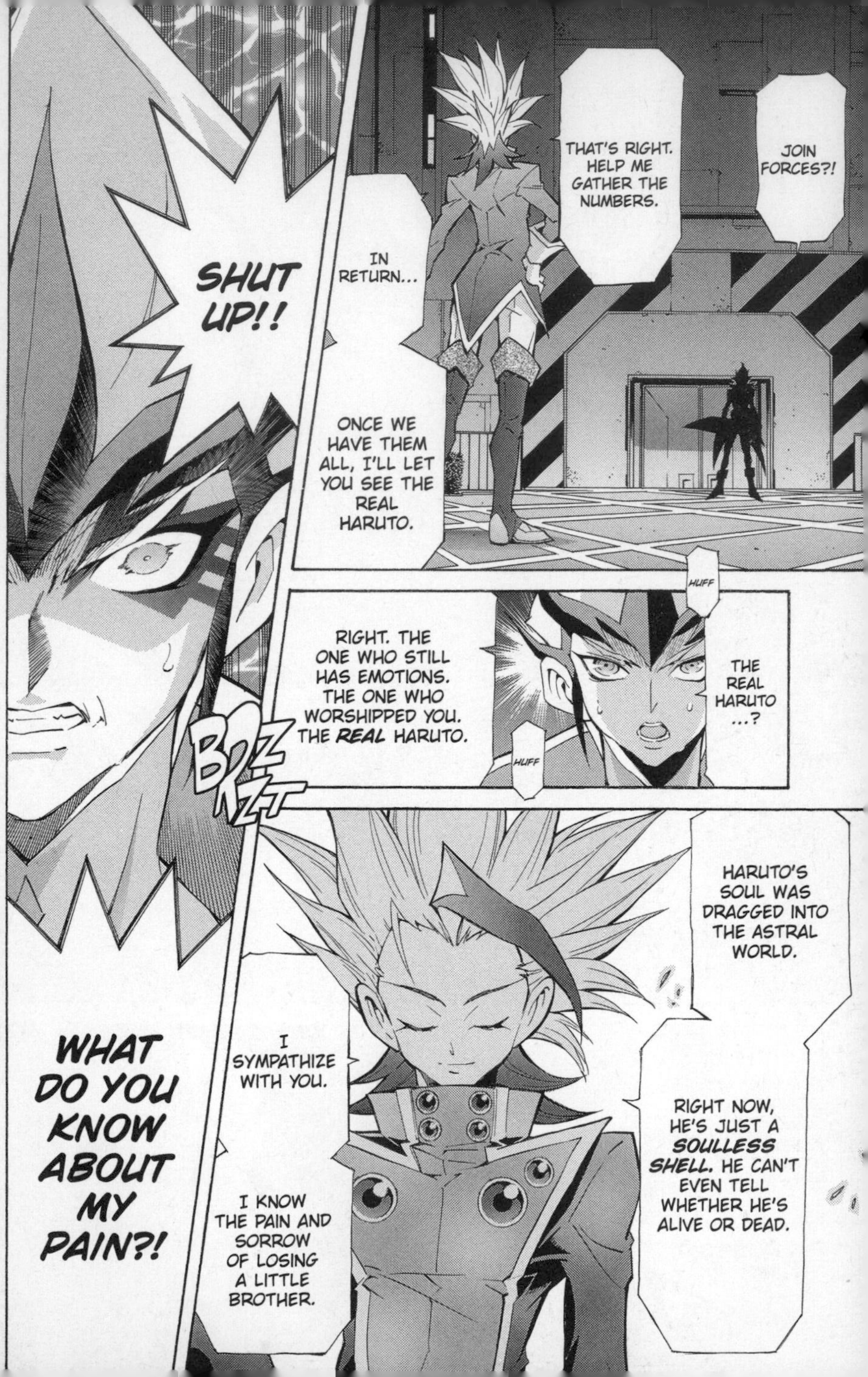
JOIN FORCES?!
THAT'S RIGHT. HELP ME GATHER THE NUMBERS.
IN RETURN...
ONCE WE HAVE THEM ALL, I'LL LET YOU SEE THE REAL HARUTO.
HUFF
THE REAL HARUTO ...?
HUFF
RIGHT. THE ONE WHO STILL HAS EMOTIONS. THE ONE WHO WORSHIPPED YOU. THE *REAL* HARUTO.
HARUTO'S SOUL WAS DRAGGED INTO THE ASTRAL WORLD.
RIGHT NOW, HE'S JUST A ***SOULLESS SHELL.*** HE CAN'T EVEN TELL WHETHER HE'S ALIVE OR DEAD.
I SYMPATHIZE WITH YOU.
I KNOW THE PAIN AND SORROW OF LOSING A LITTLE BROTHER.
SHUT UP!!
BZZ BRZZT
WHAT DO YOU KNOW ABOUT MY PAIN?!

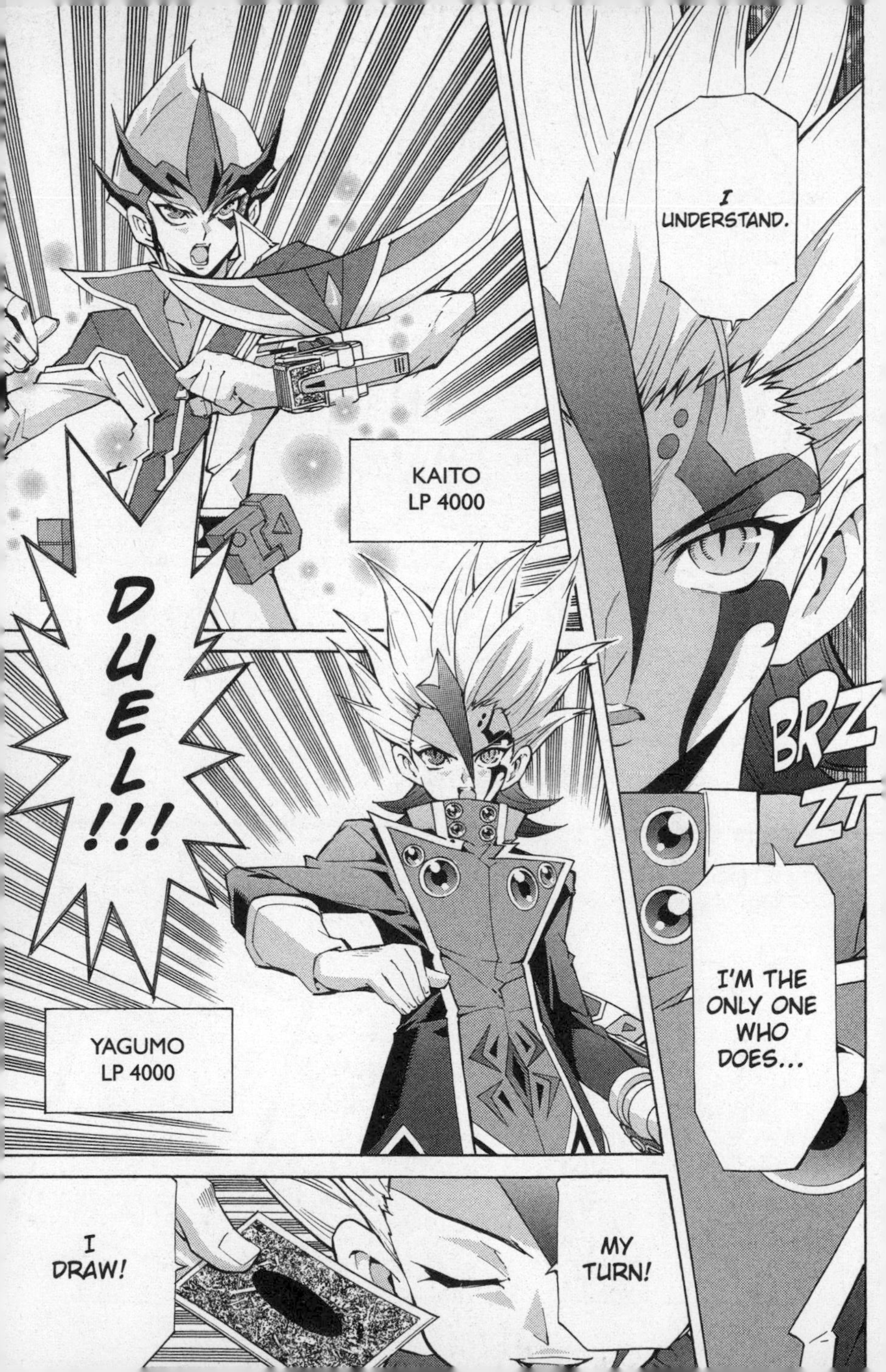
I UNDERSTAND.
BRZZT
I'M THE ONLY ONE WHO DOES...
KAITO LP 4000
DUEL!!!
YAGUMO LP 4000
MY TURN!
I DRAW!

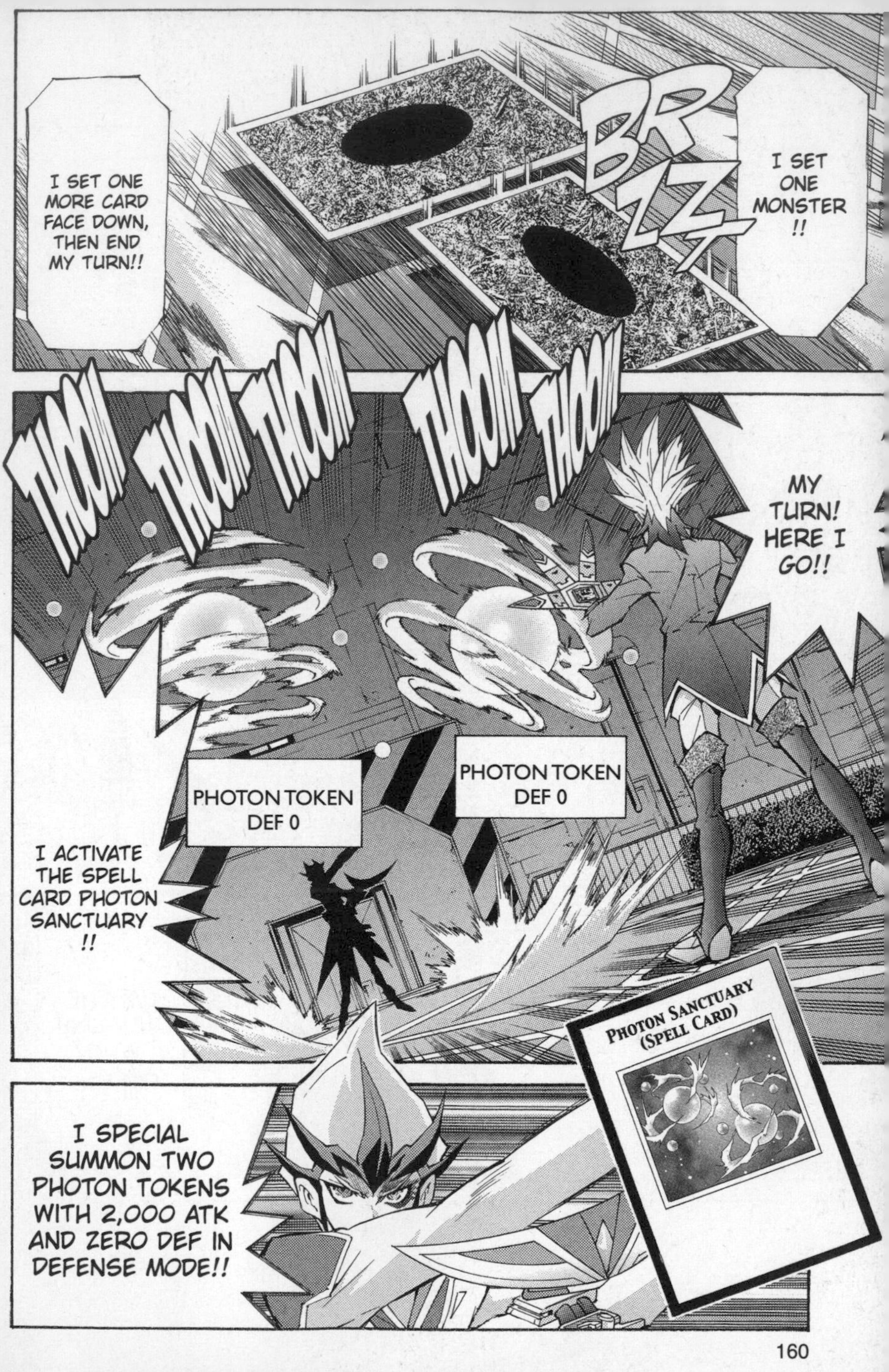
I SET ONE MONSTER!!
BRZZT
I SET ONE MORE CARD FACE DOWN, THEN END MY TURN!!
MY TURN! HERE I GO!!
THOOM
THOOM
THOOM
THOOM
THOOM
PHOTON TOKEN DEF 0
PHOTON TOKEN DEF 0
I ACTIVATE THE SPELL CARD PHOTON SANCTUARY!!
PHOTON SANCTUARY (SPELL CARD)
I SPECIAL SUMMON TWO PHOTON TOKENS WITH 2,000 ATK AND ZERO DEF IN DEFENSE MODE!!

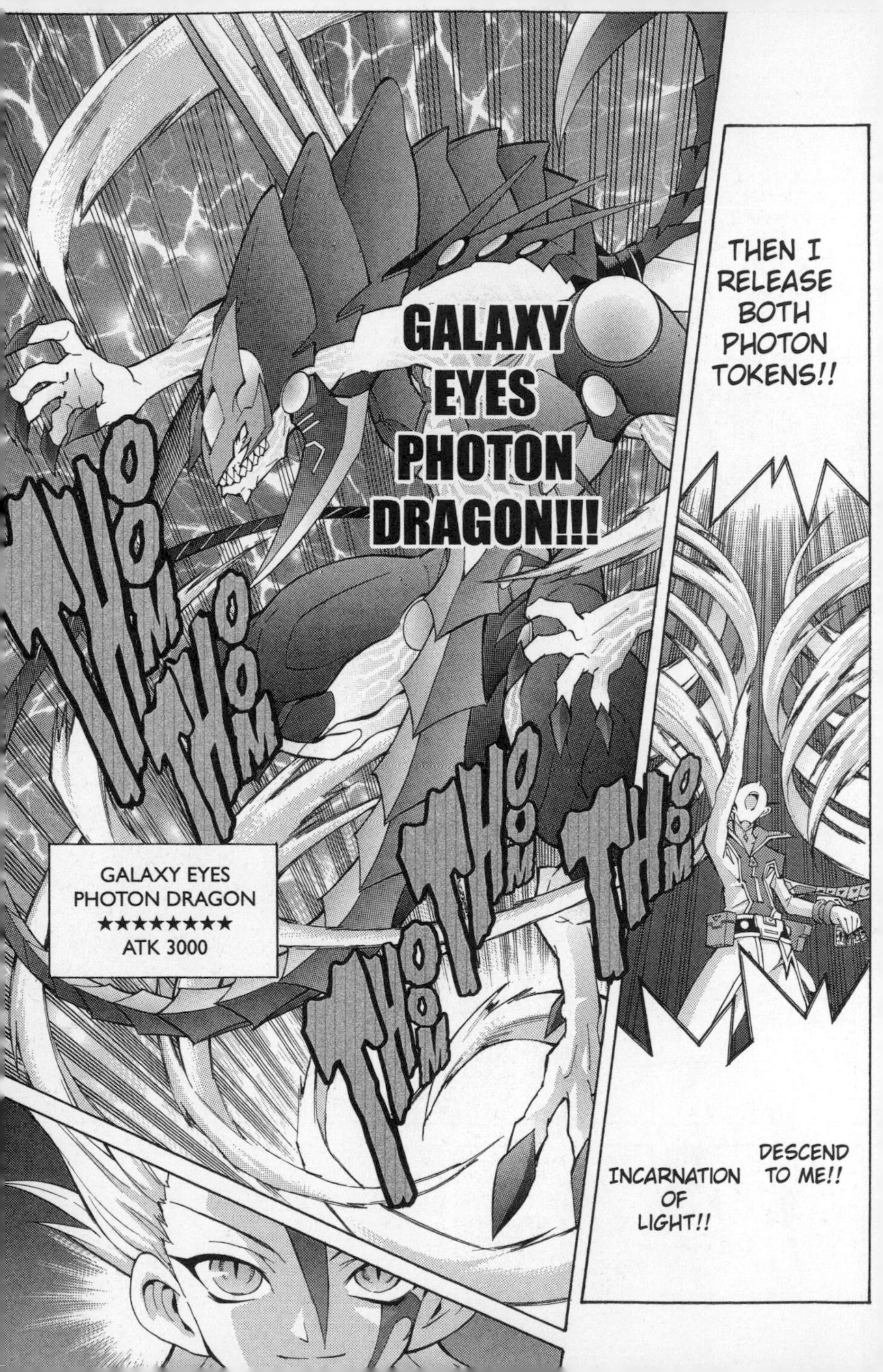
THEN I RELEASE BOTH PHOTON TOKENS!!
DESCEND TO ME!!
INCARNATION OF LIGHT!!
GALAXY EYES PHOTON DRAGON!!!!
THOOM THOOM
THOOM THOOM THOOM
GALAXY EYES PHOTON DRAGON ★★★★★★★★ ATK 3000

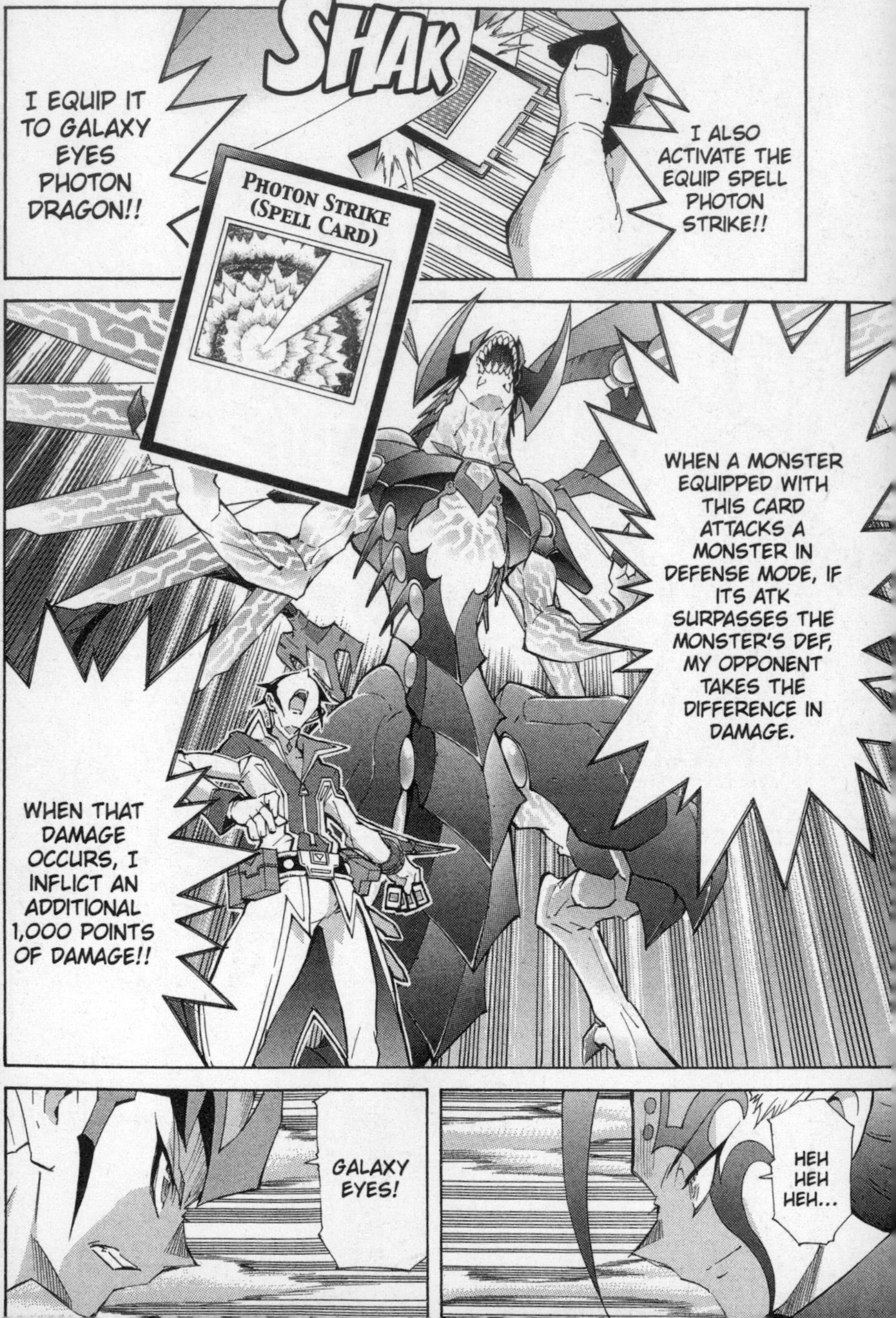
SHAK
I ALSO ACTIVATE THE EQUIP SPELL PHOTON STRIKE!!
I EQUIP IT TO GALAXY EYES PHOTON DRAGON!!
PHOTON STRIKE (SPELL CARD)
WHEN A MONSTER EQUIPPED WITH THIS CARD ATTACKS A MONSTER IN DEFENSE MODE, IF ITS ATK SURPASSES THE MONSTER'S DEF, MY OPPONENT TAKES THE DIFFERENCE IN DAMAGE.
WHEN THAT DAMAGE OCCURS, I INFLICT AN ADDITIONAL 1,000 POINTS OF DAMAGE!!
HEH HEH HEH...
GALAXY EYES!

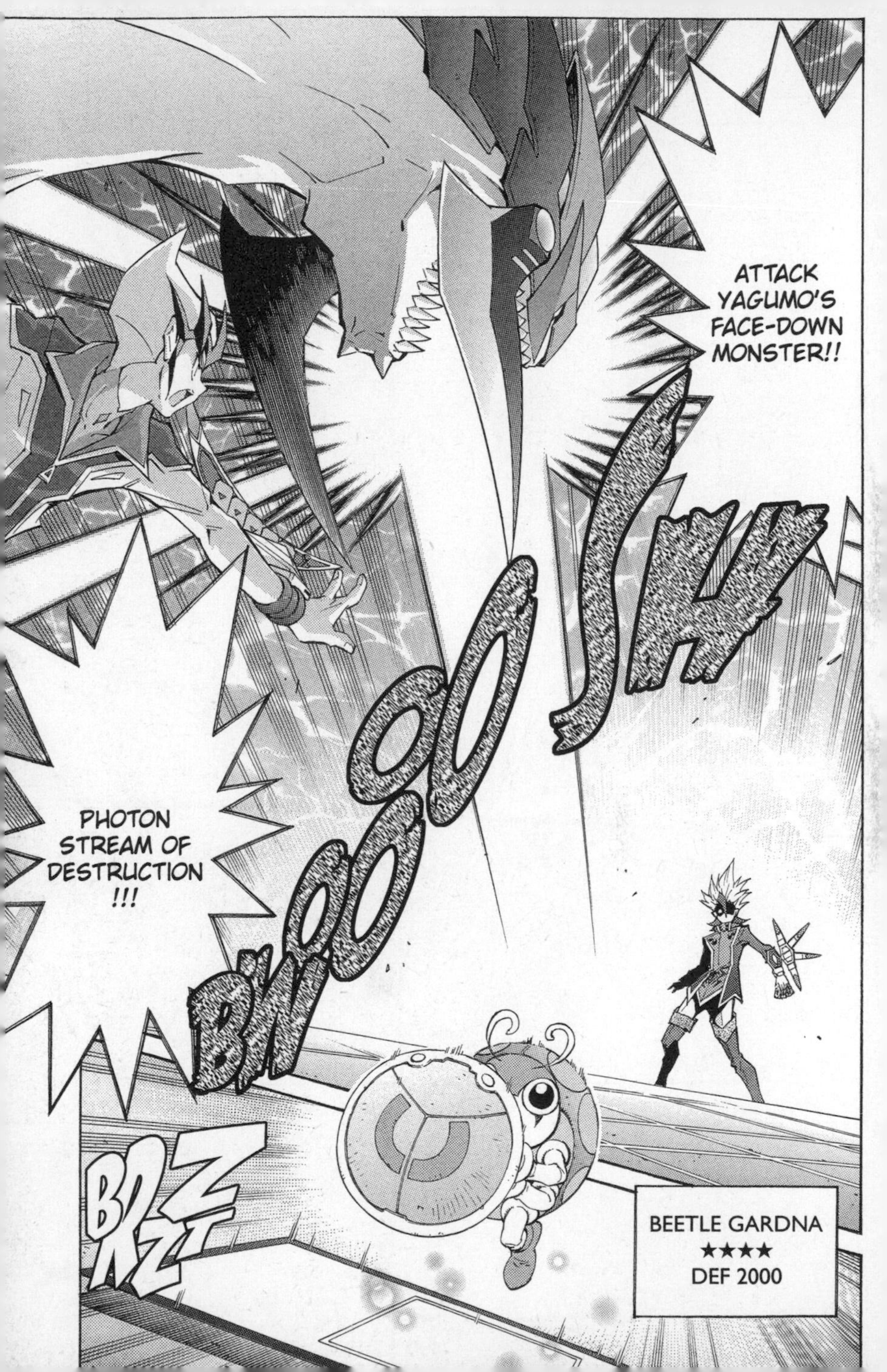
ATTACK YAGUMO'S FACE-DOWN MONSTER!!
PHOTON STREAM OF DESTRUCTION !!!
BEETLE GARDNA
★★★★
DEF 2000

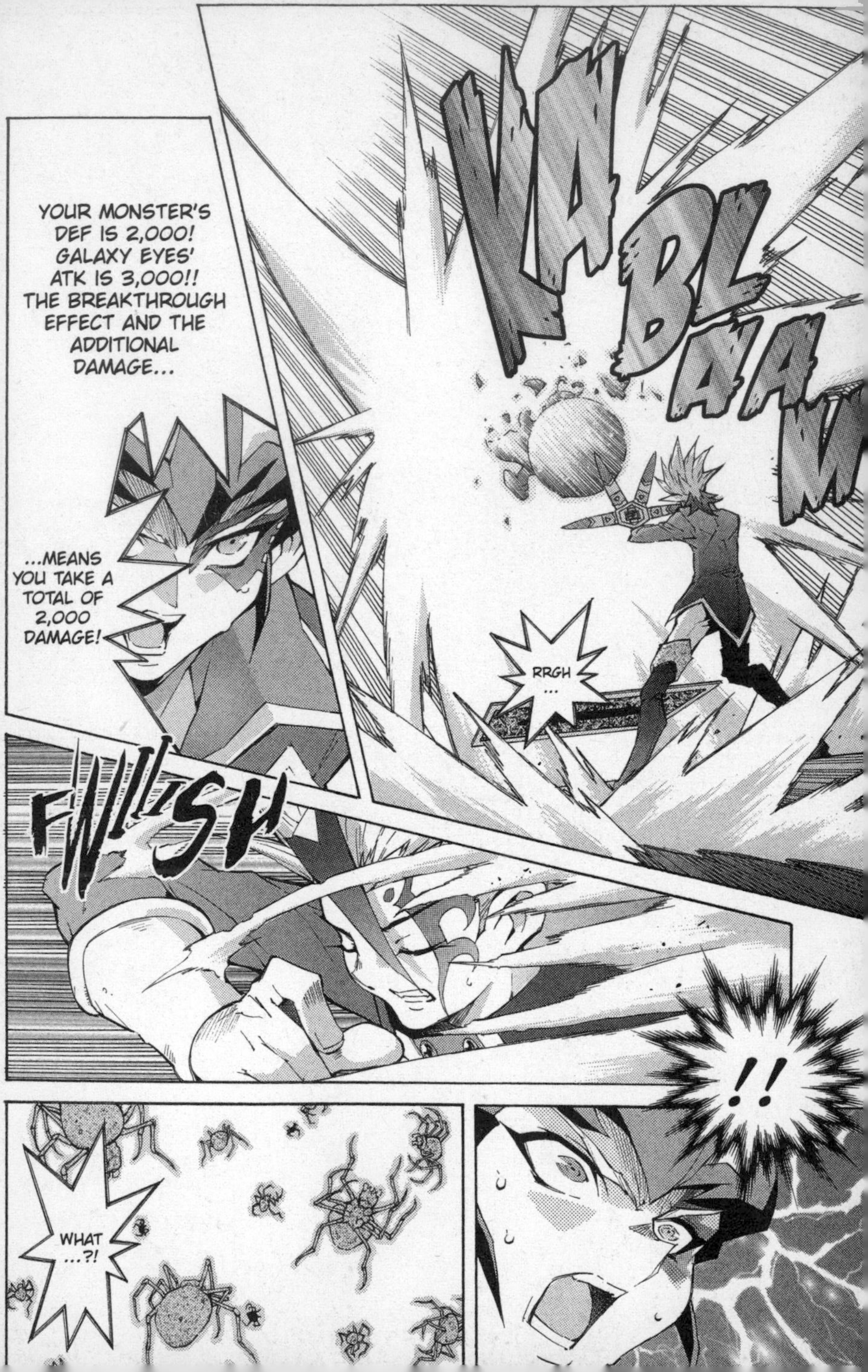
RRGH ...
YOUR MONSTER'S DEF IS 2,000! GALAXY EYES' ATK IS 3,000!! THE BREAKTHROUGH EFFECT AND THE ADDITIONAL DAMAGE...
...MEANS YOU TAKE A TOTAL OF 2,000 DAMAGE!
!!
WHAT ...?!

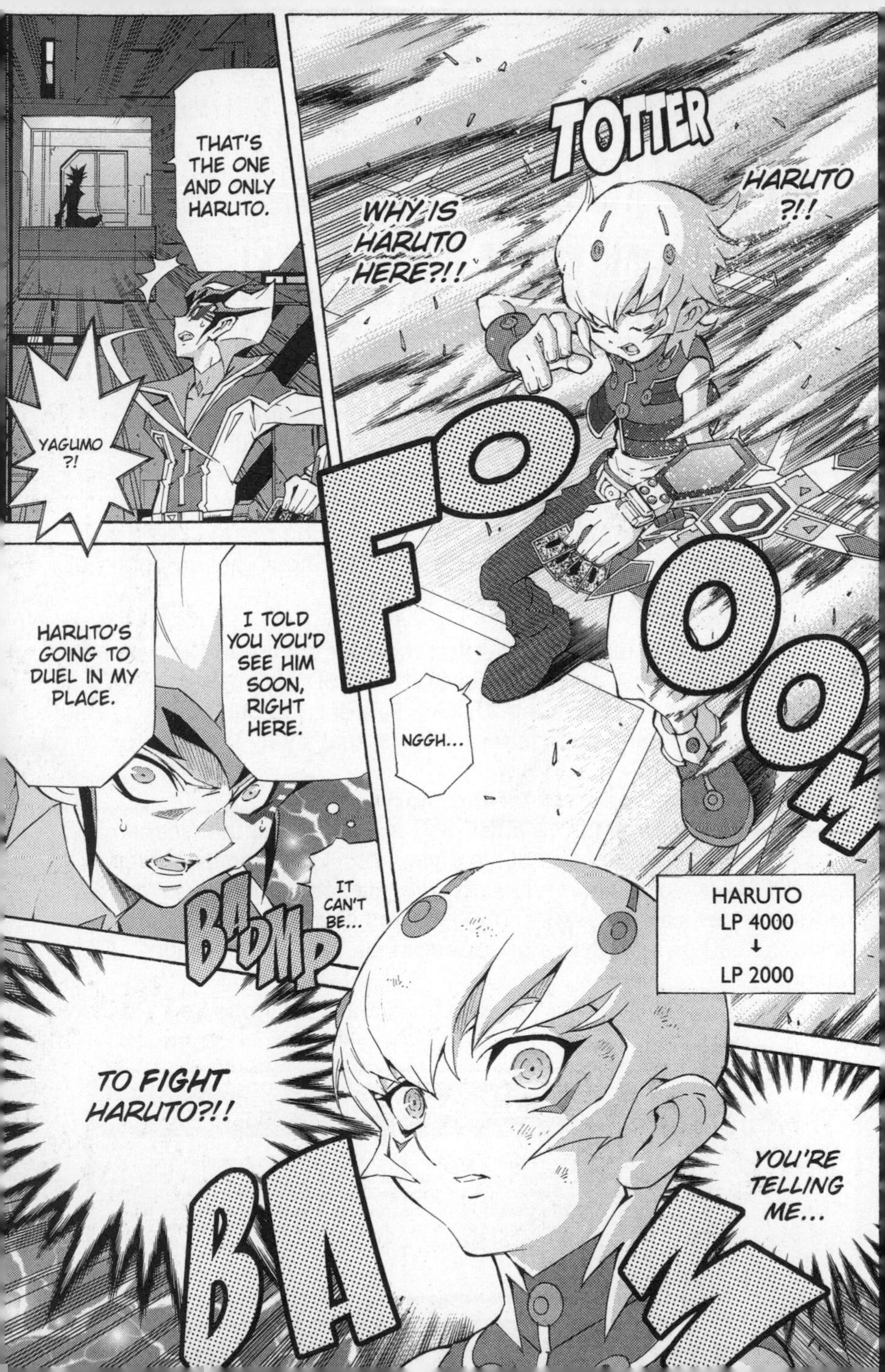
TOTTER
HARUTO ?!!
WHY IS HARUTO HERE?!!
NGGH...
FOOOM
THAT'S THE ONE AND ONLY HARUTO.
YAGUMO ?!
I TOLD YOU YOU'D SEE HIM SOON, RIGHT HERE.
HARUTO'S GOING TO DUEL IN MY PLACE.
IT CAN'T BE...
BADMP
HARUTO LP 4000 ↓ LP 2000
YOU'RE TELLING ME...
TO FIGHT HARUTO?!!
BAM

◎ SERIES COMPOSITION FOR THE ZEXAL ANIME

◎ THE AUTHOR OF THE ZEXAL MANGA

THE SAKE FLOWS... THE STORY PROGRESSES...

SHIN YOSHIDA SPEAKS:

BEHIND THE SCENES ON ZEXAL

* The difference between the manga and the anime

This is my first time working on a project that started with the manga, and it's really tough. The manga only comes out once a month, so the story is difficult to keep moving. In Yu-Gi-Oh!, when there's a duel, the story stops, but without duels, it isn't Yu-Gi-Oh! Since the manga has these two conflicting elements, I work to keep the plot moving even during a duel. The anime's the same way, though…

*Creating duels

I wrack my brains thinking, "I gave that monster such-and-such an effect. How am I going to defeat it next month?!" The 5D's manga is full of hard-core duels, so I try to keep ZEXAL different. I'm particularly careful about duel themes and atmosphere. Maybe that's why the card text is so rough. (Sorry…)

* What he pays attention to for the story

Miyoshi Sensei is an amazing artist, so I try hard to include scenes and ideas that will make the most of his style. I don't think anyone except Miyoshi Sensei would cheerfully draw difficult scenes like Galaxy Eyes cracking under water pressure. (lol) He likes it when the Numbers Club shows up, so I give them lots of appearances to keep him happy. Just kidding! (lol)

Yu-Gi-Oh! ZEXAL is building toward its climax, so I hope you'll stick with us!

A MESSAGE FROM MIYOSHI SENSEI!

You work on series composition for the anime while writing the manga whenever you get the chance. Even though you're incredibly busy, you manage to give it that special Yoshida touch, so you're awesome! And it really does make me happy when you bring out the Numbers Club! (lol)

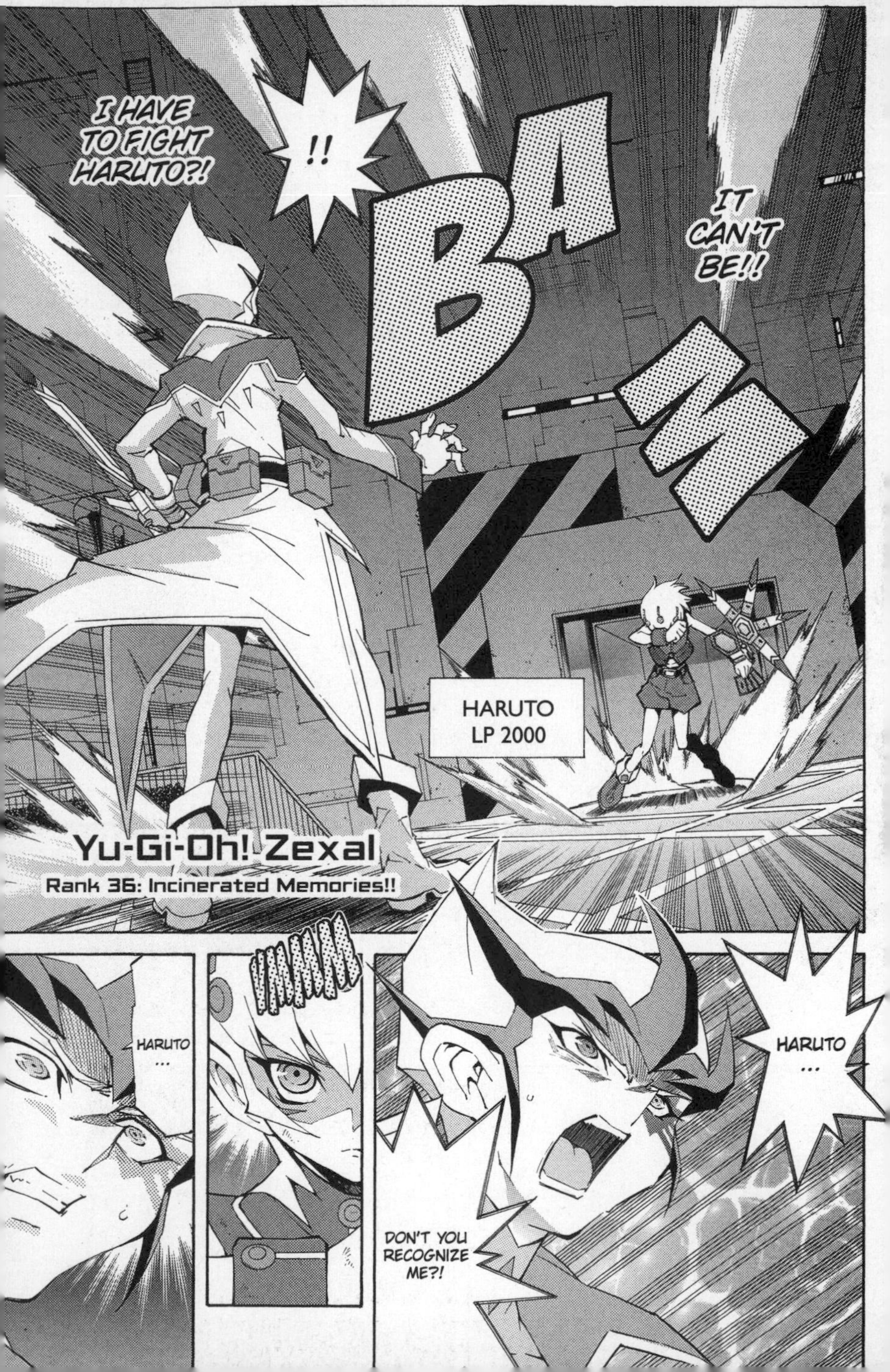
IT CAN'T BE!!
BAM
!!
I HAVE TO FIGHT HARUTO?!
HARUTO LP 2000
Yu-Gi-Oh! Zexal
Rank 36: Incinerated Memories!!
HARUTO ...
DON'T YOU RECOGNIZE ME?!
VMMM
HARUTO ...

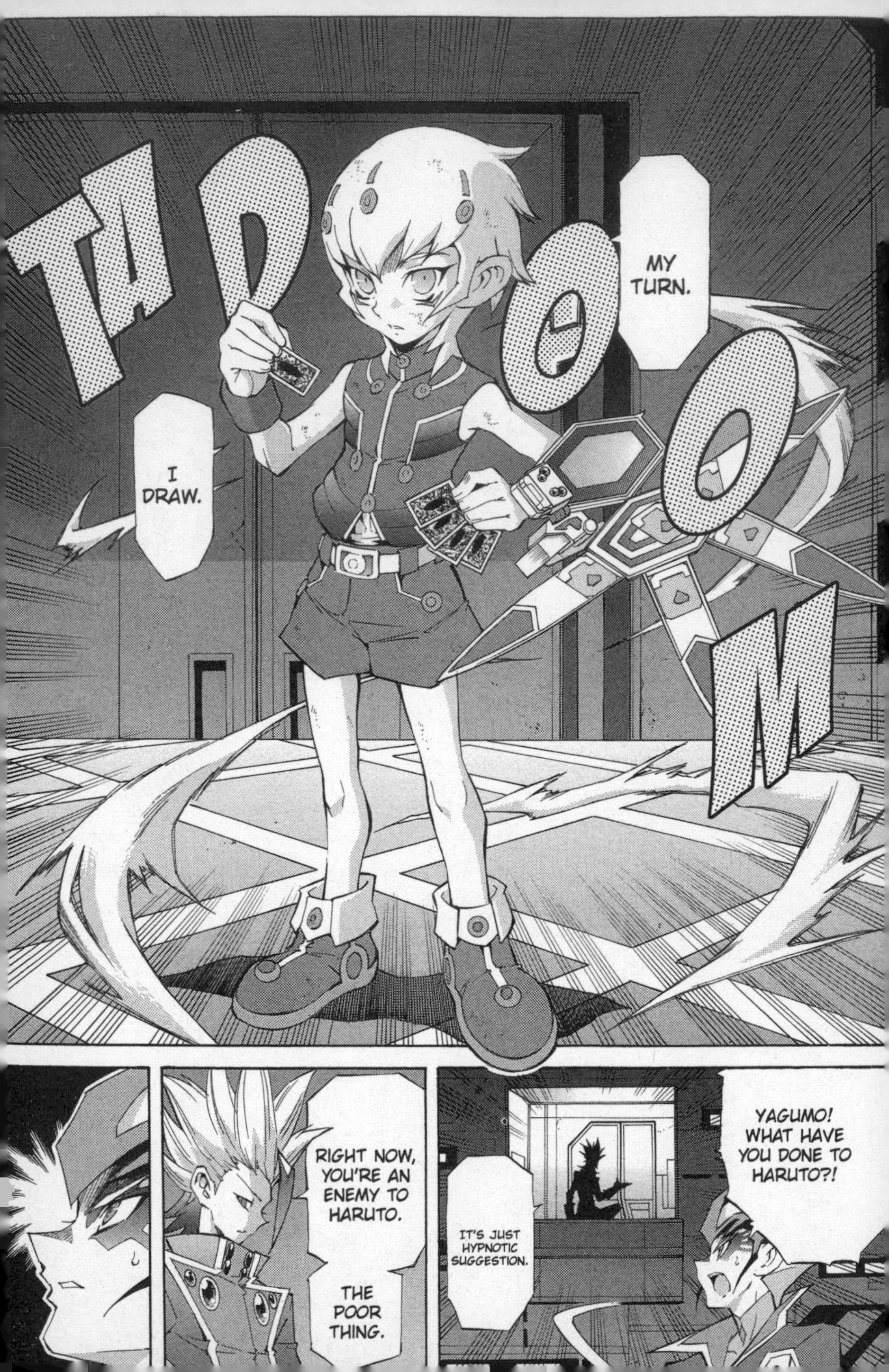
MY TURN.
TADOOOM
I DRAW.
YAGUMO! WHAT HAVE YOU DONE TO HARUTO?!
IT'S JUST HYPNOTIC SUGGESTION.
RIGHT NOW, YOU'RE AN ENEMY TO HARUTO.
THE POOR THING.

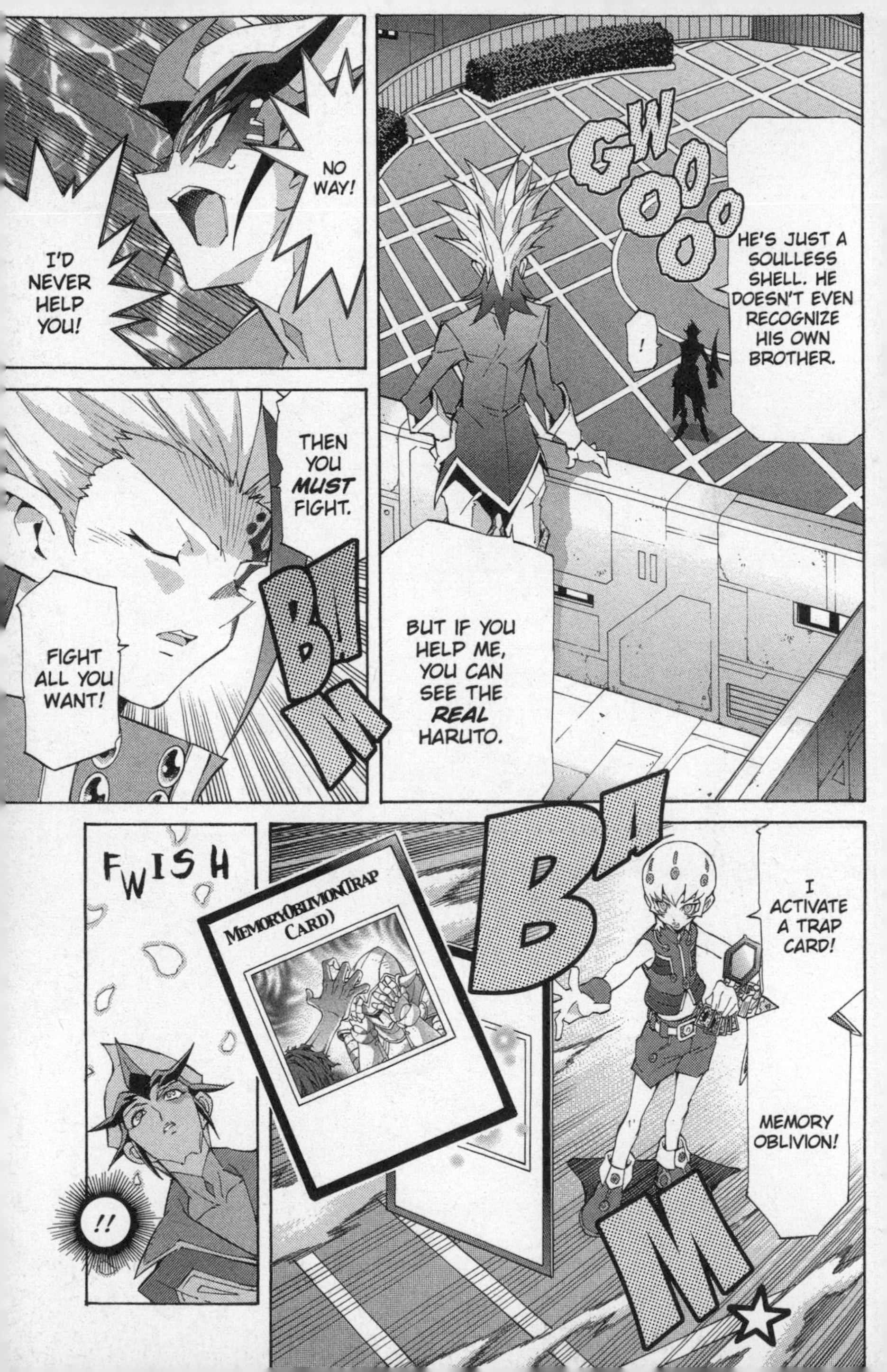
GWOOOOO
HE'S JUST A SOULLESS SHELL. HE DOESN'T EVEN RECOGNIZE HIS OWN BROTHER.
!
BUT IF YOU HELP ME, YOU CAN SEE THE REAL HARUTO.
NO WAY!
I'D NEVER HELP YOU!
THEN YOU MUST FIGHT.
BAM
FIGHT ALL YOU WANT!
I ACTIVATE A TRAP CARD!
MEMORY OBLIVION!
BAM
MEMORY OBLIVION (TRAP CARD)
FWISH
!!

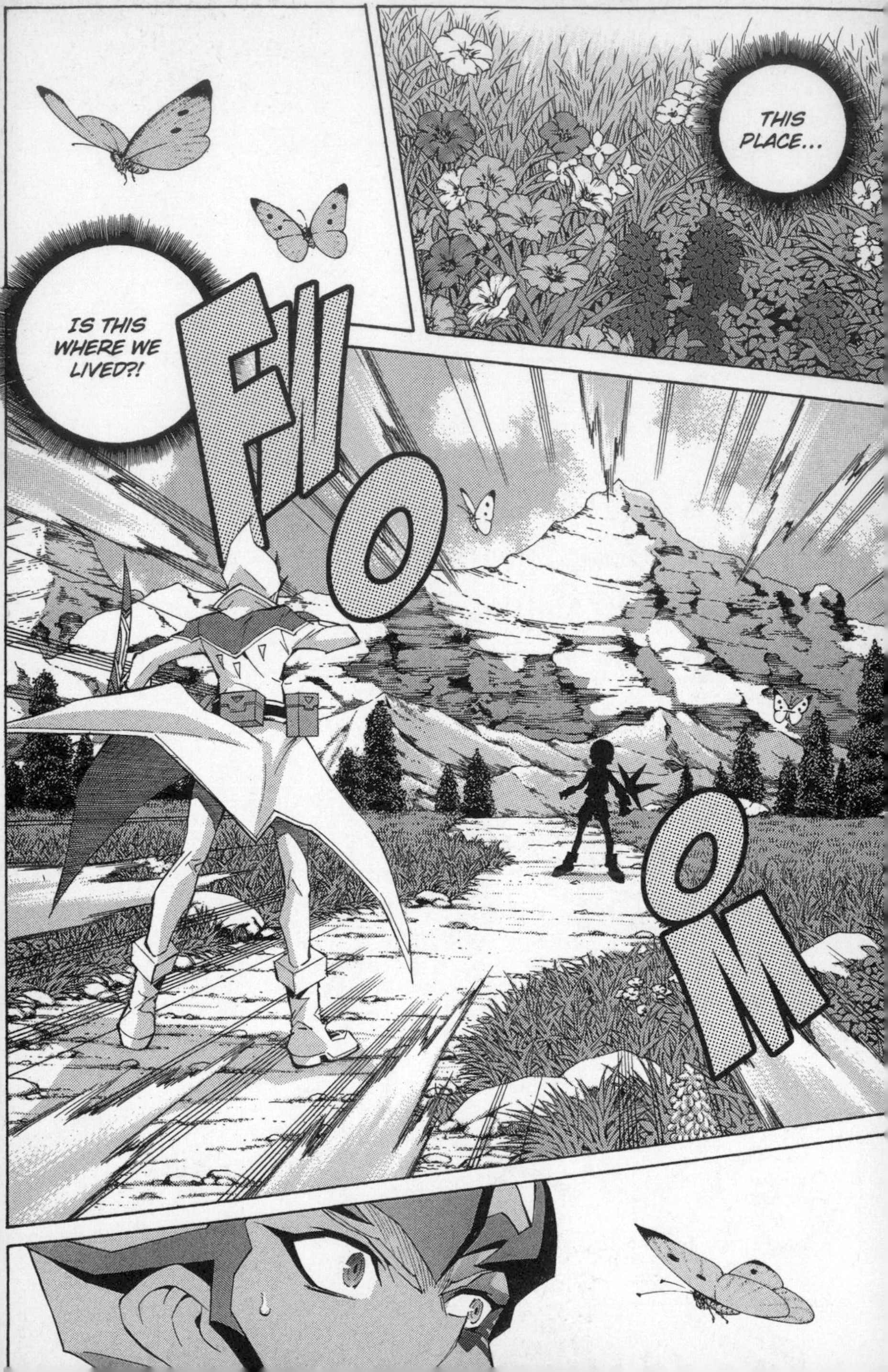
THIS PLACE...
IS THIS WHERE WE LIVED?!
FOOM

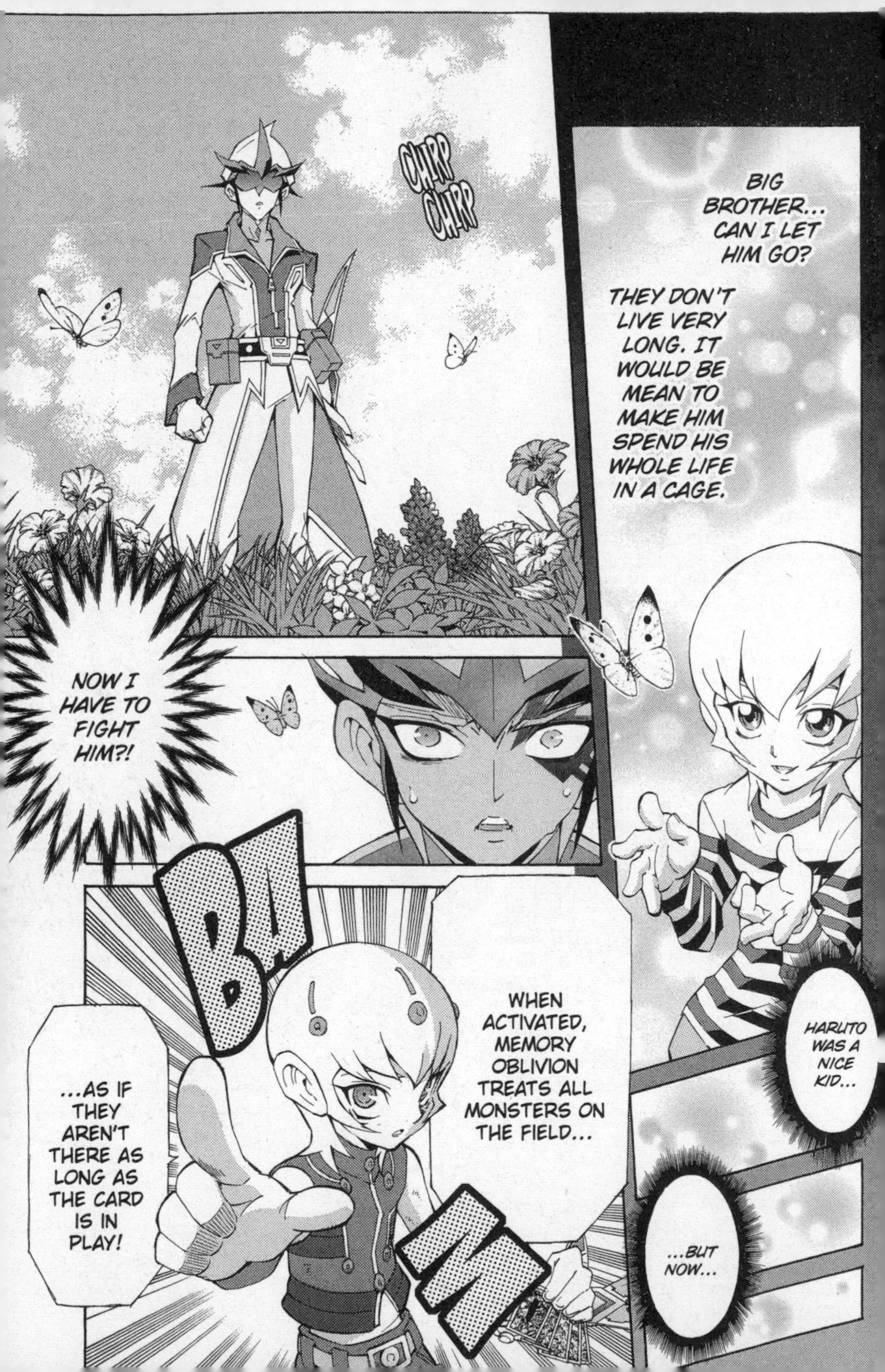
BIG BROTHER... CAN I LET HIM GO?
THEY DON'T LIVE VERY LONG. IT WOULD BE MEAN TO MAKE HIM SPEND HIS WHOLE LIFE IN A CAGE.
CHIRP CHIRP
NOW I HAVE TO FIGHT HIM?!
HARUTO WAS A NICE KID...
...BUT NOW...
BAM
WHEN ACTIVATED, MEMORY OBLIVION TREATS ALL MONSTERS ON THE FIELD...
...AS IF THEY AREN'T THERE AS LONG AS THE CARD IS IN PLAY!

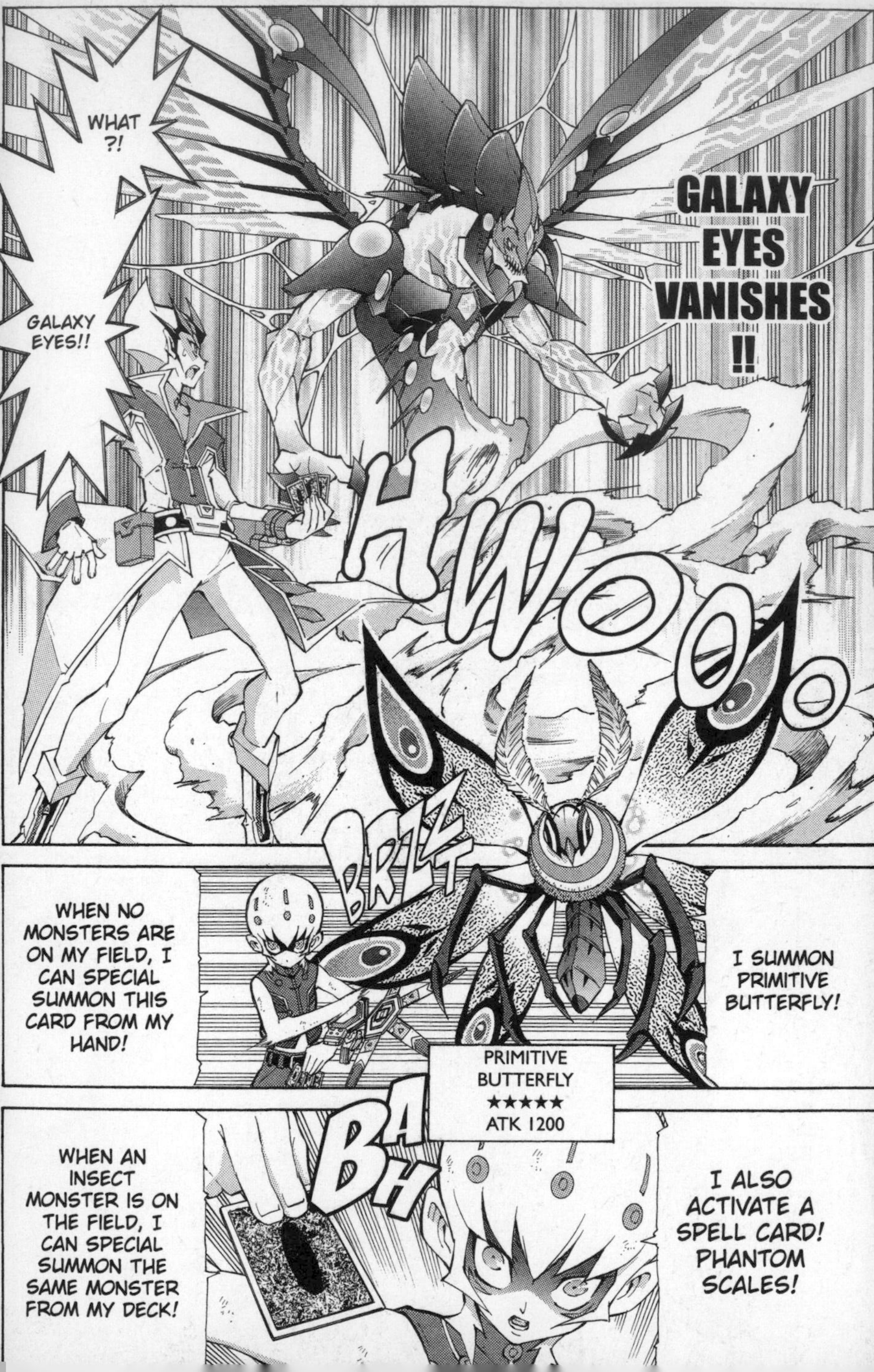
GALAXY EYES VANISHES !!
WHAT ?!
GALAXY EYES!!
HWOOO
I SUMMON PRIMITIVE BUTTERFLY!
BRZZT
WHEN NO MONSTERS ARE ON MY FIELD, I CAN SPECIAL SUMMON THIS CARD FROM MY HAND!
PRIMITIVE BUTTERFLY ★★★★★ ATK 1200
BAH
I ALSO ACTIVATE A SPELL CARD! PHANTOM SCALES!
WHEN AN INSECT MONSTER IS ON THE FIELD, I CAN SPECIAL SUMMON THE SAME MONSTER FROM MY DECK!

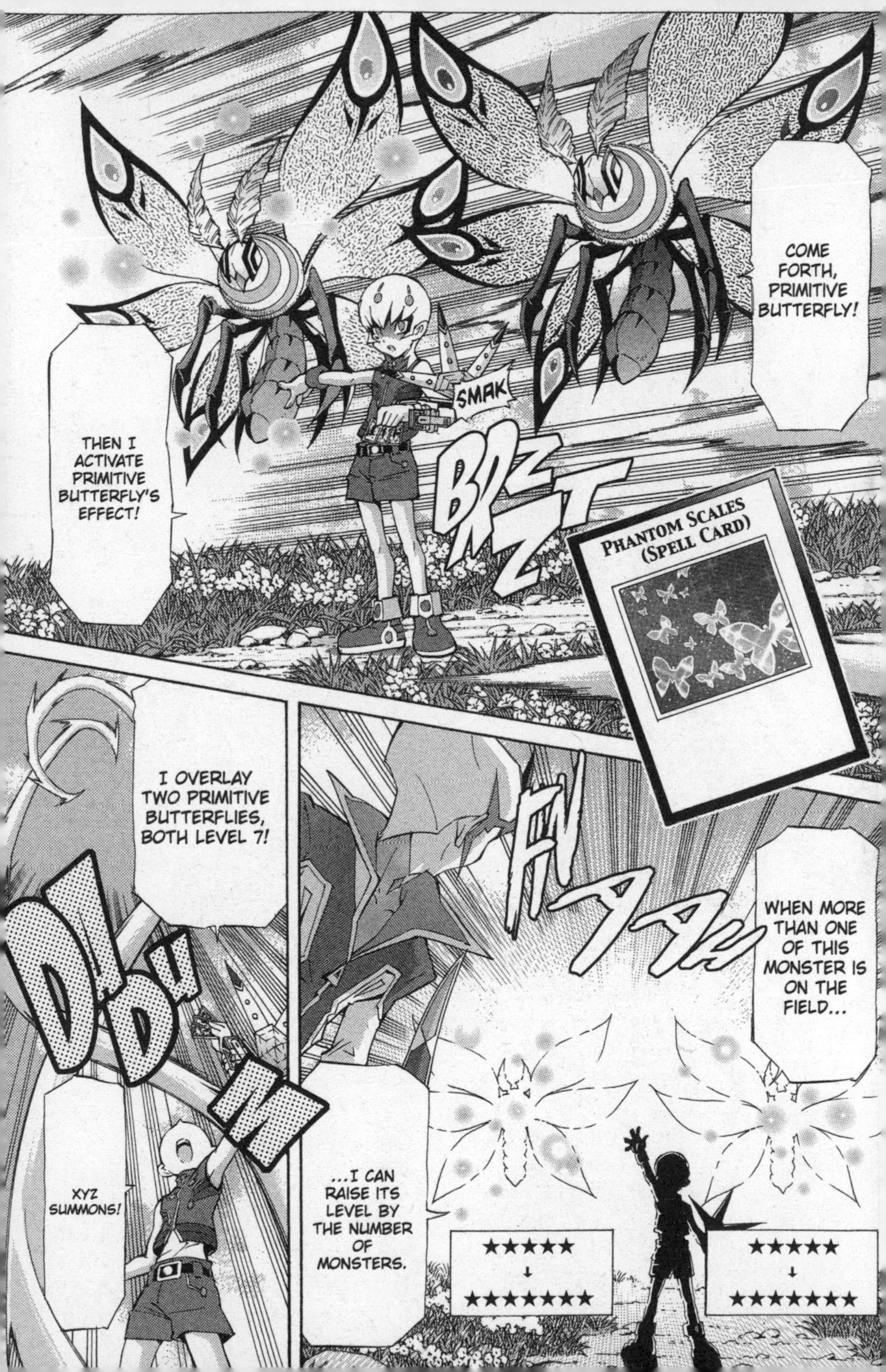
COME FORTH, PRIMITIVE BUTTERFLY!
SMAK
BRZZT
THEN I ACTIVATE PRIMITIVE BUTTERFLY'S EFFECT!
PHANTOM SCALES (SPELL CARD)
FWAAH
WHEN MORE THAN ONE OF THIS MONSTER IS ON THE FIELD...
★★★★★ ↓ ★★★★★★★
★★★★★ ↓ ★★★★★★★
...I CAN RAISE ITS LEVEL BY THE NUMBER OF MONSTERS.
I OVERLAY TWO PRIMITIVE BUTTERFLIES, BOTH LEVEL 7!
XYZ SUMMONS!

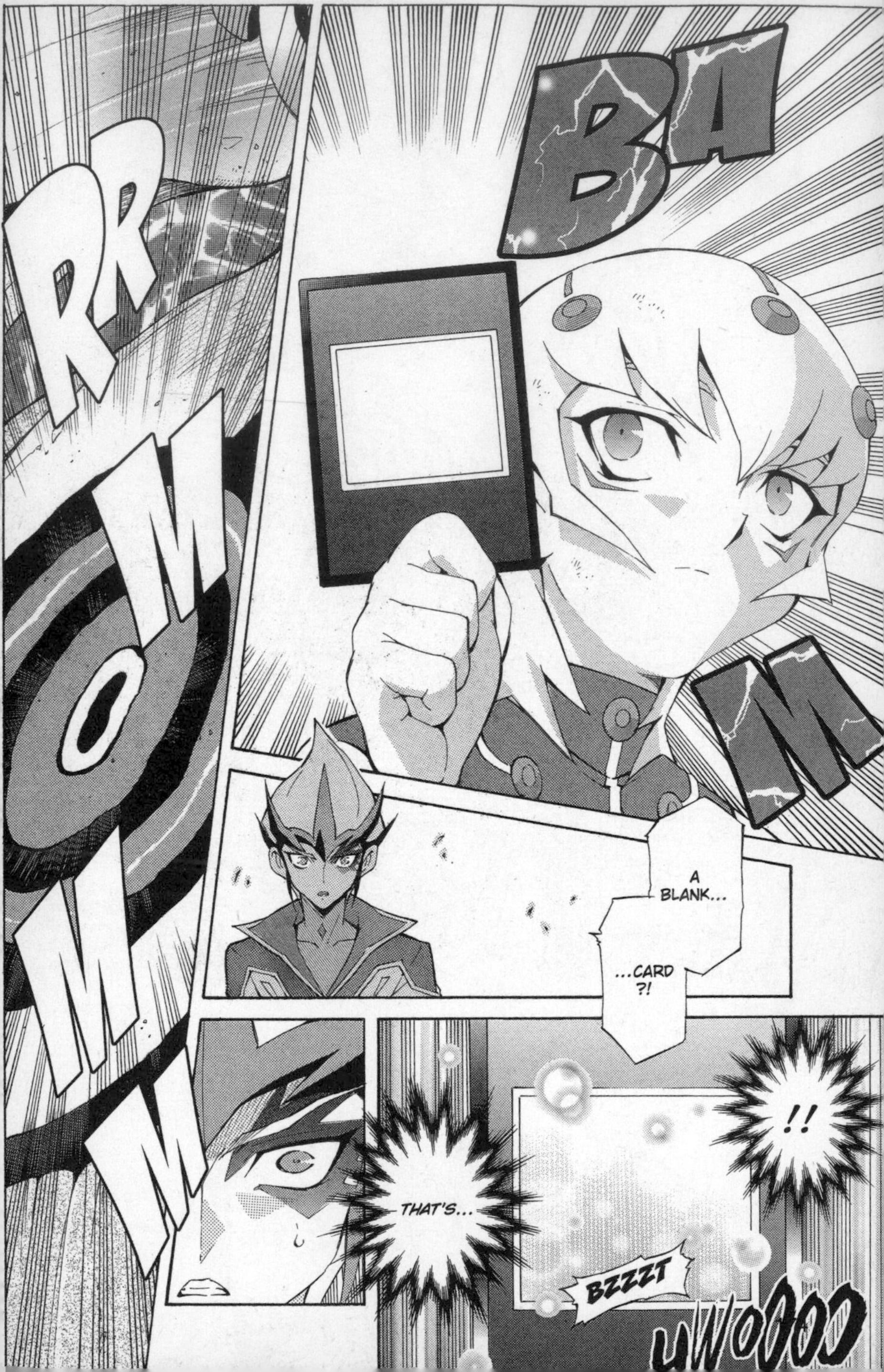
BAMM
A BLANK...
...CARD ?!
!!
BZZZT
UWOOOO
THAT'S...
RRMOMM

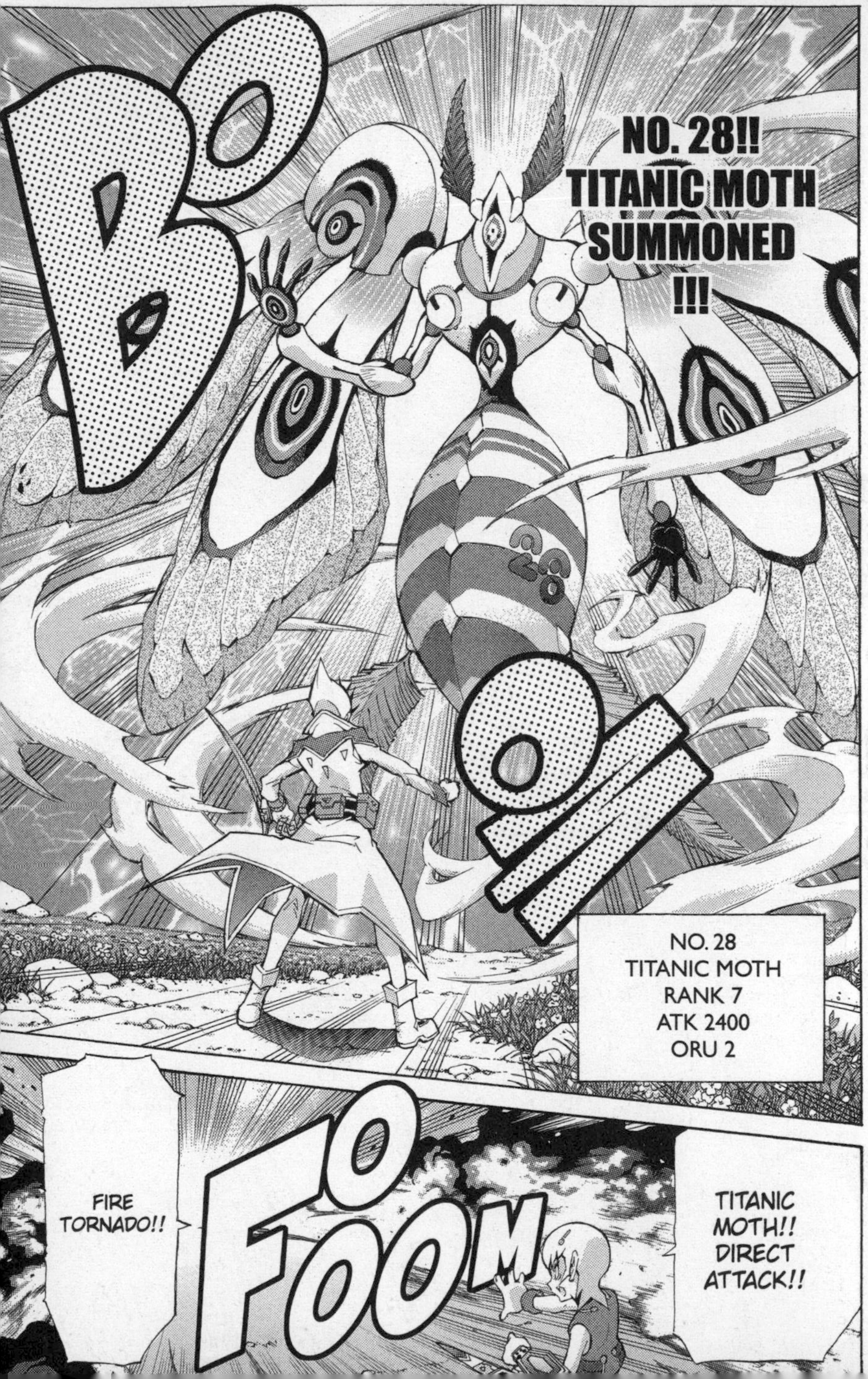
NO. 28!!
TITANIC MOTH
SUMMONED
!!!
NO. 28
TITANIC MOTH
RANK 7
ATK 2400
ORU 2
TITANIC MOTH!! DIRECT ATTACK!!
FIRE TORNADO!!

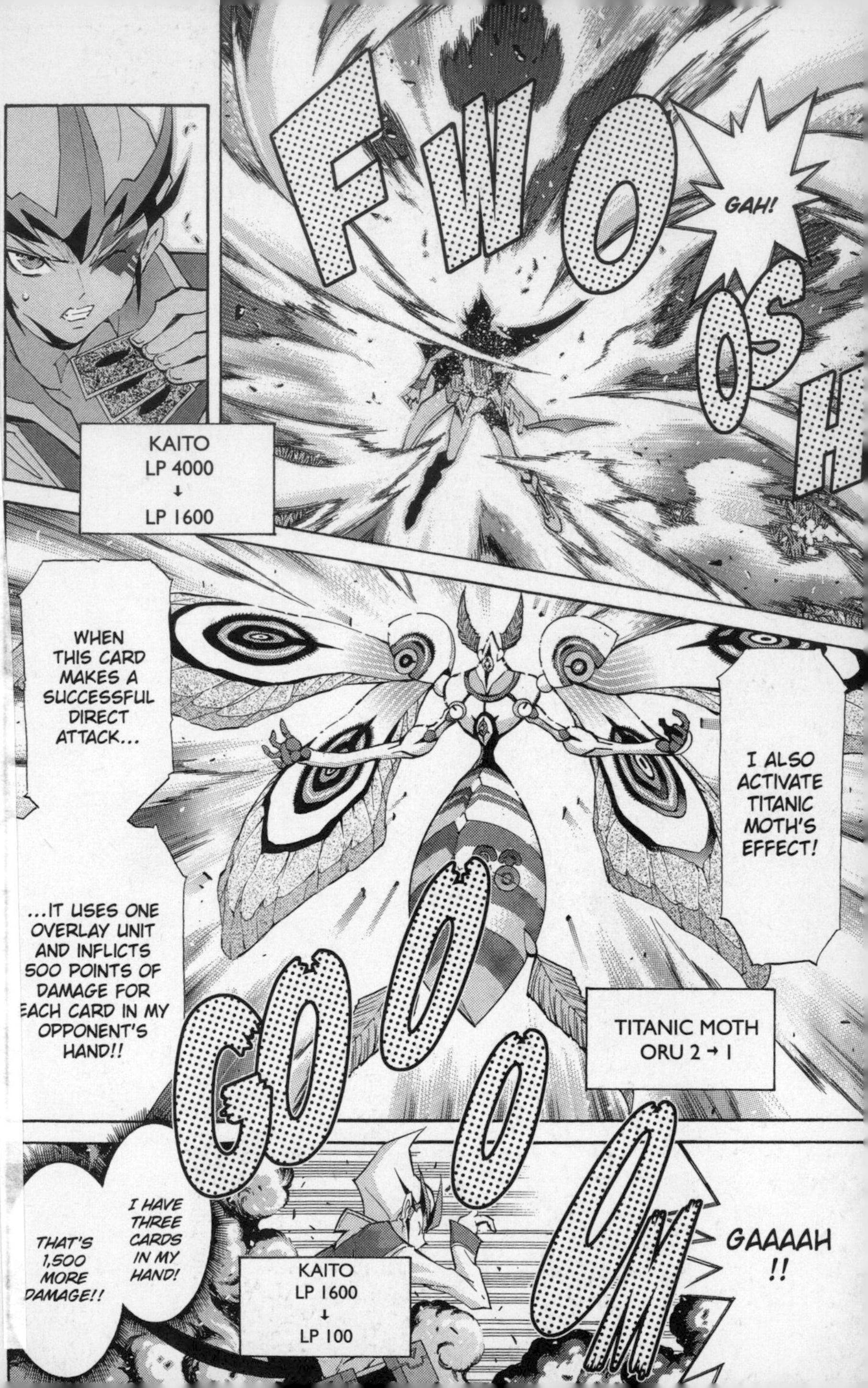
FWOOSH
GAH!
KAITO
LP 4000
↓
LP 1600
I ALSO ACTIVATE TITANIC MOTH'S EFFECT!
WHEN THIS CARD MAKES A SUCCESSFUL DIRECT ATTACK...
...IT USES ONE OVERLAY UNIT AND INFLICTS 500 POINTS OF DAMAGE FOR EACH CARD IN MY OPPONENT'S HAND!!
TITANIC MOTH
ORU 2 → 1
GOOOOM
GAAAAH!!
I HAVE THREE CARDS IN MY HAND!
THAT'S 1,500 MORE DAMAGE!!
KAITO
LP 1600
↓
LP 100

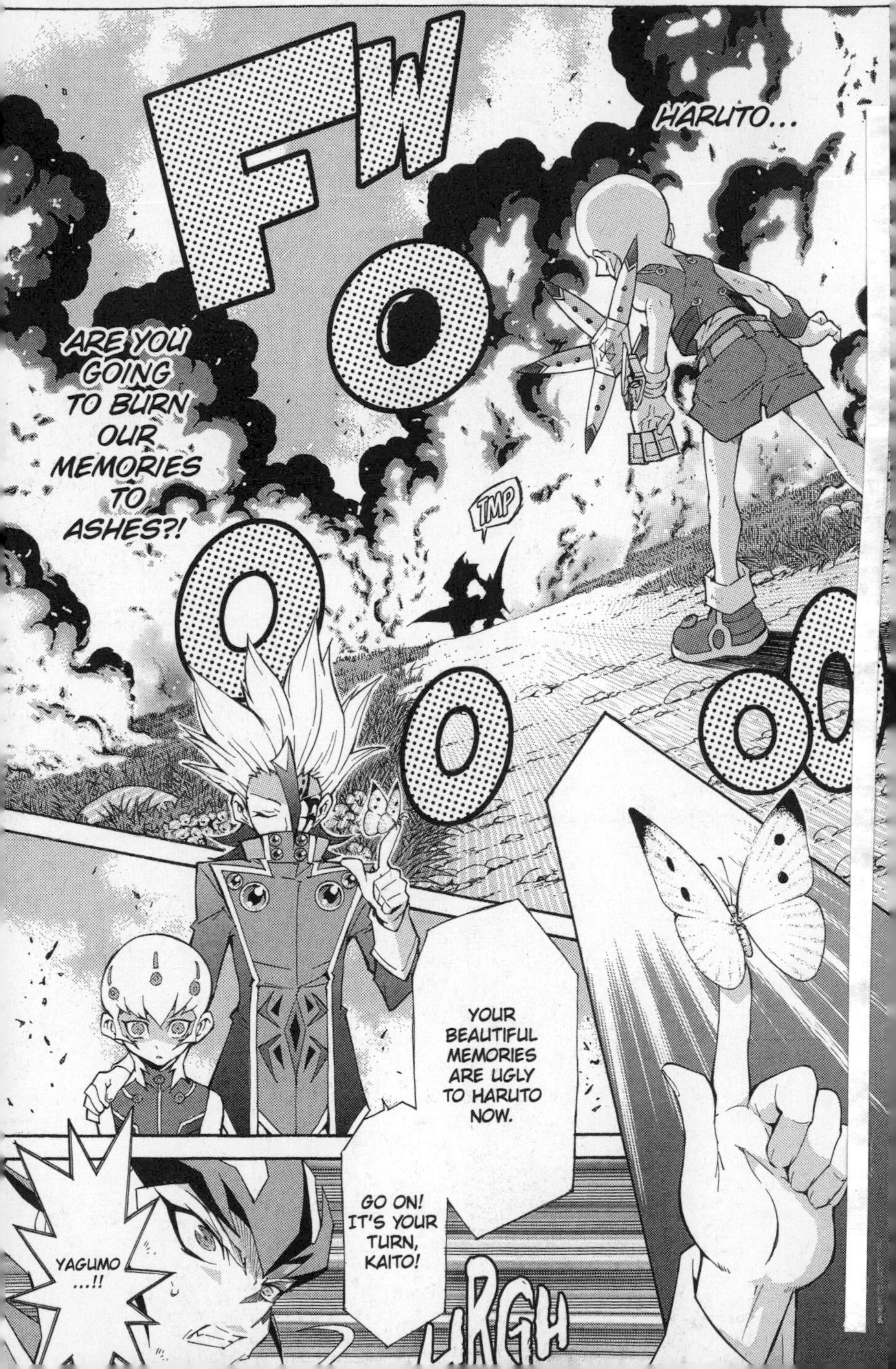
HARUTO...
FWOOOOOO
ARE YOU GOING TO BURN OUR MEMORIES TO ASHES?!
TMP
YOUR BEAUTIFUL MEMORIES ARE UGLY TO HARUTO NOW.
GO ON! IT'S YOUR TURN, KAITO!
YAGUMO ...!!
URGH

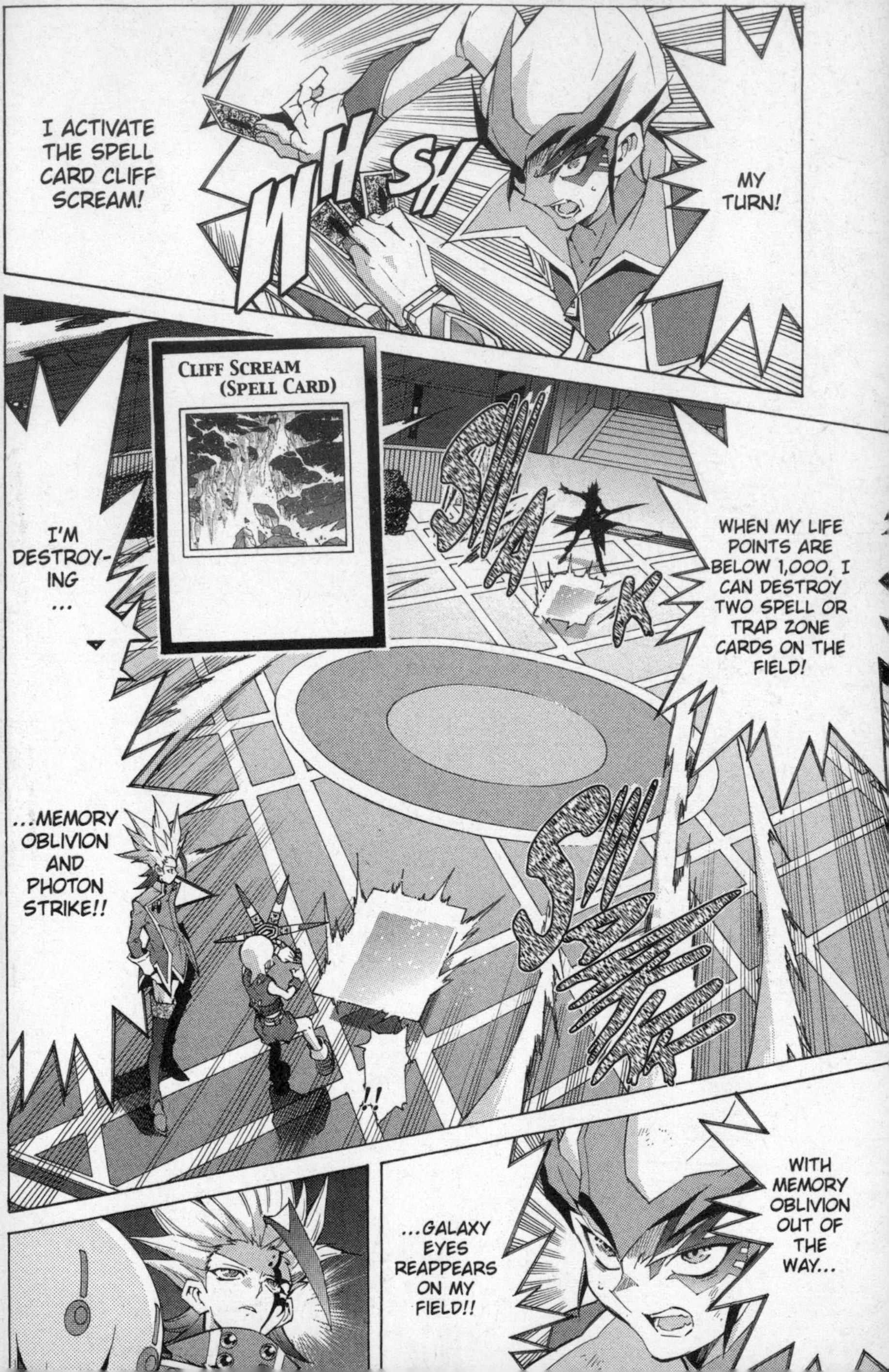
MY TURN!
I ACTIVATE THE SPELL CARD CLIFF SCREAM!
WHSH
WHEN MY LIFE POINTS ARE BELOW 1,000, I CAN DESTROY TWO SPELL OR TRAP ZONE CARDS ON THE FIELD!
CLIFF SCREAM (SPELL CARD)
I'M DESTROYING...
...MEMORY OBLIVION AND PHOTON STRIKE!!
!!
WITH MEMORY OBLIVION OUT OF THE WAY...
...GALAXY EYES REAPPEARS ON MY FIELD!!

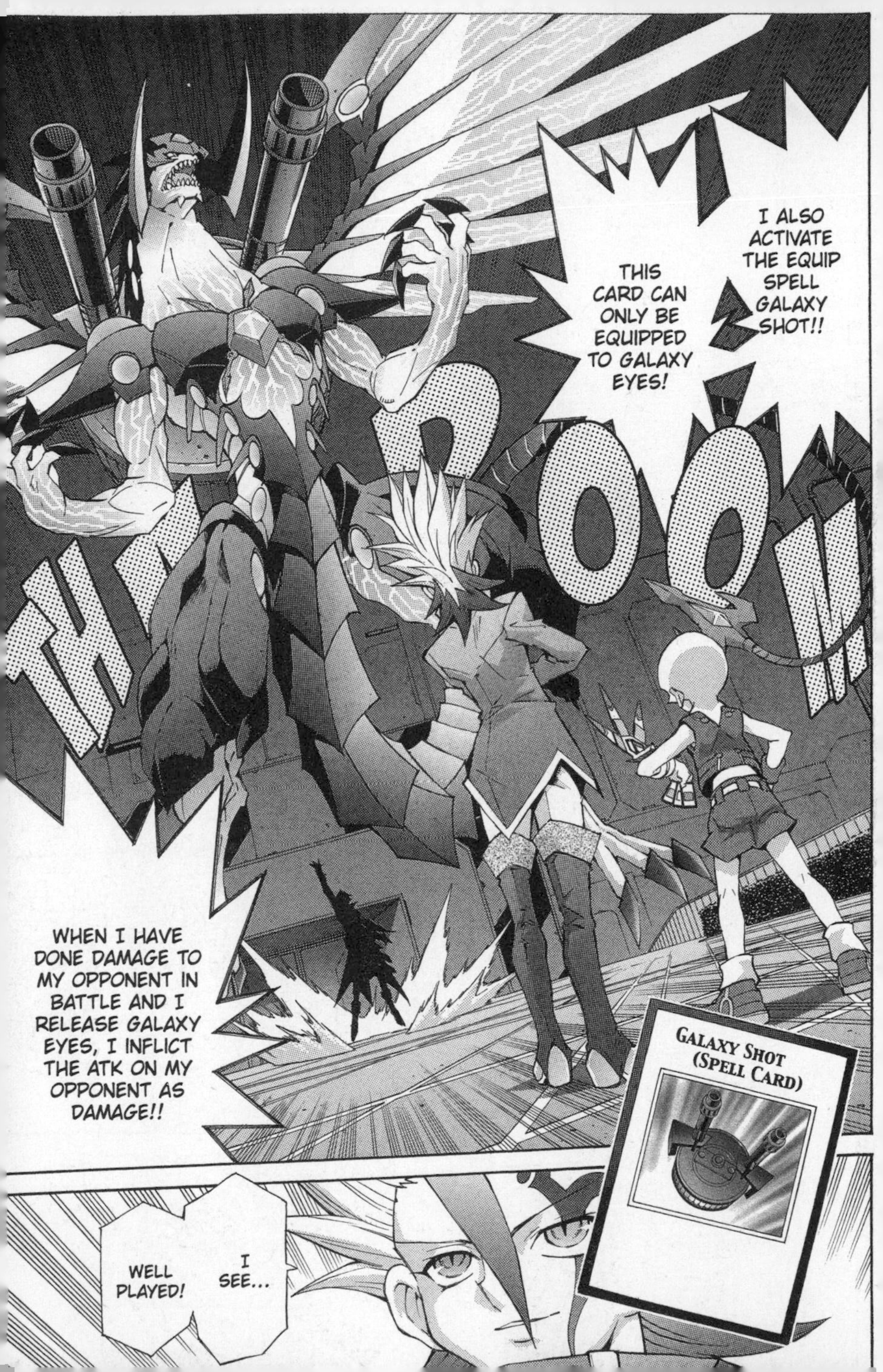
I ALSO ACTIVATE THE EQUIP SPELL GALAXY SHOT!!
THIS CARD CAN ONLY BE EQUIPPED TO GALAXY EYES!
WHEN I HAVE DONE DAMAGE TO MY OPPONENT IN BATTLE AND I RELEASE GALAXY EYES, I INFLICT THE ATK ON MY OPPONENT AS DAMAGE!!
GALAXY SHOT (SPELL CARD)
I SEE...
WELL PLAYED!

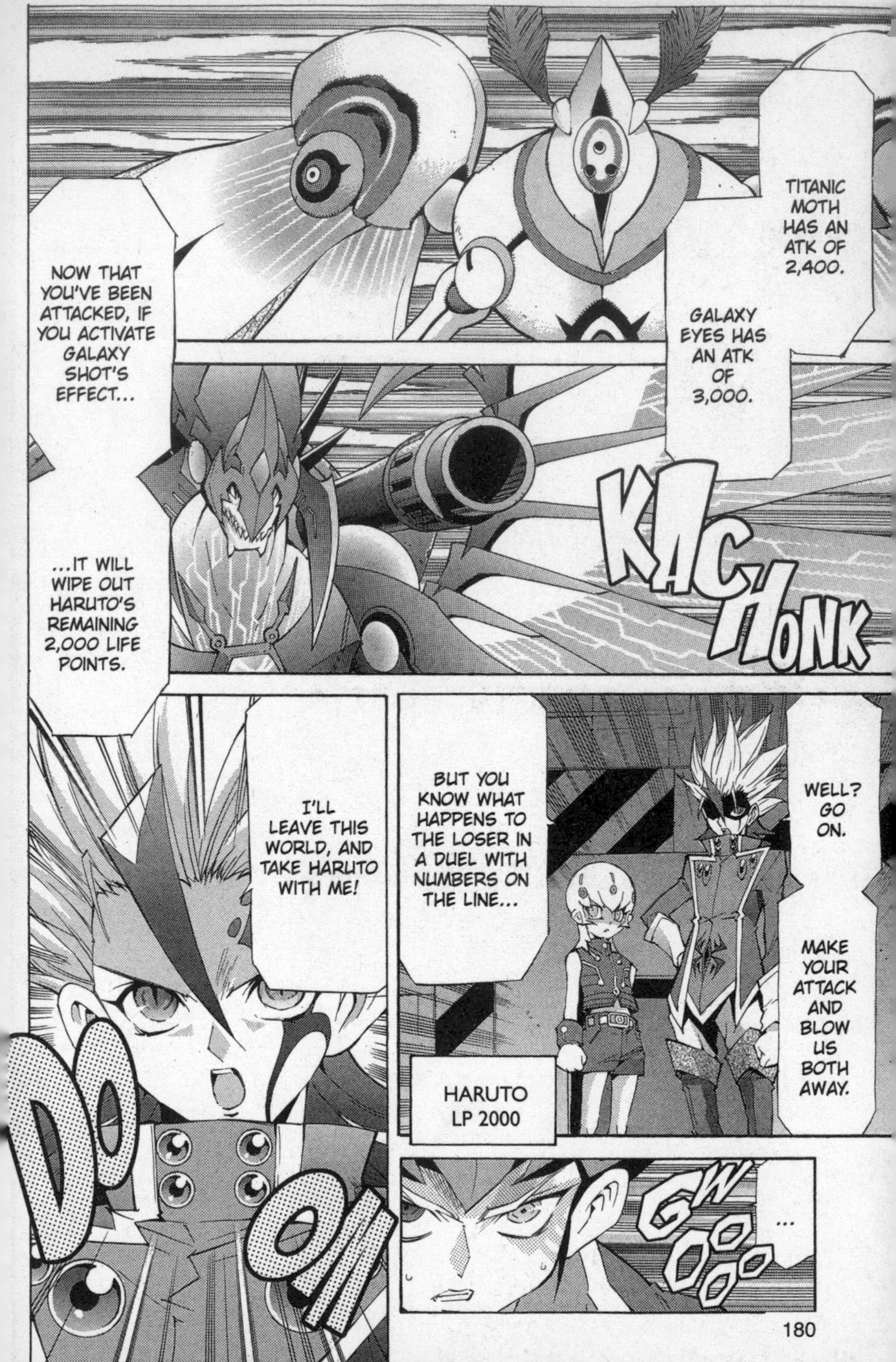
TITANIC MOTH HAS AN ATK OF 2,400.
GALAXY EYES HAS AN ATK OF 3,000.
NOW THAT YOU'VE BEEN ATTACKED, IF YOU ACTIVATE GALAXY SHOT'S EFFECT...
KACHONK
...IT WILL WIPE OUT HARUTO'S REMAINING 2,000 LIFE POINTS.
WELL? GO ON.
MAKE YOUR ATTACK AND BLOW US BOTH AWAY.
BUT YOU KNOW WHAT HAPPENS TO THE LOSER IN A DUEL WITH NUMBERS ON THE LINE...
HARUTO LP 2000
...
GWOOOOOO
I'LL LEAVE THIS WORLD, AND TAKE HARUTO WITH ME!

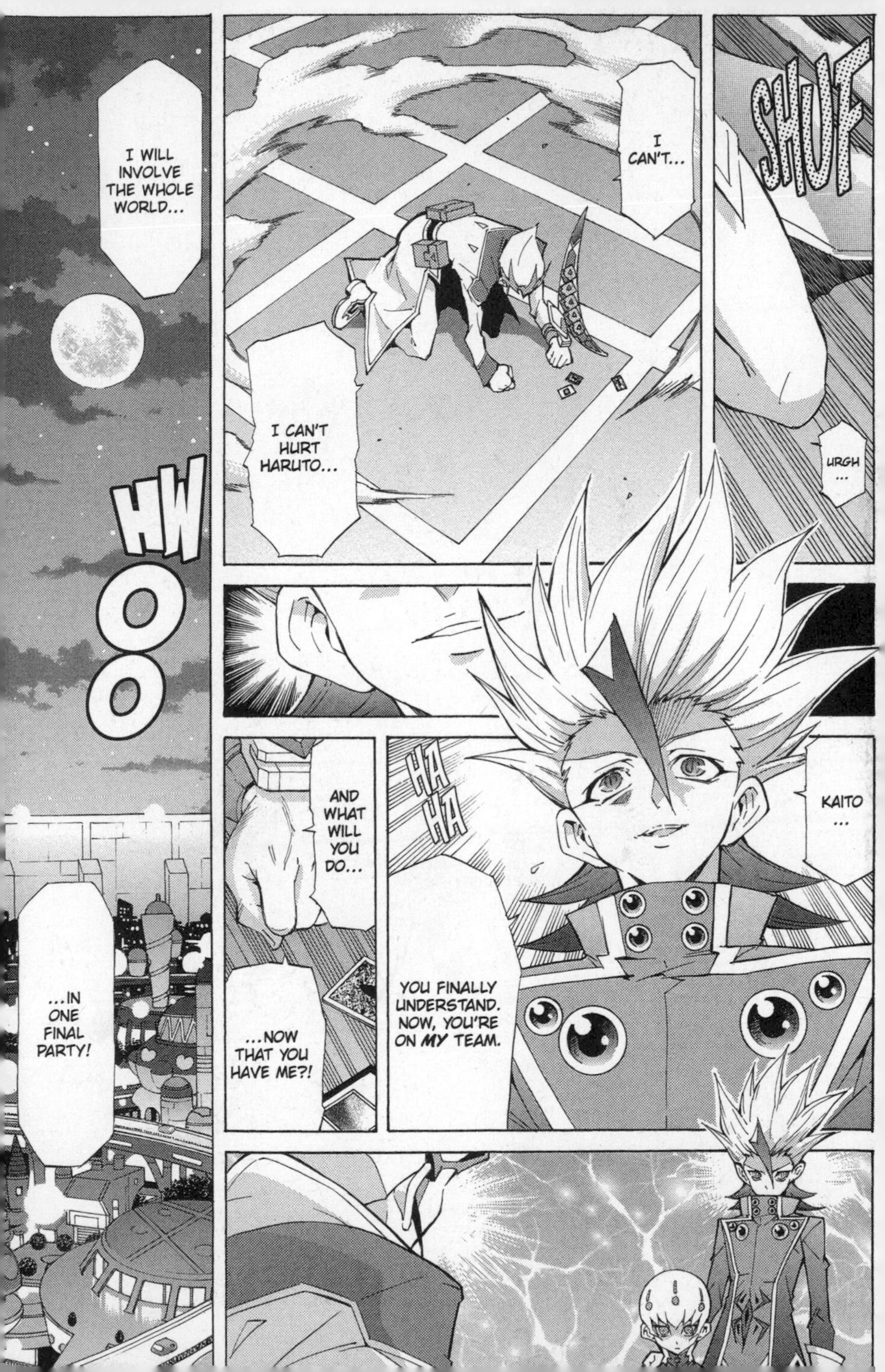
SHUF
URGH...
I CAN'T...
I CAN'T HURT HARUTO...
KAITO...
HA HA
YOU FINALLY UNDERSTAND. NOW, YOU'RE ON *MY* TEAM.
AND WHAT WILL YOU DO...
...NOW THAT YOU HAVE ME?!
I WILL INVOLVE THE WHOLE WORLD...
HWOO
...IN ONE FINAL PARTY!

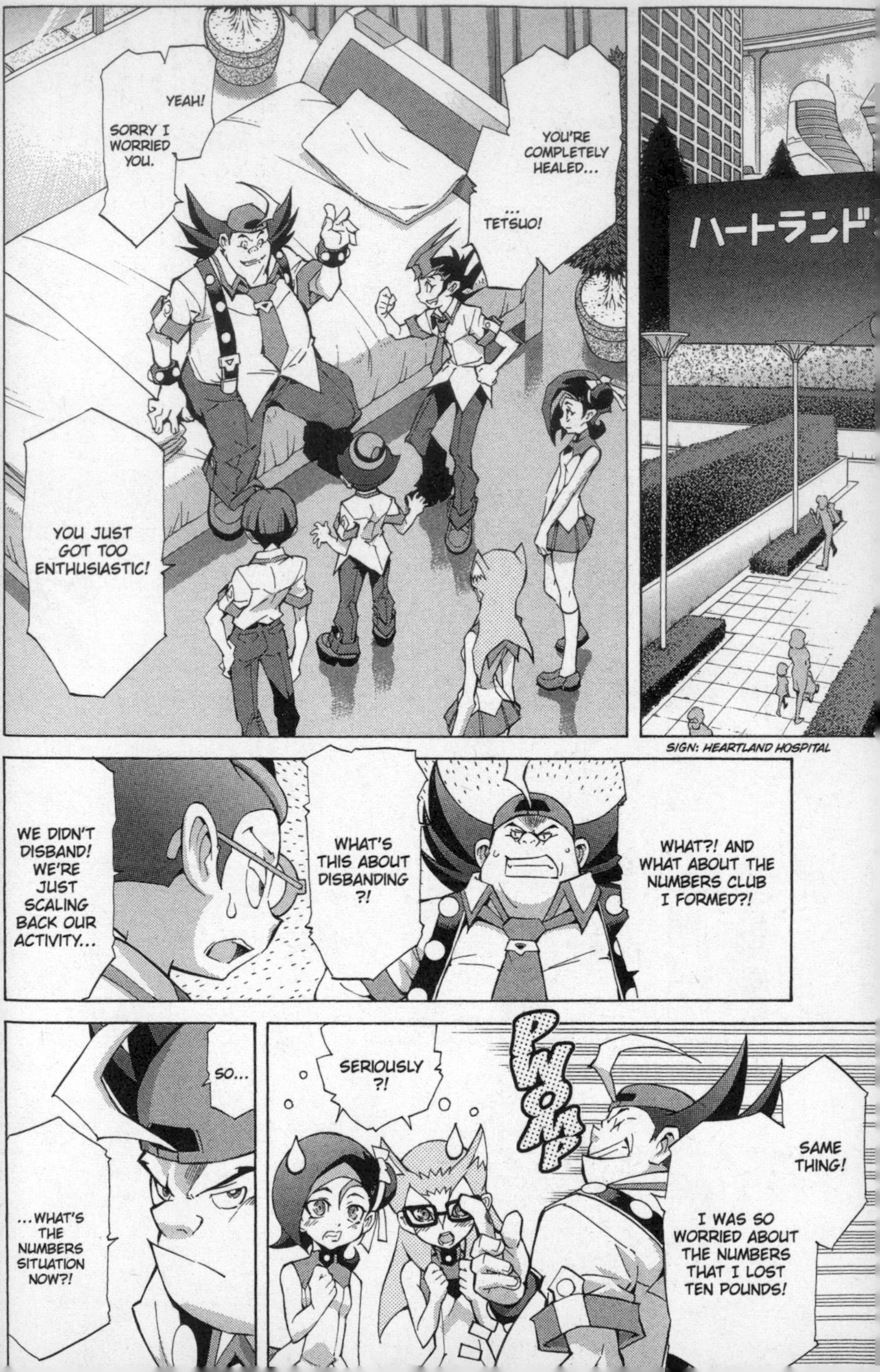
ハートランド
SIGN: HEARTLAND HOSPITAL
YOU'RE COMPLETELY HEALED...
...TETSUO!
YEAH!
SORRY I WORRIED YOU.
YOU JUST GOT TOO ENTHUSIASTIC!
WHAT?! AND WHAT ABOUT THE NUMBERS CLUB I FORMED?!
WHAT'S THIS ABOUT DISBANDING?!
WE DIDN'T DISBAND! WE'RE JUST SCALING BACK OUR ACTIVITY...
PWOMP
SAME THING!
I WAS SO WORRIED ABOUT THE NUMBERS THAT I LOST TEN POUNDS!
SERIOUSLY?!
SO...
...WHAT'S THE NUMBERS SITUATION NOW?!

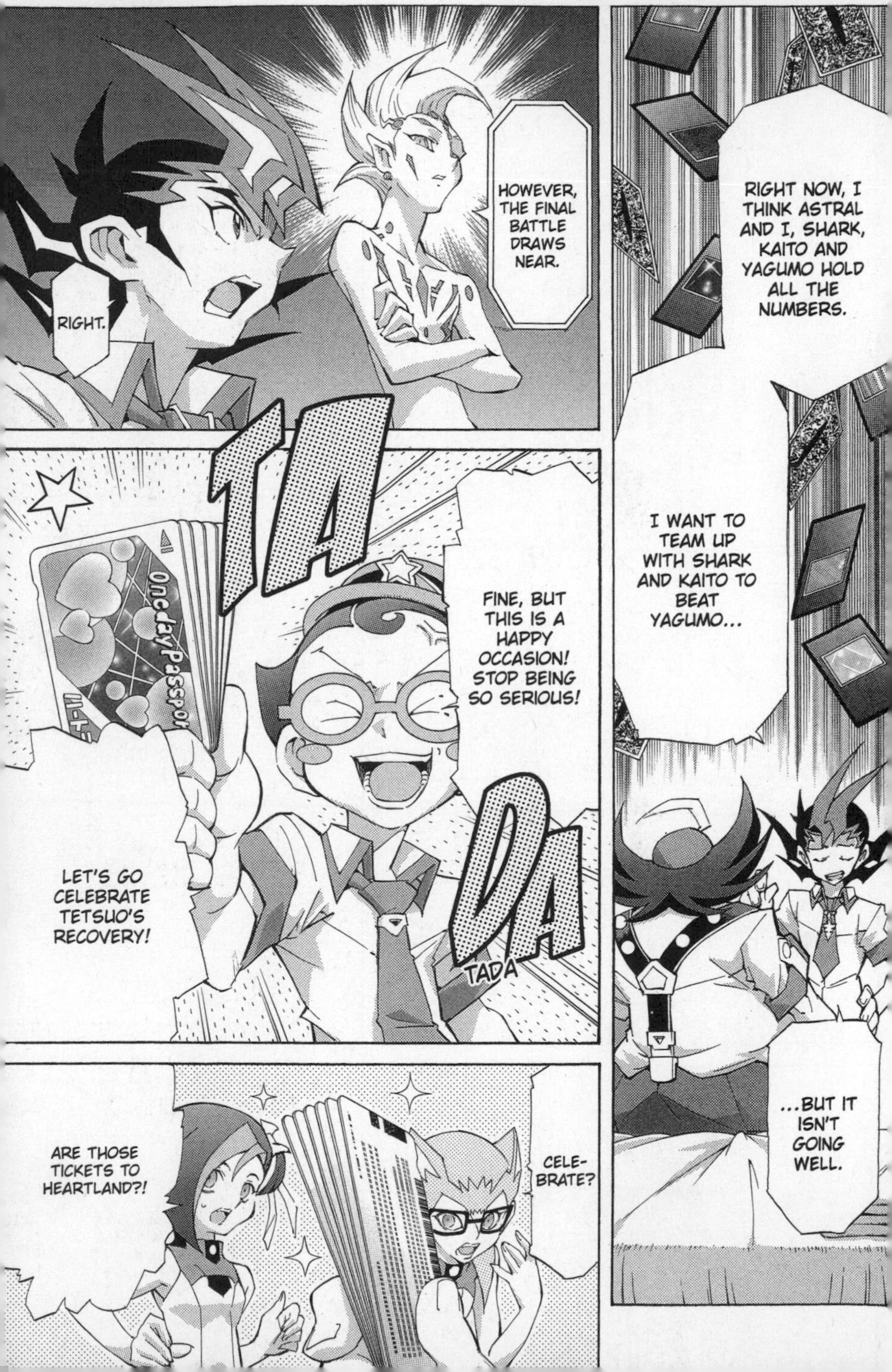
RIGHT NOW, I THINK ASTRAL AND I, SHARK, KAITO AND YAGUMO HOLD ALL THE NUMBERS.
I WANT TO TEAM UP WITH SHARK AND KAITO TO BEAT YAGUMO...
...BUT IT ISN'T GOING WELL.
HOWEVER, THE FINAL BATTLE DRAWS NEAR.
RIGHT.
TA
FINE, BUT THIS IS A HAPPY OCCASION! STOP BEING SO SERIOUS!
DA
TADA
LET'S GO CELEBRATE TETSUO'S RECOVERY!
CELE-BRATE?
ARE THOSE TICKETS TO HEARTLAND?!

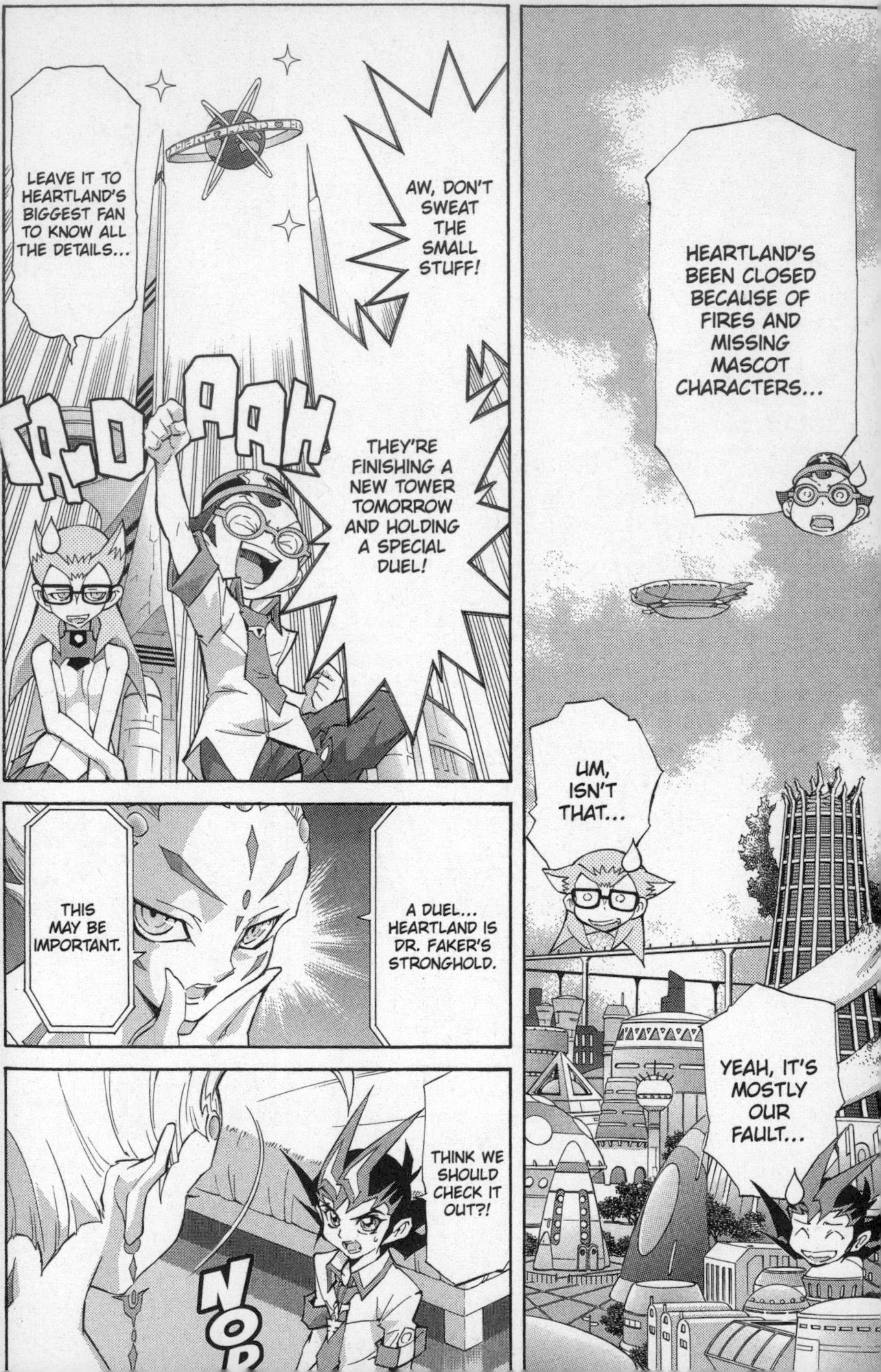
HEARTLAND'S BEEN CLOSED BECAUSE OF FIRES AND MISSING MASCOT CHARACTERS...
UM, ISN'T THAT...
YEAH, IT'S MOSTLY OUR FAULT...
AW, DON'T SWEAT THE SMALL STUFF!
LEAVE IT TO HEARTLAND'S BIGGEST FAN TO KNOW ALL THE DETAILS...
TA-DAAH
THEY'RE FINISHING A NEW TOWER TOMORROW AND HOLDING A SPECIAL DUEL!
A DUEL... HEARTLAND IS DR. FAKER'S STRONGHOLD.
THIS MAY BE IMPORTANT.
THINK WE SHOULD CHECK IT OUT?!
NOD

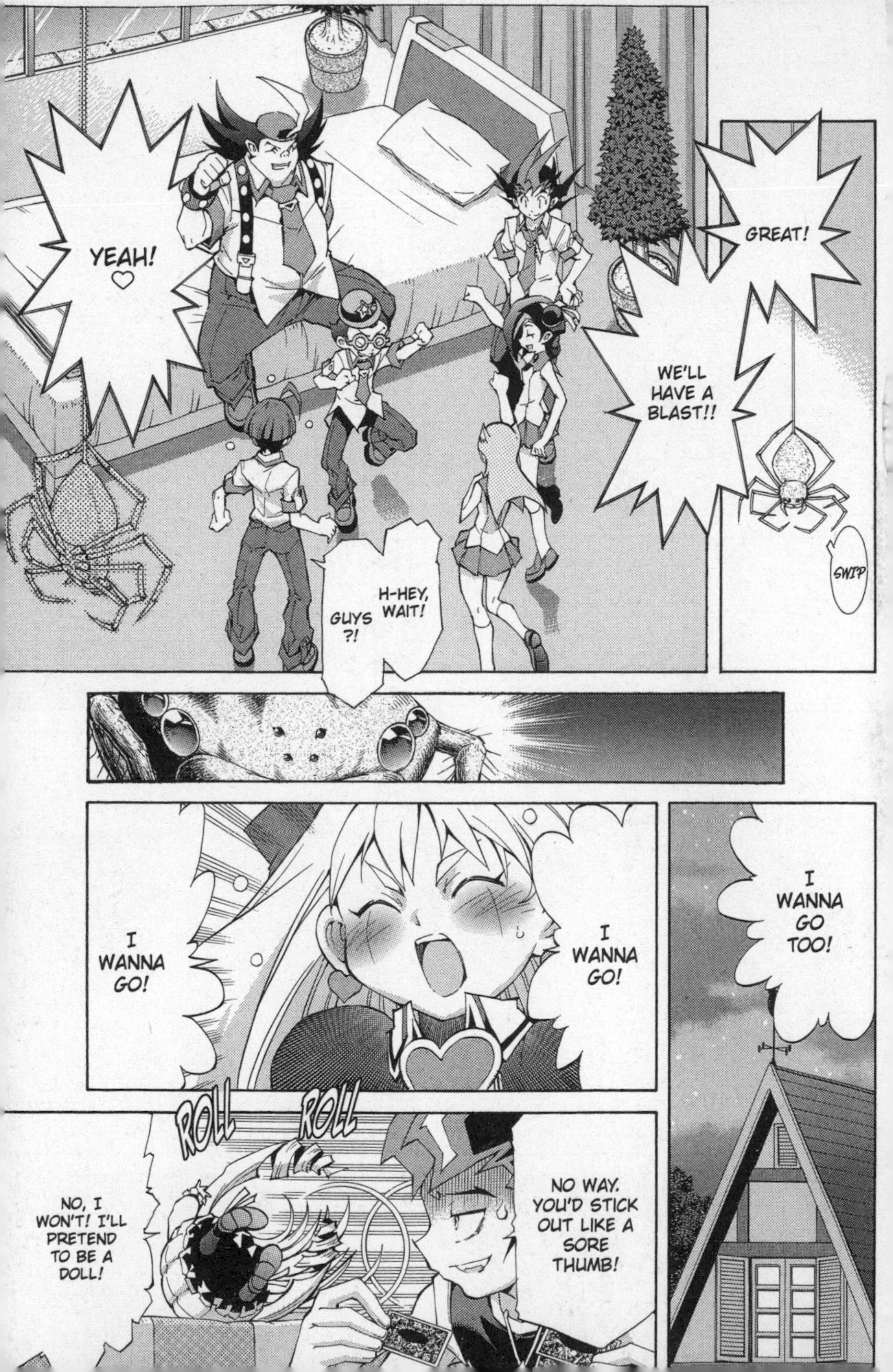
GREAT!
SWIP
WE'LL HAVE A BLAST!!
YEAH! ♡
H-HEY, WAIT!
GUYS ?!
I WANNA GO TOO!
I WANNA GO!
I WANNA GO!
ROLL
ROLL
NO WAY. YOU'D STICK OUT LIKE A SORE THUMB!
NO, I WON'T! I'LL PRETEND TO BE A DOLL!

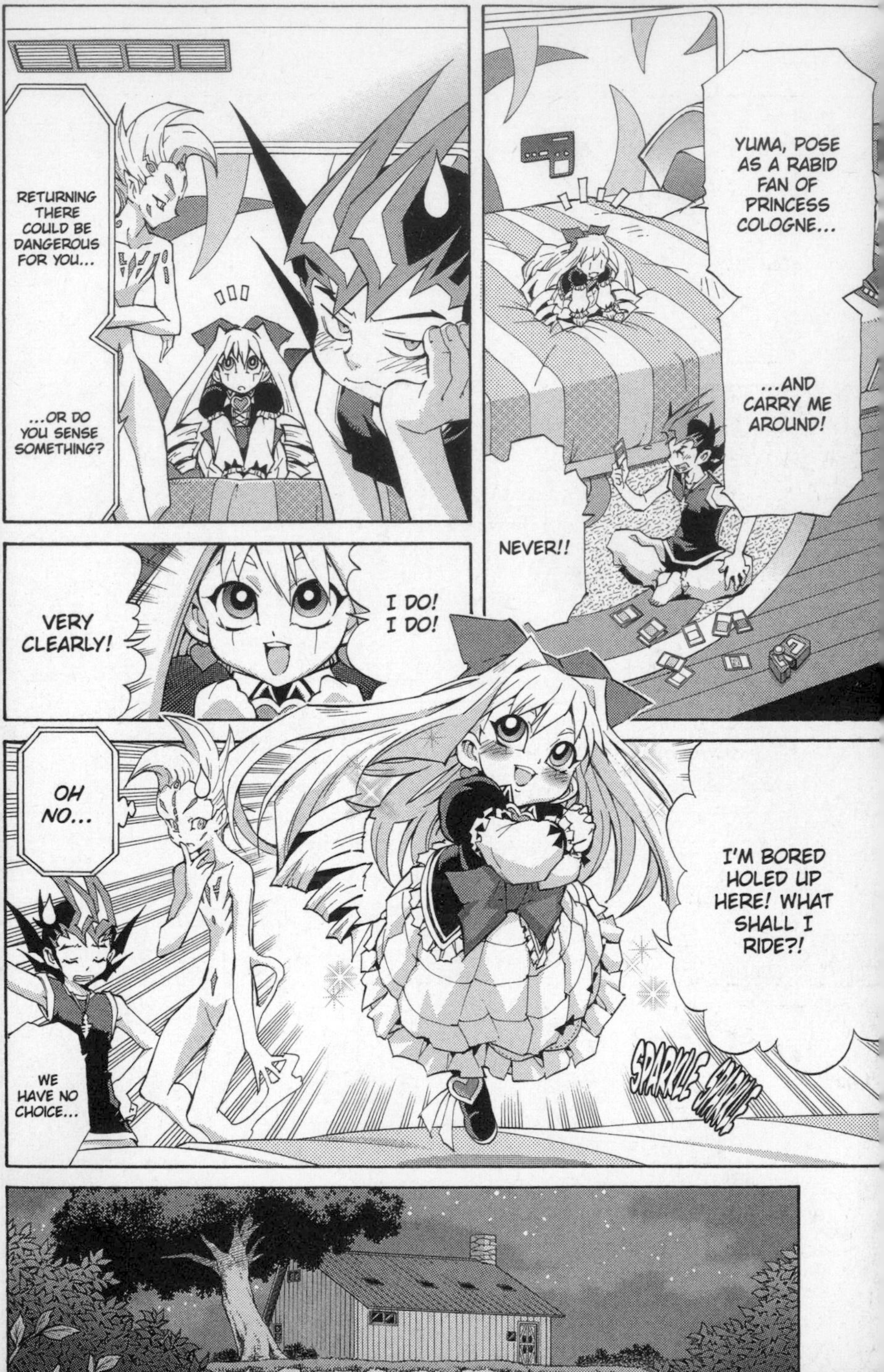
YUMA, POSE AS A RABID FAN OF PRINCESS COLOGNE...
...AND CARRY ME AROUND!
NEVER!!
RETURNING THERE COULD BE DANGEROUS FOR YOU...
...OR DO YOU SENSE SOMETHING?
I DO! I DO!
VERY CLEARLY!
I'M BORED HOLED UP HERE! WHAT SHALL I RIDE?!
SPARKLE
OH NO...
WE HAVE NO CHOICE...

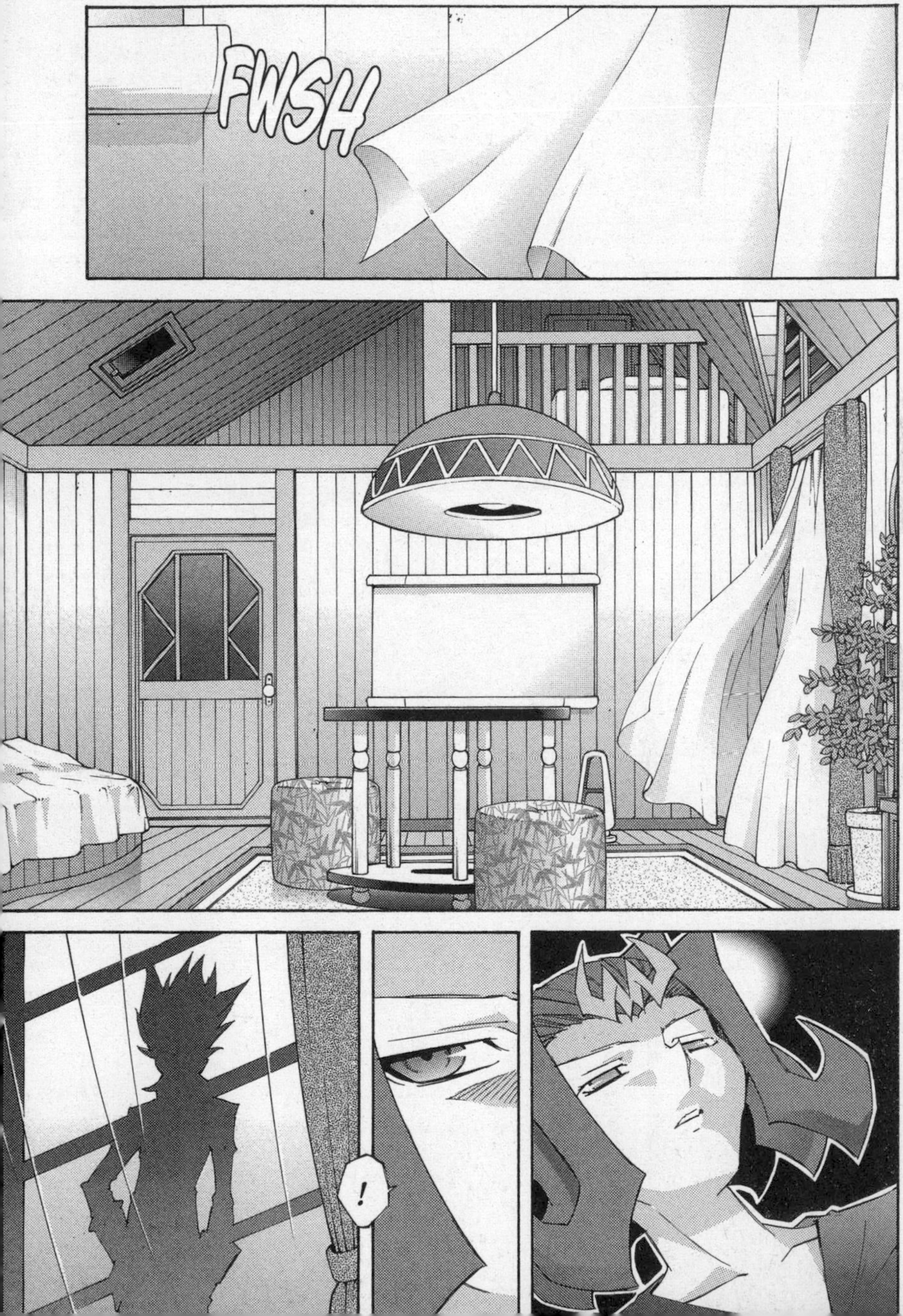
FWSH
!

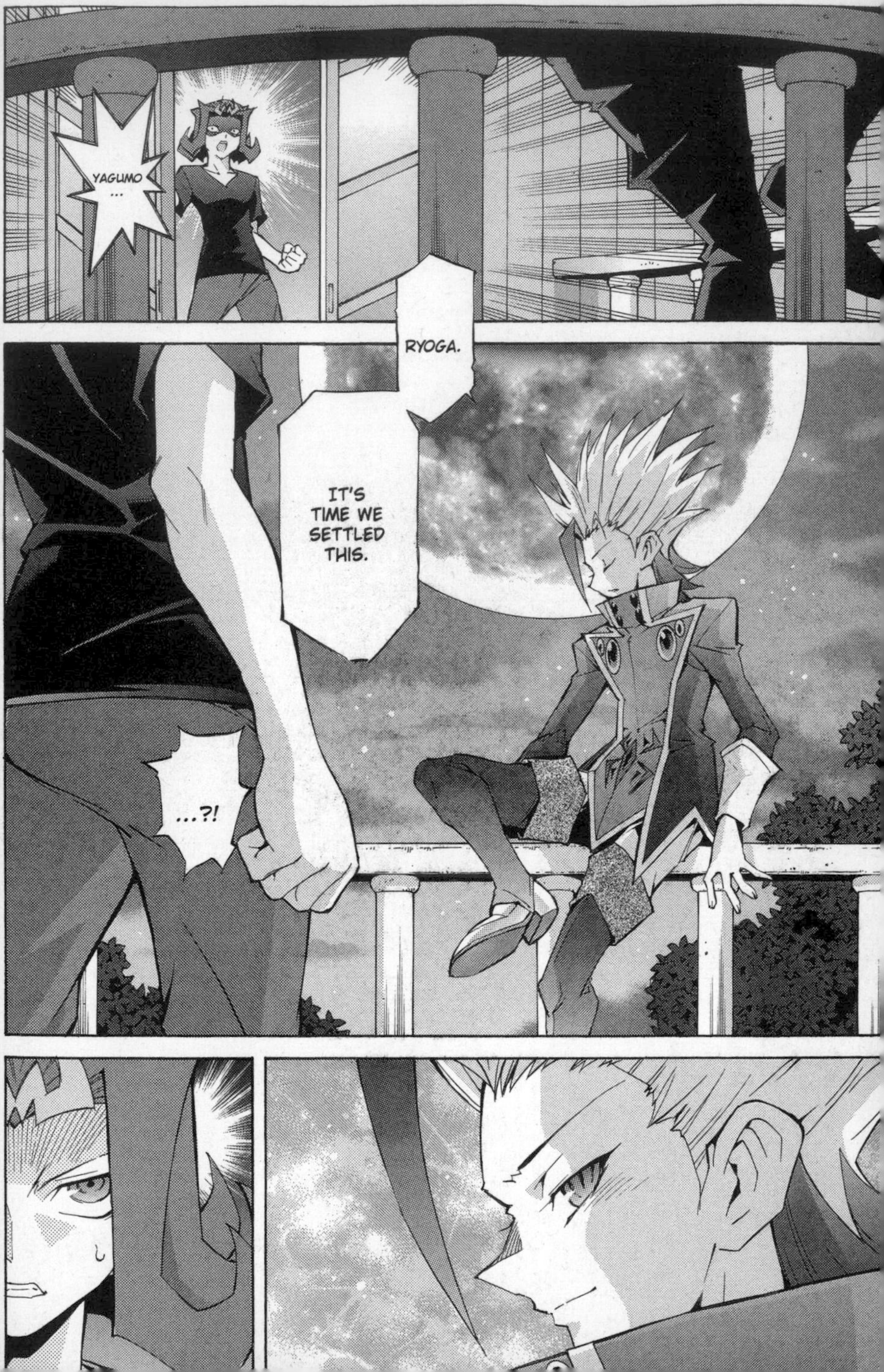
YAGUMO ...
RYOGA.
IT'S TIME WE SETTLED THIS.
...?!

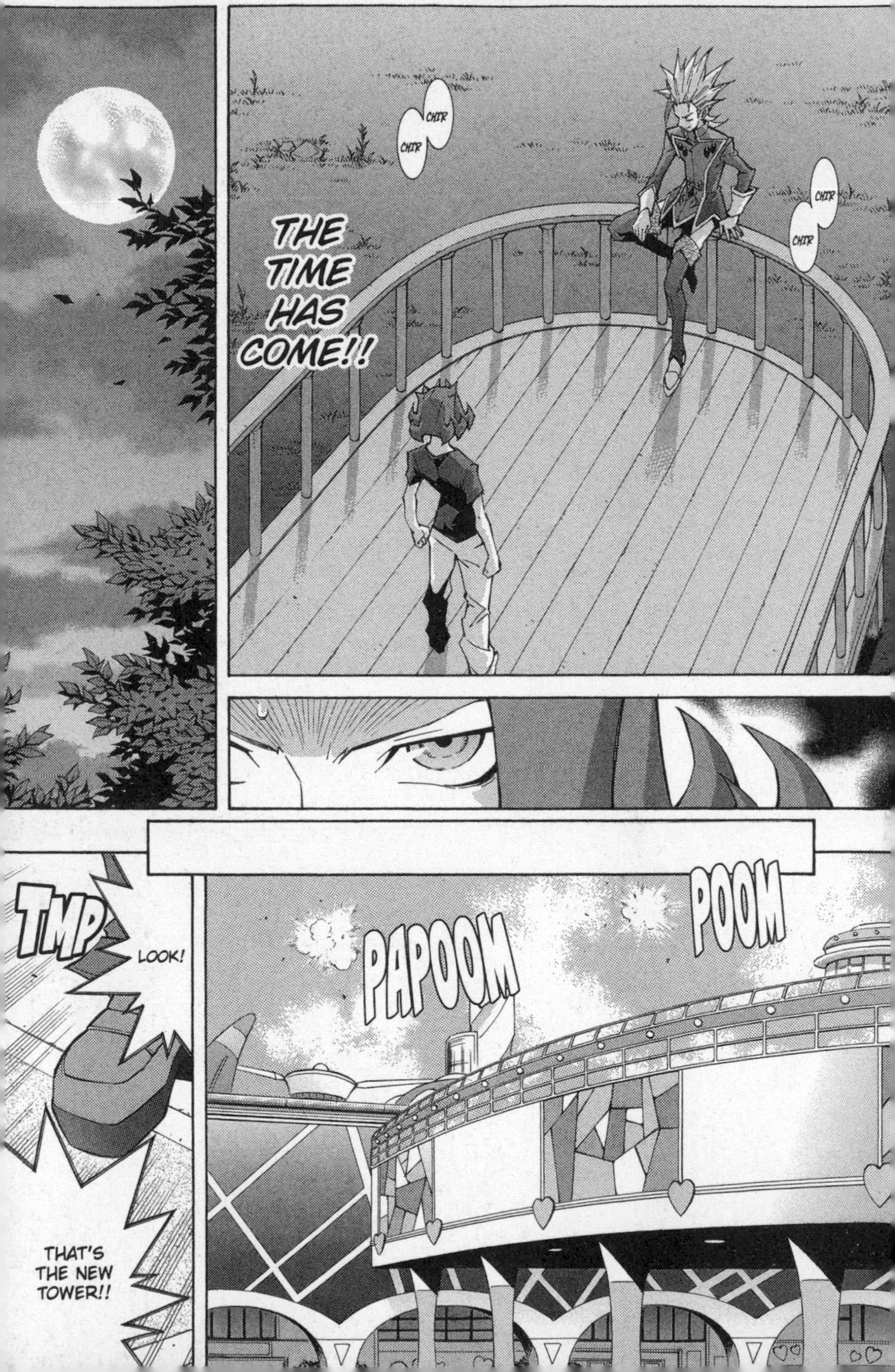
CHIR
CHIR
CHIR
CHIR
THE TIME HAS COME!!
POOM
PAPOOM
TMP
LOOK!
THAT'S THE NEW TOWER!!

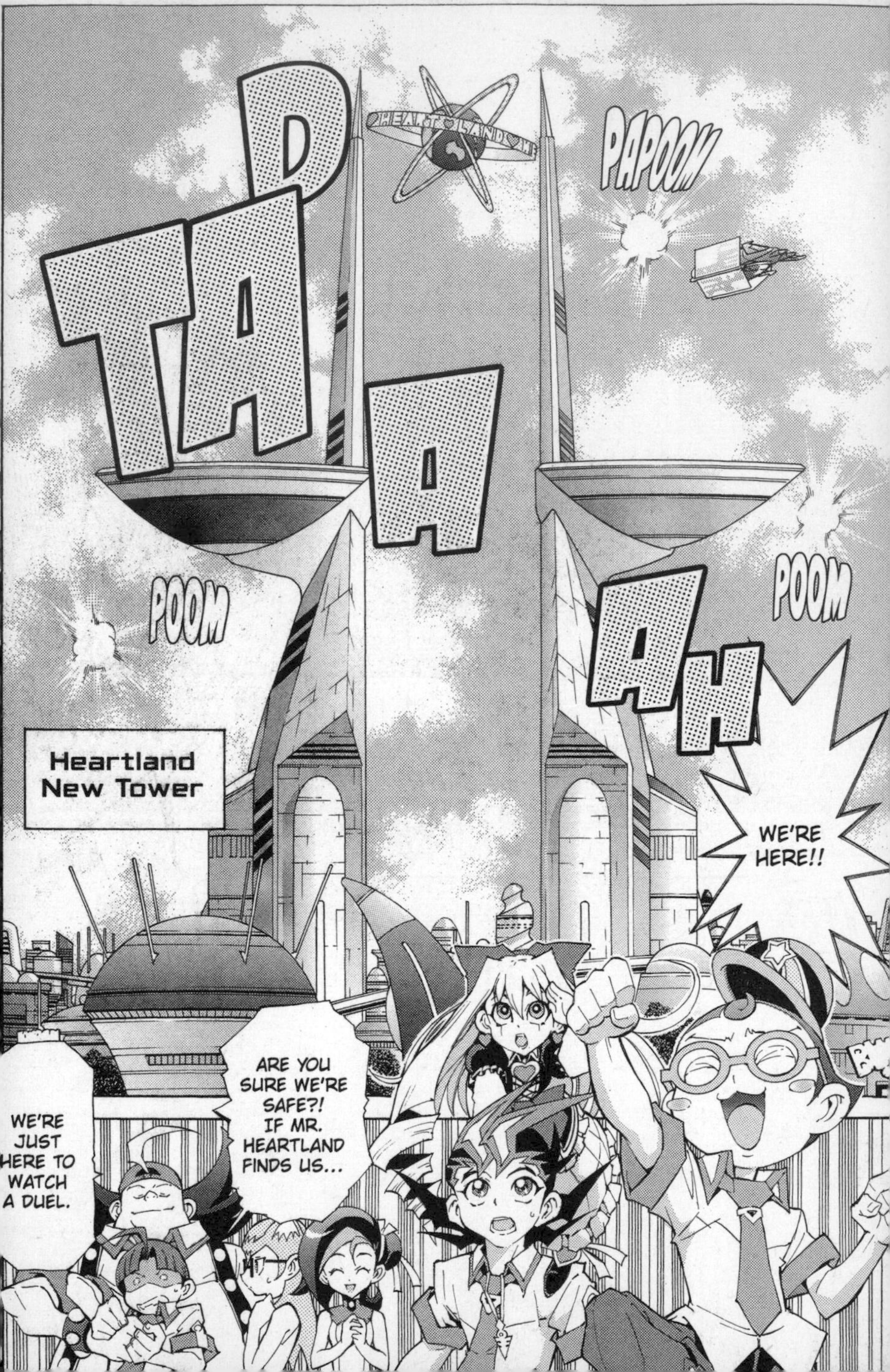
PAPOOM
TADAAH
POOM
POOM
Heartland New Tower
WE'RE HERE!!
ARE YOU SURE WE'RE SAFE?! IF MR. HEARTLAND FINDS US...
WE'RE JUST HERE TO WATCH A DUEL.

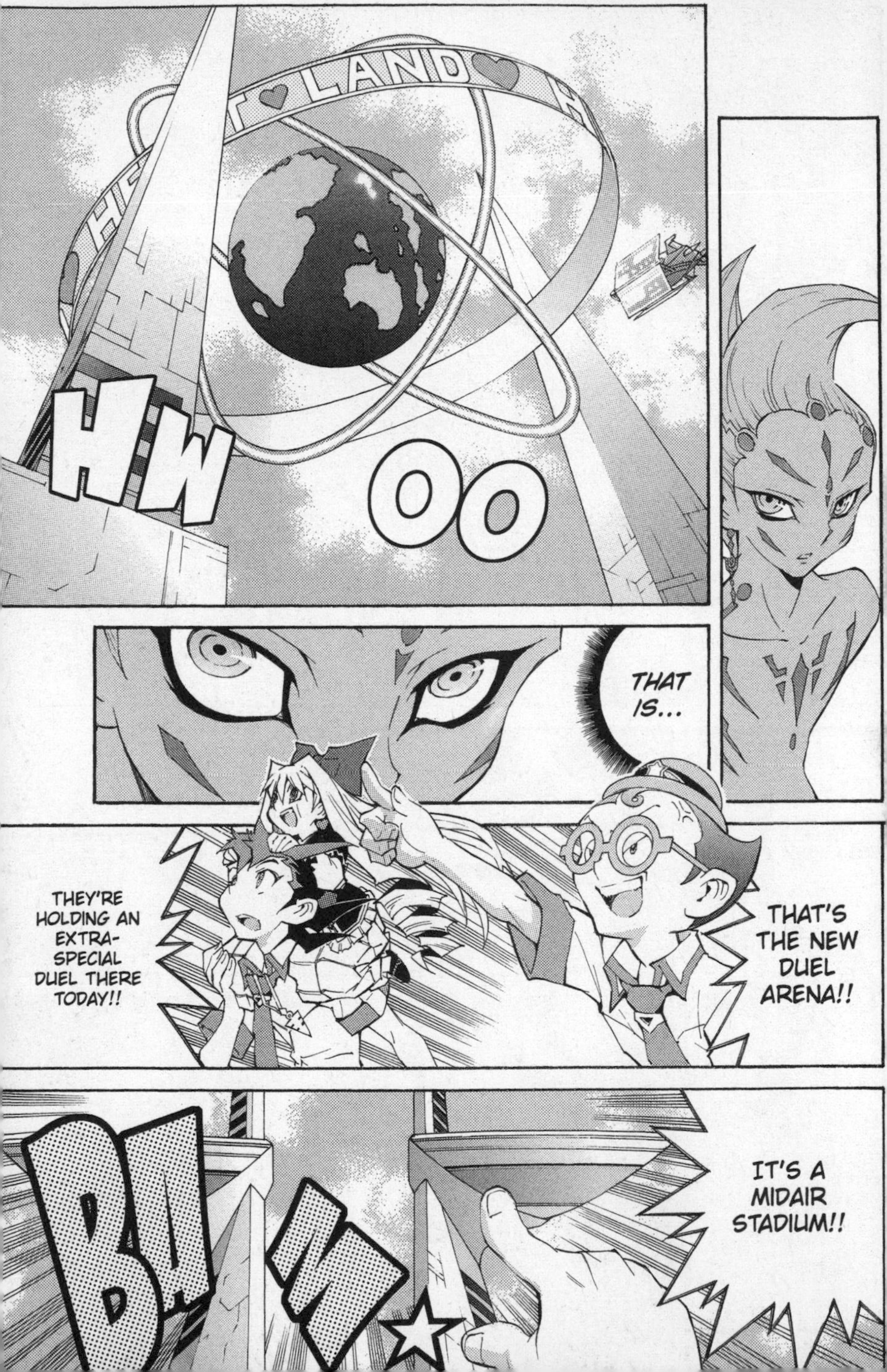
LAND
HWOO
THAT IS...
THAT'S THE NEW DUEL ARENA!!
THEY'RE HOLDING AN EXTRA-SPECIAL DUEL THERE TODAY!!
IT'S A MIDAIR STADIUM!!
BAM☆

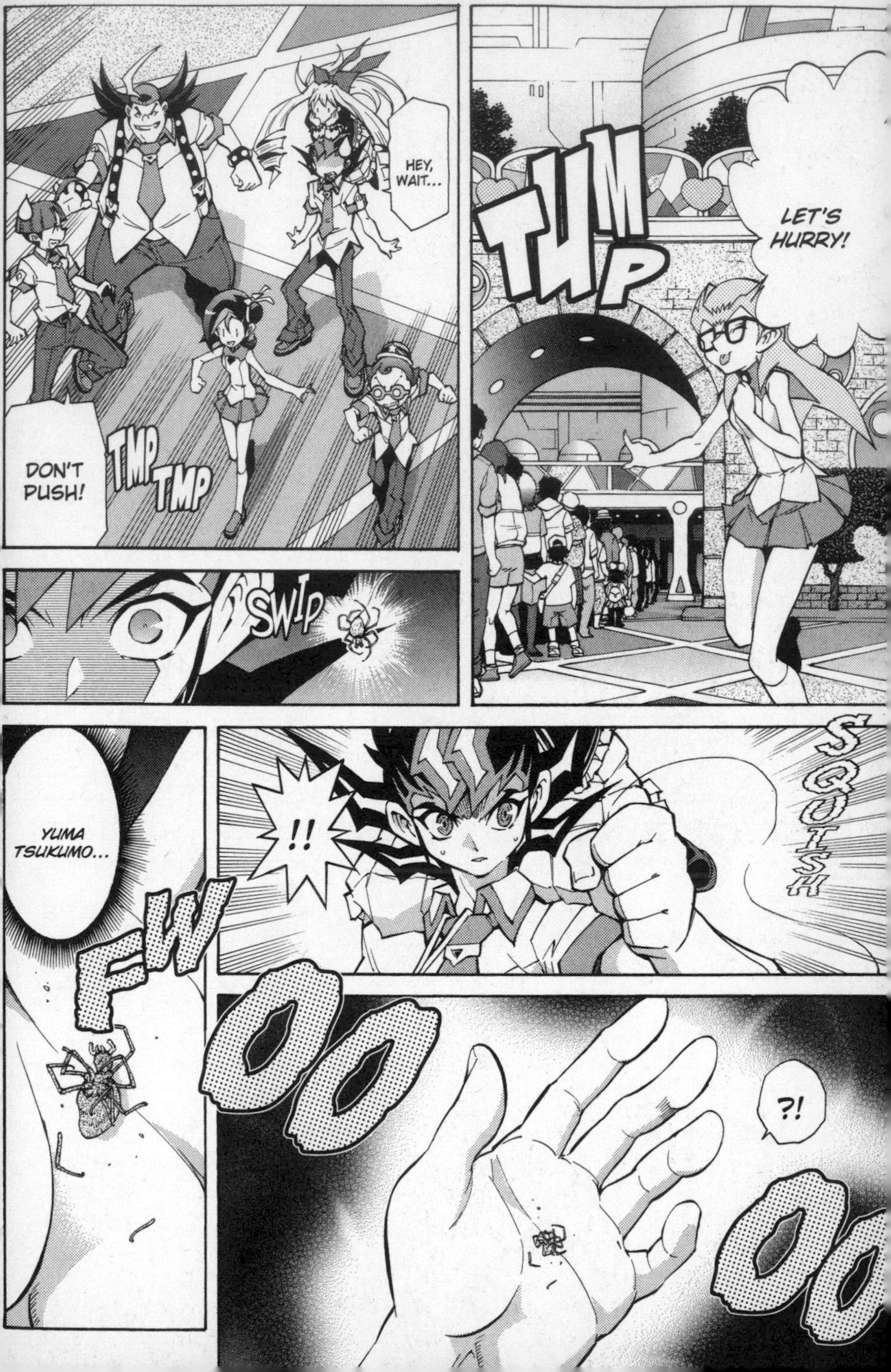
THUMP
LET'S HURRY!
HEY, WAIT...
TMP TMP
DON'T PUSH!
SWIP
SQUISH
!!
YUMA TSUKUMO...
FWOOOO
?!

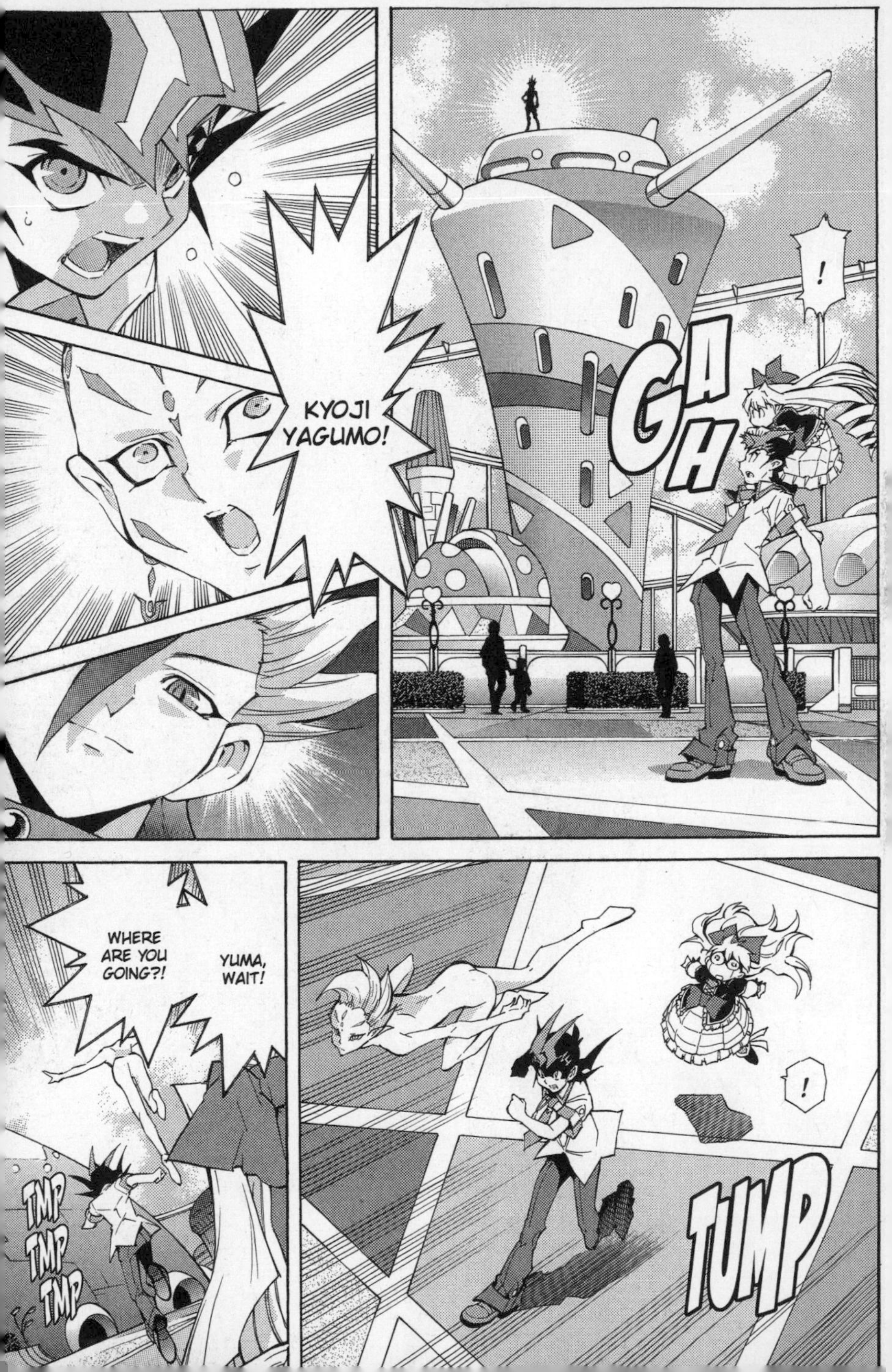
!
GAH
KYOJI YAGUMO!
!
TUMP
YUMA, WAIT!
WHERE ARE YOU GOING?!
TMP TMP TMP

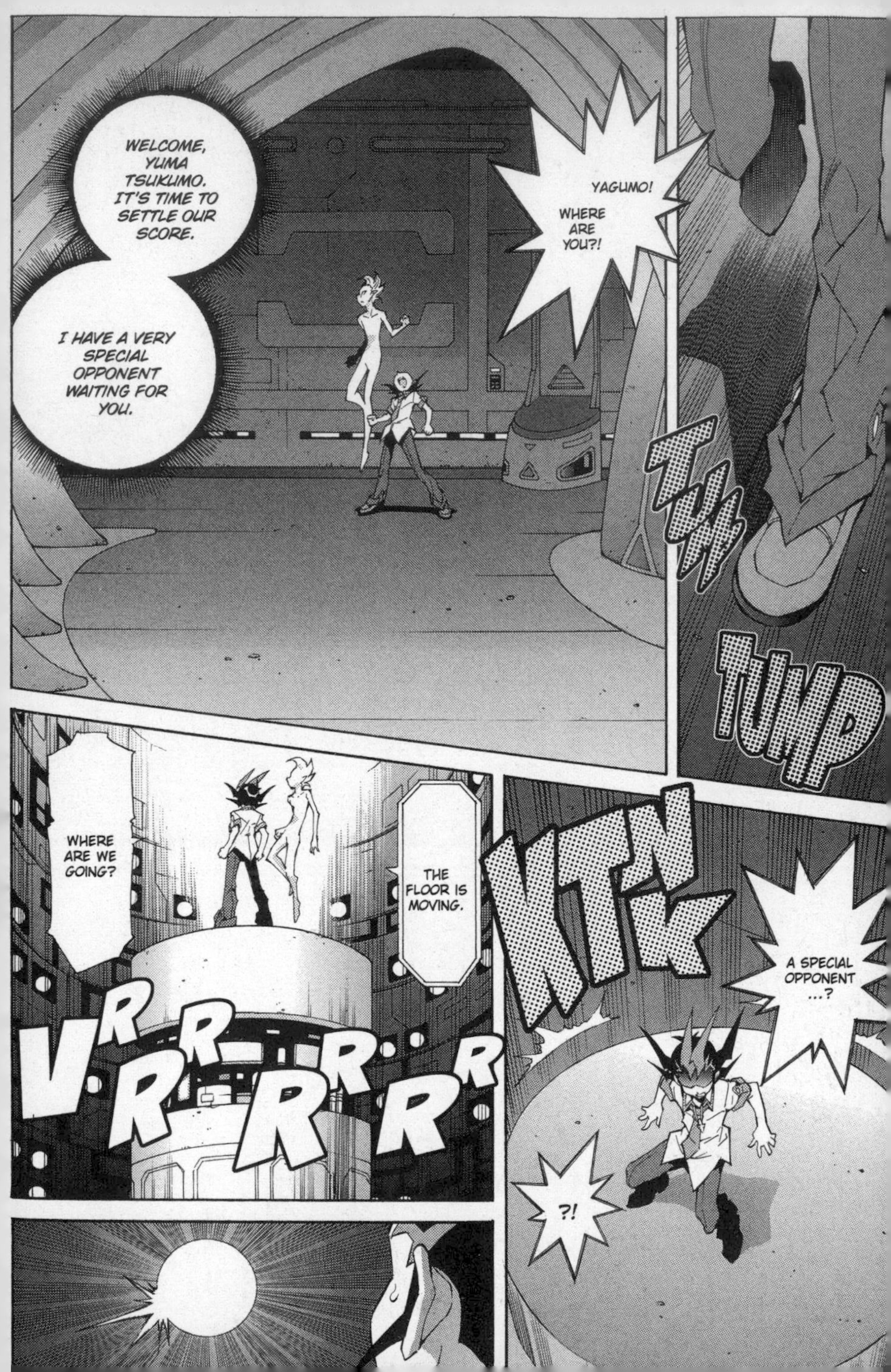
TUM
TUMP
WELCOME, YUMA TSUKUMO. IT'S TIME TO SETTLE OUR SCORE.
I HAVE A VERY SPECIAL OPPONENT WAITING FOR YOU.
YAGUMO!
WHERE ARE YOU?!
A SPECIAL OPPONENT ...?
?!
WHERE ARE WE GOING?
THE FLOOR IS MOVING.
VRR-RRRRRRR

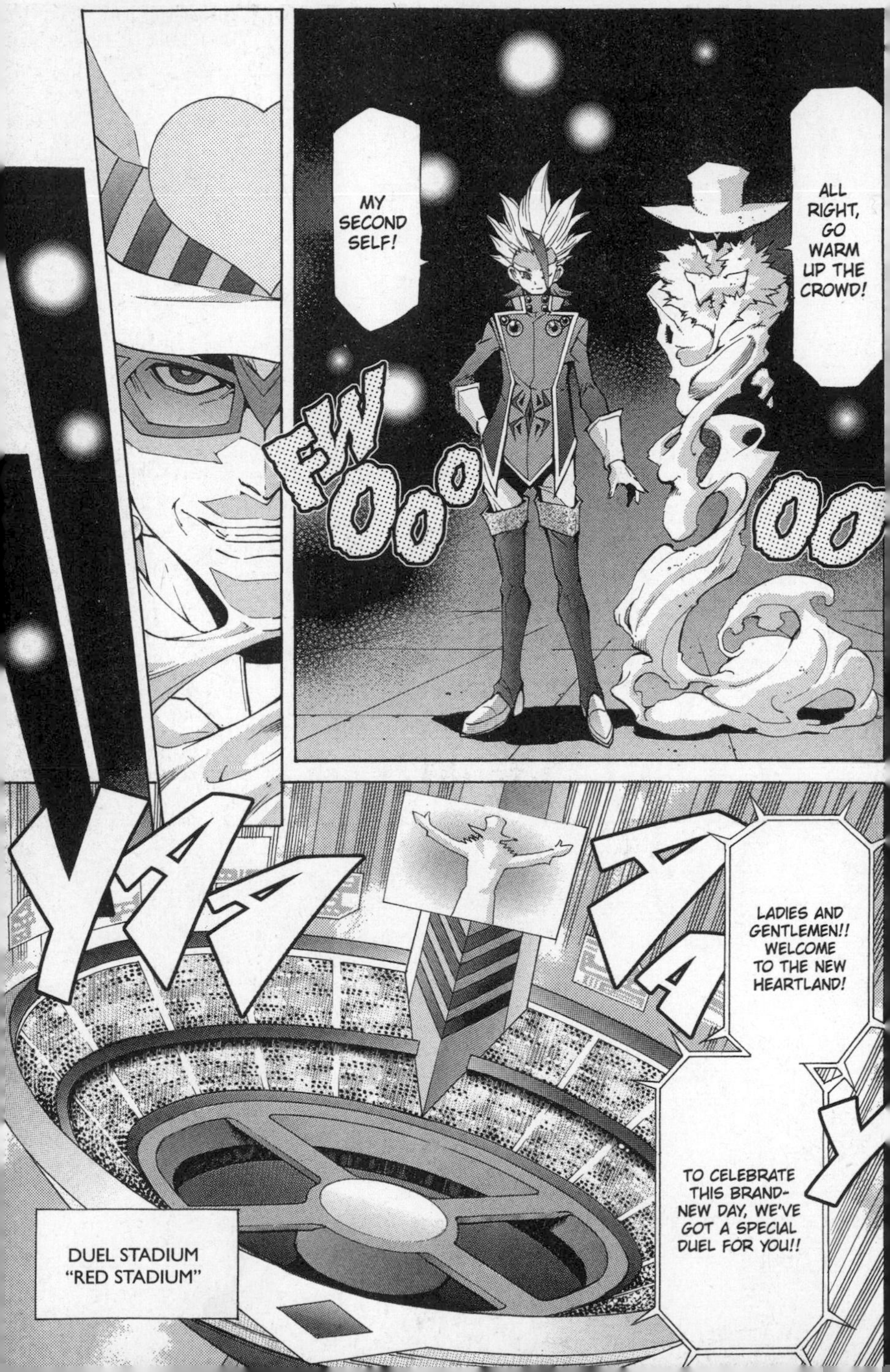

ALL RIGHT, GO WARM UP THE CROWD!
MY SECOND SELF!
FWOOOOOO
LADIES AND GENTLEMEN!! WELCOME TO THE NEW HEARTLAND!
TO CELEBRATE THIS BRAND-NEW DAY, WE'VE GOT A SPECIAL DUEL FOR YOU!!
YAAAAY
DUEL STADIUM "RED STADIUM"

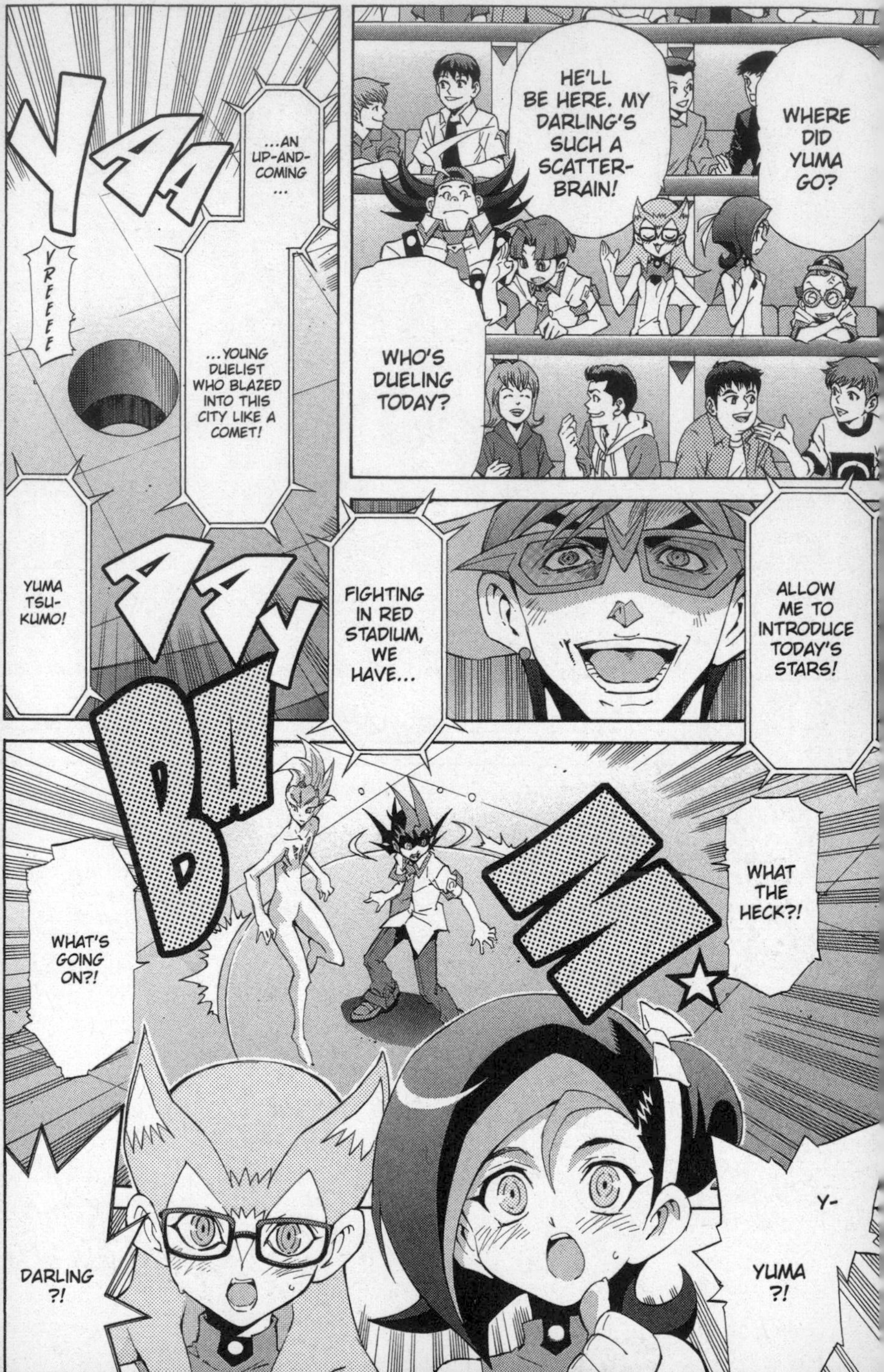
WHERE DID YUMA GO?
HE'LL BE HERE. MY DARLING'S SUCH A SCATTER-BRAIN!
WHO'S DUELING TODAY?
ALLOW ME TO INTRODUCE TODAY'S STARS!
FIGHTING IN RED STADIUM, WE HAVE...
YAA
VREEEEE
...AN UP-AND-COMING ...
...YOUNG DUELIST WHO BLAZED INTO THIS CITY LIKE A COMET!
YUMA TSU-KUMO!
AAY
BAM
WHAT THE HECK?!
WHAT'S GOING ON?!
Y-
YUMA ?!
DARLING ?!

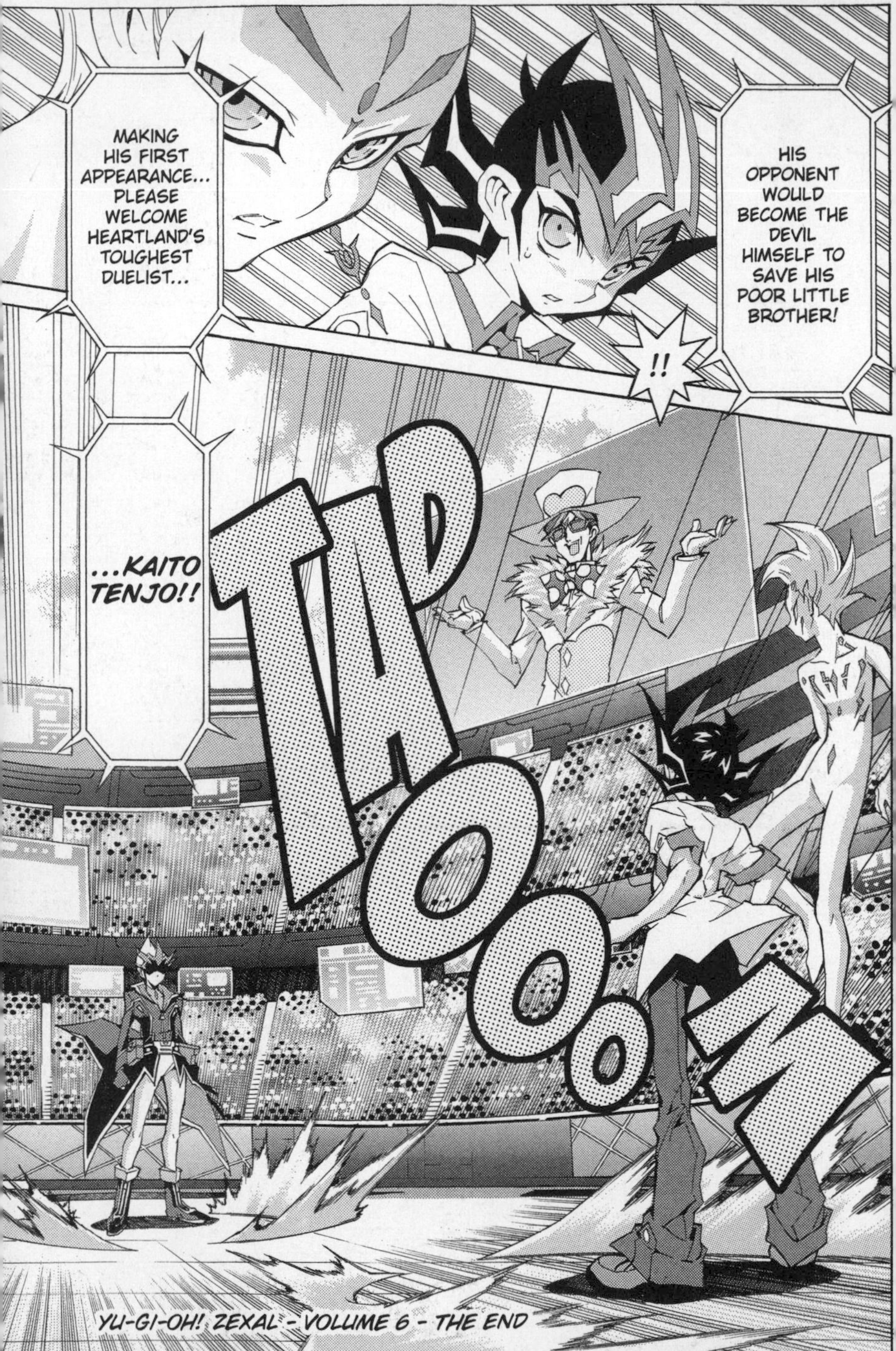
HIS OPPONENT WOULD BECOME THE DEVIL HIMSELF TO SAVE HIS POOR LITTLE BROTHER!
!!
MAKING HIS FIRST APPEARANCE... PLEASE WELCOME HEARTLAND'S TOUGHEST DUELIST...
...KAITO TENJO!!
TAPOOOM

YU-GI-OH! ZEXAL - VOLUME 6 - THE END

STAFF
Junya Uchino
Kazuo Ochiai
Masahiro Miura

Coloring
Toru Shimizu (cover)

EDITOR
Takahiko Aikawa

SUPPORT
Gallop

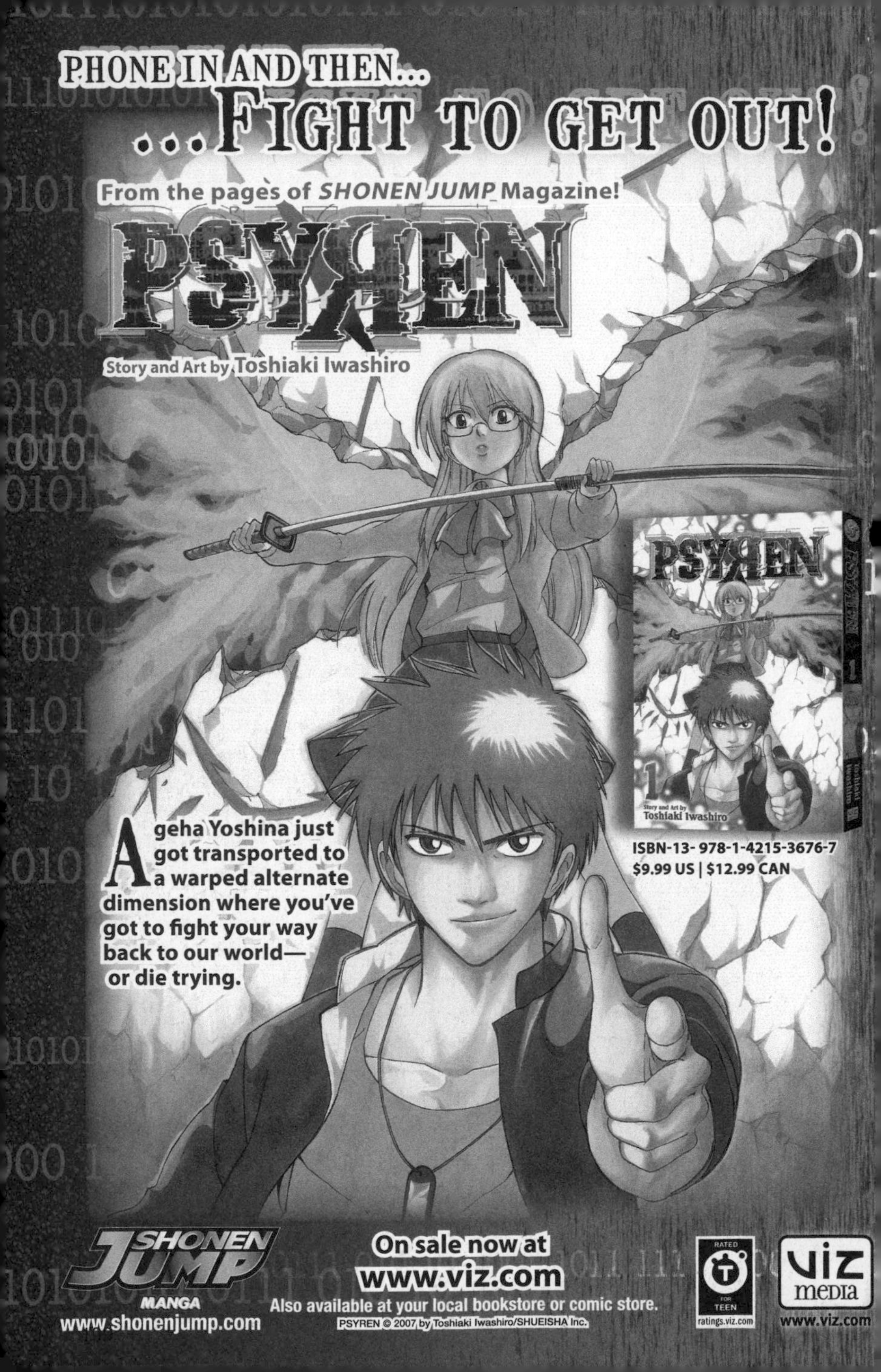
PHONE IN AND THEN...
...FIGHT TO GET OUT!
From the pages of SHONEN JUMP Magazine!
PSYREN
Story and Art by Toshiaki Iwashiro
Ageha Yoshina just got transported to a warped alternate dimension where you've got to fight your way back to our world—or die trying.
PSYREN 1
Story and Art by Toshiaki Iwashiro
ISBN-13- 978-1-4215-3676-7
$9.99 US | $12.99 CAN
SHONEN JUMP MANGA
www.shonenjump.com
On sale now at
www.viz.com
Also available at your local bookstore or comic store.
PSYREN © 2007 by Toshiaki Iwashiro/SHUEISHA Inc.
RATED T FOR TEEN
ratings.viz.com
viz media
www.viz.com

YOU ARE READING
IN THE WRONG DIRECTION!!

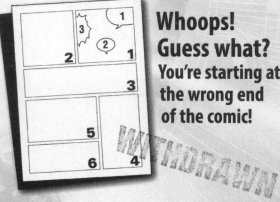

Whoops!
Guess what?
You're starting at the wrong end of the comic!

...It's true! In keeping with the original Japanese format, *Yu-Gi-Oh! ZEXAL* is meant to be read from right to left, starting in the upper-right corner.

Unlike English, which is read from left to right, Japanese is read from right to left, meaning that action, sound effects and word-balloon order are completely reversed... something which can make readers unfamiliar with Japanese feel pretty backwards themselves. For this reason, manga or Japanese comics published in the U.S. in English have sometimes been published "flopped"—that is, printed in exact reverse order, as though seen from the other side of a mirror.

By flopping pages, U.S. publishers can avoid confusing readers, but the compromise is not without its downside. For one thing, a character in a flopped manga series who once wore in the original Japanese version a T-shirt emblazoned with "M A Y" (as in "the merry month of") now wears one which reads "Y A M"! Additionally, many manga creators in Japan are themselves unhappy with the process, as some feel the mirror-imaging of their art alters their original intentions.

We are proud to bring you Shin Yoshida and Naohito Miyoshi's *Yu-Gi-Oh! ZEXAL* in the original unflopped format. For now, though, turn to the other side of the book and let the duel begin...!

—Editor